冨樫義博

Figure 1.

Yoshihiro Togashi

Yoshihiro Togashi's manga career began in 1986 at the age of 20, when he won the coveted Osamu Tezuka Award for new manga artists. He debuted in the Japanese **Weekly Shonen Jump** magazine in 1989 with the romantic comedy **Tende Shôwaru Cupid.** From 1990 to 1994 he wrote and drew the hit manga **Yu Yu Hakusho,** which was followed by the dark comedy science-fiction series **Level E,** and finally this adventure series **Hunter x Hunter,** available from VIZ Media's SHONEN JUMP Advanced imprint. In 1999 he married the manga artist Naoko Takeuchi.

HUNTER X HUNTER Volume 8
SHONEN JUMP ADVANCED Manga Edition

STORY AND ART BY
YOSHIHIRO TOGASHI

English Adaptation/Lillian Olsen
Touch-up Art & Lettering/Mark Griffin
Design/Amy Martin
Editor/Michelle Pangilinan

Printed in the U.S.A.

Published by VIZ Media, LLC
P.O. Box 77010
San Francisco, CA 94107

10 9 8 7 6 5 4
First printing, May 2006
Fourth printing, July 2015

PARENTAL ADVISORY
HUNTER X HUNTER is rated T+ for Older Teen
and is recommended for ages 16 and up.
Contains realistic violence and mature language.
ratings.viz.com

www.viz.com

www.shonenjump.com

SHONEN JUMP ADVANCED MANGA

HUNTER × HUNTER

ハンター × ハンター

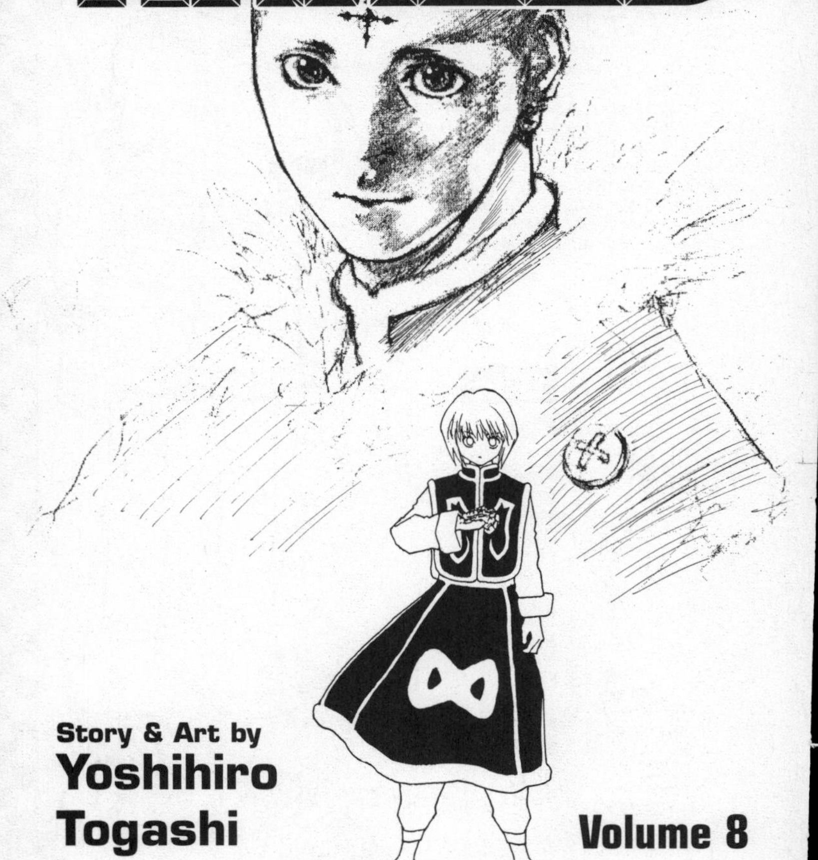

Story & Art by
Yoshihiro Togashi

Volume 8

Characters

The Story Thus Far

GON DREAMS OF BEING A HUNTER LIKE HIS FATHER AND APPLIES FOR THE LICENSING EXAM. NOW THAT HE'S PASSED, HE'S GOT HIS SIGHTS SET ON HIS RUTHLESS RIVAL HISOKA, AND HE COMES TO THE HEAVENS ARENA TO GAIN SOME MUCH-NEEDED COMBAT EXPERIENCE.

THERE, HE LEARNS OF AN AURA-BASED POWER CALLED "NEN," AND PASSES THE FINAL, SECRET PHASE OF THE HUNTER EXAM. HE ALSO WINS THE MATCH ON THE 200TH FLOOR TO QUALIFY FOR A SHOWDOWN WITH ASUKA. HISOKA IS OBVIOUSLY FAR STRONGER, BUT GON SOMEHOW MANAGES TO SOCK HISOKA IN THE FACE AND RETURN HIS BADGE. HISOKA ULTIMATELY WINS THE MATCH, BUT GON IS ABLE TO LEAVE THE HEAVENS ARENA WITH RENEWED CONFIDENCE AND DETERMINATION.

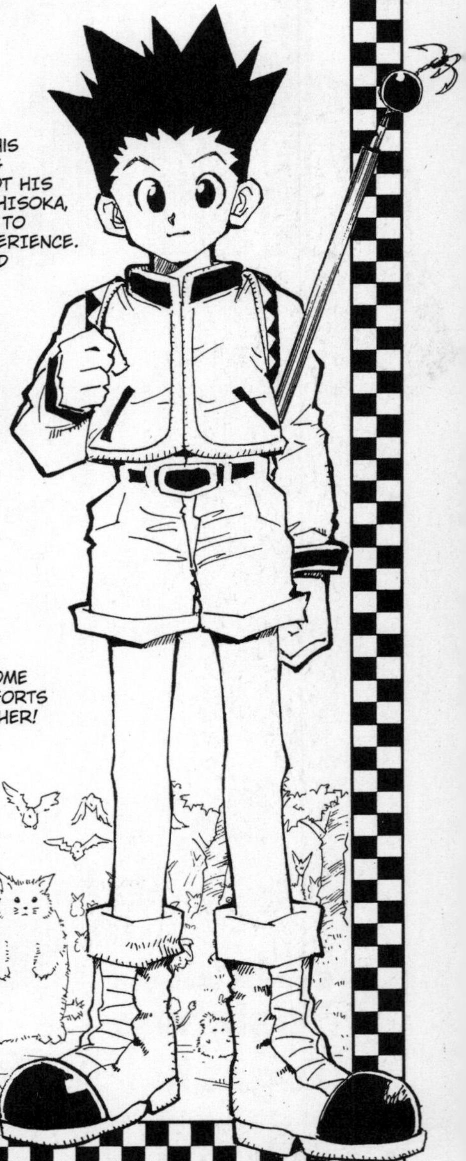

Gon

OUR EAGER HERO. HE'S BECOME A HUNTER IN HIS ONGOING EFFORTS TO BE REUNITED WITH HIS FATHER!

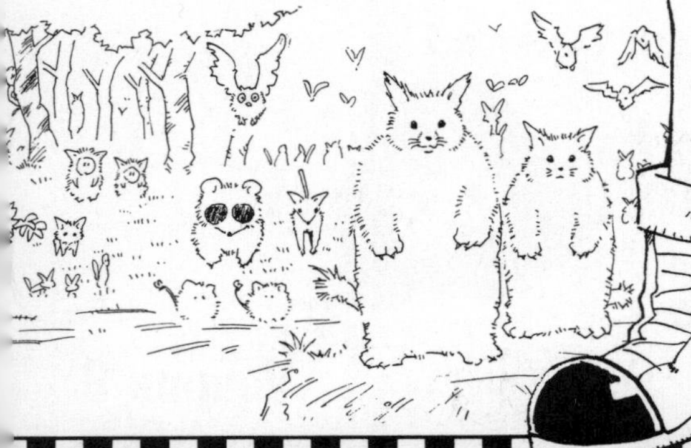

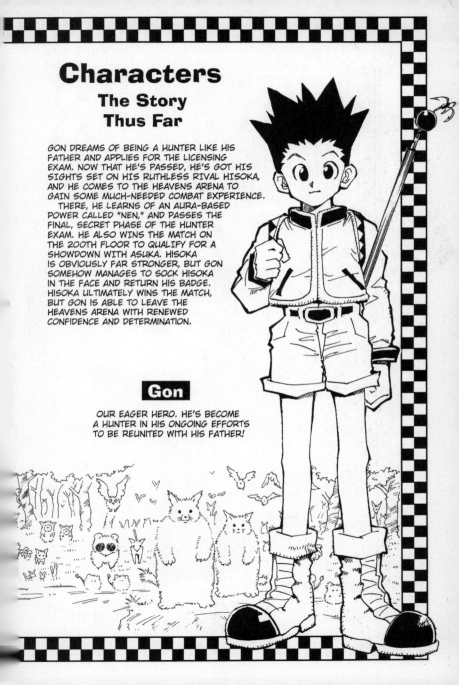

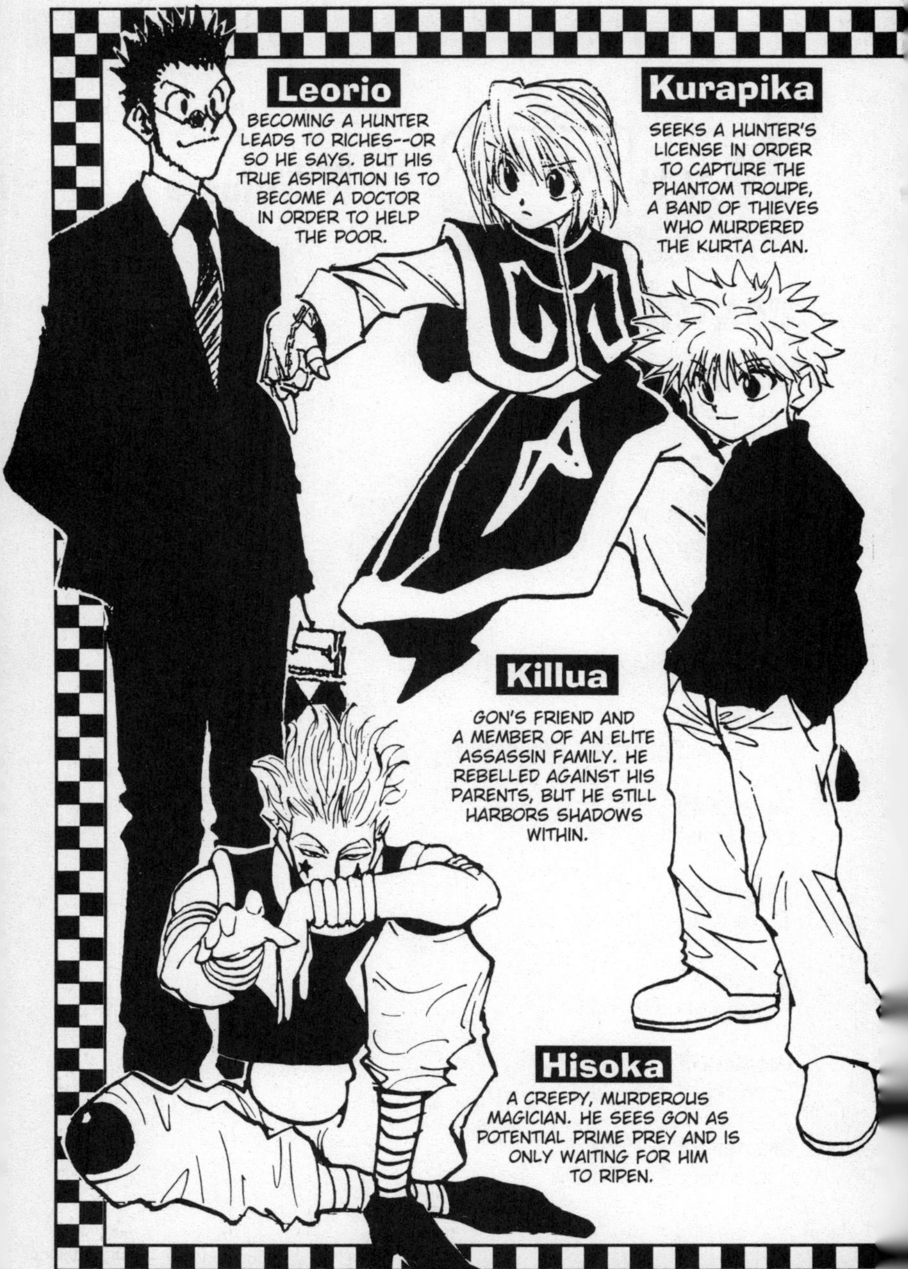
Leorio
BECOMING A HUNTER LEADS TO RICHES--OR SO HE SAYS. BUT HIS TRUE ASPIRATION IS TO BECOME A DOCTOR IN ORDER TO HELP THE POOR.
Kurapika
SEEKS A HUNTER'S LICENSE IN ORDER TO CAPTURE THE PHANTOM TROUPE, A BAND OF THIEVES WHO MURDERED THE KURTA CLAN.
Killua
GON'S FRIEND AND A MEMBER OF AN ELITE ASSASSIN FAMILY. HE REBELLED AGAINST HIS PARENTS, BUT HE STILL HARBORS SHADOWS WITHIN.
Hisoka
A CREEPY, MURDEROUS MAGICIAN. HE SEES GON AS POTENTIAL PRIME PREY AND IS ONLY WAITING FOR HIM TO RIPEN.

HUNTER×HUNTER
Volume 8

CONTENTS

Chapter 64 Homecoming

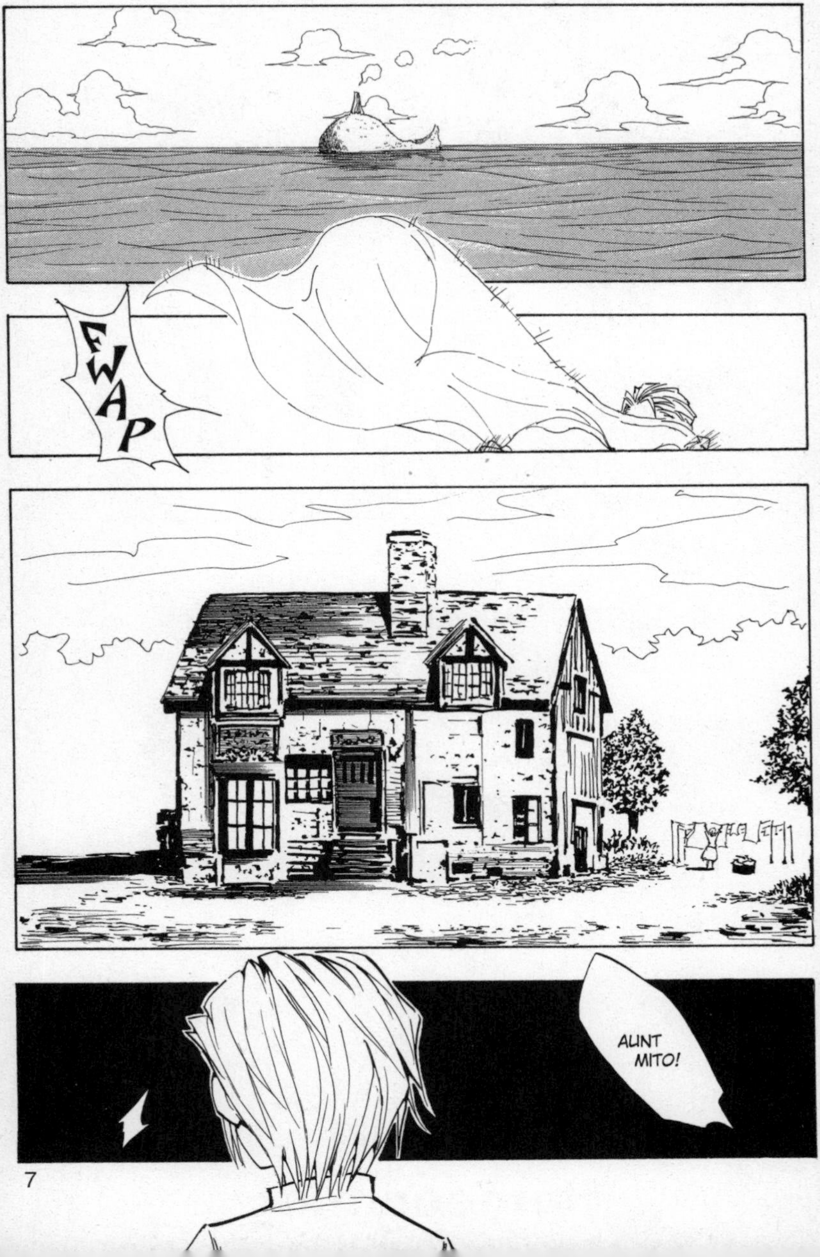
FWAP
AUNT MITO!

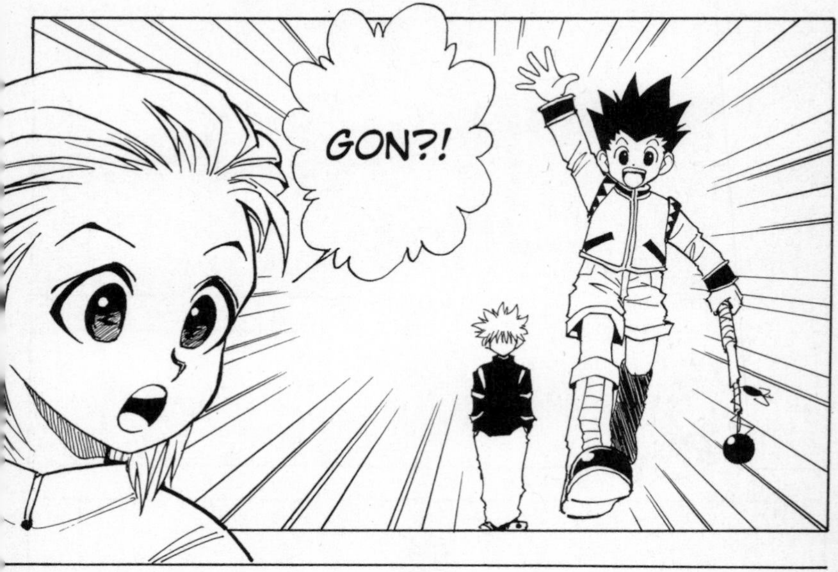
GON?!

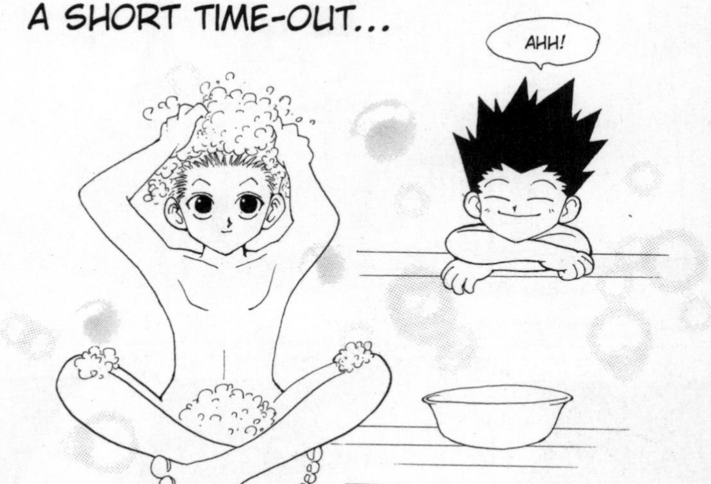
A SHORT TIME-OUT...
AHH!

Chapter 64

Homecoming

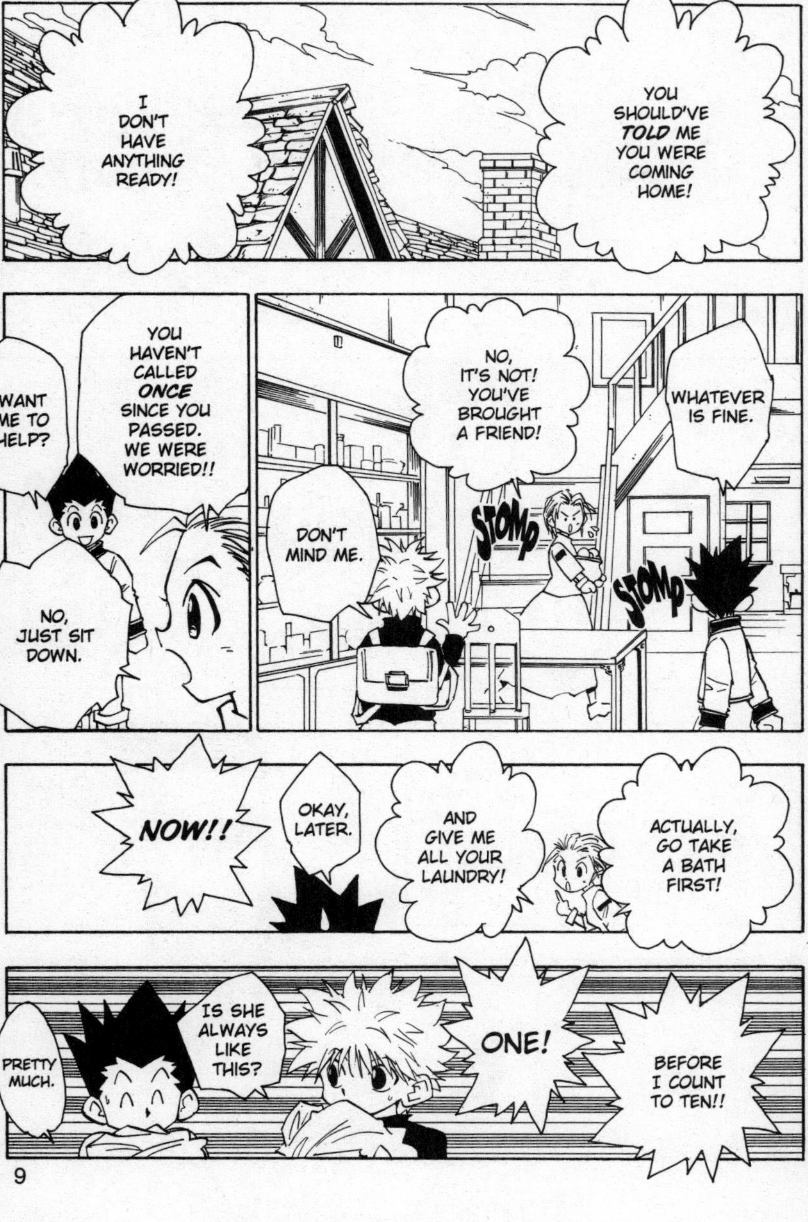
YOU SHOULD'VE TOLD ME YOU WERE COMING HOME!
I DON'T HAVE ANYTHING READY!
WHATEVER IS FINE.
NO, IT'S NOT! YOU'VE BROUGHT A FRIEND!
STOMP
STOMP
DON'T MIND ME.
YOU HAVEN'T CALLED ONCE SINCE YOU PASSED. WE WERE WORRIED!!
WANT ME TO HELP?
NO, JUST SIT DOWN.
ACTUALLY, GO TAKE A BATH FIRST!
AND GIVE ME ALL YOUR LAUNDRY!
OKAY, LATER.
NOW!!
BEFORE I COUNT TO TEN!!
ONE!
IS SHE ALWAYS LIKE THIS?
PRETTY MUCH.

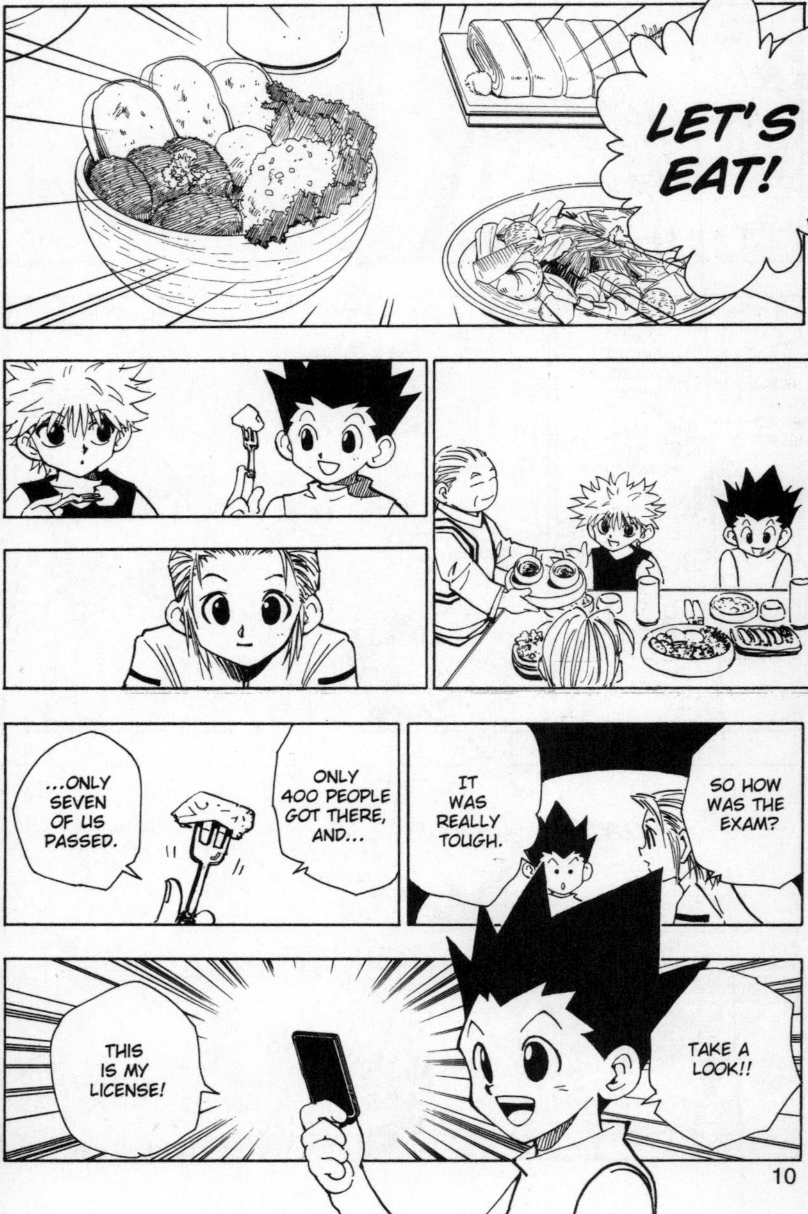
LET'S EAT!
SO HOW WAS THE EXAM?
IT WAS REALLY TOUGH.
ONLY 400 PEOPLE GOT THERE, AND...
...ONLY SEVEN OF US PASSED.
TAKE A LOOK!!
THIS IS MY LICENSE!

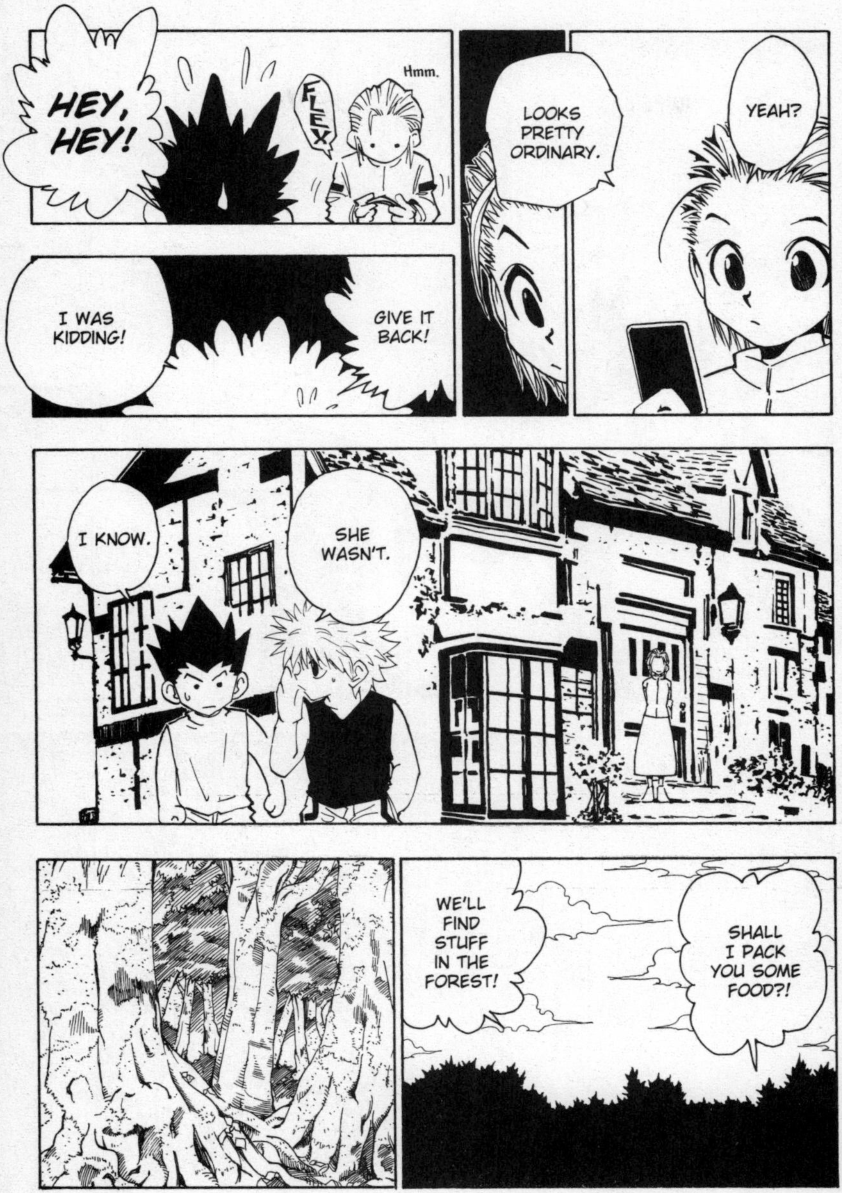
YEAH?
LOOKS PRETTY ORDINARY.
Hmm.
FLEX
HEY, HEY!
GIVE IT BACK!
I WAS KIDDING!
SHE WASN'T.
I KNOW.
SHALL I PACK YOU SOME FOOD?!
WE'LL FIND STUFF IN THE FOREST!

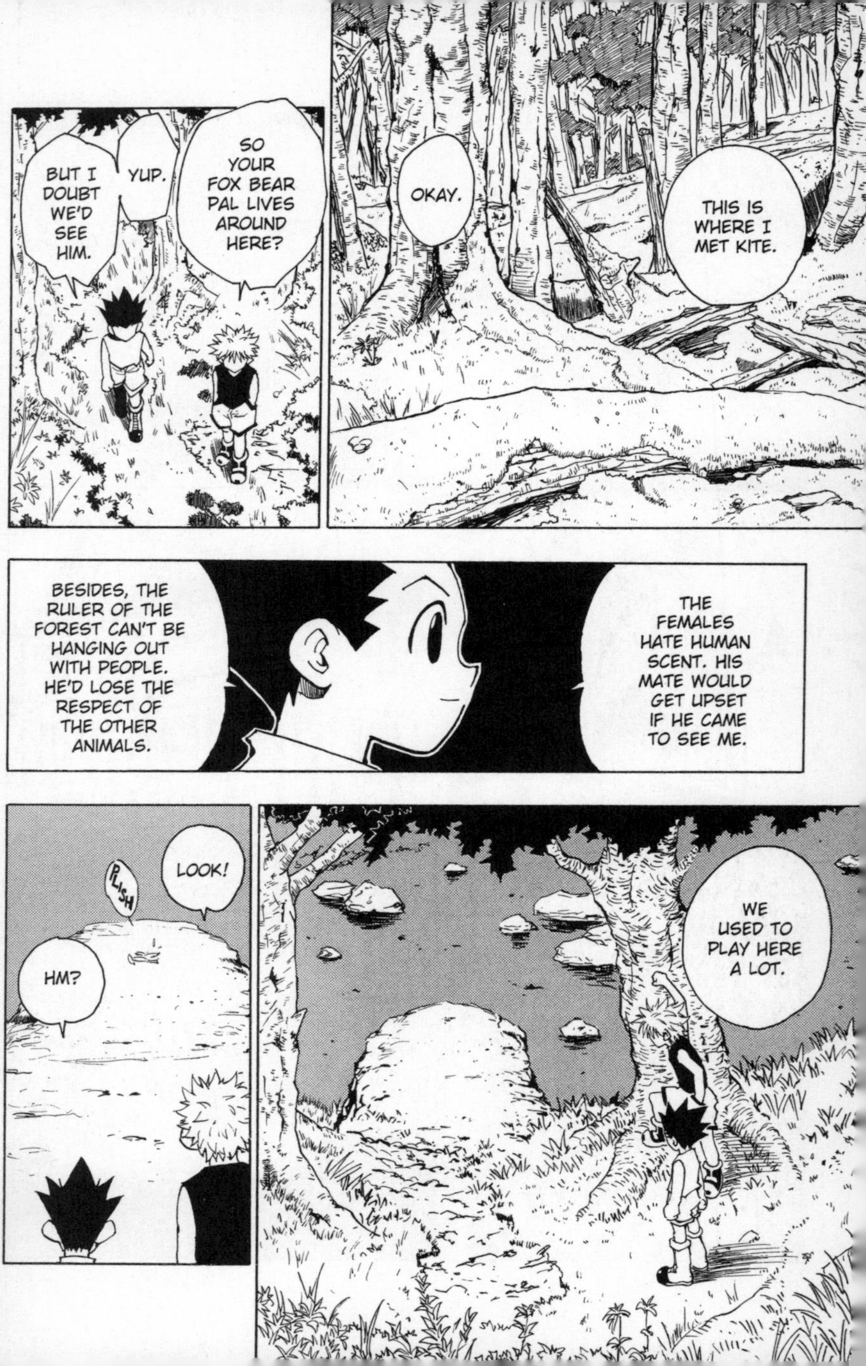
THIS IS WHERE I MET KITE.
OKAY.
SO YOUR FOX BEAR PAL LIVES AROUND HERE?
YUP.
BUT I DOUBT WE'D SEE HIM.
THE FEMALES HATE HUMAN SCENT. HIS MATE WOULD GET UPSET IF HE CAME TO SEE ME.
BESIDES, THE RULER OF THE FOREST CAN'T BE HANGING OUT WITH PEOPLE. HE'D LOSE THE RESPECT OF THE OTHER ANIMALS.
WE USED TO PLAY HERE A LOT.
LOOK!
PLISH
HM?

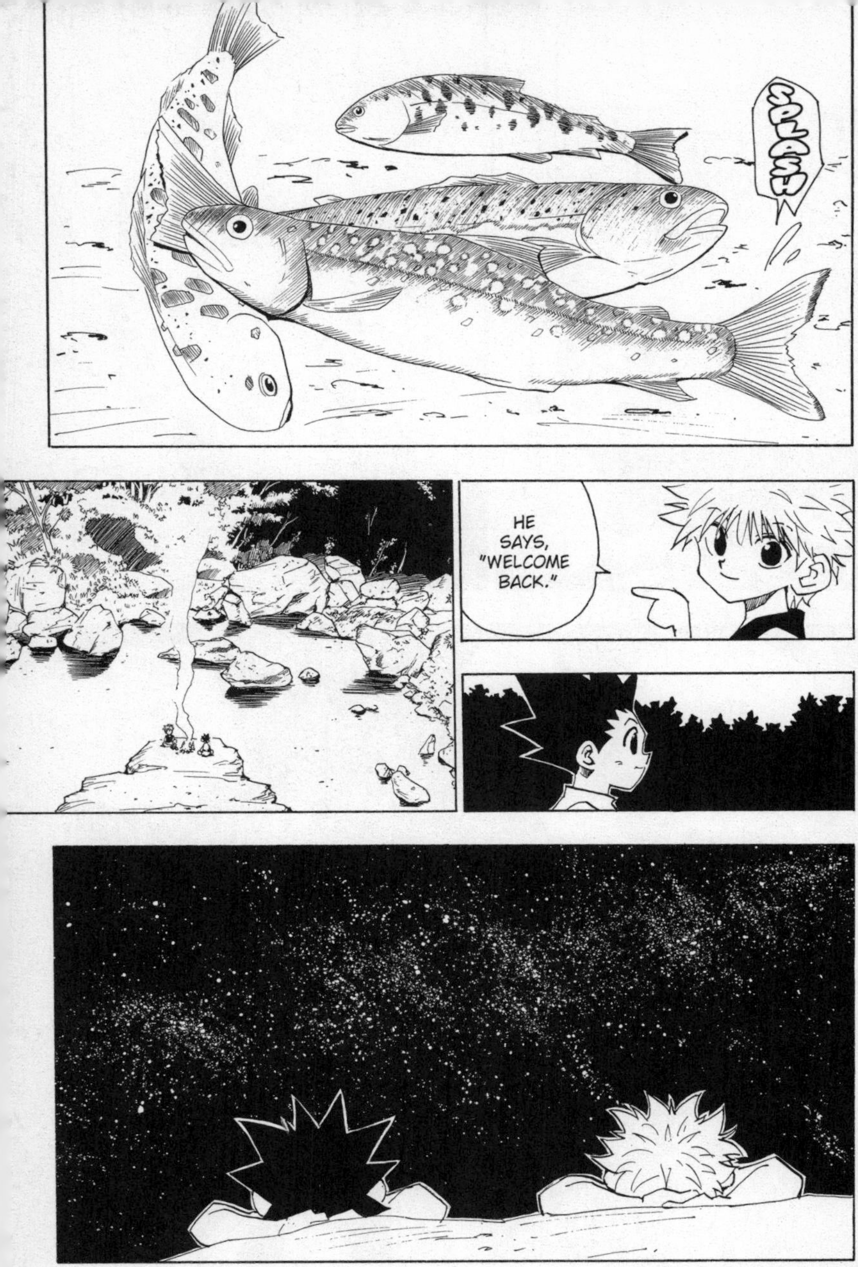
SPLASH
HE SAYS, "WELCOME BACK."

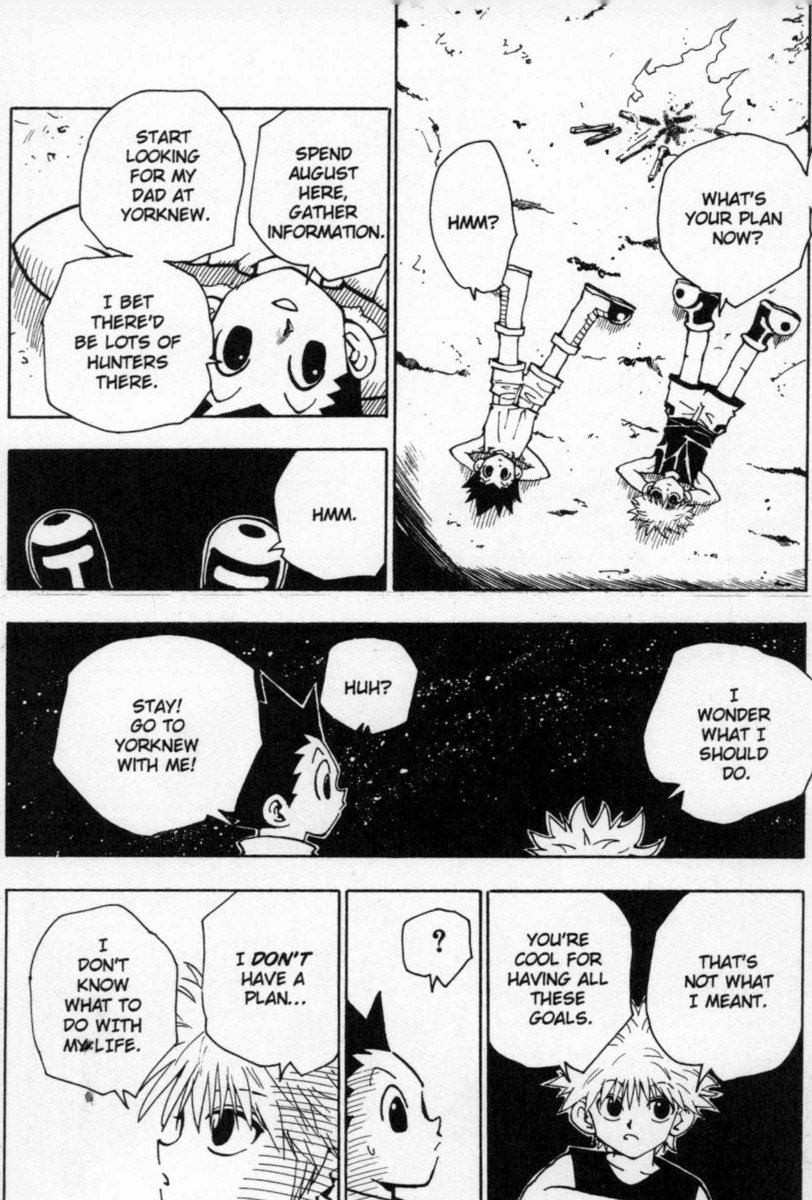
HEY.
WHAT'S YOUR PLAN NOW?
HMM?
SPEND AUGUST HERE, GATHER INFORMATION.
START LOOKING FOR MY DAD AT YORKNEW.
I BET THERE'D BE LOTS OF HUNTERS THERE.
HMM.
I WONDER WHAT I SHOULD DO.
HUH?
STAY! GO TO YORKNEW WITH ME!
THAT'S NOT WHAT I MEANT.
YOU'RE COOL FOR HAVING ALL THESE GOALS.
?
I *DON'T* HAVE A PLAN...
I DON'T KNOW WHAT TO DO WITH MY LIFE.

READ THIS WAY

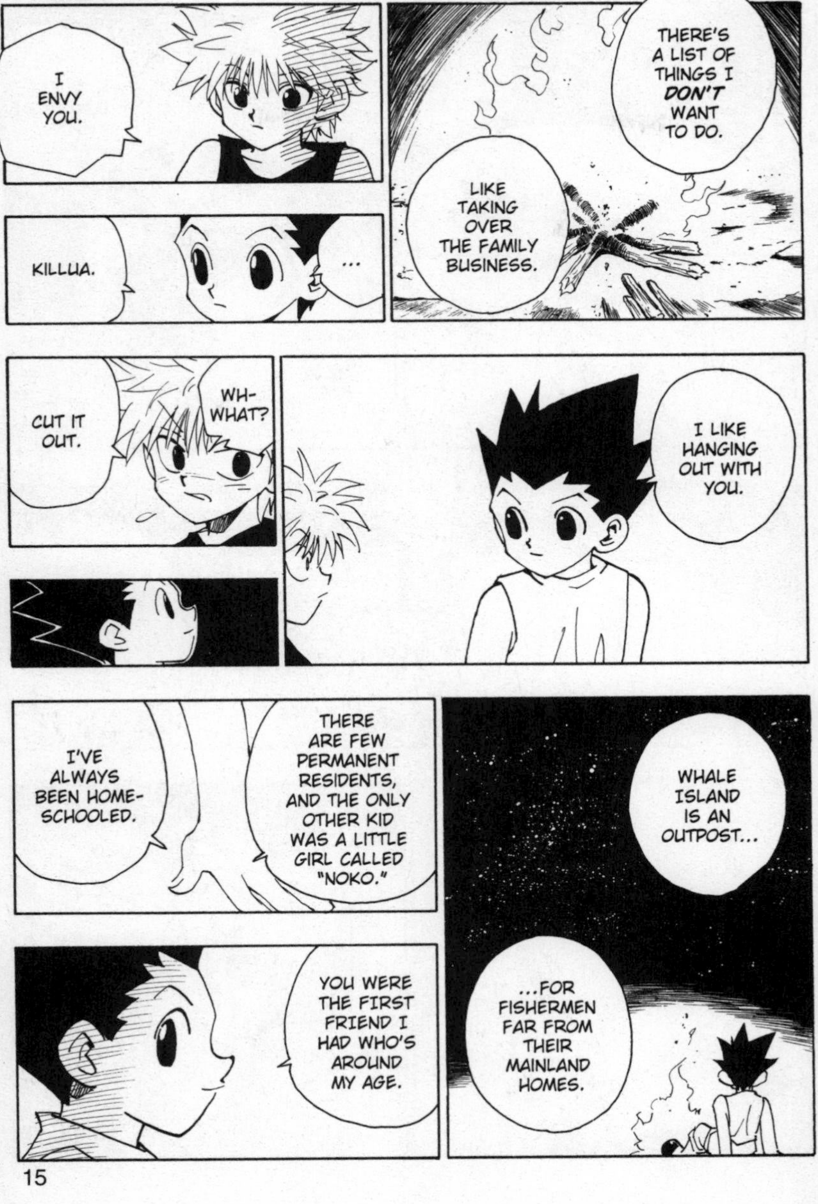
THERE'S A LIST OF THINGS I ***DON'T*** WANT TO DO.
LIKE TAKING OVER THE FAMILY BUSINESS.
I ENVY YOU.
...
KILLUA.
I LIKE HANGING OUT WITH YOU.
WH-WHAT?
CUT IT OUT.
WHALE ISLAND IS AN OUTPOST...
...FOR FISHERMEN FAR FROM THEIR MAINLAND HOMES.
THERE ARE FEW PERMANENT RESIDENTS, AND THE ONLY OTHER KID WAS A LITTLE GIRL CALLED "NOKO."
I'VE ALWAYS BEEN HOME-SCHOOLED.
YOU WERE THE FIRST FRIEND I HAD WHO'S AROUND MY AGE.

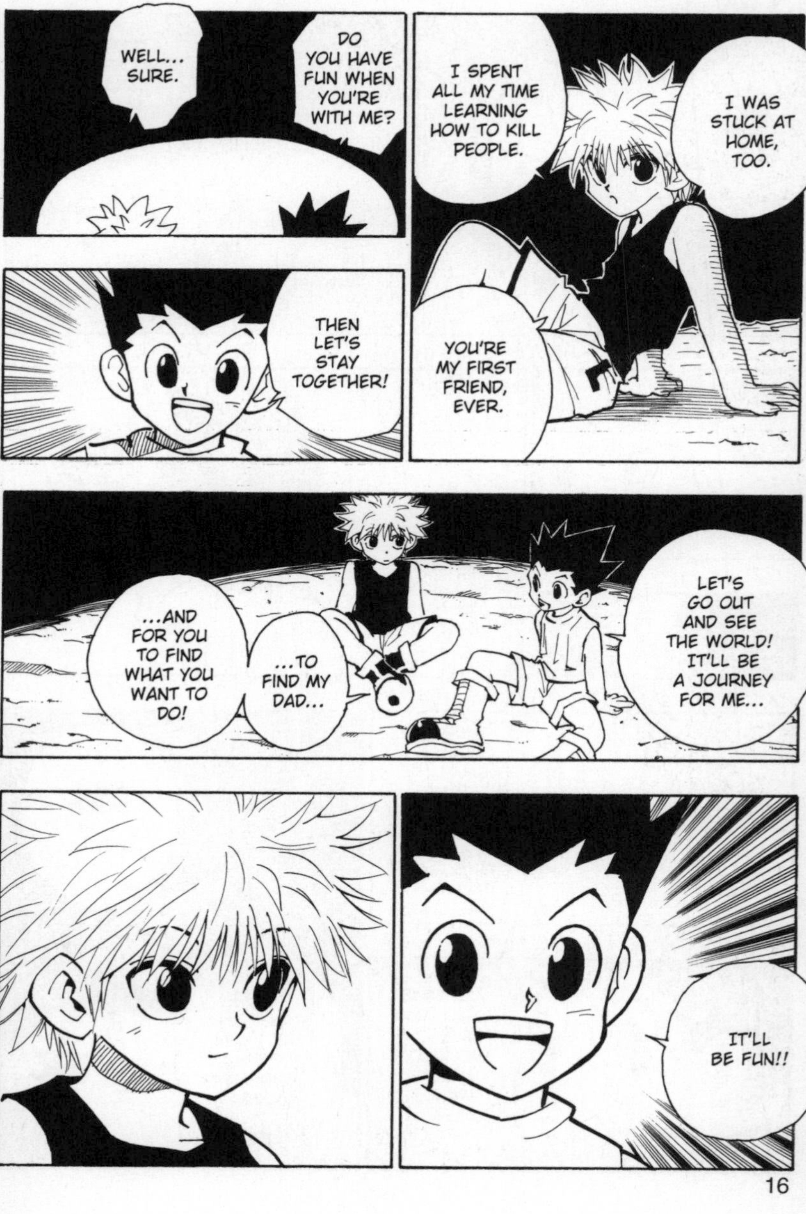
I WAS STUCK AT HOME, TOO.
I SPENT ALL MY TIME LEARNING HOW TO KILL PEOPLE.
YOU'RE MY FIRST FRIEND, EVER.
DO YOU HAVE FUN WHEN YOU'RE WITH ME?
WELL... SURE.
THEN LET'S STAY TOGETHER!
LET'S GO OUT AND SEE THE WORLD! IT'LL BE A JOURNEY FOR ME...
...TO FIND MY DAD...
...AND FOR YOU TO FIND WHAT YOU WANT TO DO!
IT'LL BE FUN!!

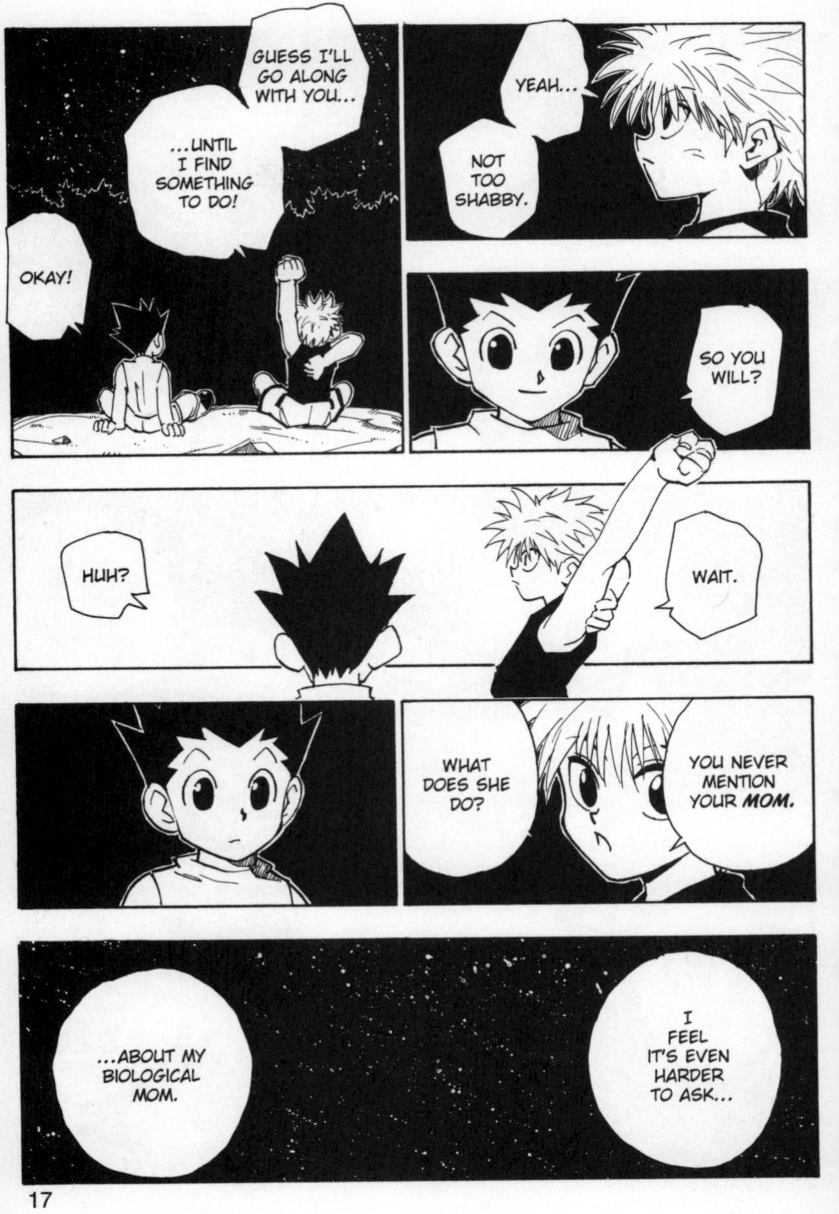
YEAH...
NOT TOO SHABBY.
SO YOU WILL?
GUESS I'LL GO ALONG WITH YOU...
...UNTIL I FIND SOMETHING TO DO!
OKAY!
WAIT.
HUH?
YOU NEVER MENTION YOUR ***MOM.***
WHAT DOES SHE DO?
I FEEL IT'S EVEN HARDER TO ASK...
...ABOUT MY BIOLOGICAL MOM.

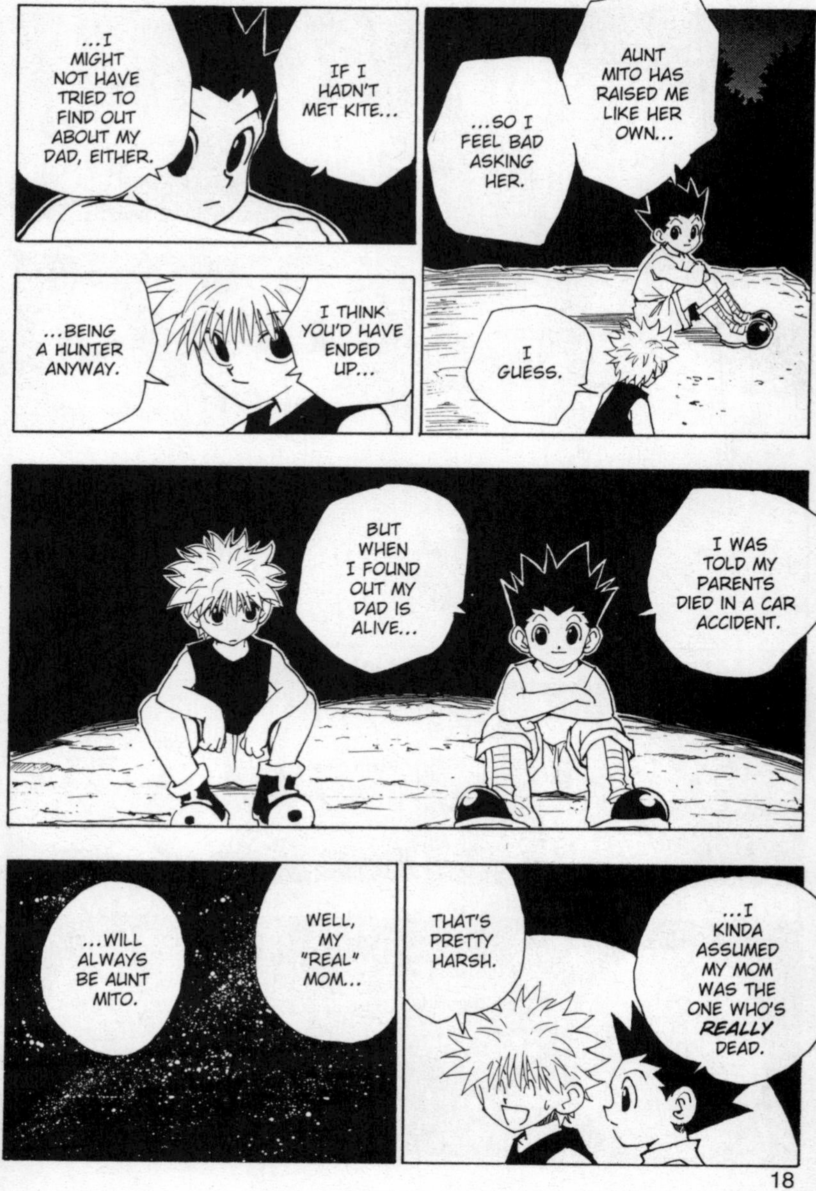
AUNT MITO HAS RAISED ME LIKE HER OWN...
...SO I FEEL BAD ASKING HER.
I GUESS.
IF I HADN'T MET KITE...
...I MIGHT NOT HAVE TRIED TO FIND OUT ABOUT MY DAD, EITHER.
I THINK YOU'D HAVE ENDED UP...
...BEING A HUNTER ANYWAY.
I WAS TOLD MY PARENTS DIED IN A CAR ACCIDENT.
BUT WHEN I FOUND OUT MY DAD IS ALIVE...
...I KINDA ASSUMED MY MOM WAS THE ONE WHO'S *REALLY* DEAD.
THAT'S PRETTY HARSH.
WELL, MY "REAL" MOM...
...WILL ALWAYS BE AUNT MITO.

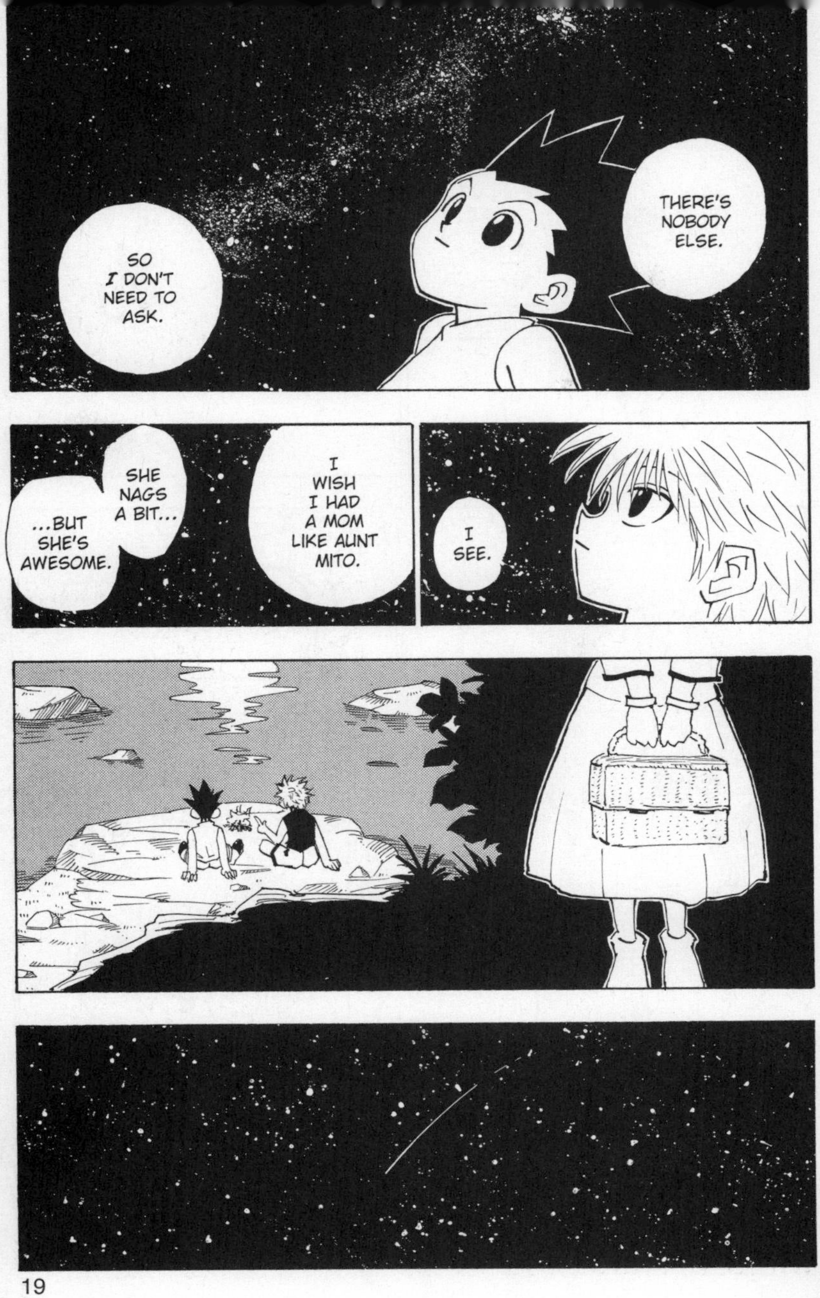
THERE'S NOBODY ELSE.
SO I DON'T NEED TO ASK.
I SEE.
I WISH I HAD A MOM LIKE AUNT MITO.
SHE NAGS A BIT...
...BUT SHE'S AWESOME.

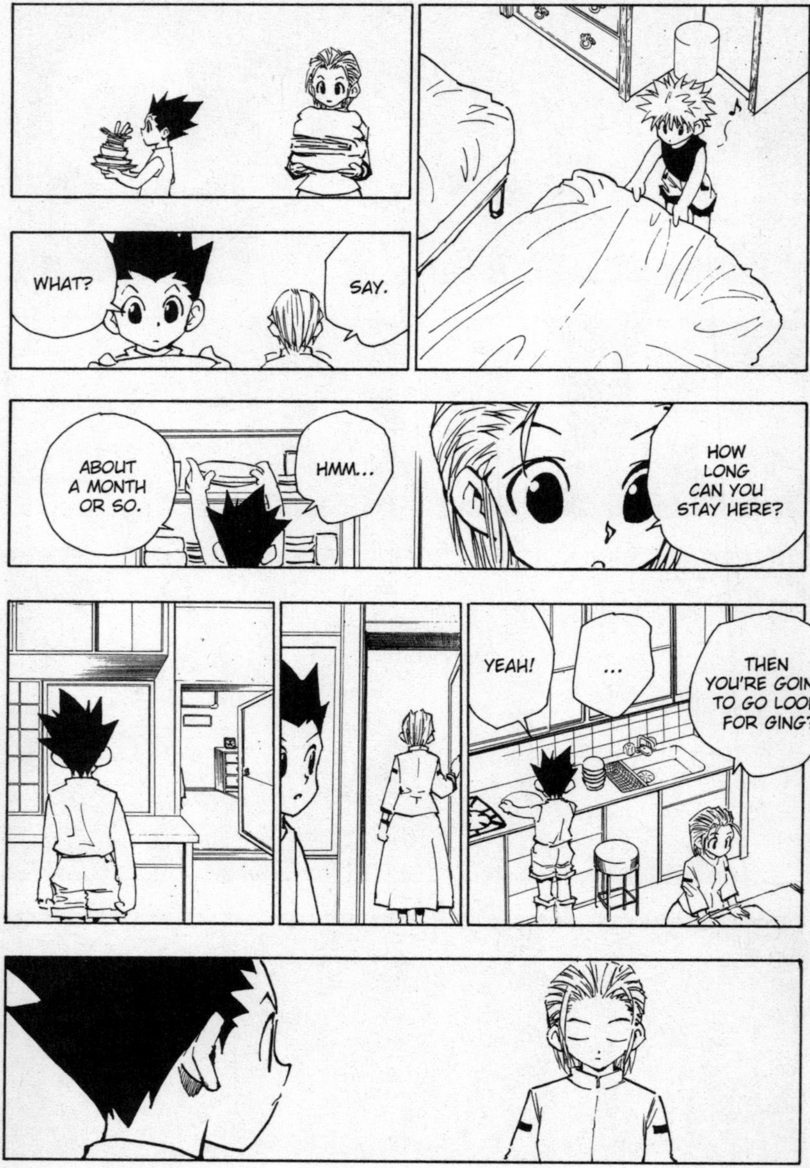
SAY.
WHAT?
HOW LONG CAN YOU STAY HERE?
HMM...
ABOUT A MONTH OR SO.
THEN YOU'RE GOING TO GO LOOK FOR GING?
...
YEAH!

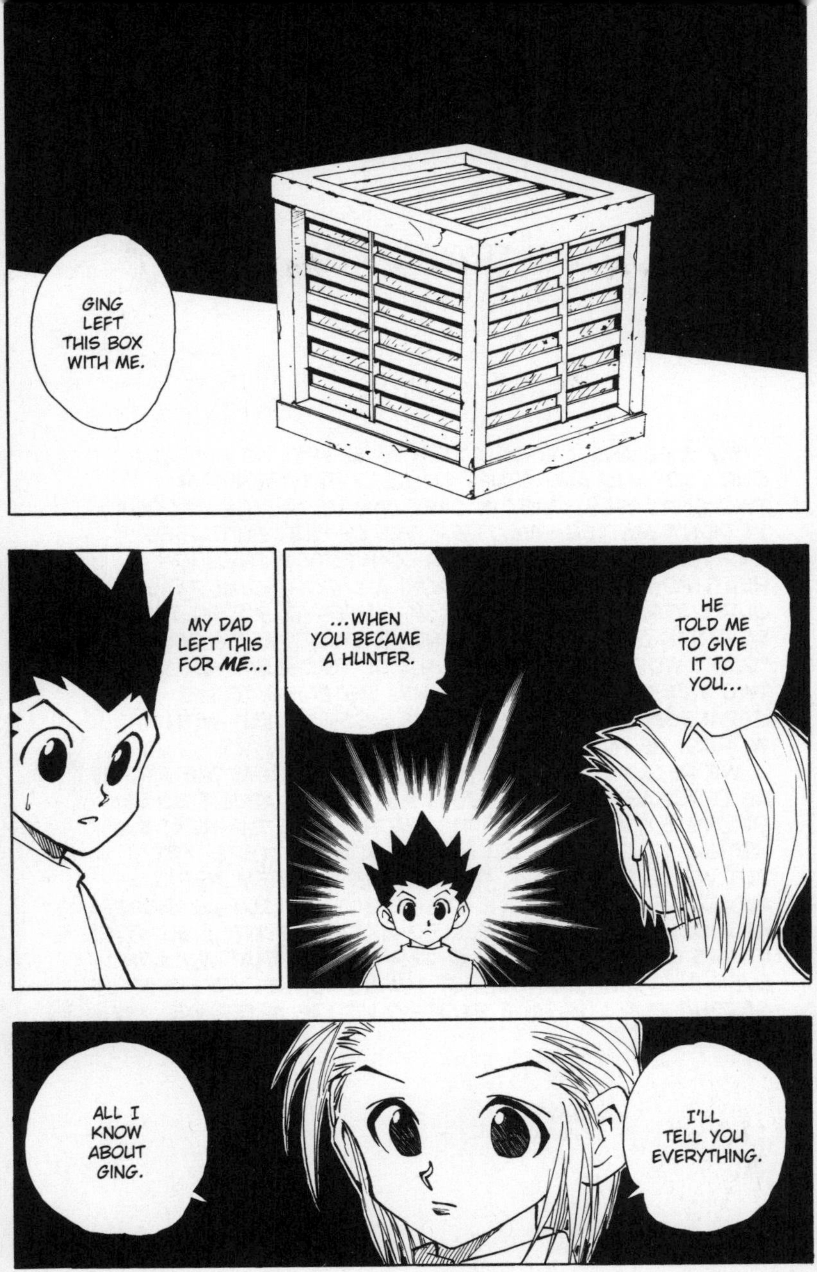
GING LEFT THIS BOX WITH ME.
HE TOLD ME TO GIVE IT TO YOU...
...WHEN YOU BECAME A HUNTER.
MY DAD LEFT THIS FOR *ME*...
I'LL TELL YOU EVERYTHING.
ALL I KNOW ABOUT GING.

OUR EGYPTIAN TRAVEL LOG
NO. 1

MY WIFE AND I TOOK A TRIP TO EGYPT. WE DIVIDED OUR CLOTHING AND STUFF EQUALLY BETWEEN OUR TWO SUITCASES, JUST IN CASE ONE OF THEM GOT LOST. IT DIDN'T MATTER--*NEITHER* ONE OF OUR SUITCASES ARRIVED IN EGYPT. WE HAD A CONNECTION THROUGH HEATHROW AIRPORT IN LONDON, AND FOR SOME REASON, OUR LUGGAGE GOT SENT BACK TO TOKYO. WE TOLD OUR EGYPTIAN GUIDE ABOUT IT, AND HE JUST KEPT SAYING, "DON'T WORRY. IT'S ALL RIGHT. NO PROBLEM." IN THE TWO WEEKS WE SPENT WITH HIM LISTENING TO HIS JAPANESE, HE APPEARED TO BE MOST FLUENT WITH THESE WORDS. HE MUST USE THEM ALL THE TIME.

WE RECEIVED 840 EGYPTIAN POUNDS FROM THE AIRLINE AS (PROBABLY) AN APOLOGY. A POUND IS ABOUT 30 YEN (17 CENTS). WE LIVED ON THIS MONEY FOR THE NEXT DAY. WE HAD HEARD THAT ALL EGYPTIAN BILLS WERE DIRTY, BUT WE WERE WRONG. ONLY *SOME* OF THEM WERE *REALLY* FILTHY. THE ONE-POUND BILL WE GOT AS CHANGE AT A SOUVENIR SHOP SMELLED LIKE CAT BUTT. I SUPPOSE IT WAS BETTER THAN THE OTHER PLACES THAT WOULDN'T EVEN GIVE ANY CHANGE, BUT I'M NOT SURE. WE ENDED UP GETTING OUR LUGGAGE BACK 30 HOURS AFTER WE ARRIVED.

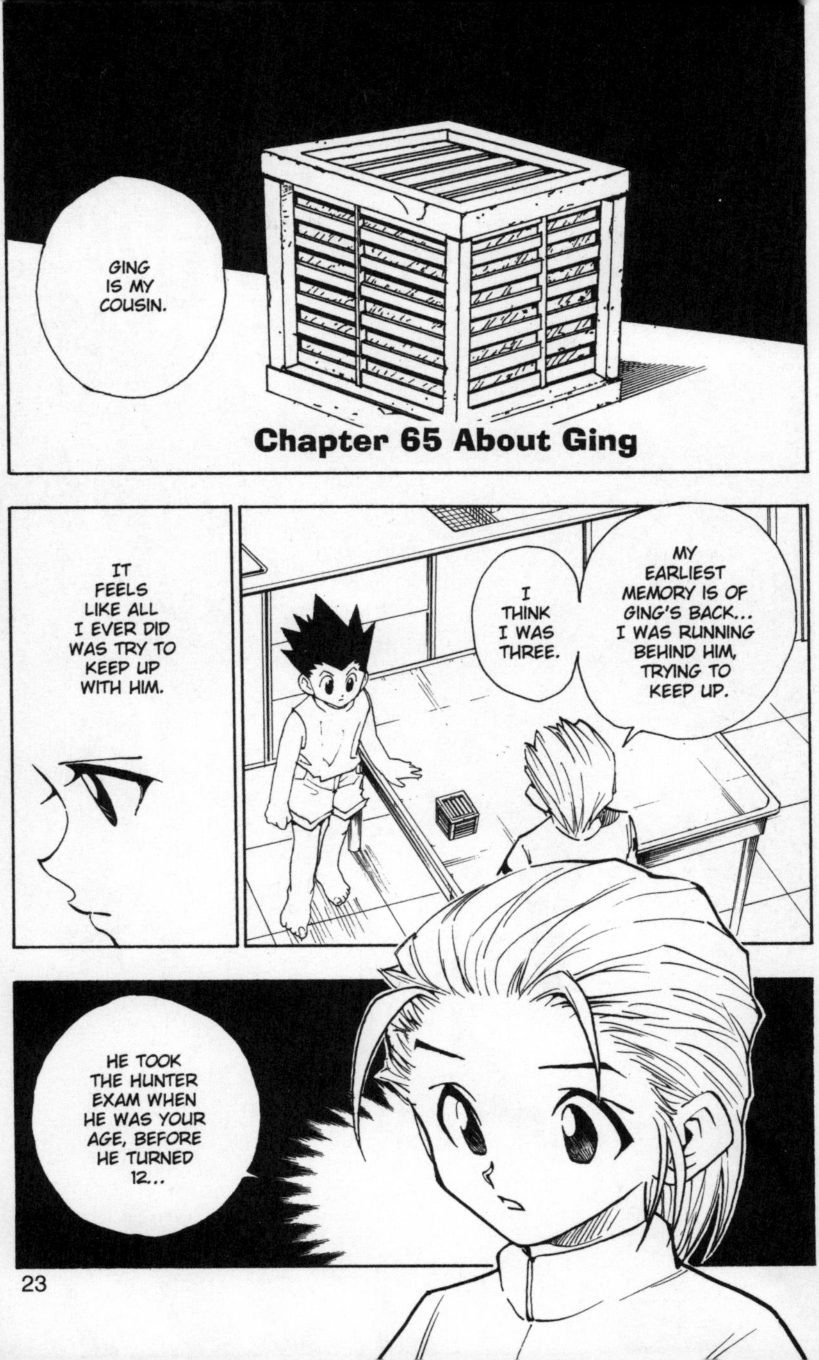
GING IS MY COUSIN.
Chapter 65 About Ging
MY EARLIEST MEMORY IS OF GING'S BACK... I WAS RUNNING BEHIND HIM, TRYING TO KEEP UP.
I THINK I WAS THREE.
IT FEELS LIKE ALL I EVER DID WAS TRY TO KEEP UP WITH HIM.
HE TOOK THE HUNTER EXAM WHEN HE WAS YOUR AGE, BEFORE HE TURNED 12...

Chapter 65
About Ging

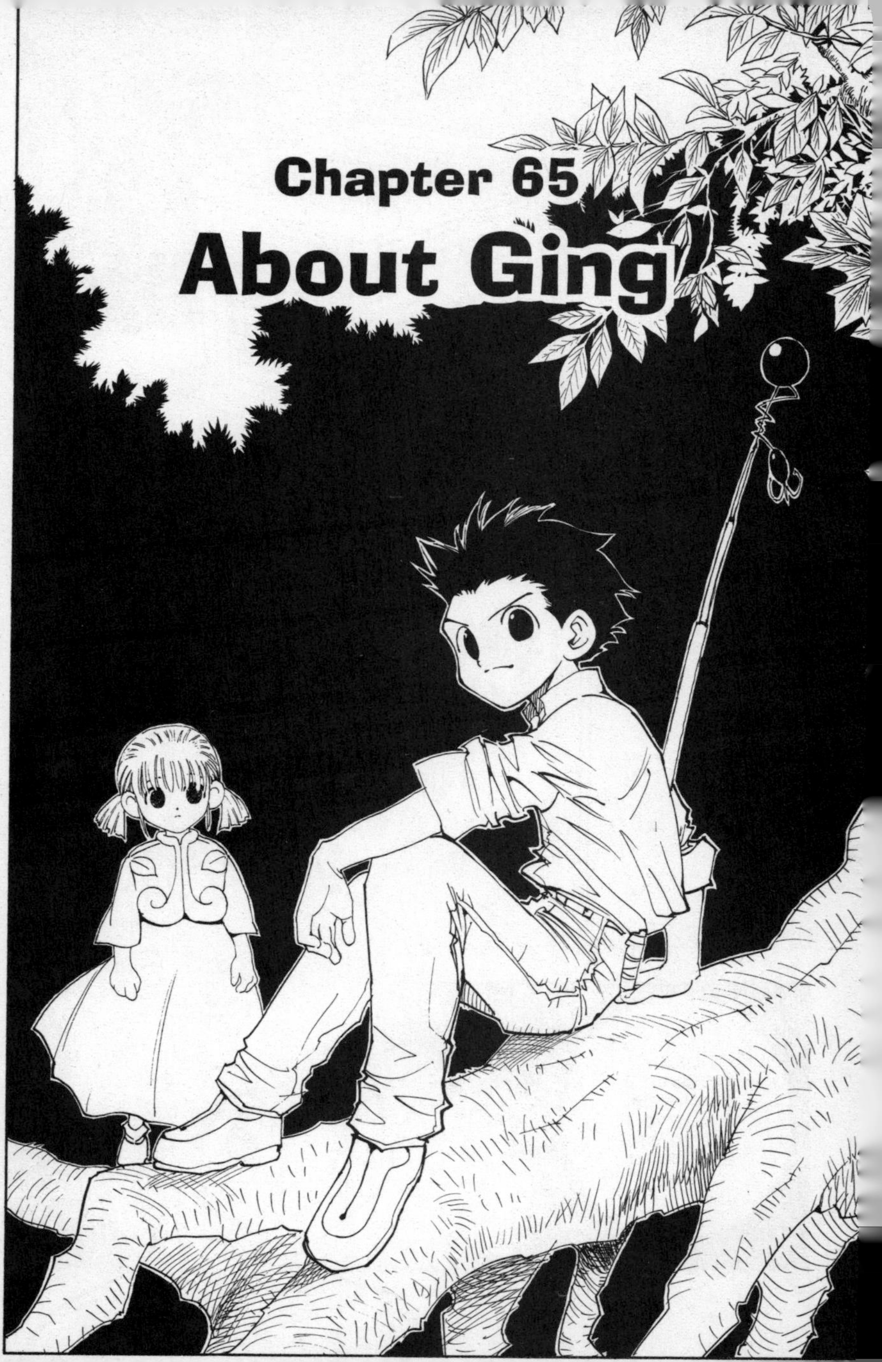

READ THIS WAY

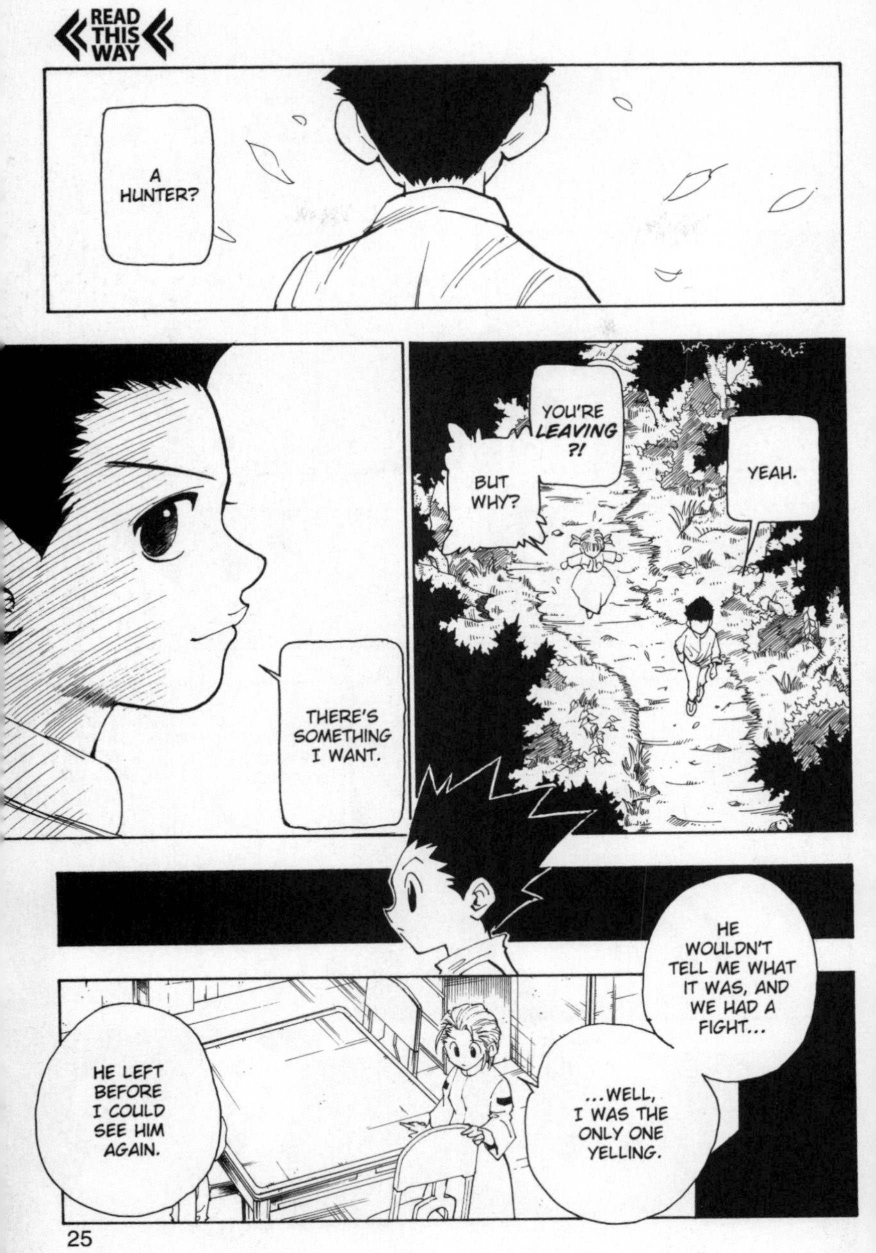
A HUNTER?
YOU'RE LEAVING?!
YEAH.
BUT WHY?
THERE'S SOMETHING I WANT.
HE WOULDN'T TELL ME WHAT IT WAS, AND WE HAD A FIGHT...
...WELL, I WAS THE ONLY ONE YELLING.
HE LEFT BEFORE I COULD SEE HIM AGAIN.

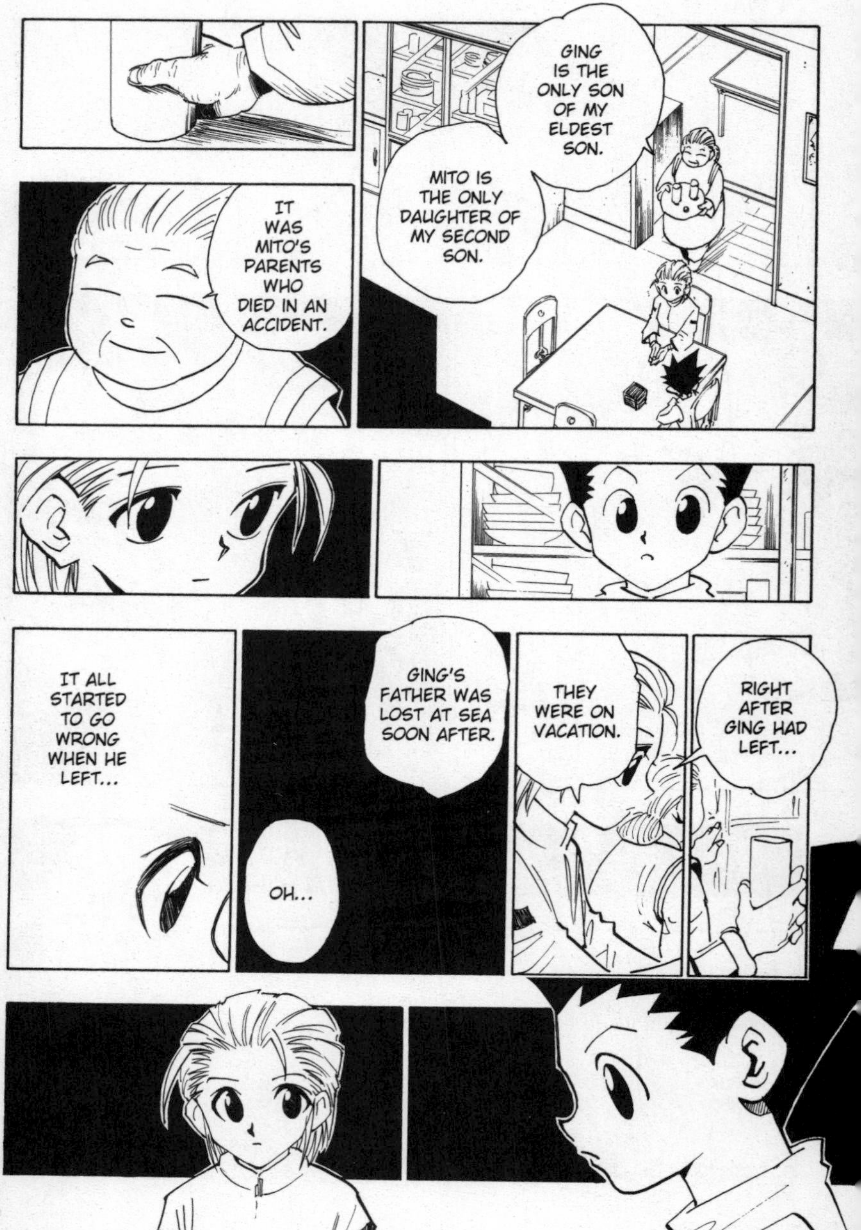
GING IS THE ONLY SON OF MY ELDEST SON.
MITO IS THE ONLY DAUGHTER OF MY SECOND SON.
IT WAS MITO'S PARENTS WHO DIED IN AN ACCIDENT.
RIGHT AFTER GING HAD LEFT...
THEY WERE ON VACATION.
GING'S FATHER WAS LOST AT SEA SOON AFTER.
OH...
IT ALL STARTED TO GO WRONG WHEN HE LEFT...

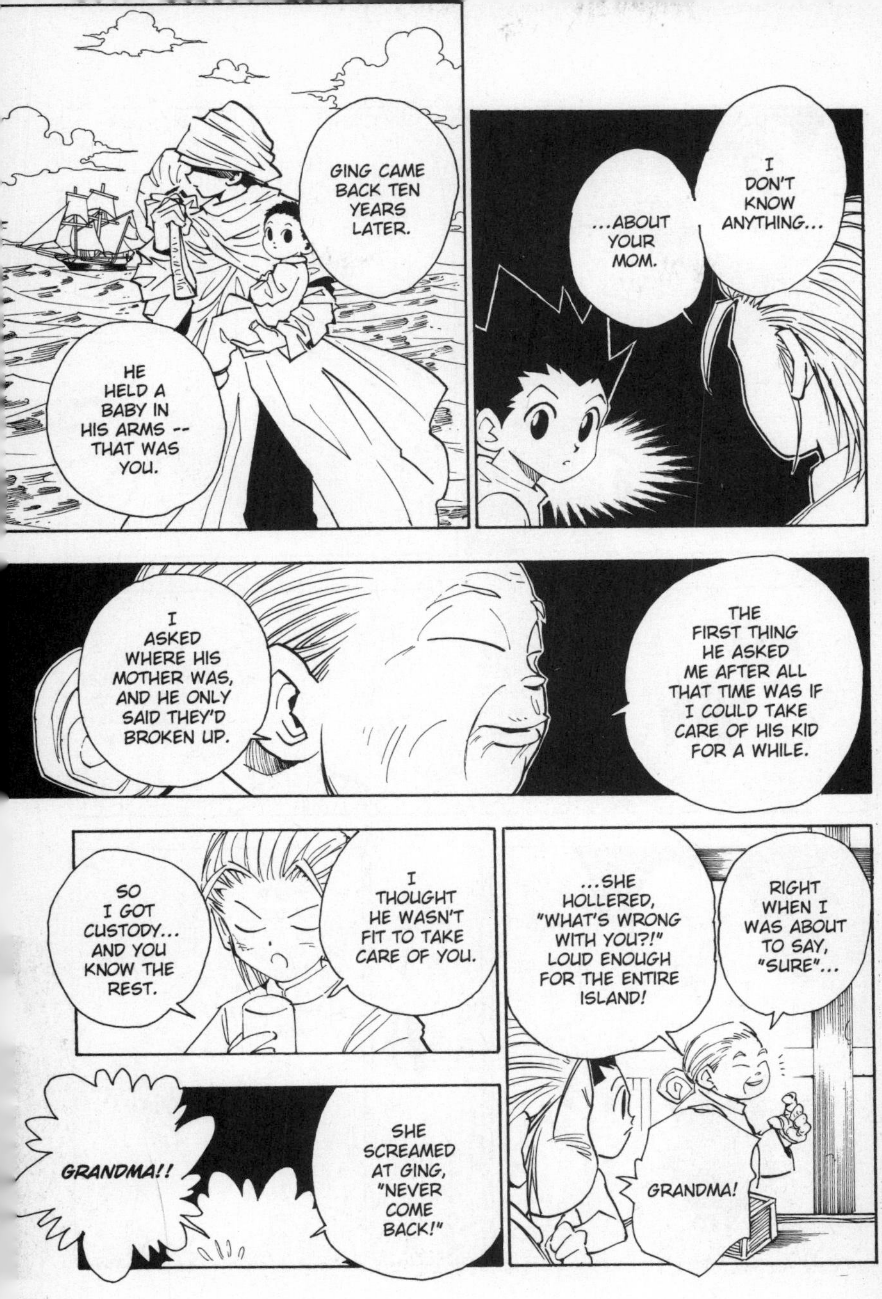
I DON'T KNOW ANYTHING...
...ABOUT YOUR MOM.
GING CAME BACK TEN YEARS LATER.
HE HELD A BABY IN HIS ARMS -- THAT WAS YOU.
THE FIRST THING HE ASKED ME AFTER ALL THAT TIME WAS IF I COULD TAKE CARE OF HIS KID FOR A WHILE.
I ASKED WHERE HIS MOTHER WAS, AND HE ONLY SAID THEY'D BROKEN UP.
RIGHT WHEN I WAS ABOUT TO SAY, "SURE"...
...SHE HOLLERED, "WHAT'S WRONG WITH YOU?!" LOUD ENOUGH FOR THE ENTIRE ISLAND!
GRANDMA!
I THOUGHT HE WASN'T FIT TO TAKE CARE OF YOU.
SO I GOT CUSTODY... AND YOU KNOW THE REST.
SHE SCREAMED AT GING, "NEVER COME BACK!"
GRANDMA!!

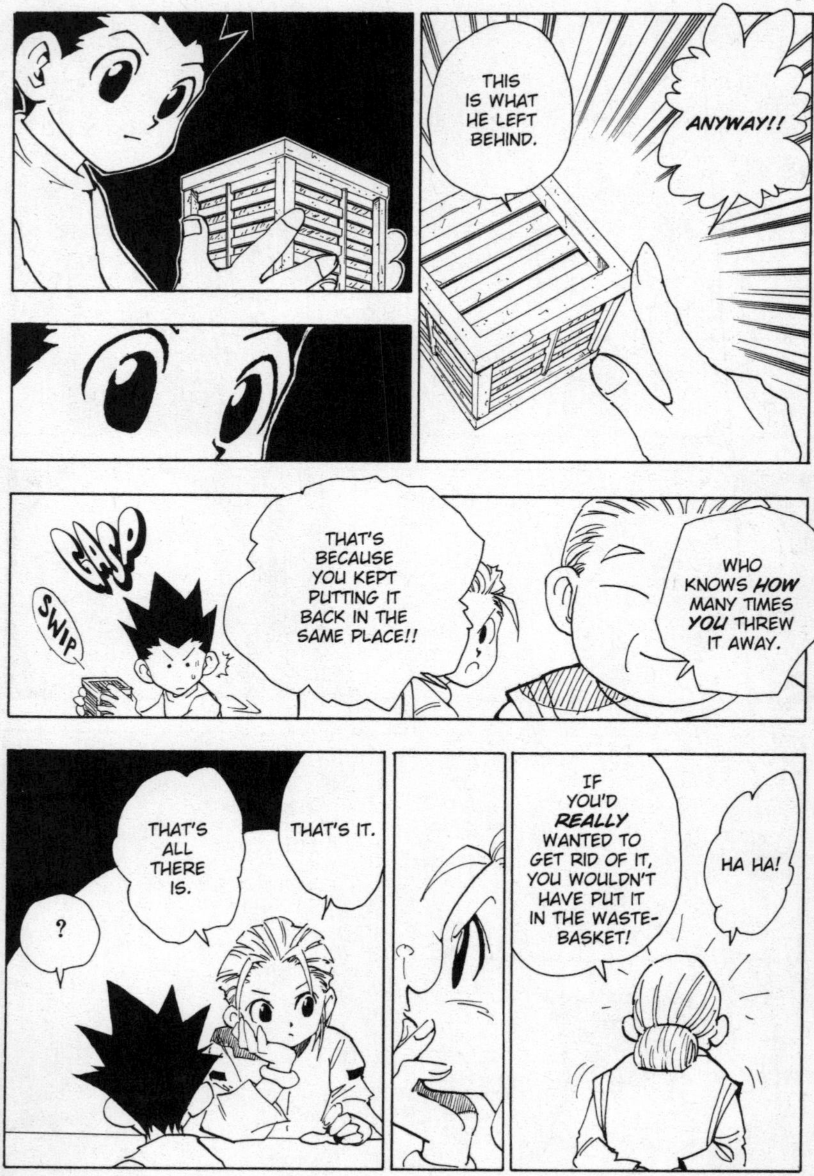
ANYWAY!!
THIS IS WHAT HE LEFT BEHIND.
WHO KNOWS HOW MANY TIMES YOU THREW IT AWAY.
THAT'S BECAUSE YOU KEPT PUTTING IT BACK IN THE SAME PLACE!!
GASP
SWIP
HA HA!
IF YOU'D REALLY WANTED TO GET RID OF IT, YOU WOULDN'T HAVE PUT IT IN THE WASTE-BASKET!
THAT'S IT.
THAT'S ALL THERE IS.
?

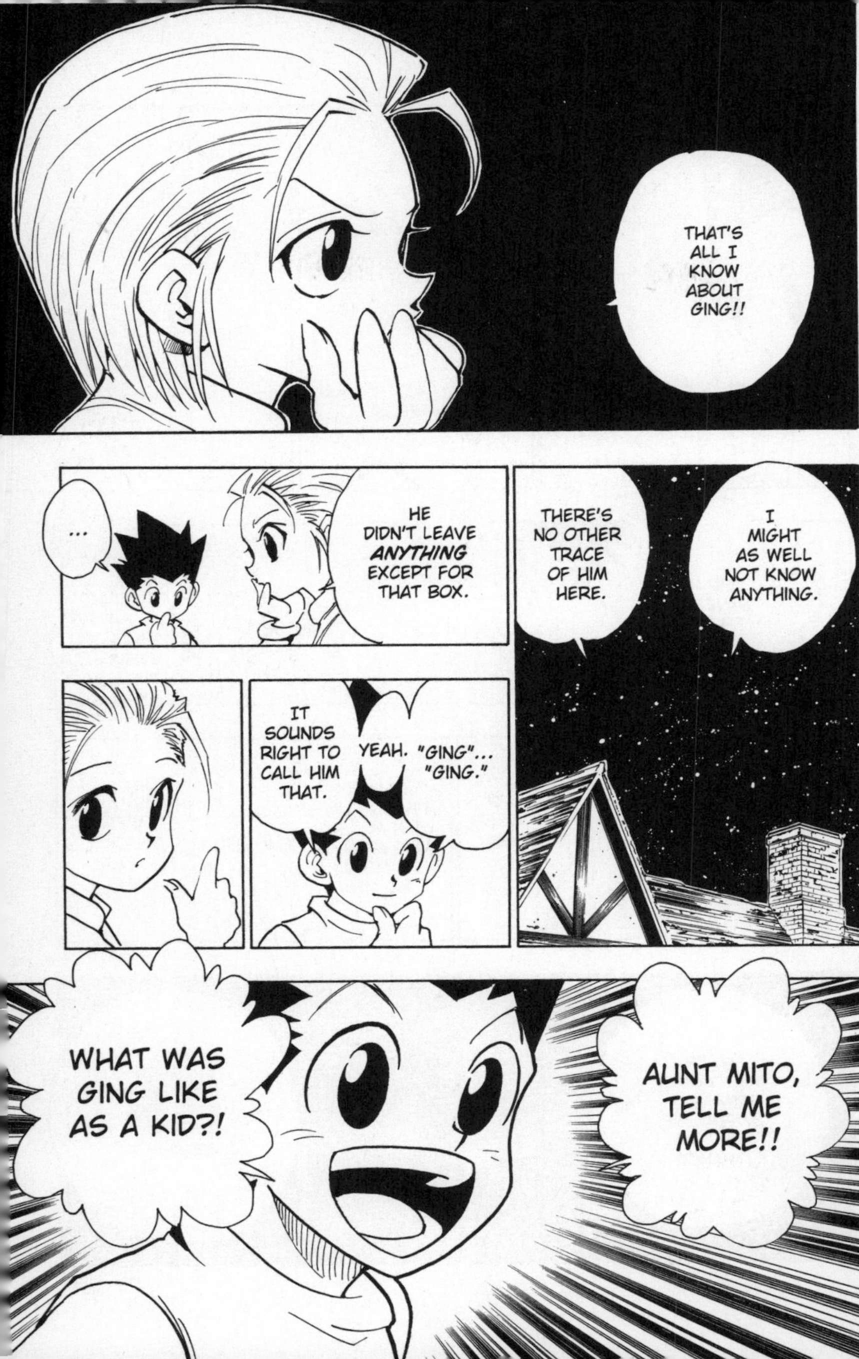
THAT'S ALL I KNOW ABOUT GING!!
I MIGHT AS WELL NOT KNOW ANYTHING.
THERE'S NO OTHER TRACE OF HIM HERE.
HE DIDN'T LEAVE *ANYTHING* EXCEPT FOR THAT BOX.
...
YEAH. "GING"... "GING."
IT SOUNDS RIGHT TO CALL HIM THAT.
AUNT MITO, TELL ME MORE!!
WHAT WAS GING LIKE AS A KID?!

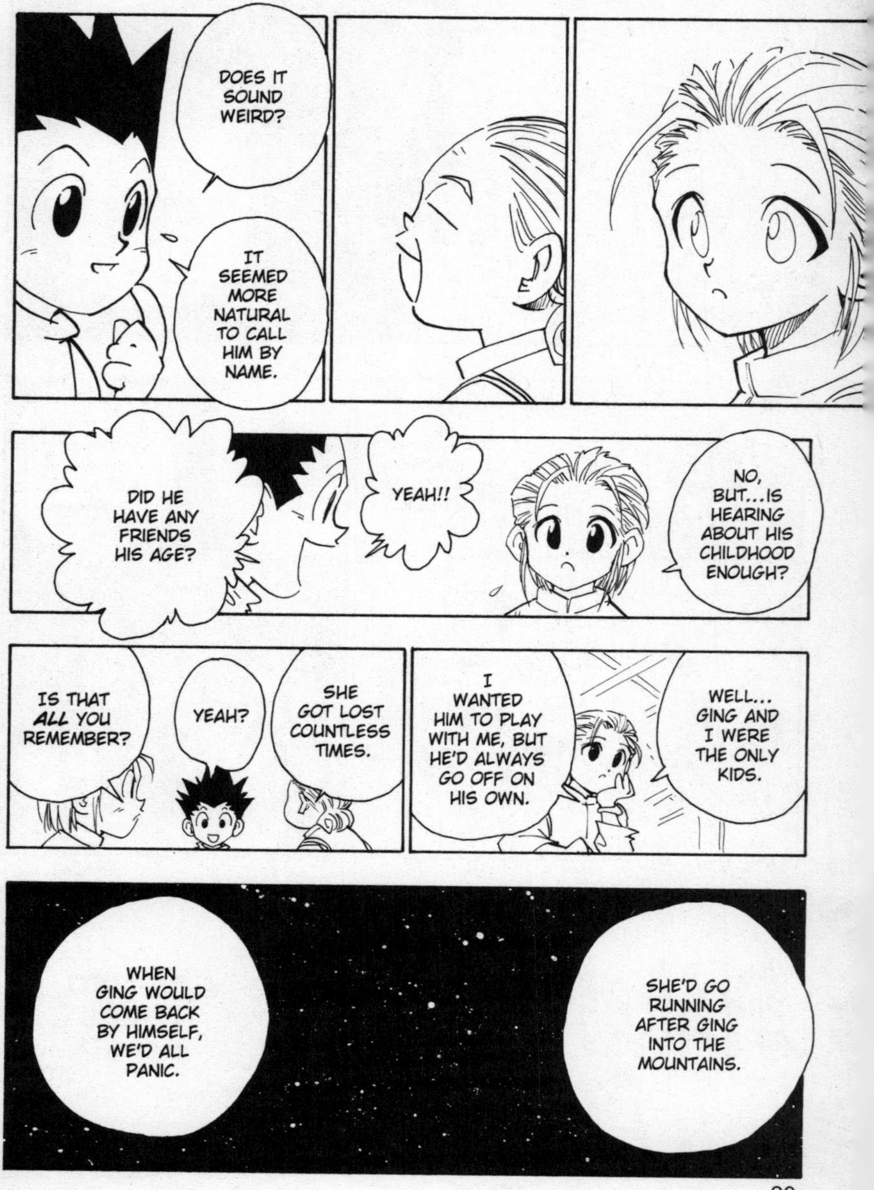
DOES IT SOUND WEIRD?
IT SEEMED MORE NATURAL TO CALL HIM BY NAME.
NO, BUT...IS HEARING ABOUT HIS CHILDHOOD ENOUGH?
YEAH!!
DID HE HAVE ANY FRIENDS HIS AGE?
WELL... GING AND I WERE THE ONLY KIDS.
I WANTED HIM TO PLAY WITH ME, BUT HE'D ALWAYS GO OFF ON HIS OWN.
SHE GOT LOST COUNTLESS TIMES.
YEAH?
IS THAT *ALL* YOU REMEMBER?
SHE'D GO RUNNING AFTER GING INTO THE MOUNTAINS.
WHEN GING WOULD COME BACK BY HIMSELF, WE'D ALL PANIC.

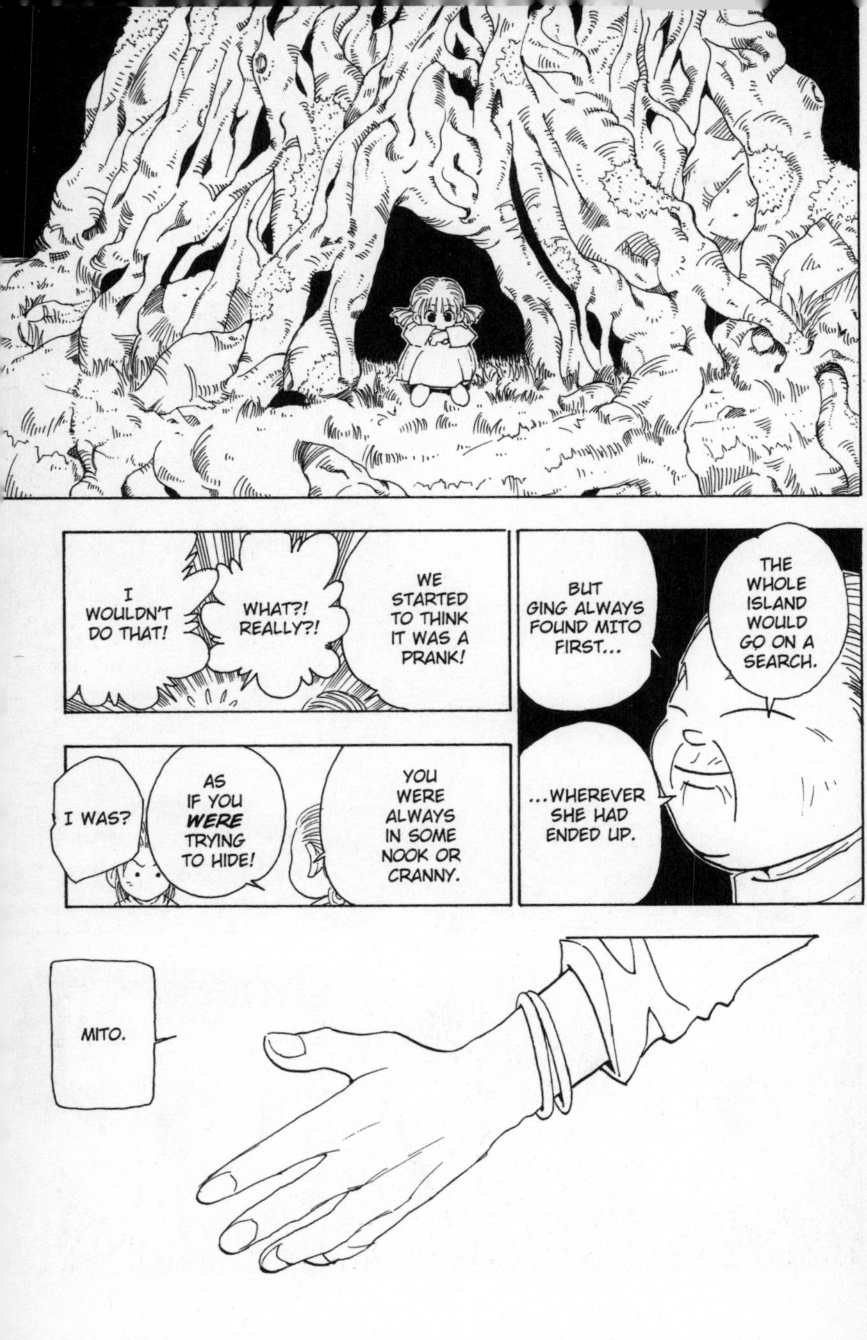
THE WHOLE ISLAND WOULD GO ON A SEARCH.
BUT GING ALWAYS FOUND MITO FIRST...
...WHEREVER SHE HAD ENDED UP.
WE STARTED TO THINK IT WAS A PRANK!
WHAT?! REALLY?!
I WOULDN'T DO THAT!
YOU WERE ALWAYS IN SOME NOOK OR CRANNY.
AS IF YOU *WERE* TRYING TO HIDE!
I WAS?
MITO.

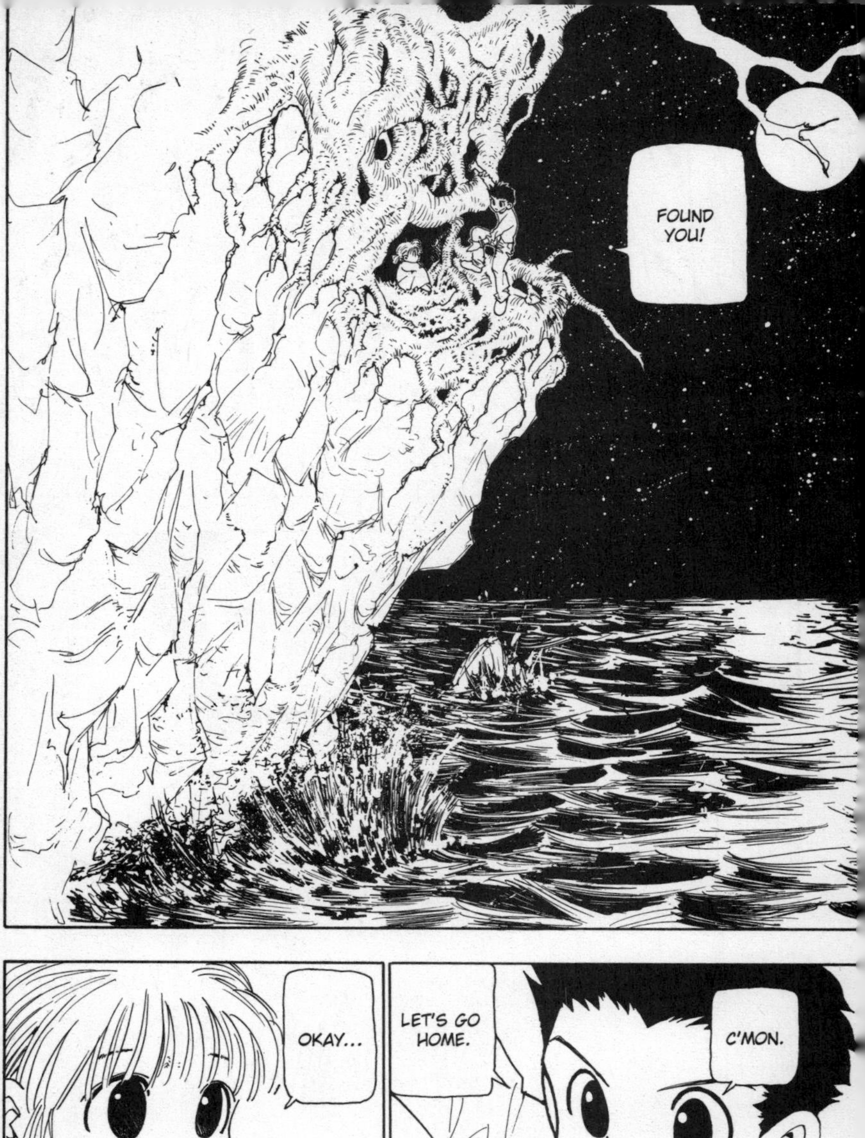
FOUND YOU!
C'MON.
LET'S GO HOME.
OKAY...

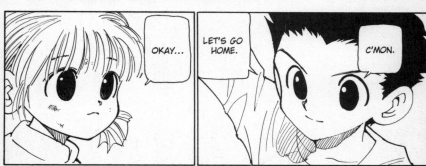

READ THIS WAY

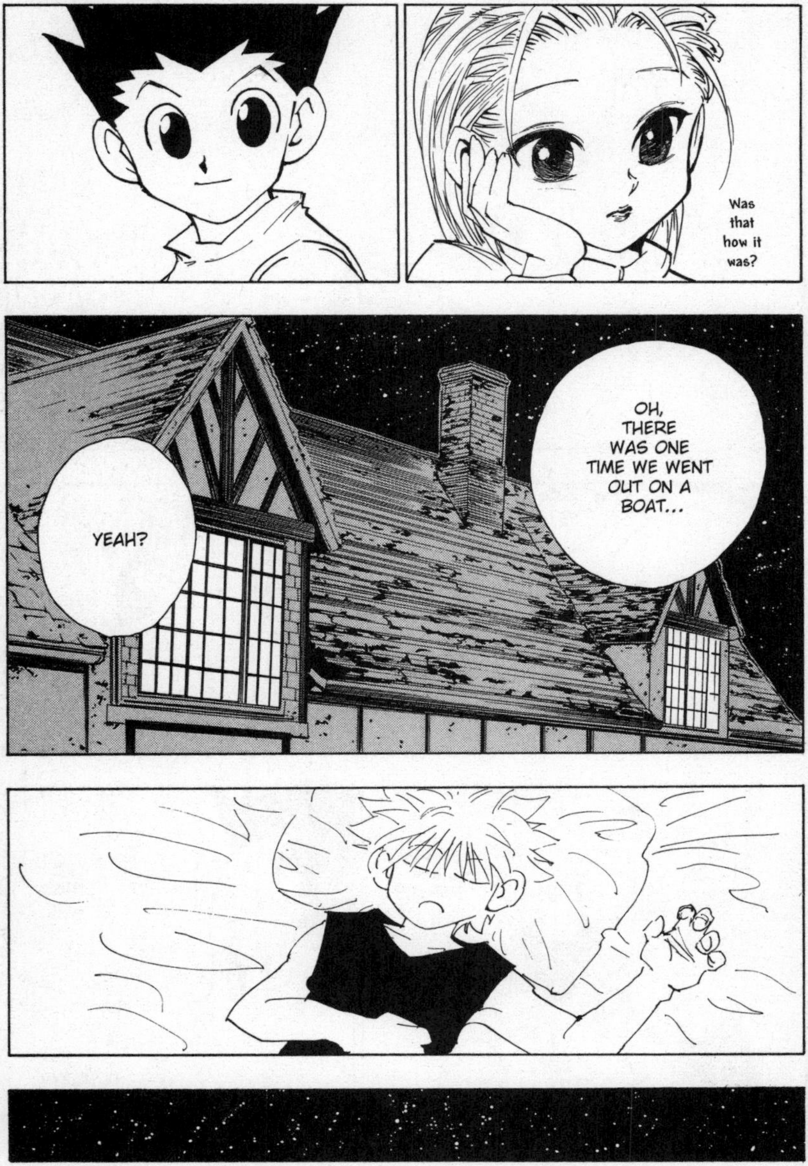
Was that how it was?
OH, THERE WAS ONE TIME WE WENT OUT ON A BOAT...
YEAH?

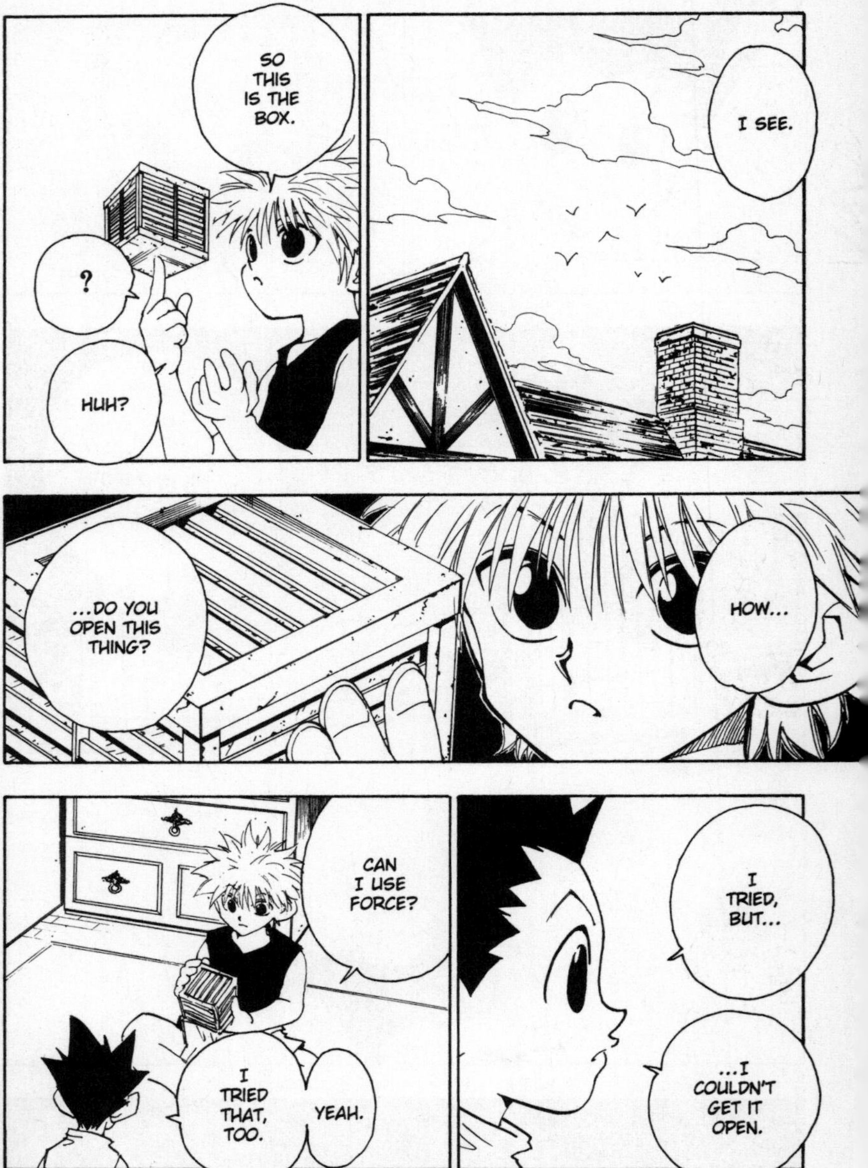
I SEE.
SO THIS IS THE BOX.
?
HUH?
HOW...
...DO YOU OPEN THIS THING?
I TRIED, BUT...
...I COULDN'T GET IT OPEN.
CAN I USE FORCE?
YEAH.
I TRIED THAT, TOO.

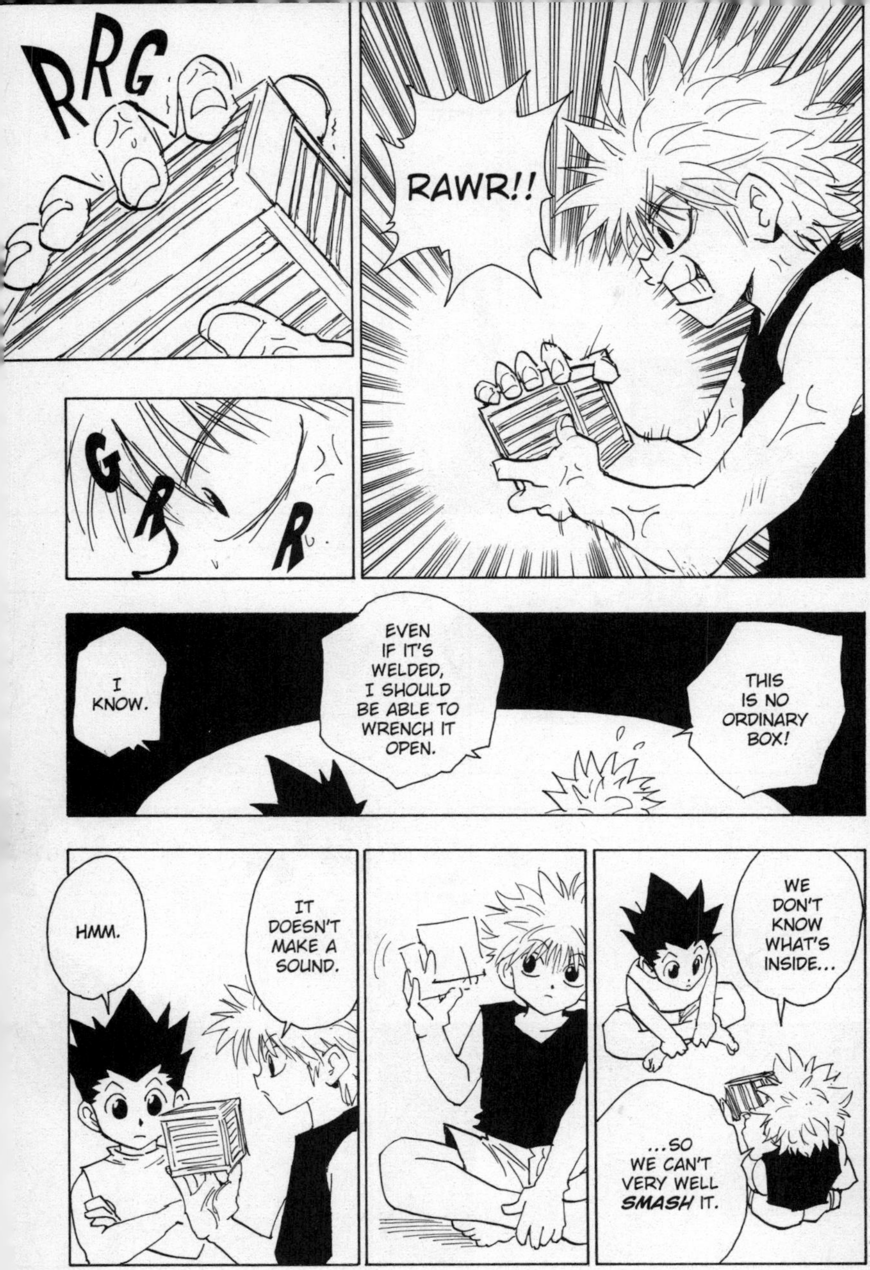
RAWR!!
RRG
GRR
THIS IS NO ORDINARY BOX!
EVEN IF IT'S WELDED, I SHOULD BE ABLE TO WRENCH IT OPEN.
I KNOW.
WE DON'T KNOW WHAT'S INSIDE...
...SO WE CAN'T VERY WELL *SMASH* IT.
IT DOESN'T MAKE A SOUND.
HMM.

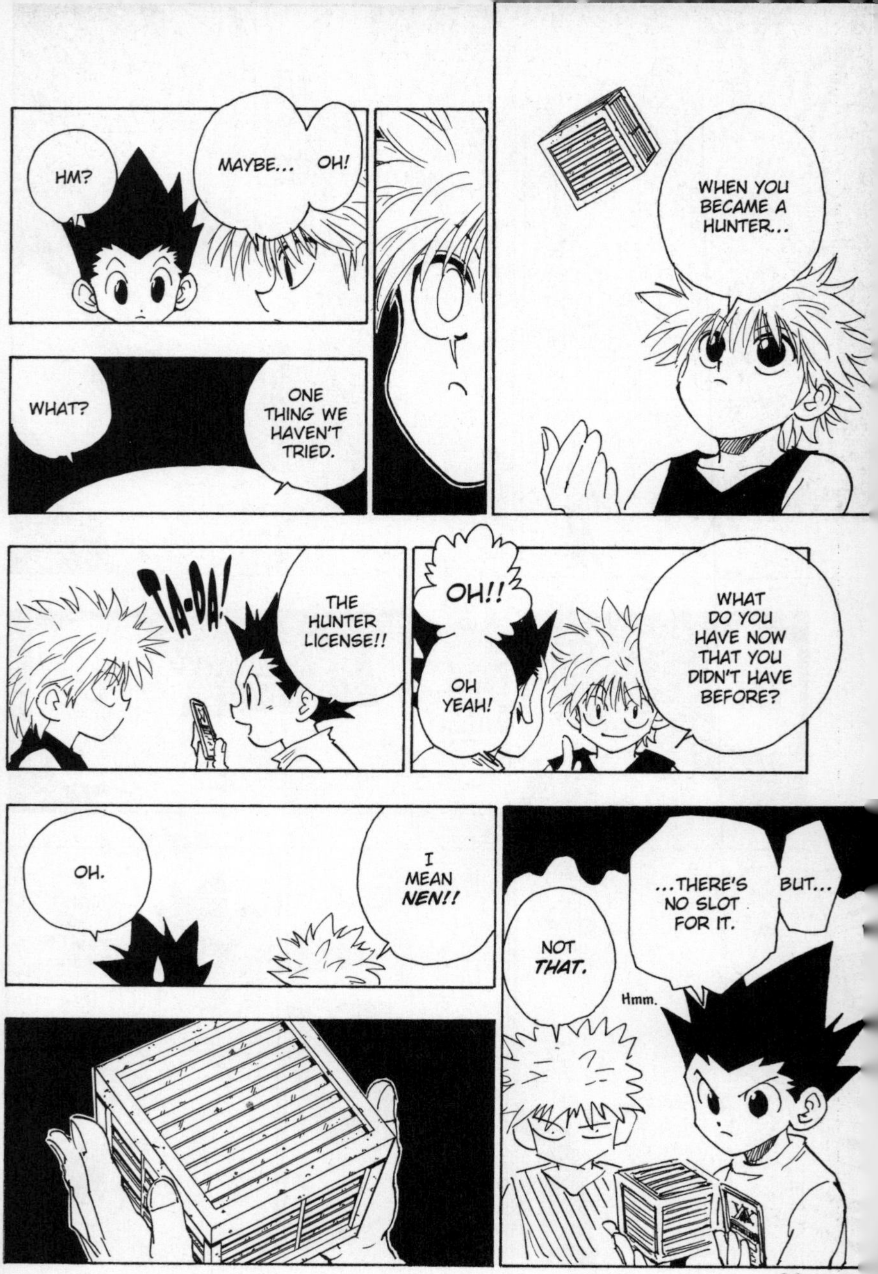
WHEN YOU BECAME A HUNTER...
MAYBE... OH!
HM?
ONE THING WE HAVEN'T TRIED.
WHAT?
WHAT DO YOU HAVE NOW THAT YOU DIDN'T HAVE BEFORE?
OH!!
OH YEAH!
THE HUNTER LICENSE!!
TA-DA!
BUT...
...THERE'S NO SLOT FOR IT.
NOT *THAT*.
Hmm.
I MEAN *NEN!!*
OH.

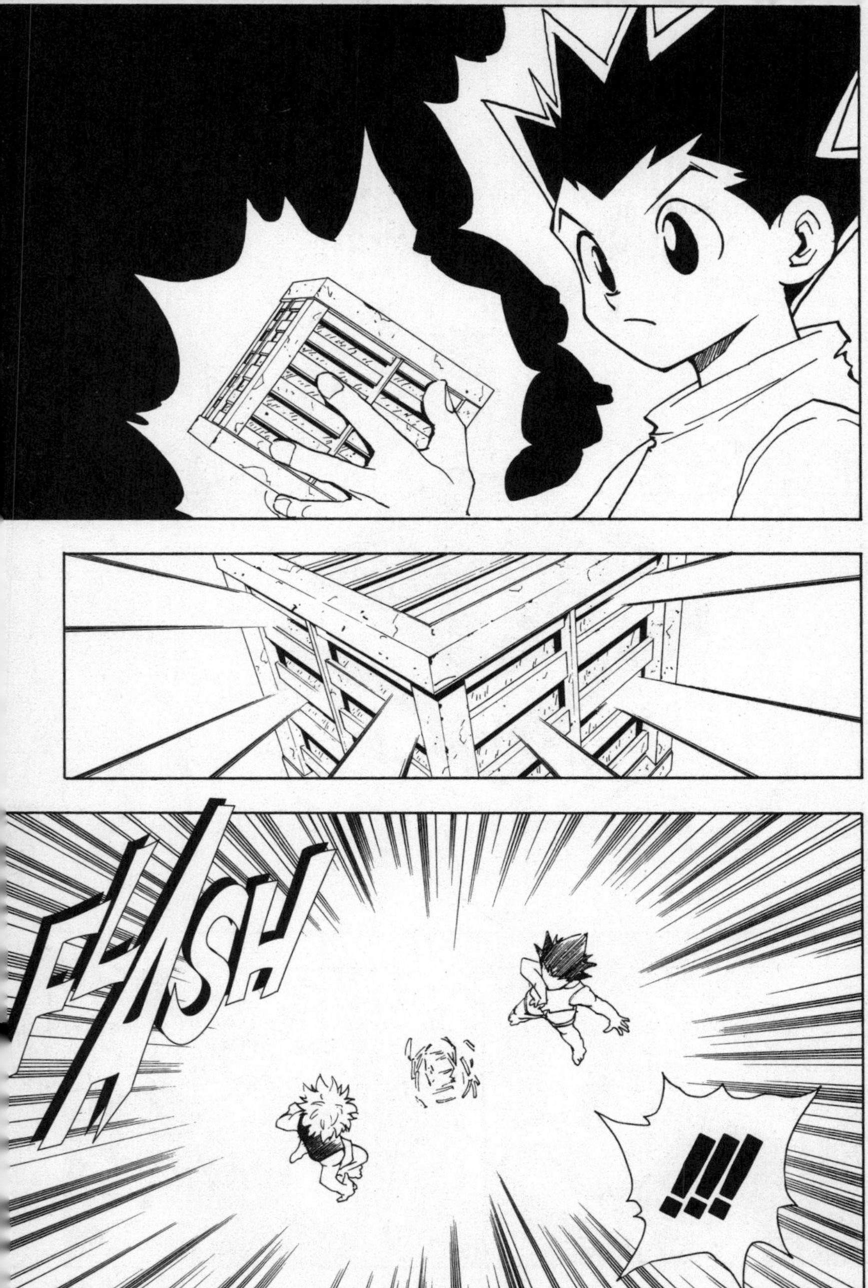
FLASH
!!!

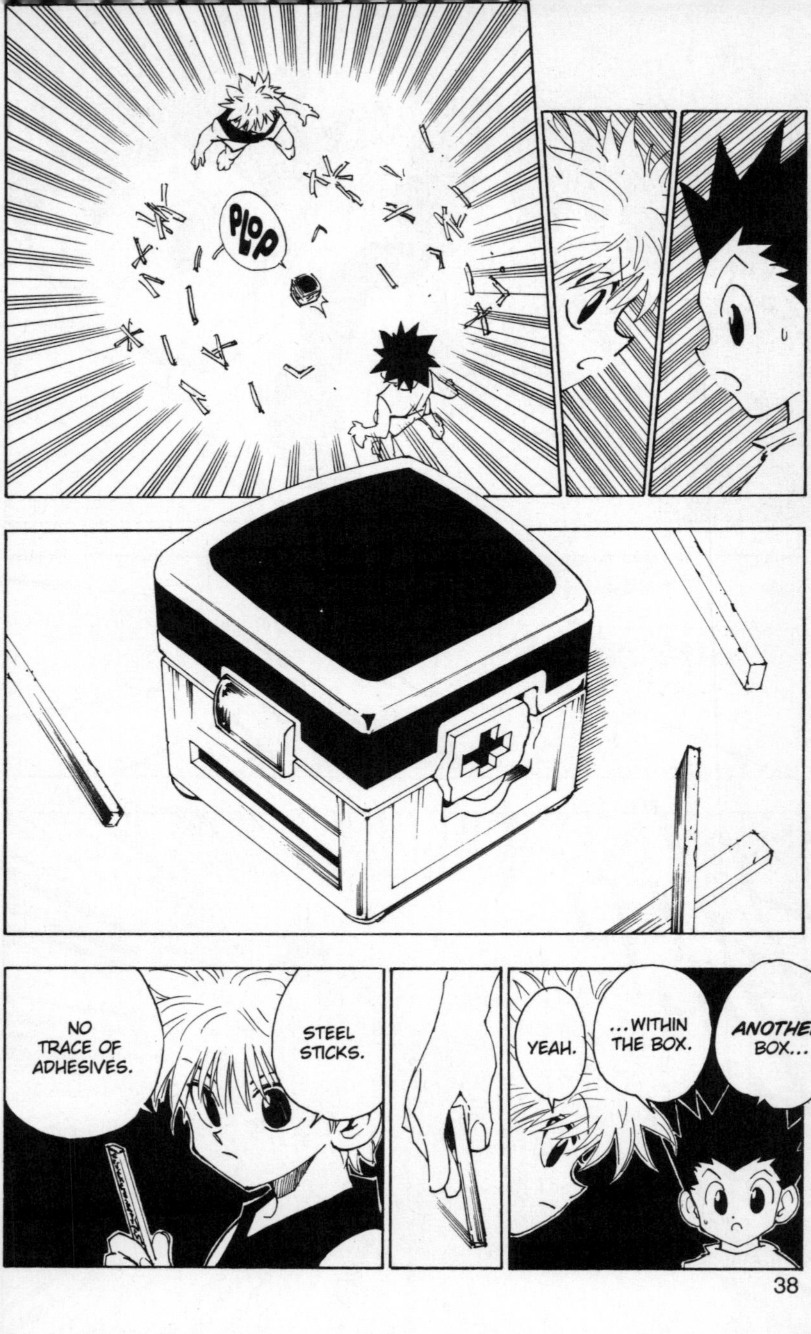
PLOP
ANOTHER BOX...
...WITHIN THE BOX.
YEAH.
STEEL STICKS.
NO TRACE OF ADHESIVES.

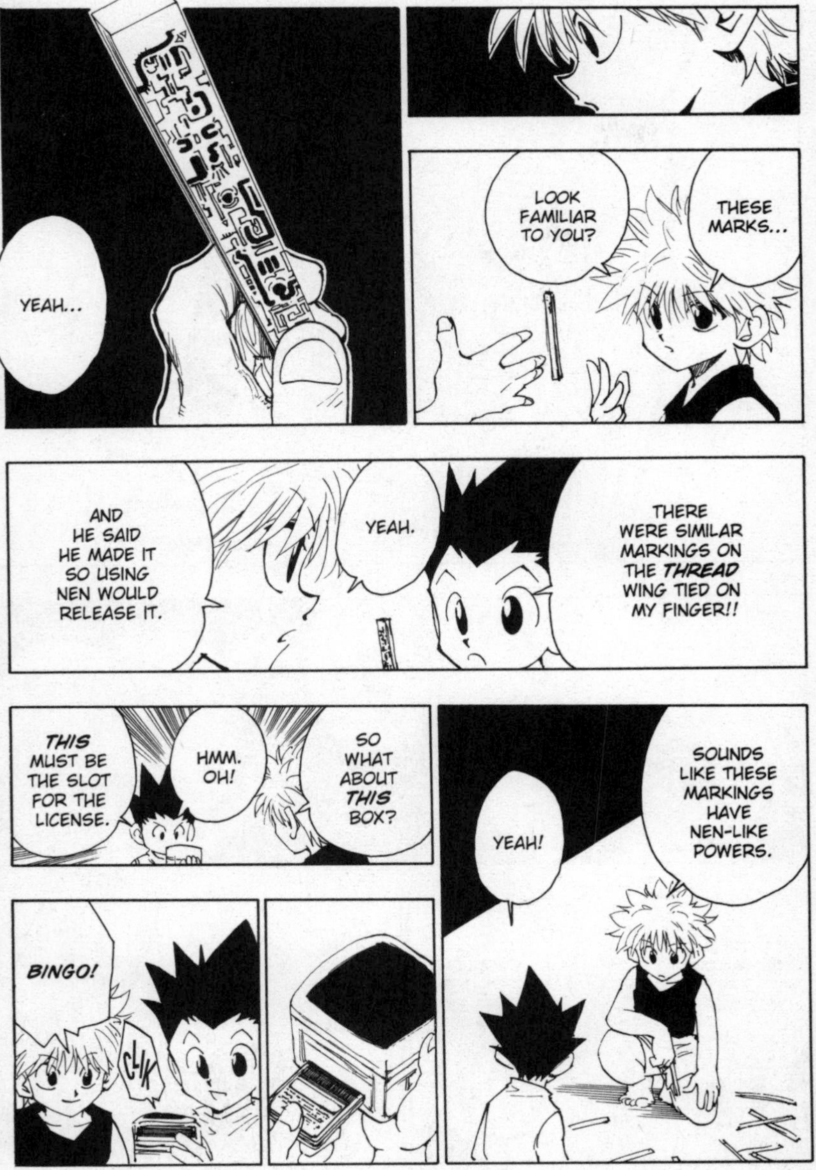
THESE MARKS...
LOOK FAMILIAR TO YOU?
YEAH...
THERE WERE SIMILAR MARKINGS ON THE *THREAD* WING TIED ON MY FINGER!!
YEAH.
AND HE SAID HE MADE IT SO USING NEN WOULD RELEASE IT.
SOUNDS LIKE THESE MARKINGS HAVE NEN-LIKE POWERS.
YEAH!
SO WHAT ABOUT *THIS* BOX?
HMM. OH!
THIS MUST BE THE SLOT FOR THE LICENSE.
CLIK
BINGO!

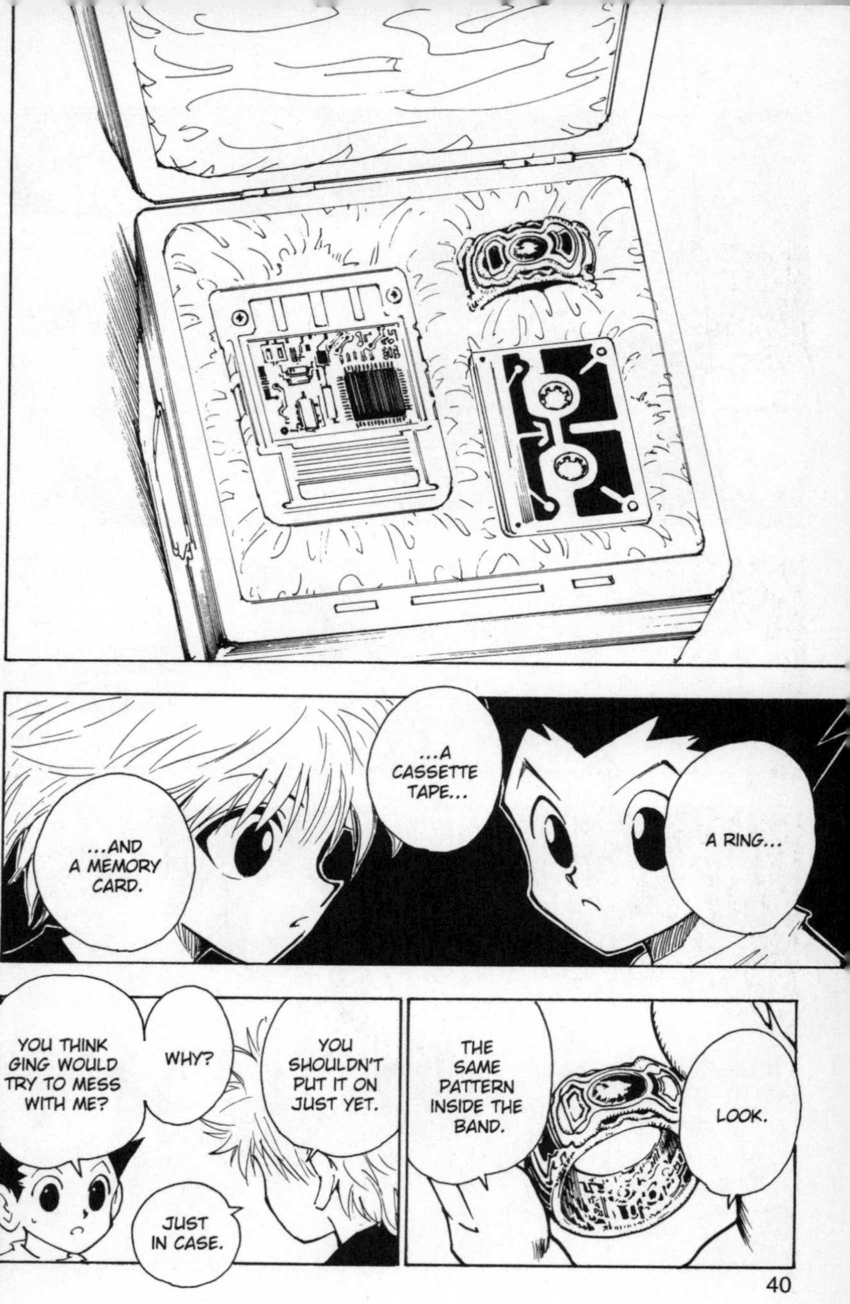
A RING...
...A CASSETTE TAPE...
...AND A MEMORY CARD.
LOOK.
THE SAME PATTERN INSIDE THE BAND.
YOU SHOULDN'T PUT IT ON JUST YET.
WHY?
YOU THINK GING WOULD TRY TO MESS WITH ME?
JUST IN CASE.

READ THIS WAY

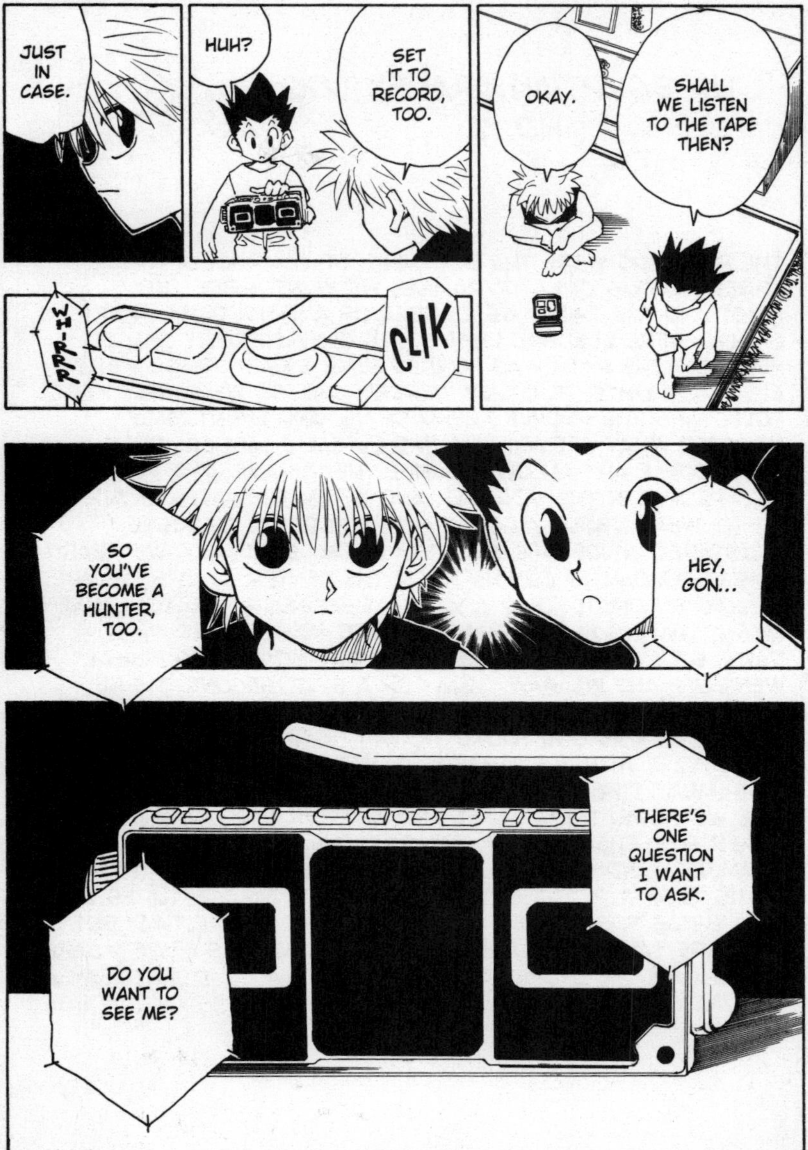
SHALL WE LISTEN TO THE TAPE THEN?
OKAY.
SET IT TO RECORD, TOO.
HUH?
JUST IN CASE.
CLIK
WHIRRR
HEY, GON...
SO YOU'VE BECOME A HUNTER, TOO.
THERE'S ONE QUESTION I WANT TO ASK.
DO YOU WANT TO SEE ME?

OUR EGYPTIAN TRAVEL LOG NO. 2

THE PYRAMIDS WERE THE BIG THING, OF COURSE. OF THE THREE FAMOUS GREAT PYRAMIDS, WE WENT INSIDE THE FIRST AND THE THIRD. WE CLIMBED UP A LONG, DARK SHAFT (THERE WERE ELECTRIC LIGHTS, BUT THEY WEREN'T ON). IT FELT LIKE THE PATH WAS FORKED (LIKE I SAID, THERE WERE ELECTRIC LIGHTS, BUT THEY WEREN'T ON), SO WE SIMPLY KEPT FOLLOWING THE PEOPLE AHEAD OF US, AND EVENTUALLY REACHED WHAT SEEMED LIKE THE BURIAL CHAMBER. ONLY 300 PEOPLE ARE ALLOWED INSIDE THE PYRAMID PER DAY (150 PEOPLE IN THE MORNING, AND 150 IN THE AFTERNOON). THERE WERE ABOUT A DOZEN OTHER FOREIGN TOURISTS CLUSTERED INSIDE THIS 5m X 10m ROOM. SUDDENLY, WE HEARD THIS ODD MOANING COMING FROM THE CENTER OF THE CHAMBER. IT WAS A MONOTONOUS VOICE THAT SOUNDED LIKE, "OHHMM," LIKE A CHORUS ENDLESSLY TUNING TO MIDDLE C. IT WAS DARK, SO I COULDN'T REALLY TELL, BUT SOMEONE'S FLASH WENT OFF AND WE SAW THEM FOR A SPLIT SECOND. THERE WERE ABOUT FIVE OR SIX WESTERNERS (MOSTLY OLD MEN, BUT THERE WAS ONE YOUNG WOMAN, TOO) HOLDING HANDS IN A CIRCLE, WITH THEIR HANDS RAISED HIGH, ALL MOANING, "OHHHMM." I BET THE OTHER TOURISTS WERE WEIRDED OUT LIKE WE WERE. THEN, THESE PEOPLE STARTED HUGGING EACH OTHER ECSTATICALLY AND CLUNG TO THE WALLS OF THE CHAMBER--AND STARTED MOANING AGAIN. WHENEVER THE REST OF US TOOK A PICTURE, THEY SAID, "DON'T TAKE PICTURES OF US." I WAS TOO SCARED TO SAY ANYTHING AT THE TIME, BUT WE WERE TAKING PICTURES OF THE CHAMBER! AS IF WE'D CARE ABOUT RANDOM, STUPID PEOPLE! BUT ACTUALLY, I DID SNEAK A PICTURE OF THEM, TOO.

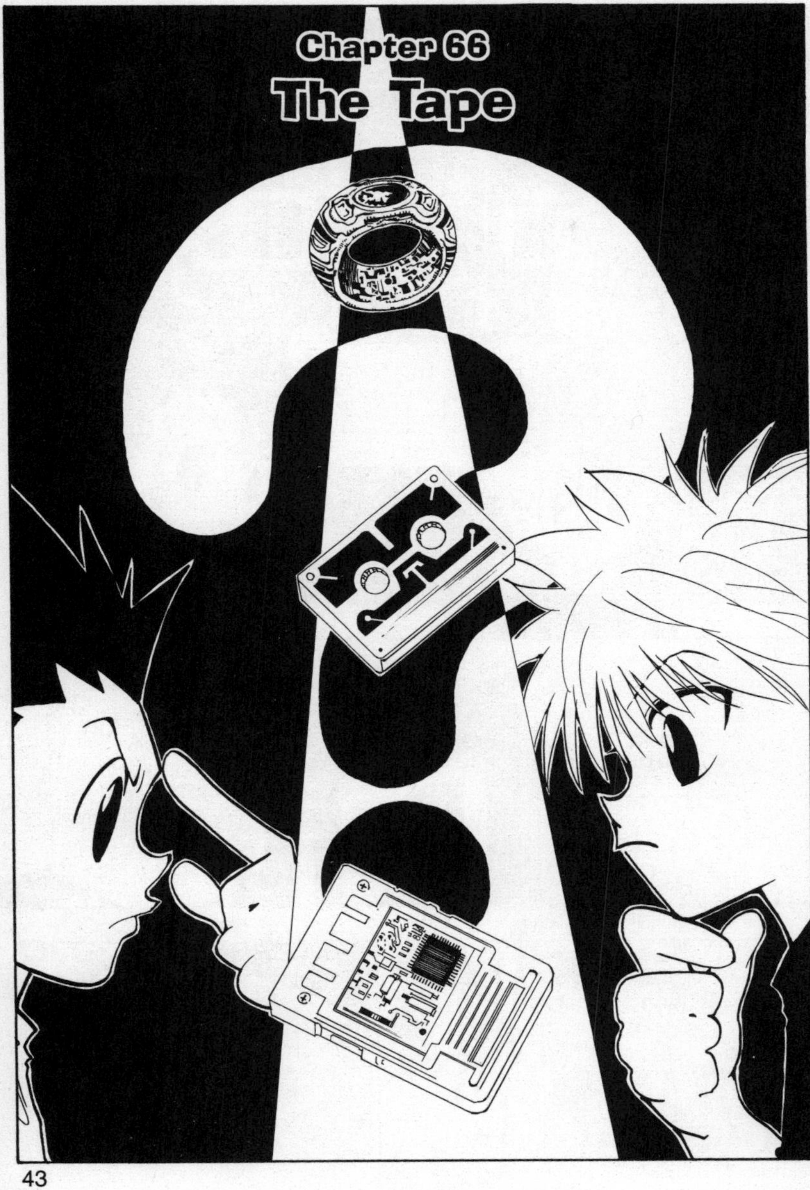
Chapter 66
The Tape

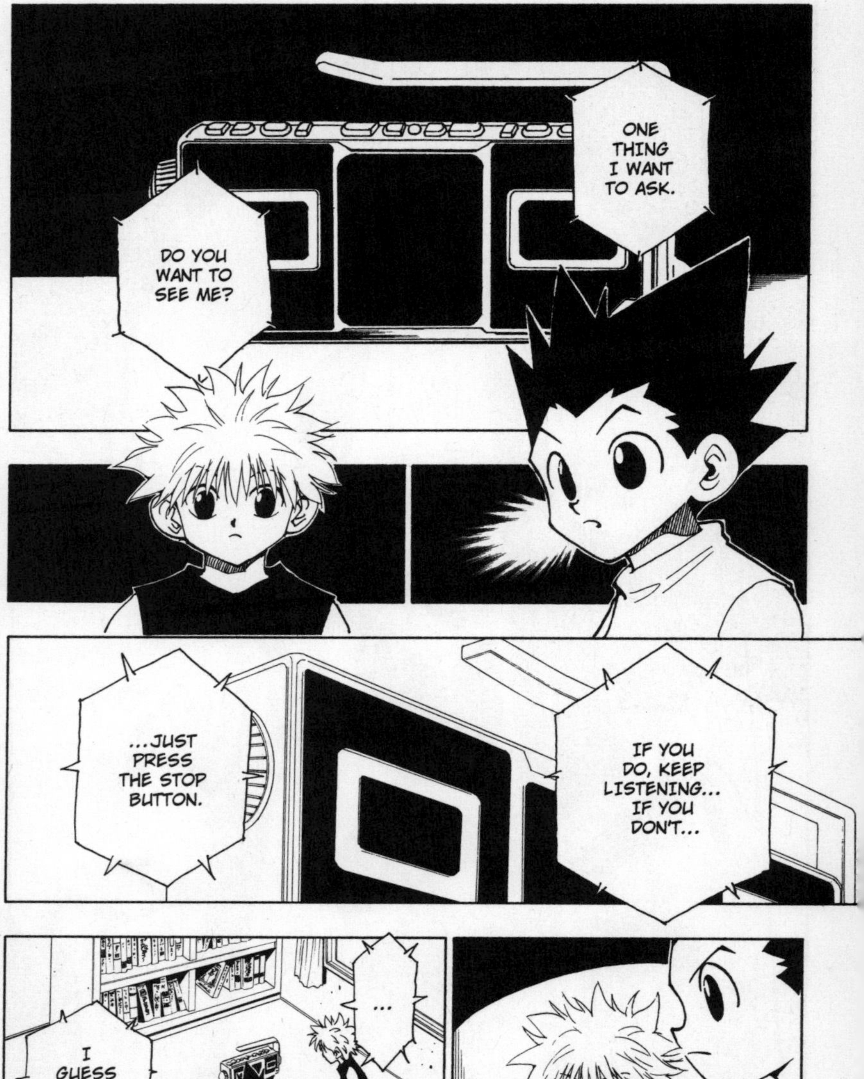
ONE THING I WANT TO ASK.
DO YOU WANT TO SEE ME?
IF YOU DO, KEEP LISTENING... IF YOU DON'T...
...JUST PRESS THE STOP BUTTON.
...
I GUESS THAT'S A "YES."

READ THIS WAY

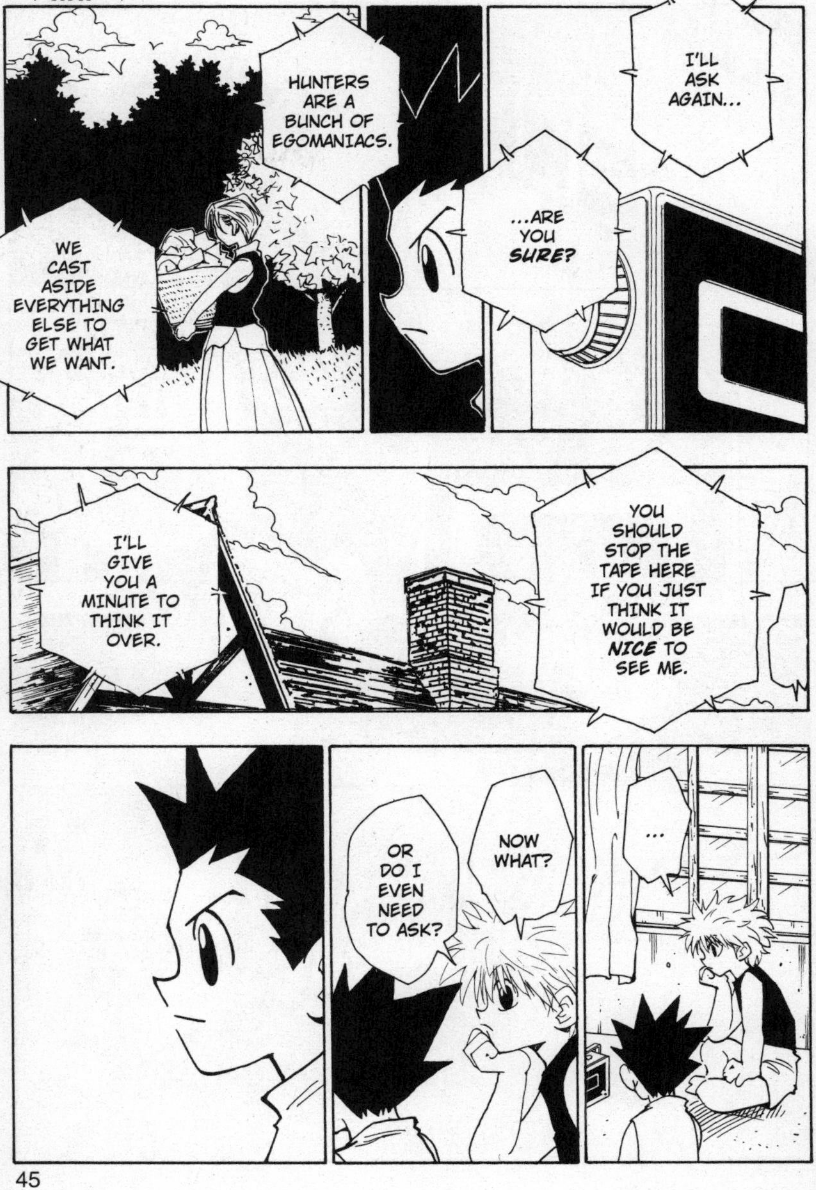
I'LL ASK AGAIN...
...ARE YOU *SURE?*
HUNTERS ARE A BUNCH OF EGOMANIACS.
WE CAST ASIDE EVERYTHING ELSE TO GET WHAT WE WANT.
YOU SHOULD STOP THE TAPE HERE IF YOU JUST THINK IT WOULD BE *NICE* TO SEE ME.
I'LL GIVE YOU A MINUTE TO THINK IT OVER.
...
NOW WHAT?
OR DO I EVEN NEED TO ASK?

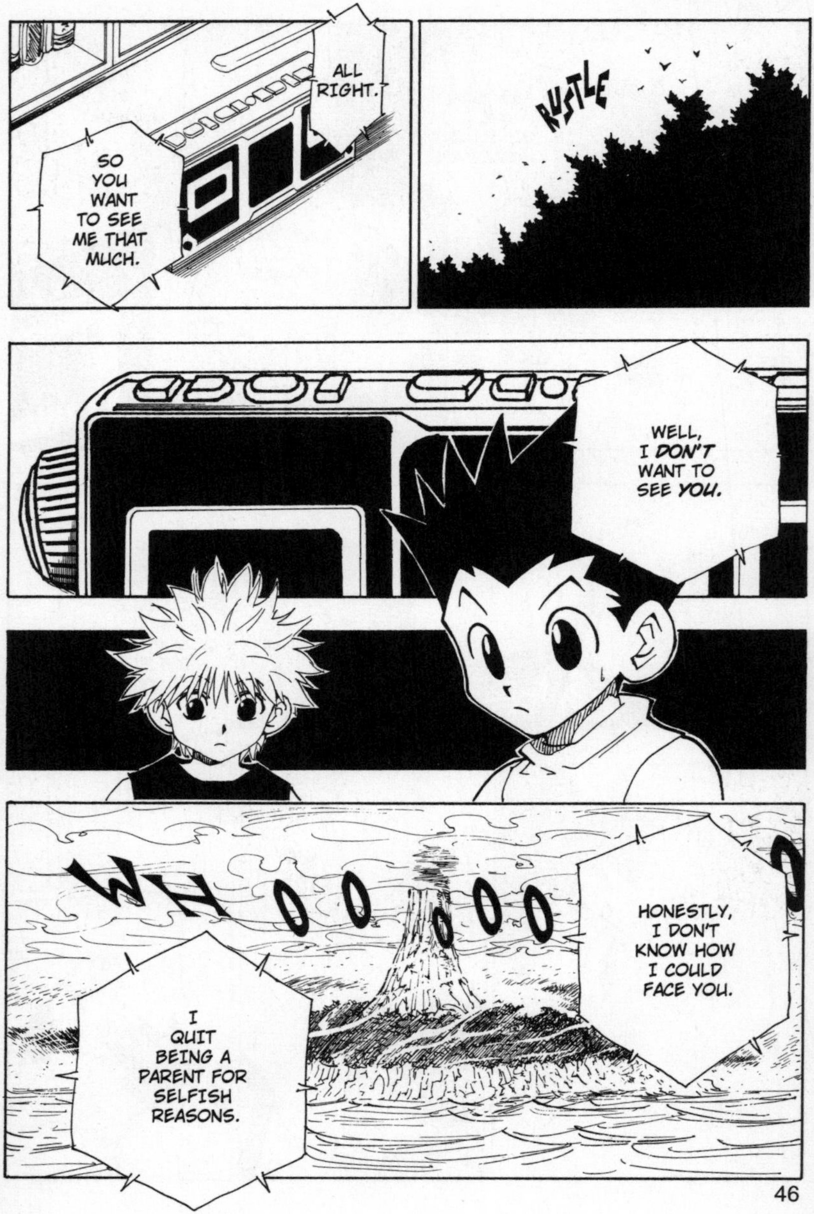
RUSTLE
ALL RIGHT.
SO YOU WANT TO SEE ME THAT MUCH.
WELL, I *DON'T* WANT TO SEE *YOU*.
HONESTLY, I DON'T KNOW HOW I COULD FACE YOU.
WHOOOOOO
I QUIT BEING A PARENT FOR SELFISH REASONS.

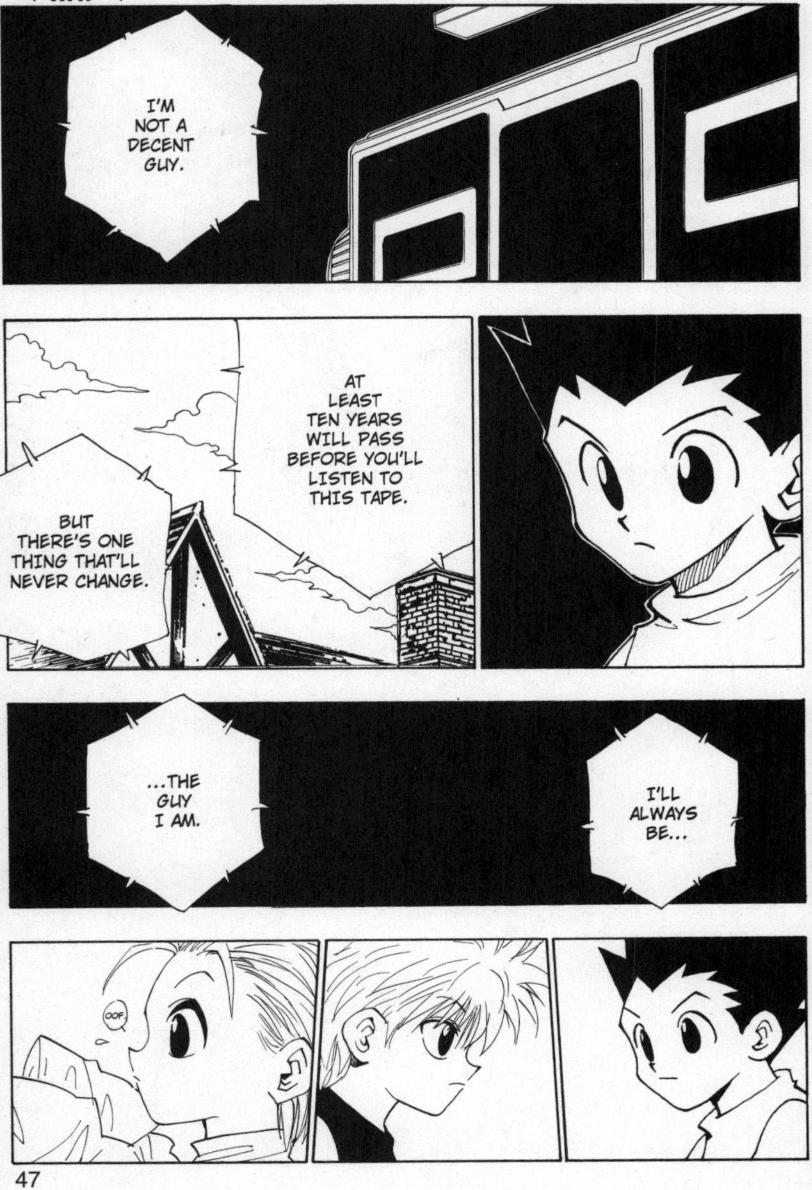
READ THIS WAY
I'M NOT A DECENT GUY.
AT LEAST TEN YEARS WILL PASS BEFORE YOU'LL LISTEN TO THIS TAPE.
BUT THERE'S ONE THING THAT'LL NEVER CHANGE.
I'LL ALWAYS BE...
...THE GUY I AM.
OOF.

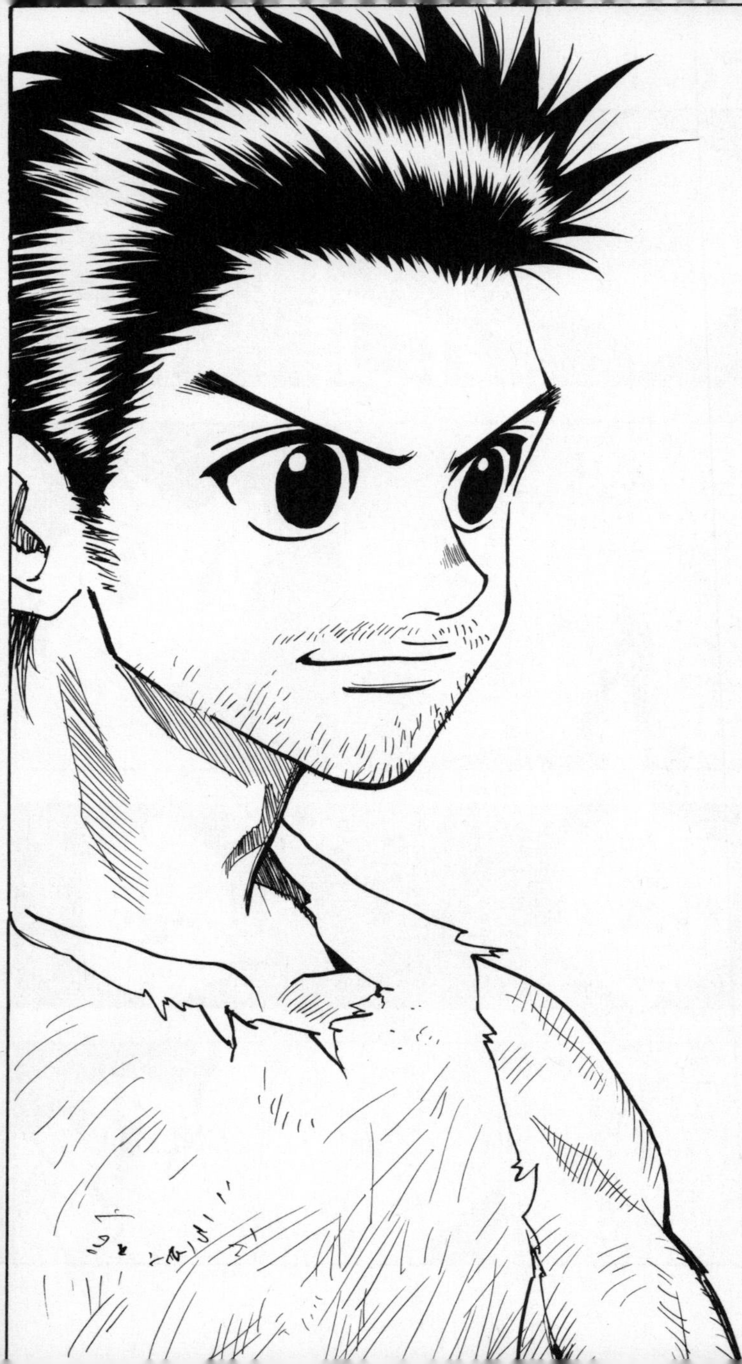

READ THIS WAY

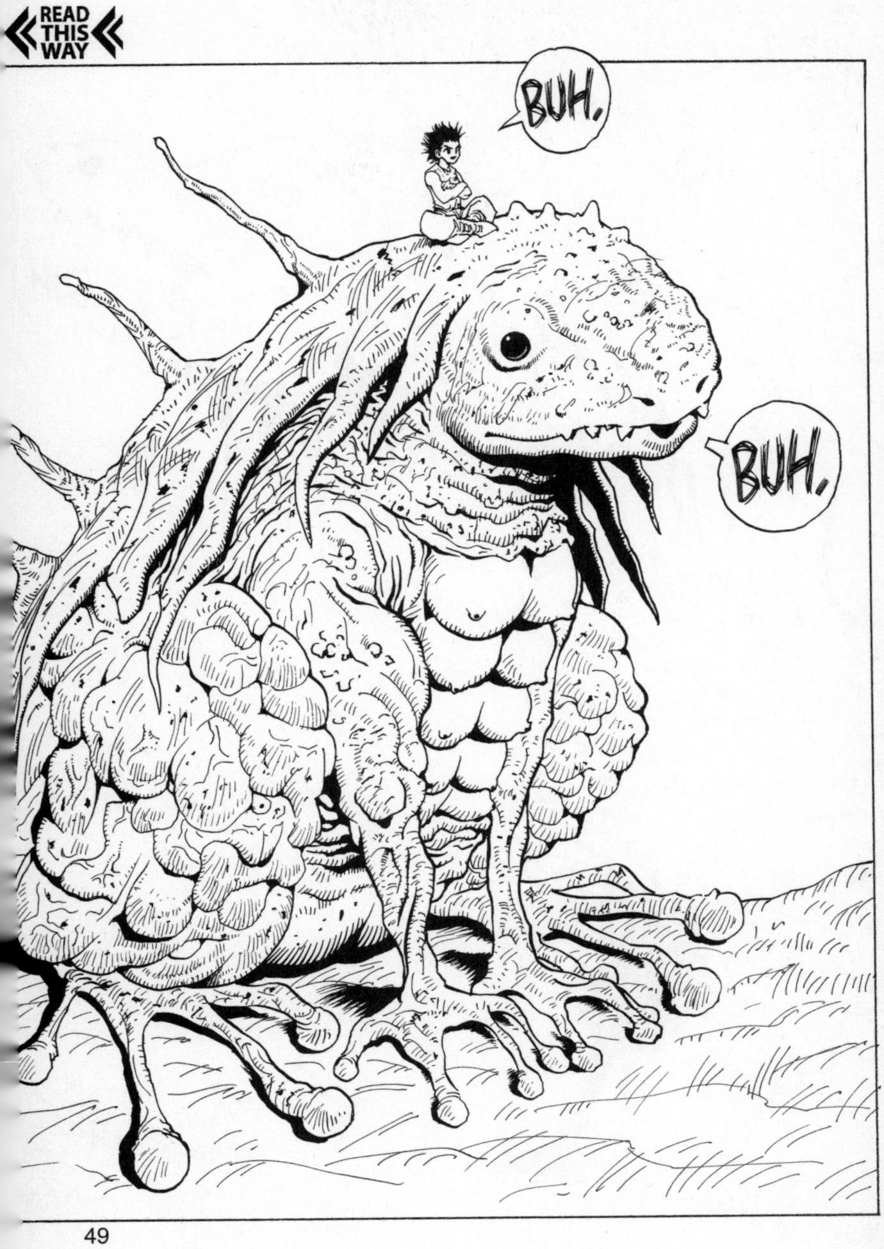
BUH.
BUH.

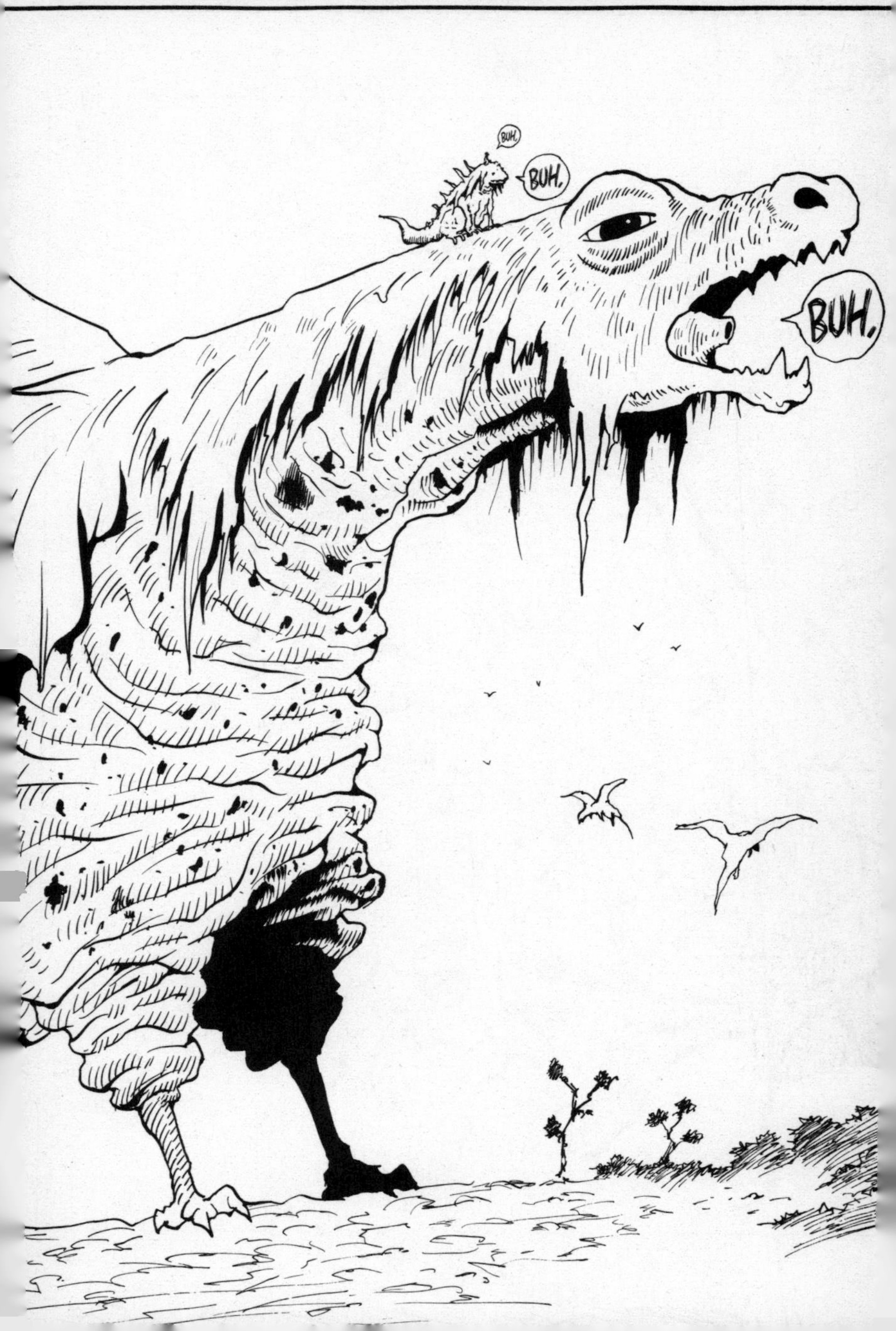
BUH.
BUH.
BUH.

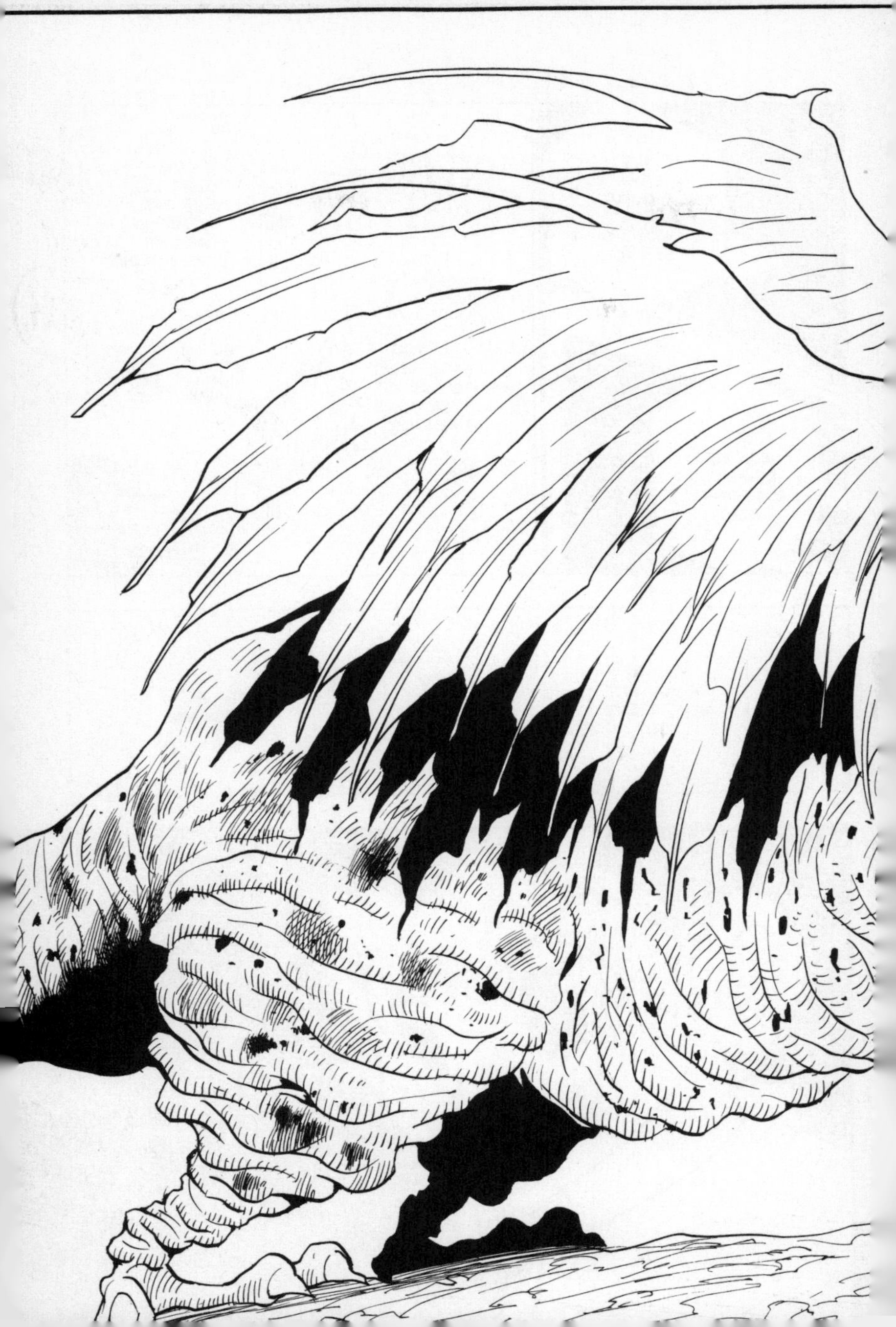

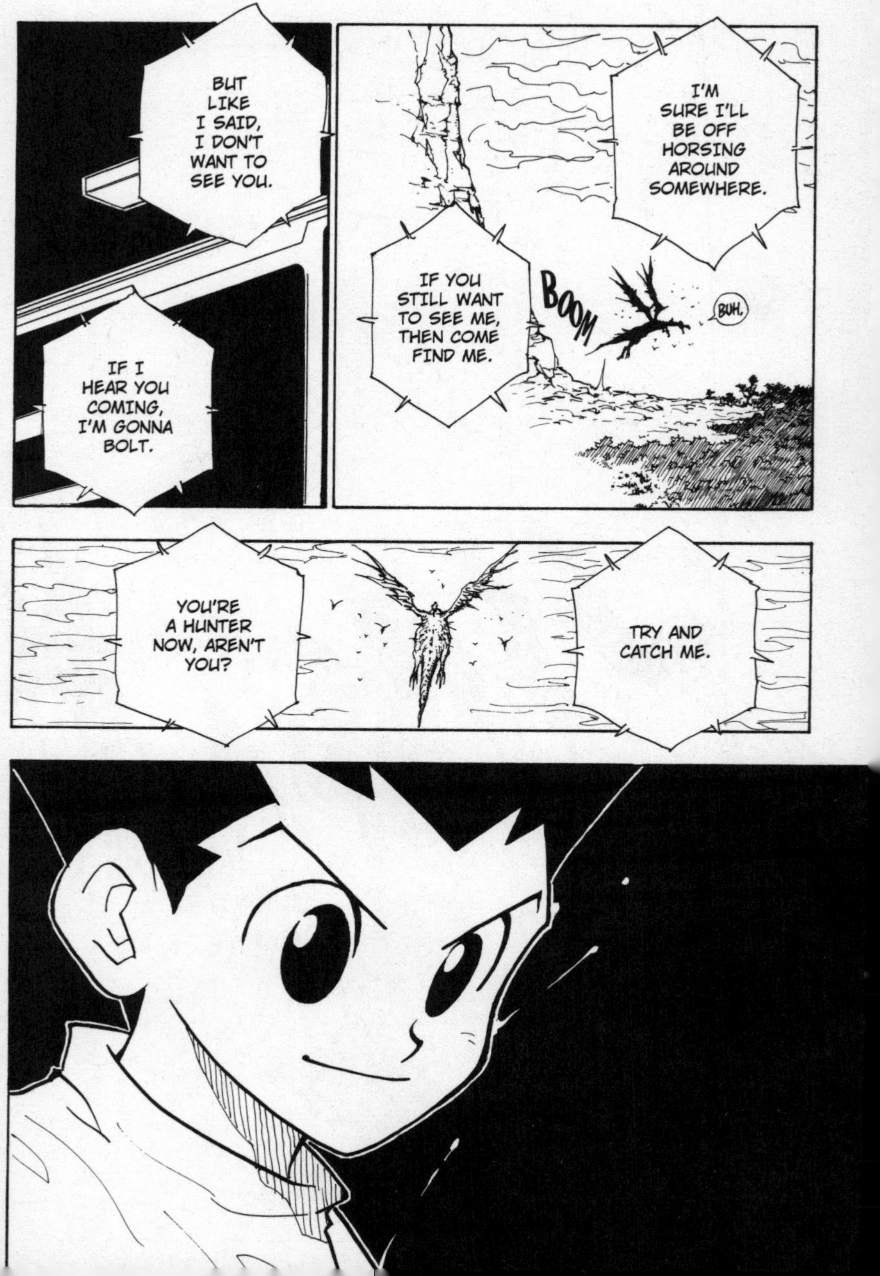
I'M SURE I'LL BE OFF HORSING AROUND SOMEWHERE.
BUH.
BOOM
IF YOU STILL WANT TO SEE ME, THEN COME FIND ME.
BUT LIKE I SAID, I DON'T WANT TO SEE YOU.
IF I HEAR YOU COMING, I'M GONNA BOLT.
TRY AND CATCH ME.
YOU'RE A HUNTER NOW, AREN'T YOU?

READ THIS WAY

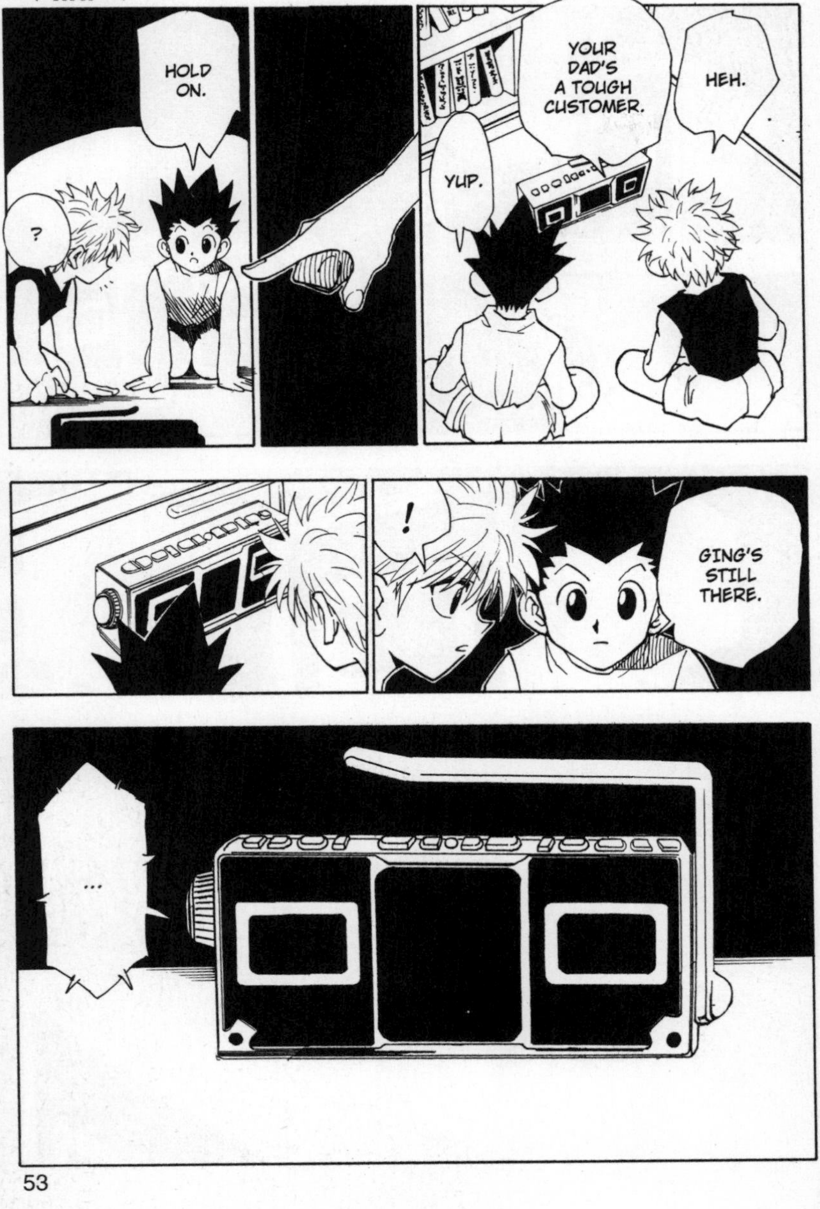
HEH.
YOUR DAD'S A TOUGH CUSTOMER.
YUP.
HOLD ON.
?
GING'S STILL THERE.
!
...

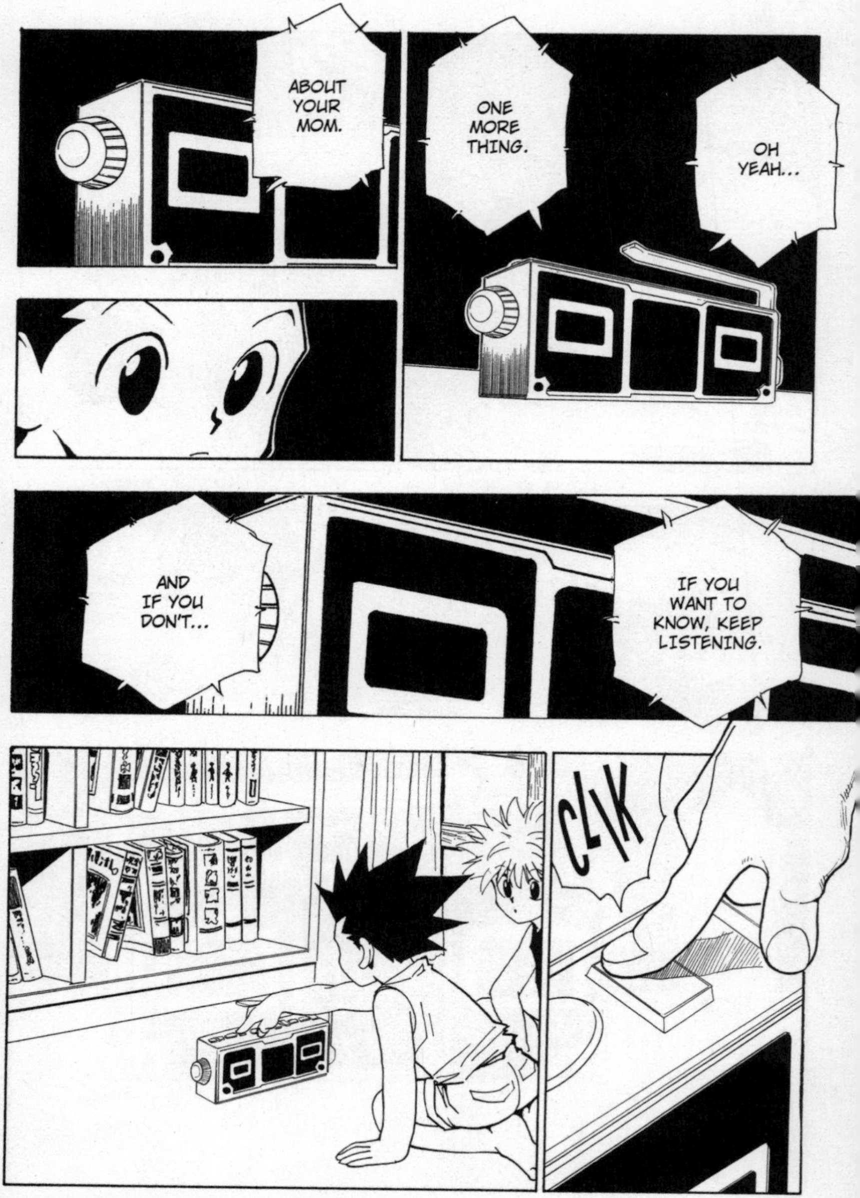
OH YEAH...
ONE MORE THING.
ABOUT YOUR MOM.
IF YOU WANT TO KNOW, KEEP LISTENING.
AND IF YOU DON'T...
CLIK

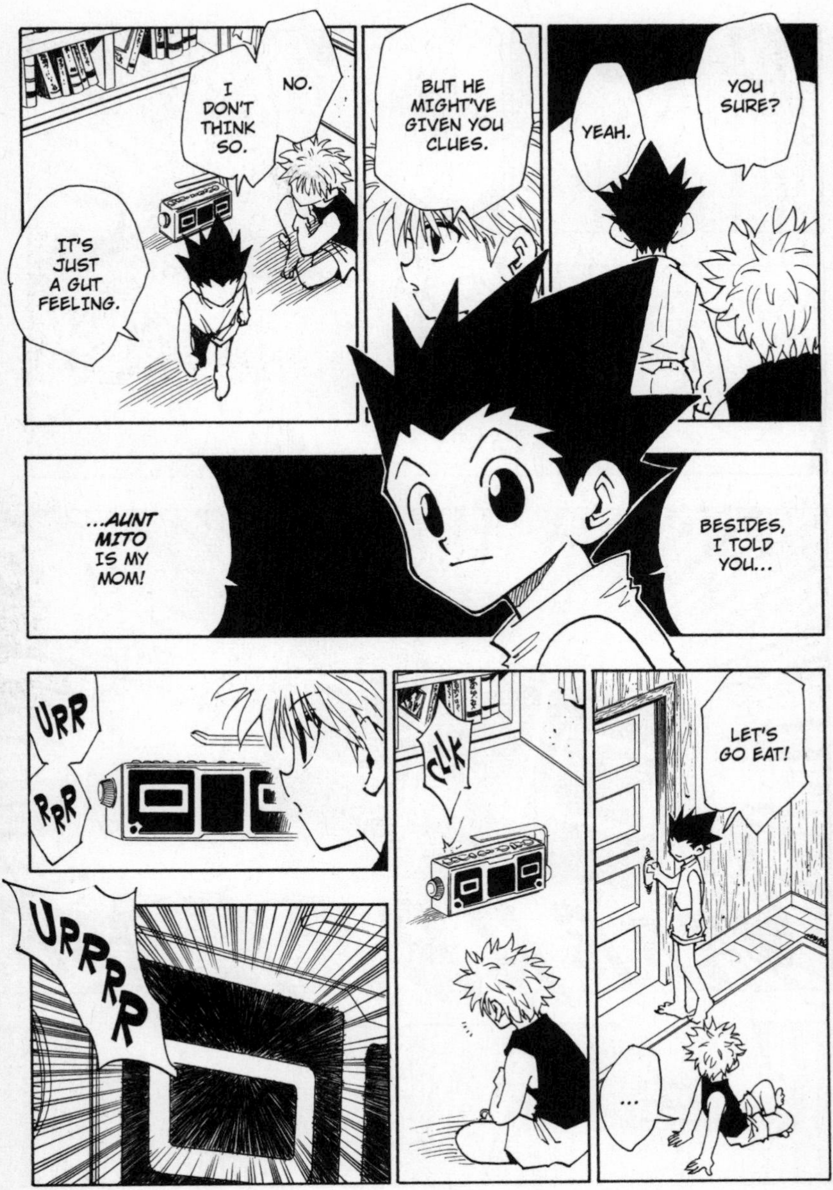
YOU SURE?
YEAH.
BUT HE MIGHT'VE GIVEN YOU CLUES.
NO.
I DON'T THINK SO.
IT'S JUST A GUT FEELING.
BESIDES, I TOLD YOU...
...AUNT MITO IS MY MOM!
LET'S GO EAT!
...
CLIK
URR
RRR
URRRRR

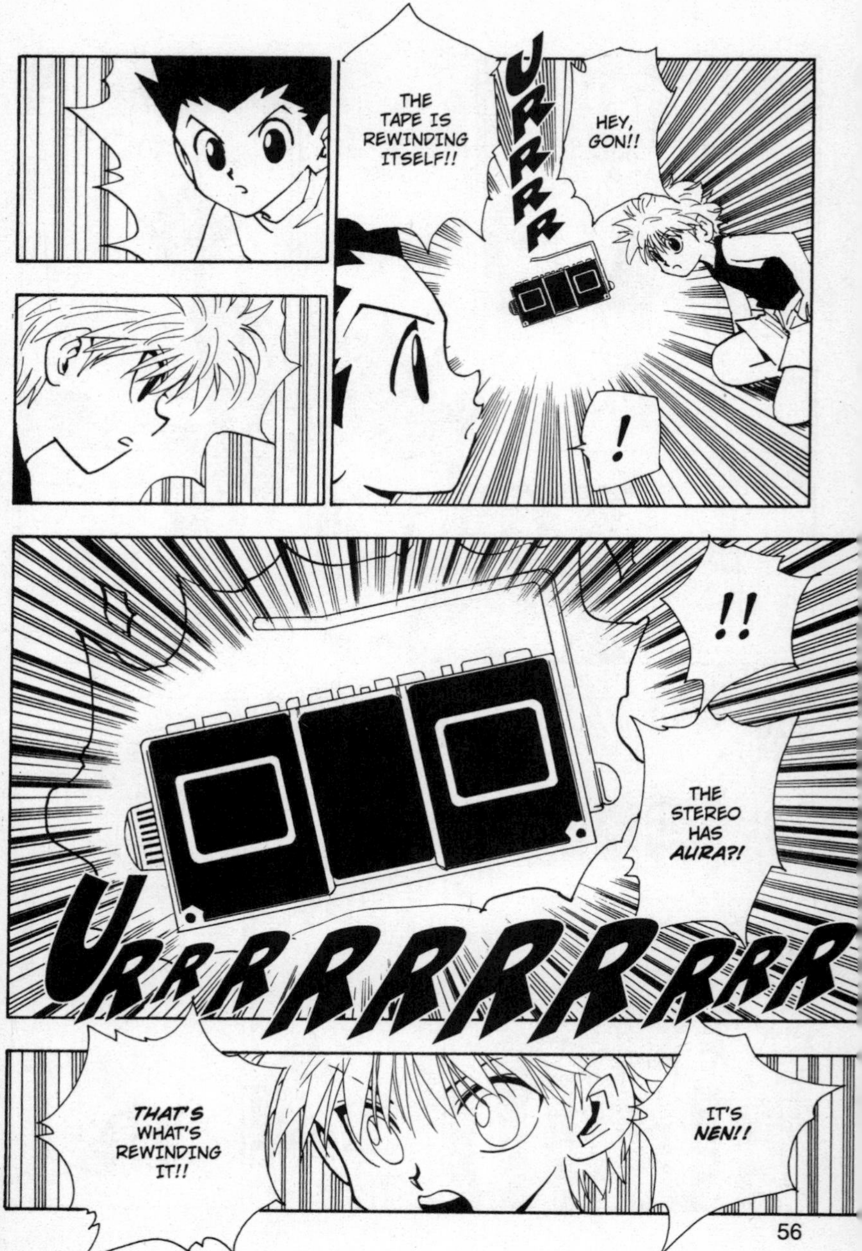
HEY, GON!!
URRRR
THE TAPE IS REWINDING ITSELF!!
!
!!
THE STEREO HAS *AURA?!*
URRRRRRRRRRRR
IT'S *NEN!!*
THAT'S WHAT'S REWINDING IT!!

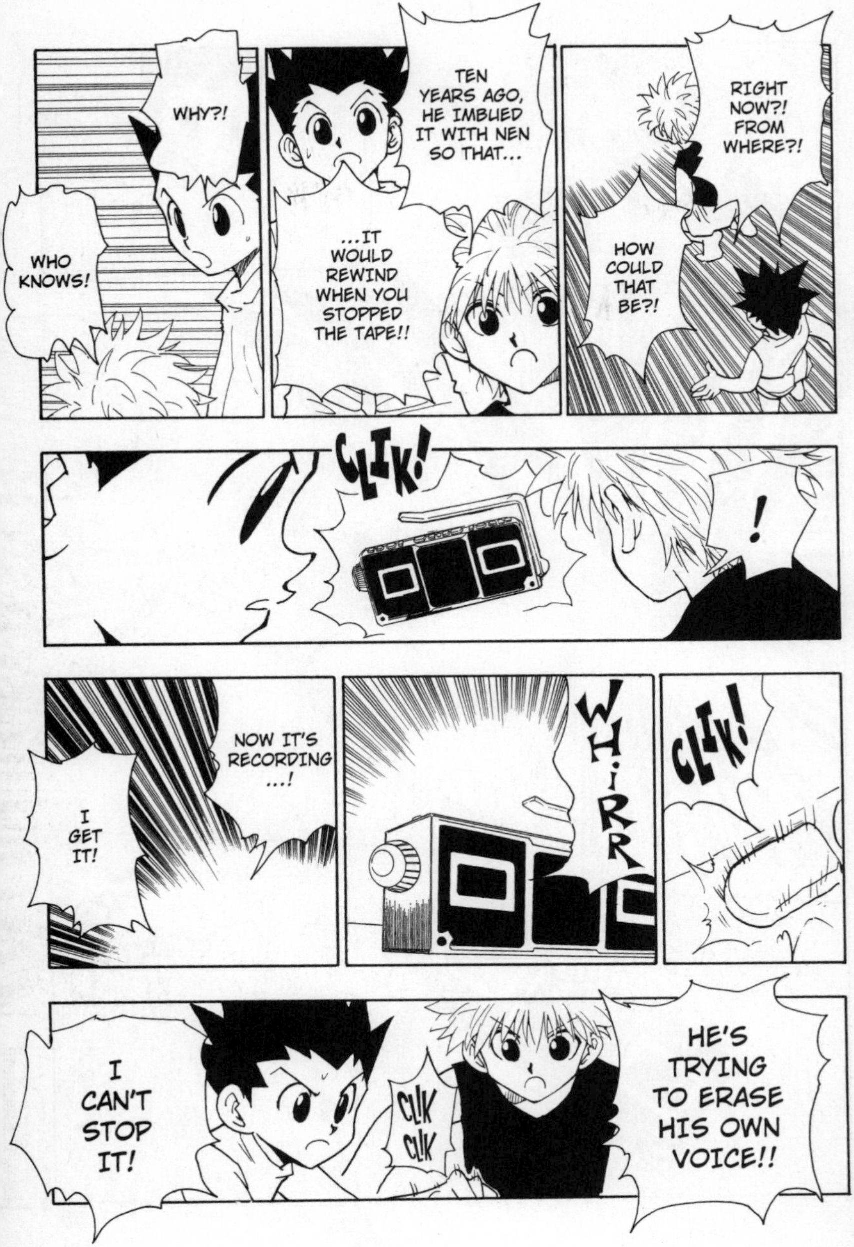
RIGHT NOW?! FROM WHERE?!
HOW COULD THAT BE?!
TEN YEARS AGO, HE IMBUED IT WITH NEN SO THAT...
...IT WOULD REWIND WHEN YOU STOPPED THE TAPE!!
WHY?!
WHO KNOWS!
!
CLIK!
CLIK!
WHIRR
NOW IT'S RECORDING ...!
I GET IT!
HE'S TRYING TO ERASE HIS OWN VOICE!!
CLIK CLIK
I CAN'T STOP IT!

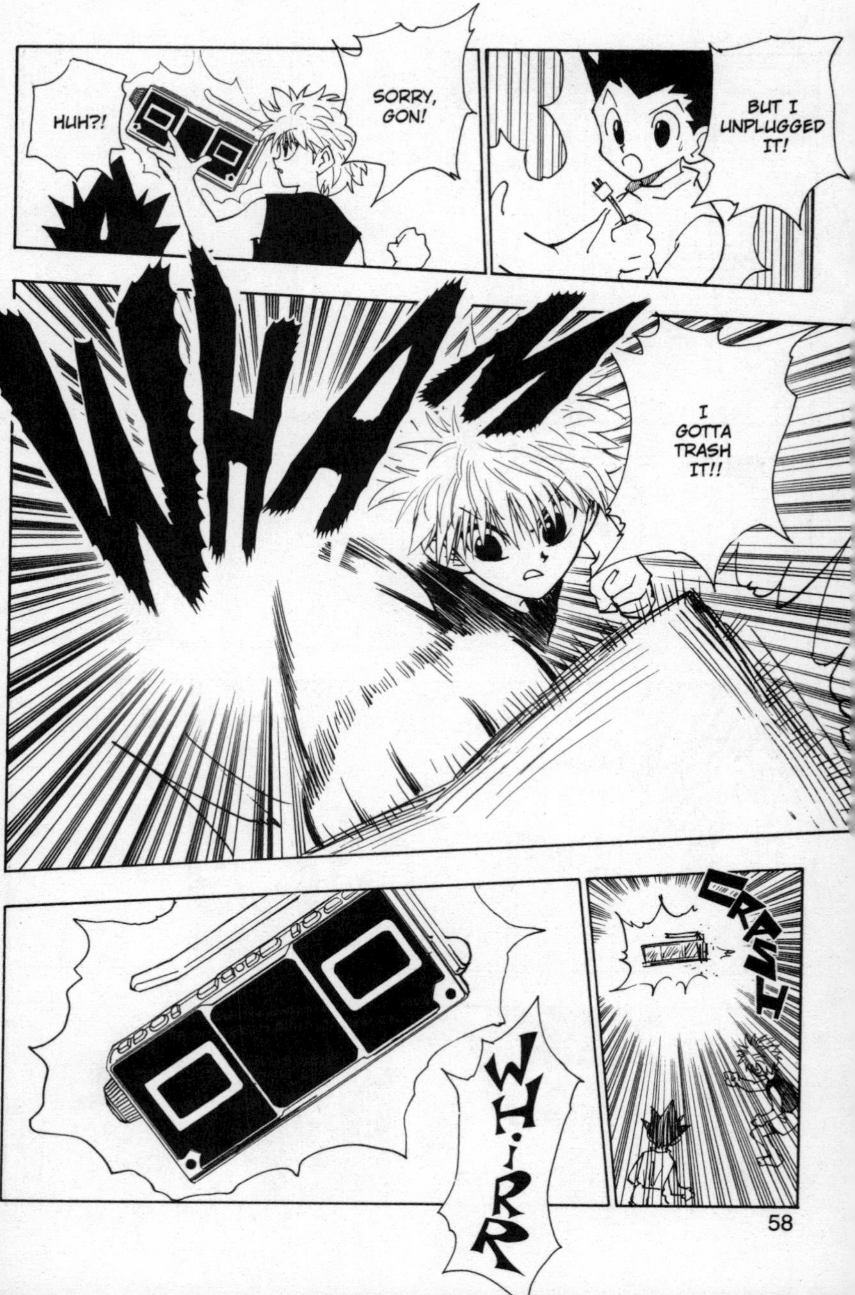

BUT I UNPLUGGED IT!
SORRY, GON!
HUH?!
I GOTTA TRASH IT!!
WHAM
CRASH
WHIRR

READ THIS WAY

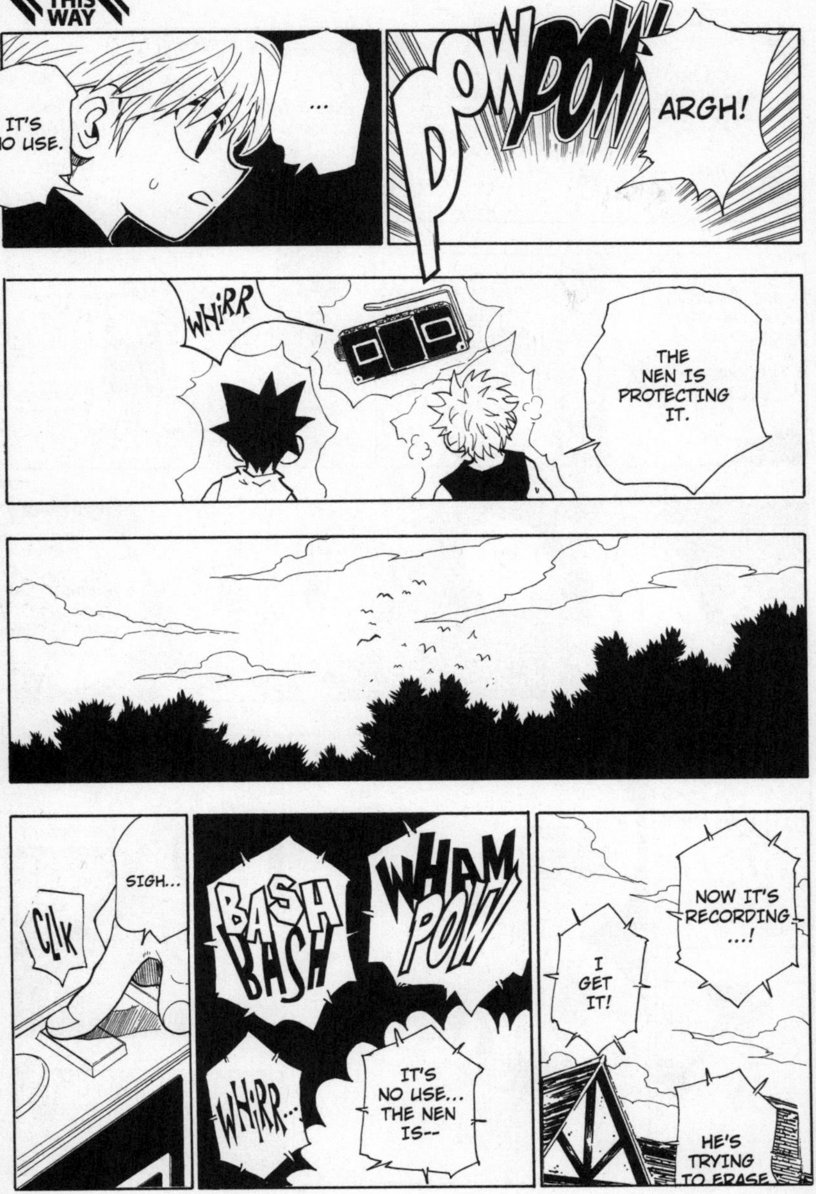
POWPOW
ARGH!
...
IT'S NO USE.
THE NEN IS PROTECTING IT.
WHIRR
NOW IT'S RECORDING...!
I GET IT!
HE'S TRYING TO ERASE
WHAM POW
BASH BASH
IT'S NO USE... THE NEN IS--
WHIRR...
SIGH...
CLIK

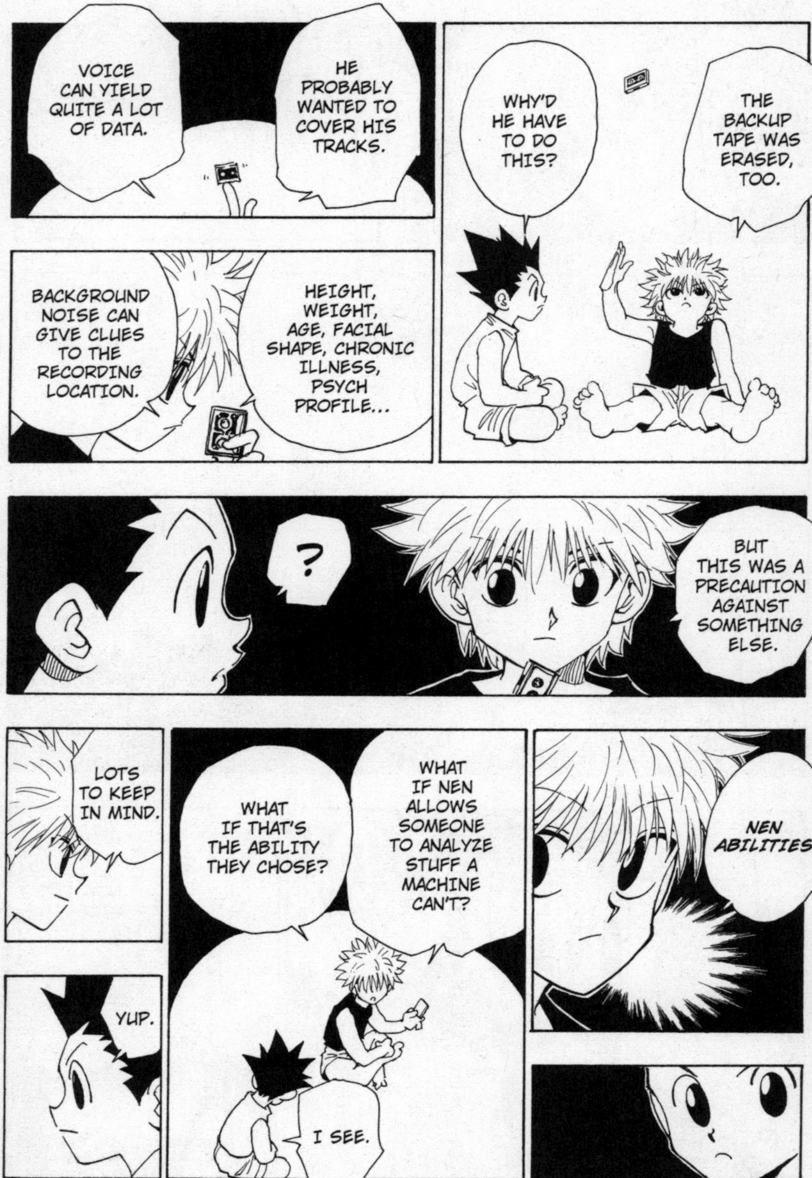
THE BACKUP TAPE WAS ERASED, TOO.
WHY'D HE HAVE TO DO THIS?
HE PROBABLY WANTED TO COVER HIS TRACKS.
VOICE CAN YIELD QUITE A LOT OF DATA.
HEIGHT, WEIGHT, AGE, FACIAL SHAPE, CHRONIC ILLNESS, PSYCH PROFILE...
BACKGROUND NOISE CAN GIVE CLUES TO THE RECORDING LOCATION.
BUT THIS WAS A PRECAUTION AGAINST SOMETHING ELSE.
?
NEN ABILITIES.
WHAT IF NEN ALLOWS SOMEONE TO ANALYZE STUFF A MACHINE CAN'T?
WHAT IF THAT'S THE ABILITY THEY CHOSE?
I SEE.
LOTS TO KEEP IN MIND.
YUP.

READ THIS WAY

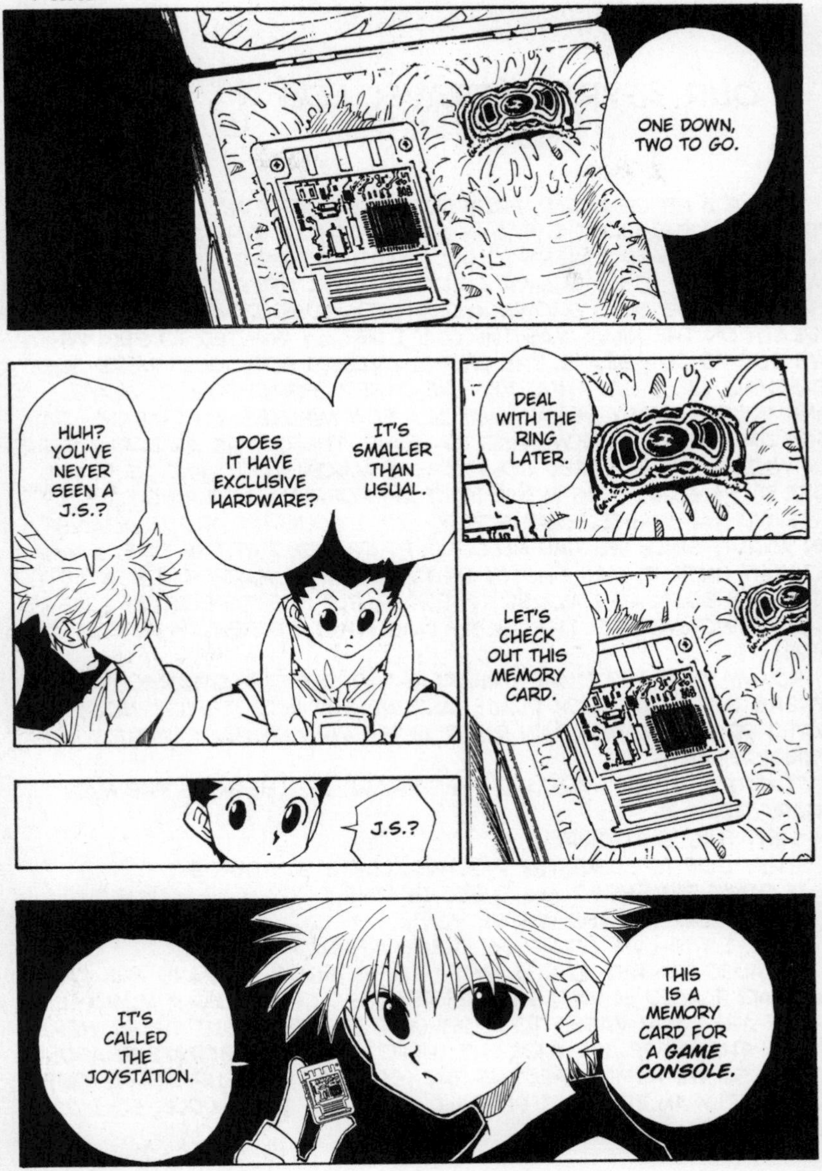
ONE DOWN, TWO TO GO.
DEAL WITH THE RING LATER.
LET'S CHECK OUT THIS MEMORY CARD.
IT'S SMALLER THAN USUAL.
DOES IT HAVE EXCLUSIVE HARDWARE?
HUH? YOU'VE NEVER SEEN A J.S.?
J.S.?
THIS IS A MEMORY CARD FOR A *GAME CONSOLE.*
IT'S CALLED THE JOYSTATION.

OUR EGYPTIAN TRAVEL LOG NO. 3

I HAVE A BIT OF A SAD, FRUSTRATING MEMORY ABOUT THE MOVIE "DEATH ON THE NILE." I WAS IN GRADE SCHOOL WHEN IT CAME OUT IN THEATERS, AND I WENT TO SEE IT WITH A FRIEND AND HIS FATHER. MOVIES USED TO BE SHOWN AS DOUBLE FEATURES AT THE TIME, AND THIS ONE WAS ALSO SHOWN ALONG WITH SOME OTHER MYSTERY MOVIE. "DEATH ON THE NILE" WAS THE ONE I REALLY WANTED TO SEE. WHEN WE GOT TO OUR SEATS, THE ENDING CREDITS FOR "NILE" WERE JUST FINISHING UP. I SAT THROUGH THE OTHER (FORGETTABLE) MOVIE, AND "NILE" FINALLY BEGAN. BUT IN A FEW MINUTES, MY FRIEND'S DAD GOT UP AND TOLD US WE HAD TO LEAVE. THERE WAS AN EARLY SCENE IN WHICH THE ENGAGED COUPLE WAS MAKING OUT, AND HE DIDN'T LIKE IT. HE SAID, "THIS MOVIE ISN'T APPROPRIATE FOR KIDS." I FELT LIKE WE HAD WASTED OUR MONEY, BUT I COULDN'T ARGUE AGAINST AN ADULT. SINCE WE HAD NO CONCEPT OF VIDEO AT THE TIME, I HAD TO WAIT UNTIL IT WAS SHOWN ON TV. IT DIDN'T HAPPEN. I RENTED THE VIDEO AS SOON AS I MOVED TO TOKYO, BUT THE TAPE DIDN'T CONTAIN THE ENDING CREDITS. THAT SONG WAS WHAT I'D REALLY WANTED TO HEAR...!

SO, MY WIFE AND I HAD BREAKFAST AT THE OLD CATARACT HOTEL WHERE THE MOVIE TOOK PLACE, AND WE GOT INTO A "NILE" MOOD. WE WATCHED THE MOVIE AGAIN RIGHT AFTER WE GOT BACK. HERE WERE OUR COMMENTS.

"THERE'S NOBODY AROUND THE PYRAMIDS?! (BESIDES THE MAIN CHARACTERS.)"

"HEY, THIS ISN'T CAIRO."

"THEY GOT TO CLIMB THE PYRAMID. LUCKY BASTARDS."

"I DON'T REMEMBER ALL THESE DEATHS."

"I'D FORGOTTEN THE WHOLE MOVIE."

"MAN, I WISH WE COULD GO THERE AGAIN..."

WE ALSO RENTED "THE MUMMY." THE INTERNAL ORGANS ARE TAKEN OUT AND PLACED IN VASES IN THE PROCESS OF MAKING A MUMMY. THERE ARE FOUR VASES TO A SET (SEE FIGURE 1), BUT THERE WERE FIVE IN THE MOVIE. WE THOUGHT THERE WAS A DELIBERATE REASON FOR IT, SO WE KEPT EXPECTING THE ISSUE TO COME UP. TURNS OUT IT WAS SIMPLY AN ERROR. I DID FALL ASLEEP IN THE MIDDLE, SO I CAN'T BE TOO SURE.

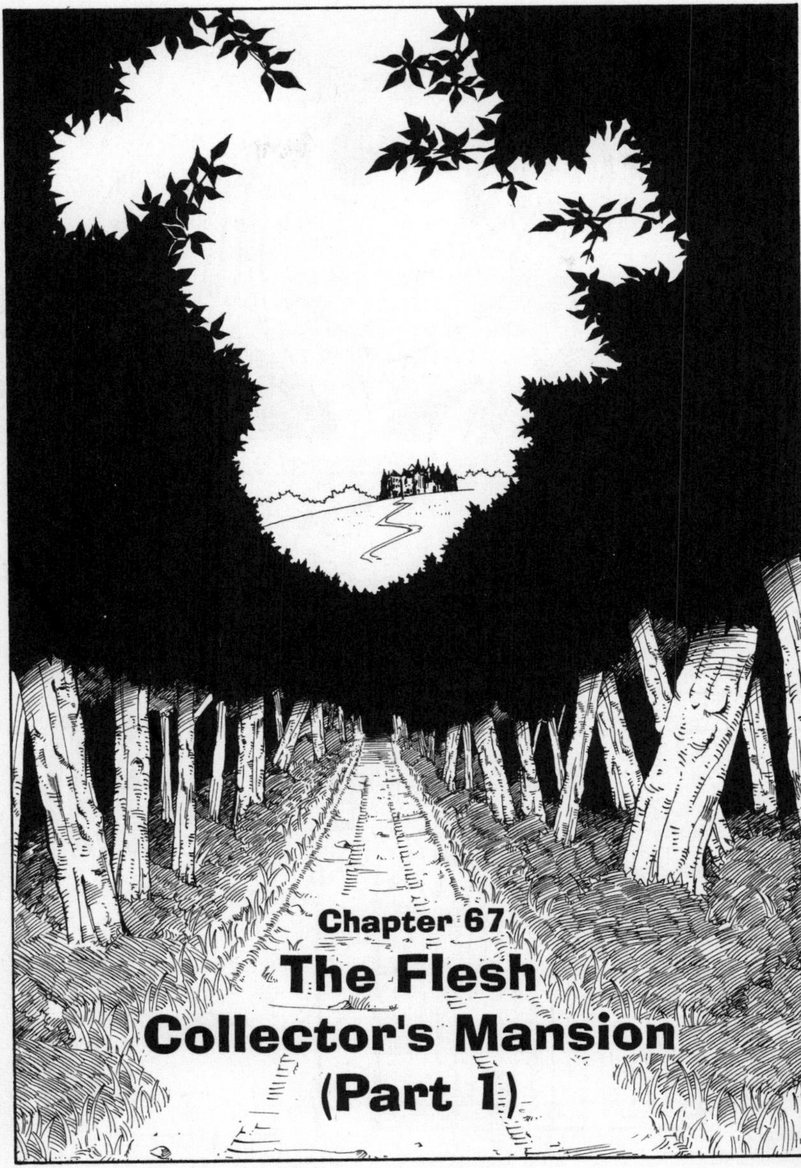
Chapter 67
The Flesh Collector's Mansion (Part 1)

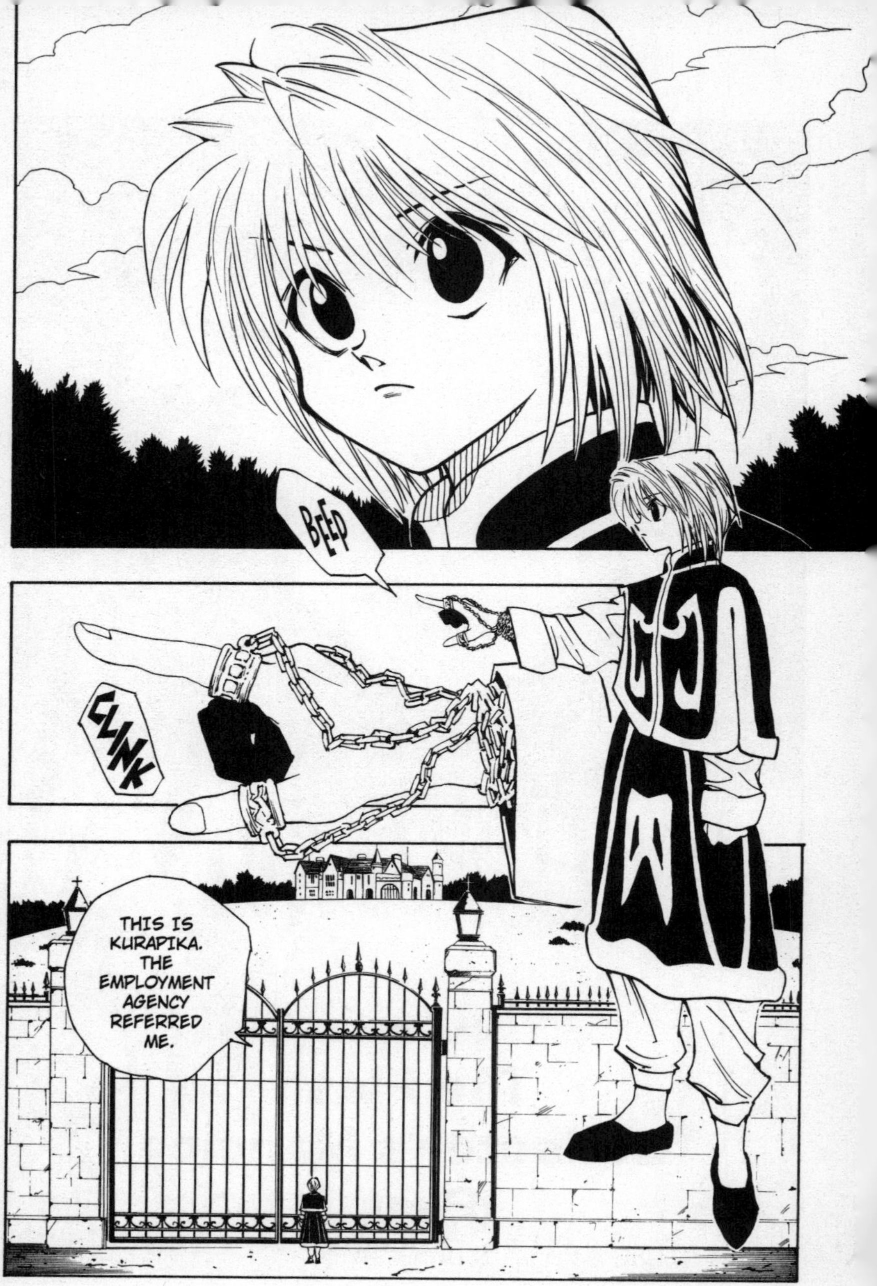
BEEP
CLINK
THIS IS KURAPIKA. THE EMPLOYMENT AGENCY REFERRED ME.

READ THIS WAY

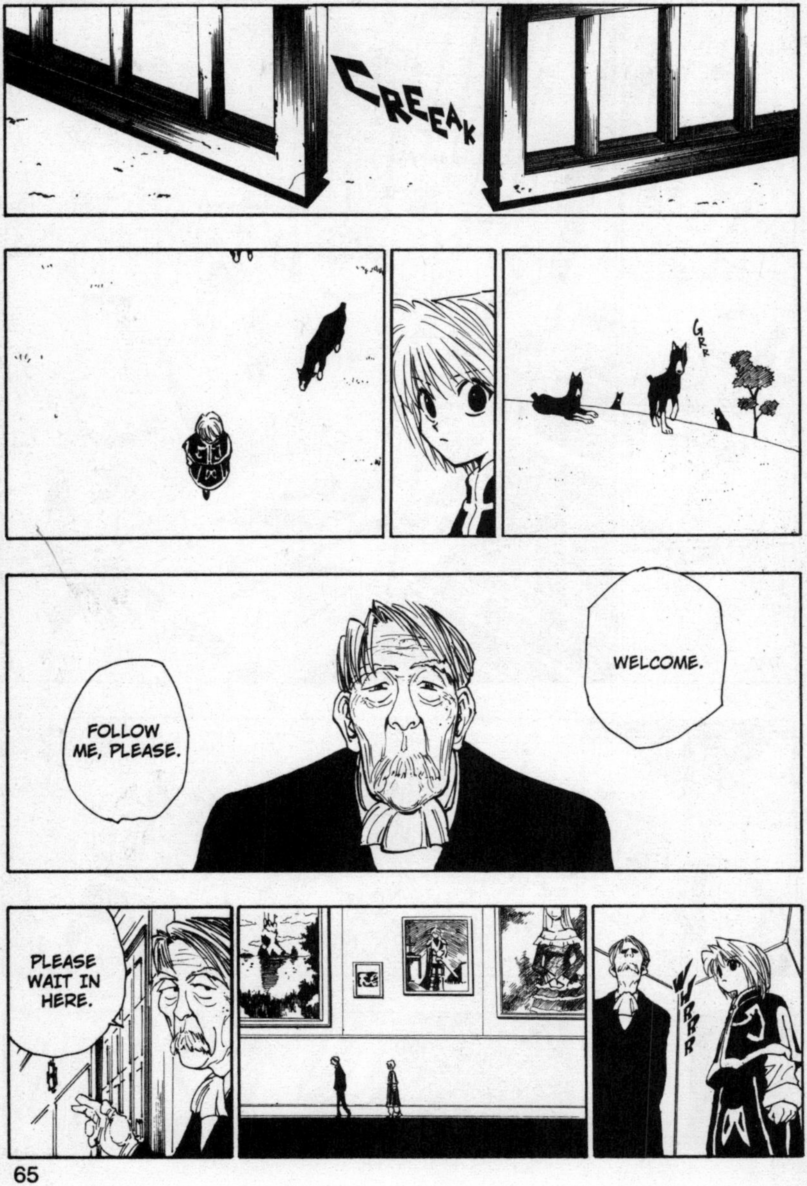
CREEAK
GRR
WELCOME.
FOLLOW ME, PLEASE.
WHRRR
PLEASE WAIT IN HERE.

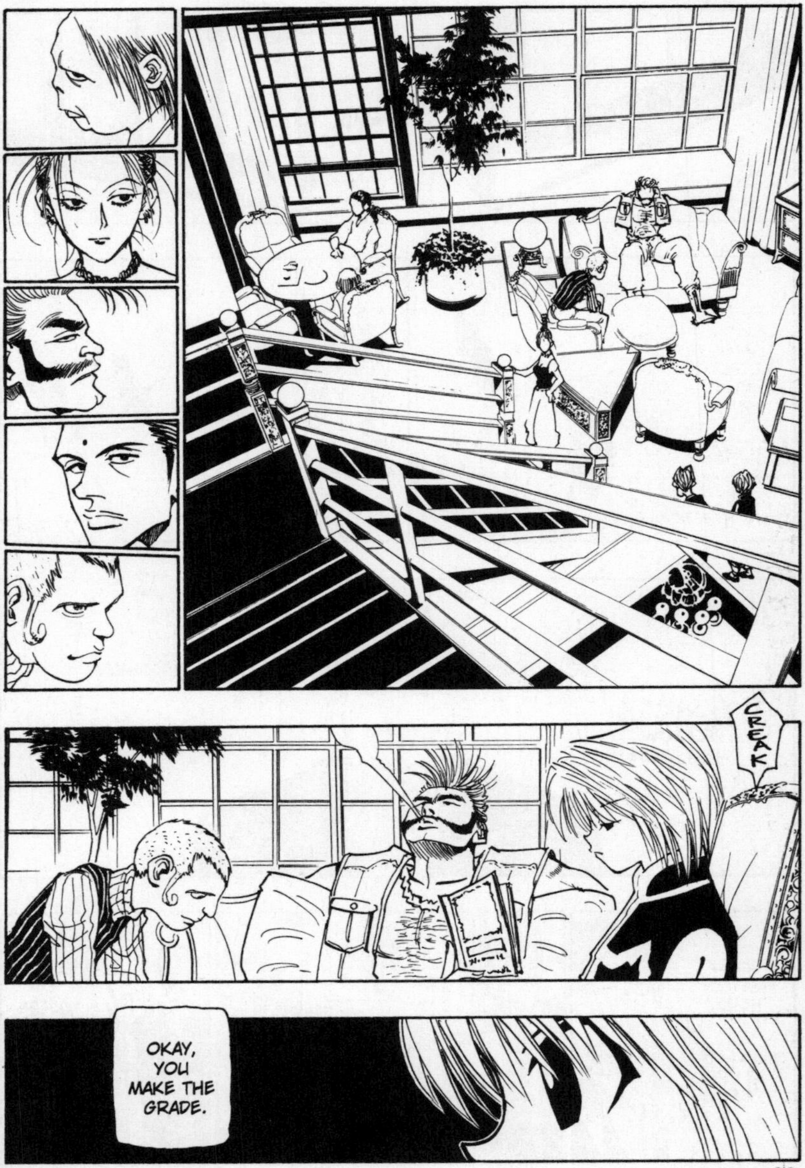
CREAK
OKAY, YOU MAKE THE GRADE.

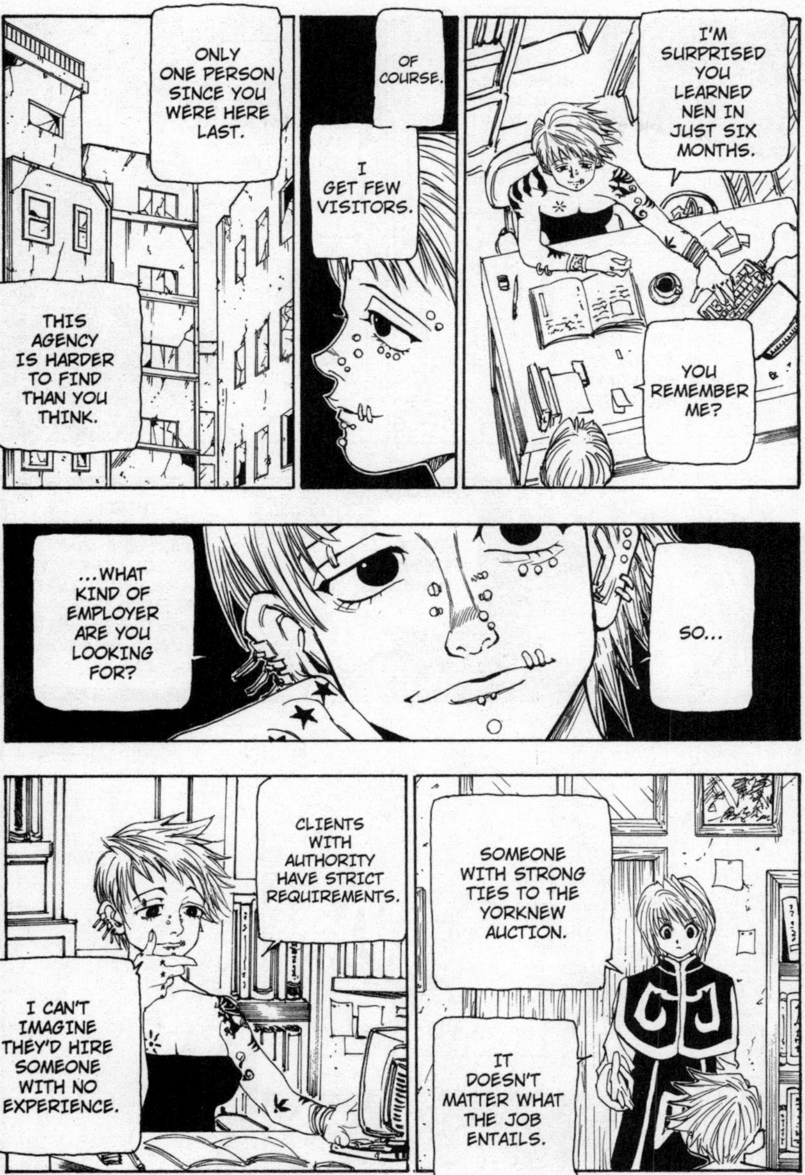
I'M SURPRISED YOU LEARNED NEN IN JUST SIX MONTHS.
YOU REMEMBER ME?
OF COURSE.
I GET FEW VISITORS.
ONLY ONE PERSON SINCE YOU WERE HERE LAST.
THIS AGENCY IS HARDER TO FIND THAN YOU THINK.
SO...
...WHAT KIND OF EMPLOYER ARE YOU LOOKING FOR?
SOMEONE WITH STRONG TIES TO THE YORKNEW AUCTION.
IT DOESN'T MATTER WHAT THE JOB ENTAILS.
CLIENTS WITH AUTHORITY HAVE STRICT REQUIREMENTS.
I CAN'T IMAGINE THEY'D HIRE SOMEONE WITH NO EXPERIENCE.

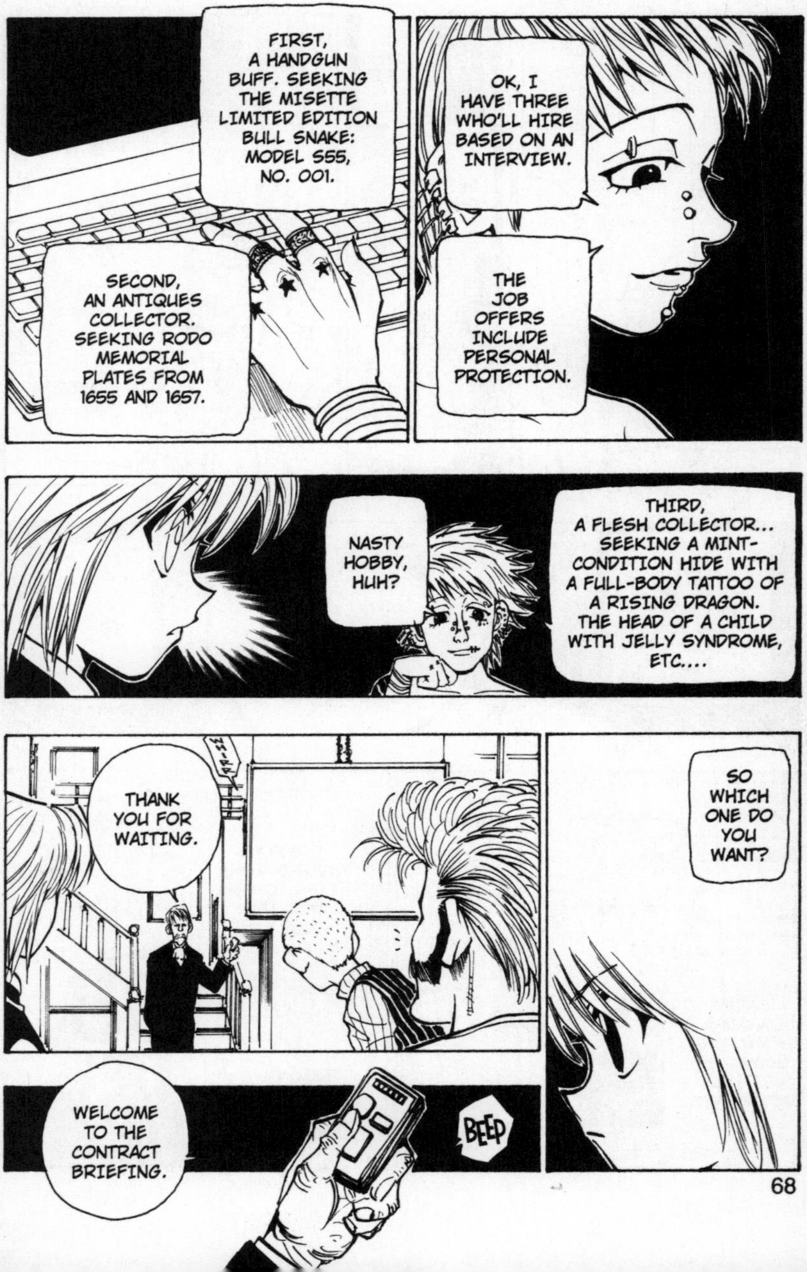
OK, I HAVE THREE WHO'LL HIRE BASED ON AN INTERVIEW.
THE JOB OFFERS INCLUDE PERSONAL PROTECTION.
FIRST, A HANDGUN BUFF. SEEKING THE MISETTE LIMITED EDITION BULL SNAKE: MODEL S55, NO. 001.
SECOND, AN ANTIQUES COLLECTOR. SEEKING RODO MEMORIAL PLATES FROM 1655 AND 1657.
THIRD, A FLESH COLLECTOR... SEEKING A MINT-CONDITION HIDE WITH A FULL-BODY TATTOO OF A RISING DRAGON. THE HEAD OF A CHILD WITH JELLY SYNDROME, ETC....
NASTY HOBBY, HUH?
SO WHICH ONE DO YOU WANT?
WHIRR
THANK YOU FOR WAITING.
BEEP
WELCOME TO THE CONTRACT BRIEFING.

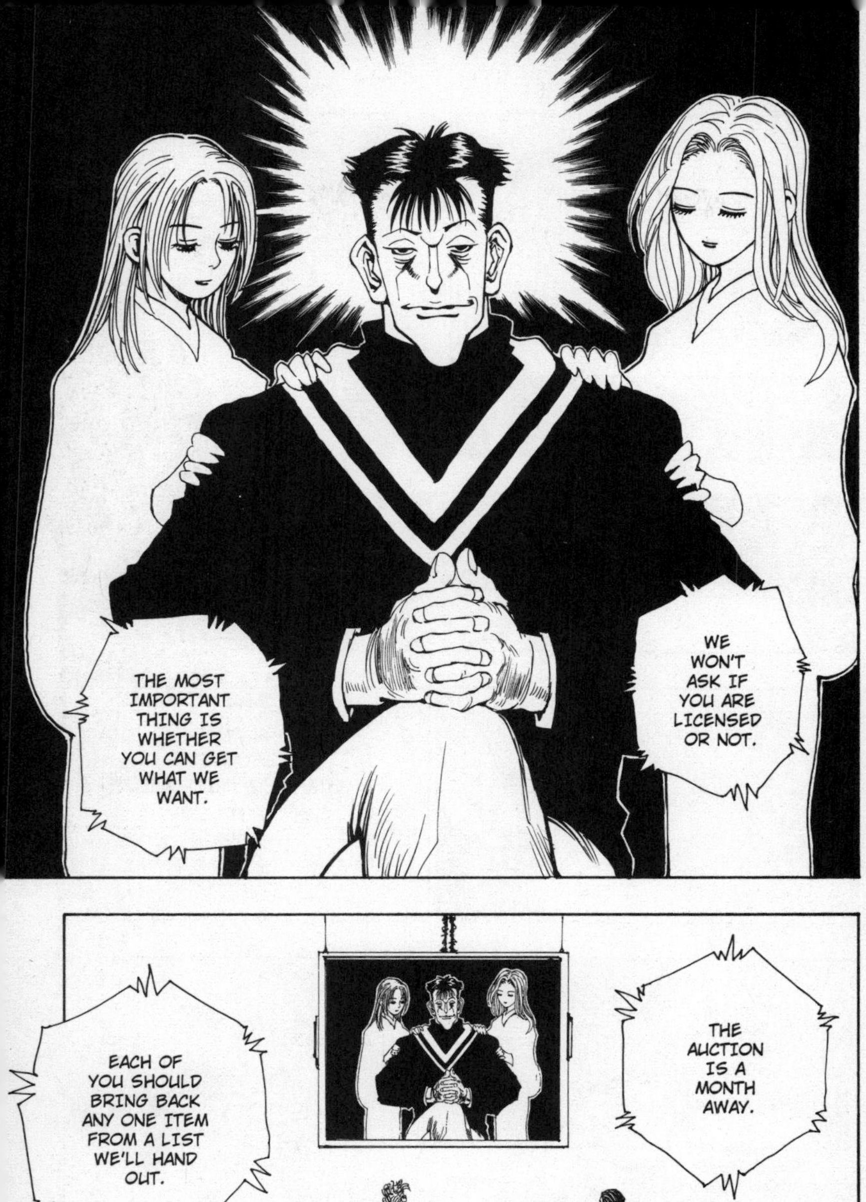
WE WON'T ASK IF YOU ARE LICENSED OR NOT.
THE MOST IMPORTANT THING IS WHETHER YOU CAN GET WHAT WE WANT.
THE AUCTION IS A MONTH AWAY.
EACH OF YOU SHOULD BRING BACK ANY ONE ITEM FROM A LIST WE'LL HAND OUT.

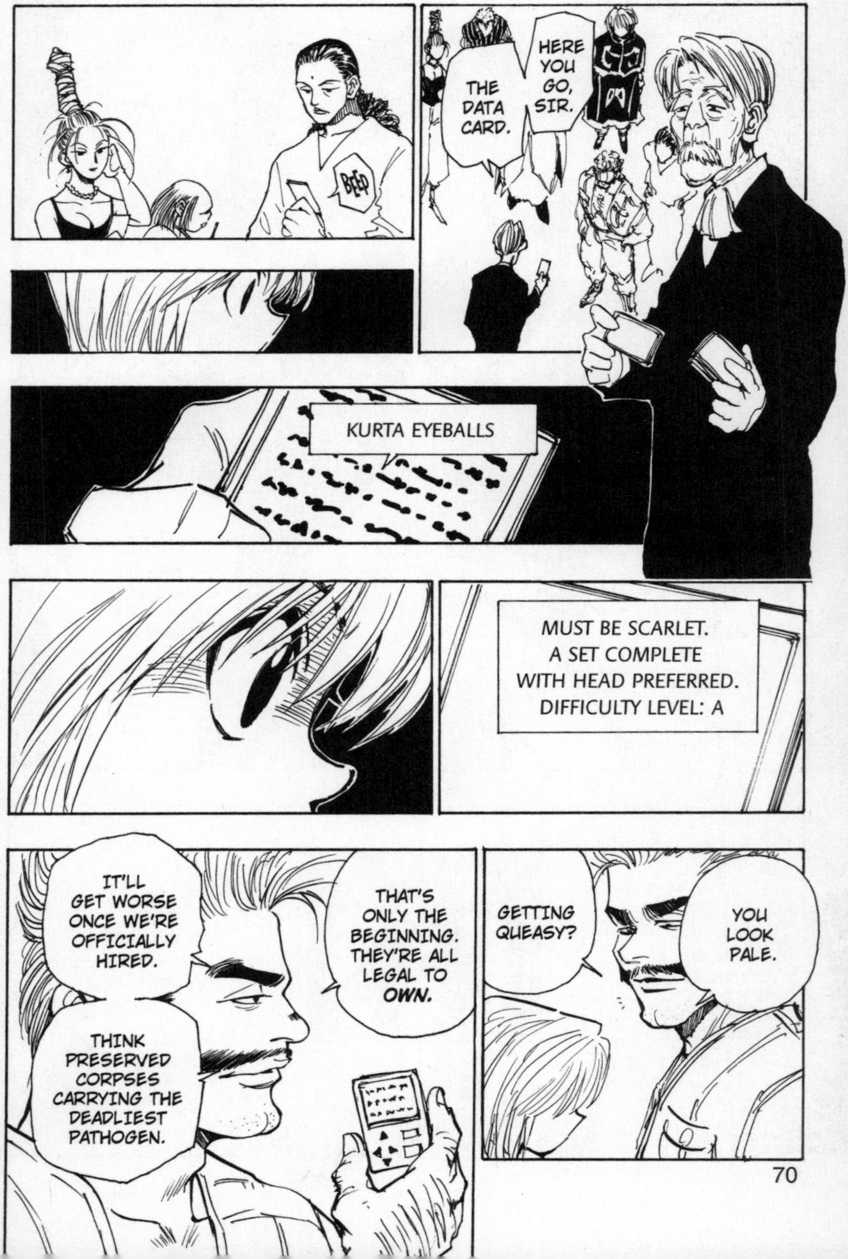
HERE YOU GO, SIR.
THE DATA CARD.
BEEP
KURTA EYEBALLS
MUST BE SCARLET. A SET COMPLETE WITH HEAD PREFERRED. DIFFICULTY LEVEL: A
YOU LOOK PALE.
GETTING QUEASY?
THAT'S ONLY THE BEGINNING. THEY'RE ALL LEGAL TO *OWN.*
IT'LL GET WORSE ONCE WE'RE OFFICIALLY HIRED.
THINK PRESERVED CORPSES CARRYING THE DEADLIEST PATHOGEN.

READ THIS WAY

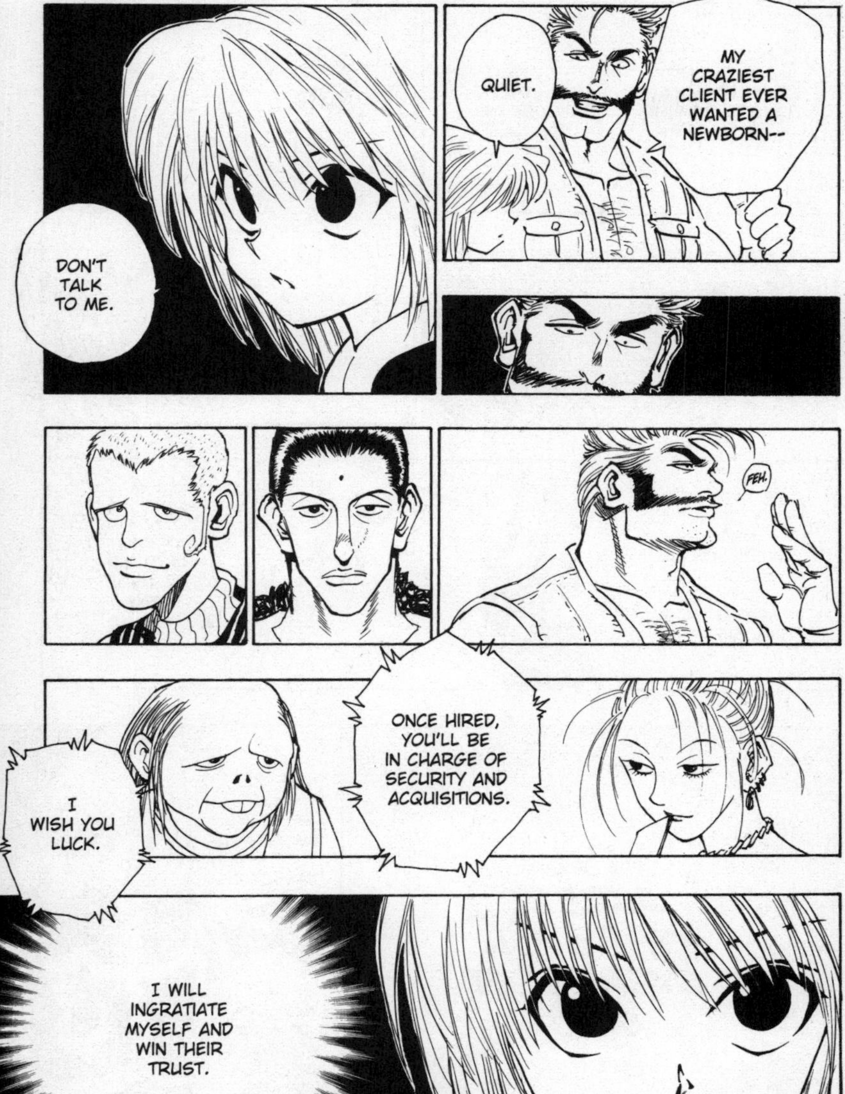
MY CRAZIEST CLIENT EVER WANTED A NEWBORN--
QUIET.
DON'T TALK TO ME.
FEH.
ONCE HIRED, YOU'LL BE IN CHARGE OF SECURITY AND ACQUISITIONS.
I WISH YOU LUCK.
I WILL INGRATIATE MYSELF AND WIN THEIR TRUST.

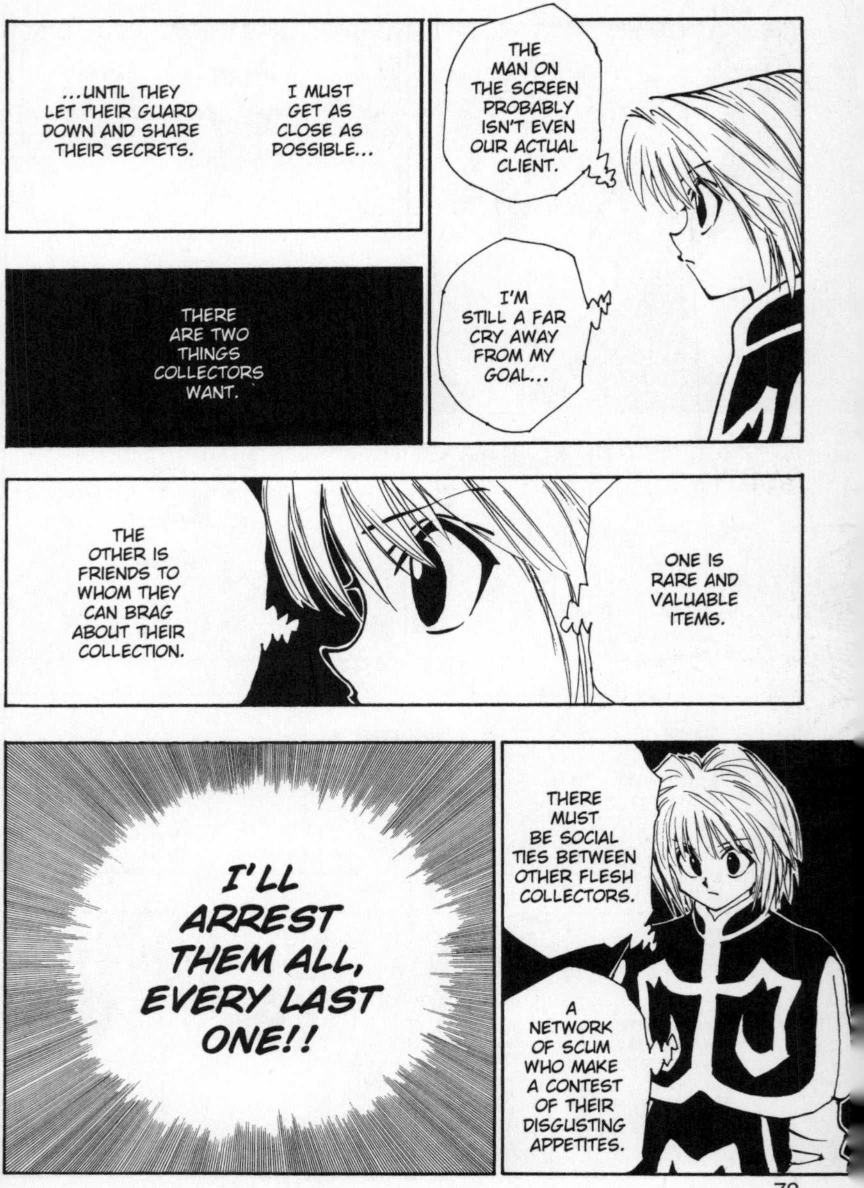
THE MAN ON THE SCREEN PROBABLY ISN'T EVEN OUR ACTUAL CLIENT.
I'M STILL A FAR CRY AWAY FROM MY GOAL...
I MUST GET AS CLOSE AS POSSIBLE...
...UNTIL THEY LET THEIR GUARD DOWN AND SHARE THEIR SECRETS.
THERE ARE TWO THINGS COLLECTORS WANT.
ONE IS RARE AND VALUABLE ITEMS.
THE OTHER IS FRIENDS TO WHOM THEY CAN BRAG ABOUT THEIR COLLECTION.
THERE MUST BE SOCIAL TIES BETWEEN OTHER FLESH COLLECTORS.
A NETWORK OF SCUM WHO MAKE A CONTEST OF THEIR DISGUSTING APPETITES.
I'LL ARREST THEM ALL, EVERY LAST ONE!!

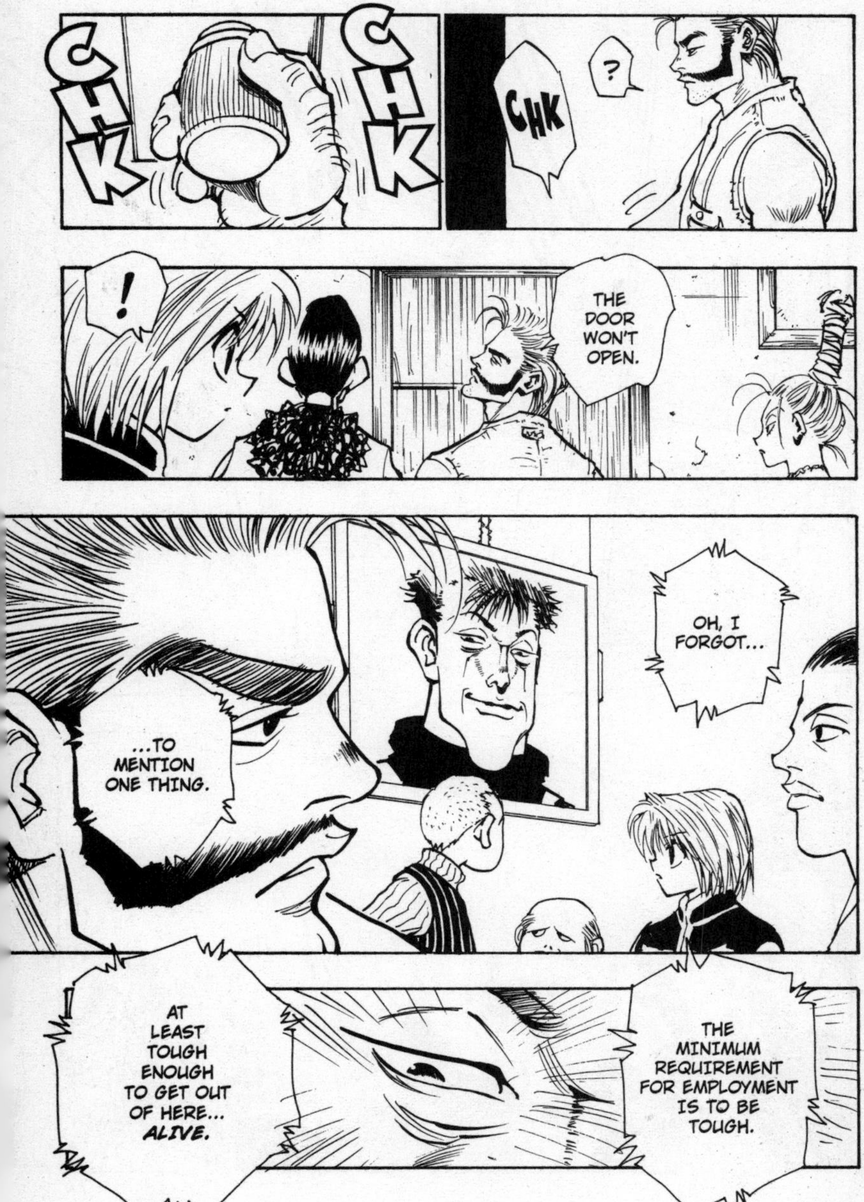
CHK
?
CHK
CHK
THE DOOR WON'T OPEN.
!
OH, I FORGOT...
...TO MENTION ONE THING.
THE MINIMUM REQUIREMENT FOR EMPLOYMENT IS TO BE TOUGH.
AT LEAST TOUGH ENOUGH TO GET OUT OF HERE... *ALIVE.*

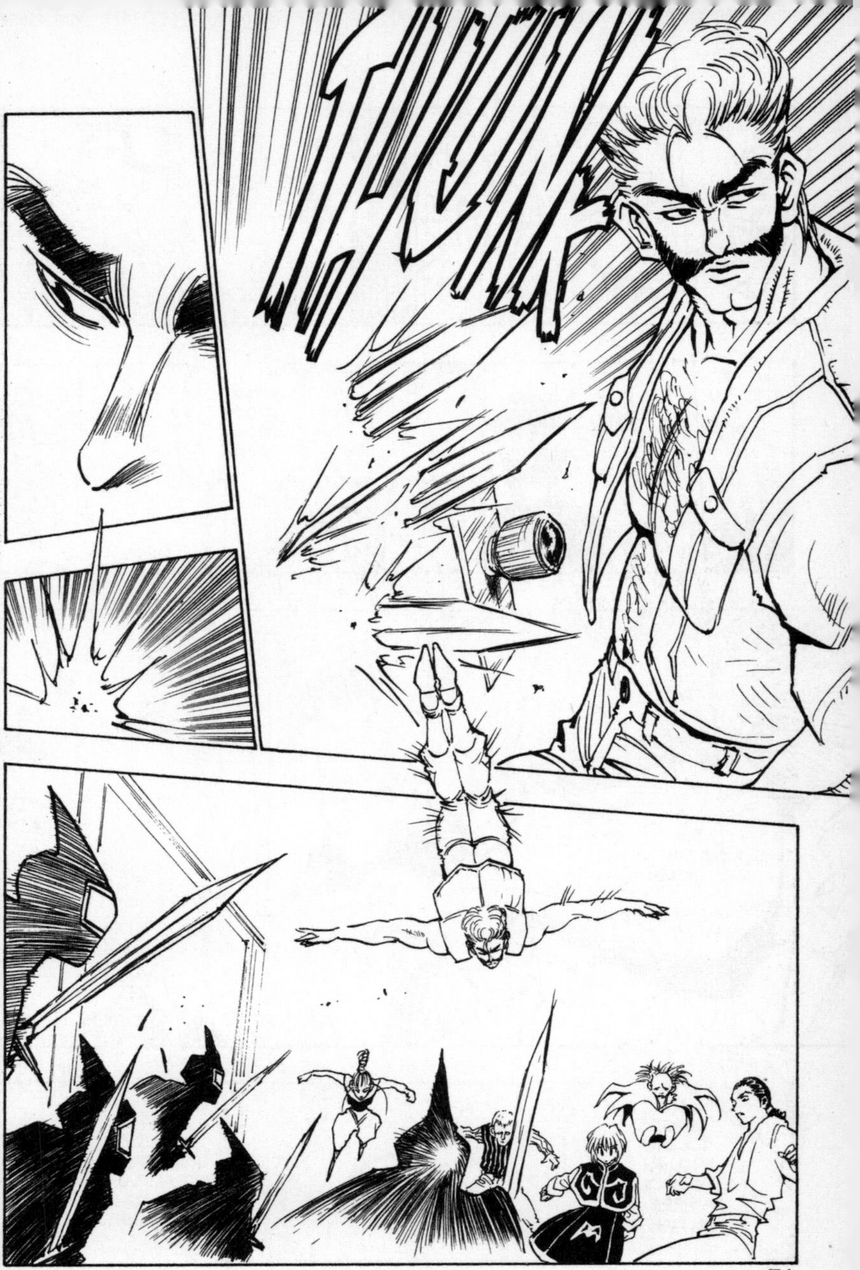

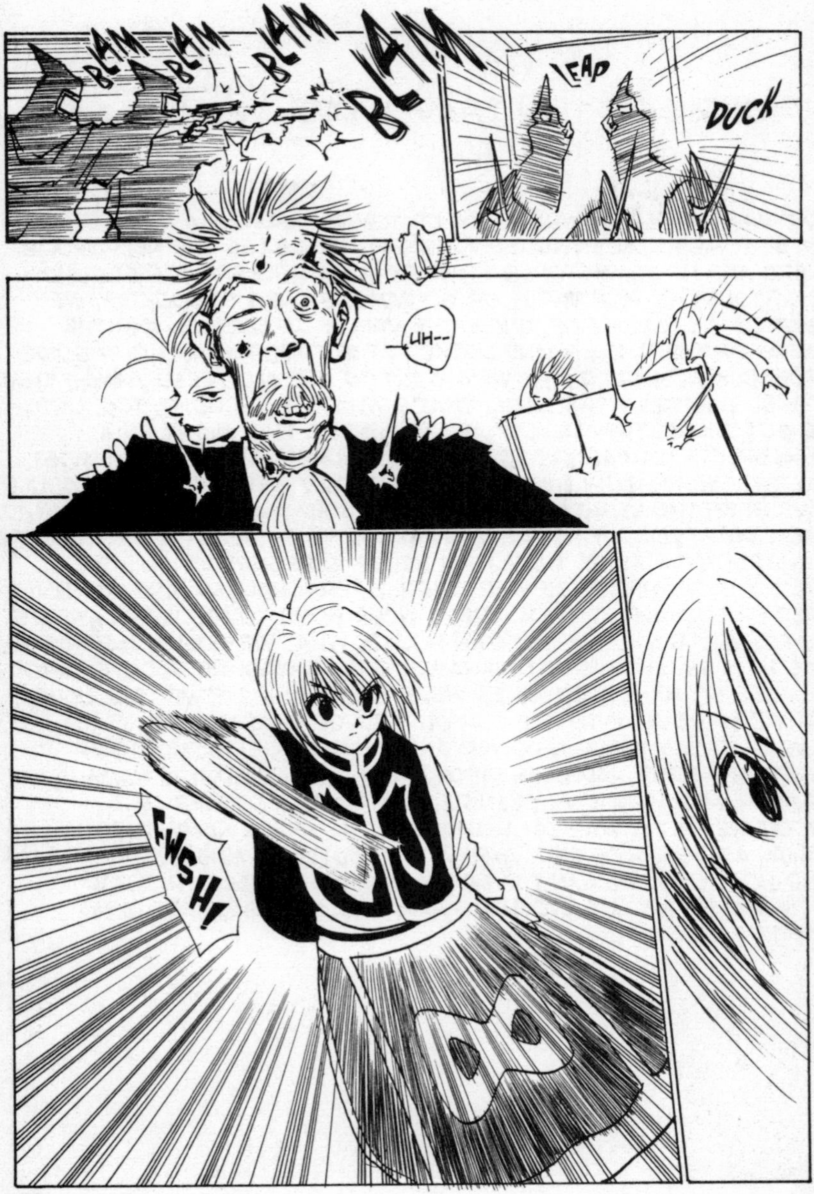
LEAP
DUCK
BLAM BLAM BLAM BLAM
--UH--
FWSH!

OUR EGYPTIAN TRAVEL LOG NO. 4

WE WENT TO SEE A WHOLE LOT OF TOMBS. THERE'S A MASS OF ROYAL TOMBS CONCENTRATED IN THIS PLACE CALLED THE NECROPOLIS. THERE ARE NO TOMBSTONES--THEY'RE JUST HOLES IN THE GROUND. MOST TOURISTS PICK THREE OR SO FAMOUS ONES TO LOOK AT. WE WENT TO THE VALLEY OF KINGS, THE VALLEY OF QUEENS, AND THE TOMBS OF THE NOBLES, AND LOOKED AT 15 TOMBS IN ALL. OUR GUIDE PROBABLY WONDERED WHY WE'D WANT TO SEE ALL THESE THINGS THAT LOOKED BASICALLY THE SAME. THAT'S WHAT WE THOUGHT, TOO, UNTIL WE GOT THERE. THEY REALLY ARE DIFFERENT. THIS MIGHT BE A DISRESPECTFUL REACTION TOWARDS SOMEONE'S GRAVE, BUT I MUST SAY THEY WERE HIGHLY INTRIGUING. AND THEY WERE BRIGHT. IT COULD HAVE BEEN THE LIGHTS, BUT THE DECORATED WALLS WERE VERY VIVID. I COULDN'T FEEL ANY NEGATIVE IMPRESSIONS OF DEATH. (I'M NOT SURE IF THAT'S BECAUSE OF THEIR FIRM BELIEF IN RESURRECTION.) THE INTERIORS OF THE TOMBS WERE HIGHLY PERSONALIZED, AND WE NEVER TIRED OF LOOKING AT THEM. THERE WERE SOME TOMBS WITH LAYOUTS THAT I WOULD LIKE FOR MY OWN HOUSE. WHAT WE FOUND SURPRISING WAS HOW SMALL KING TUTANKHAMEN'S TOMB WAS. HE BECAME FAMOUS BECAUSE SO MANY TREASURES WERE FOUND IN HIS TOMB UNTOUCHED, BUT WE WERE ABLE TO SEE FOR OURSELVES THAT HE WAS COMPARATIVELY WEAK IN POWER AS A PHARAOH. IF SOME OTHER PHARAOH'S TOMB HAD BEEN DISCOVERED UNSCATHED, THE NAME TUTANKHAMEN WOULD'VE BEEN RELEGATED TO A CORNER OF A BROCHURE. YET IT WAS STILL AMAZING. THE SHEER NUMBER OF BURIAL ACCESSORIES DISPLAYED AT THE EGYPTIAN MUSEUM WAS MIND-BOGGLING. WE CAN'T EVEN IMAGINE THE JEWELS THAT HAD BEEN STOLEN FROM THE OTHER PHARAOHS' TOMBS. THERE IS NO WAY TO KNOW.

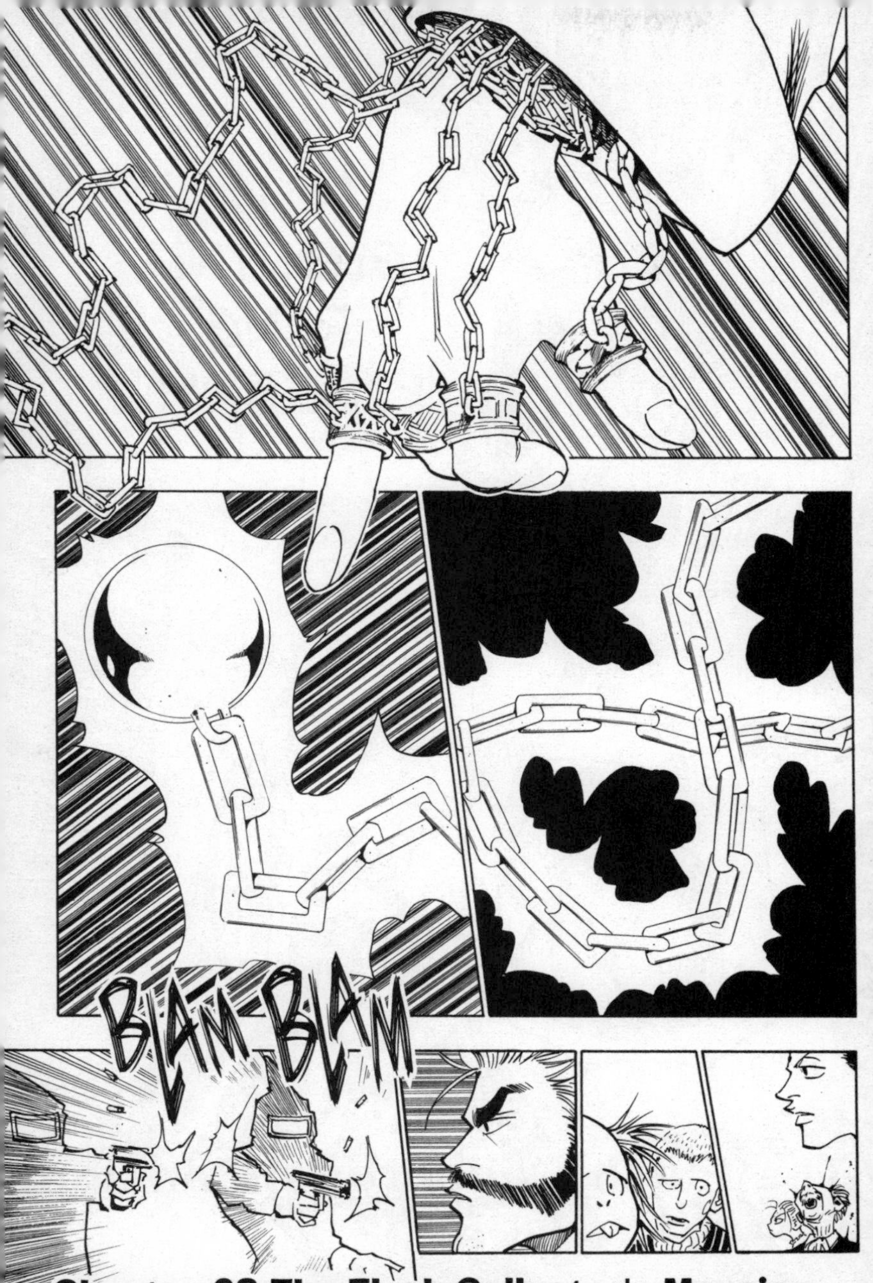
BLAM BLAM

Chapter 68 The Flesh Collector's Mansion (Part 2)

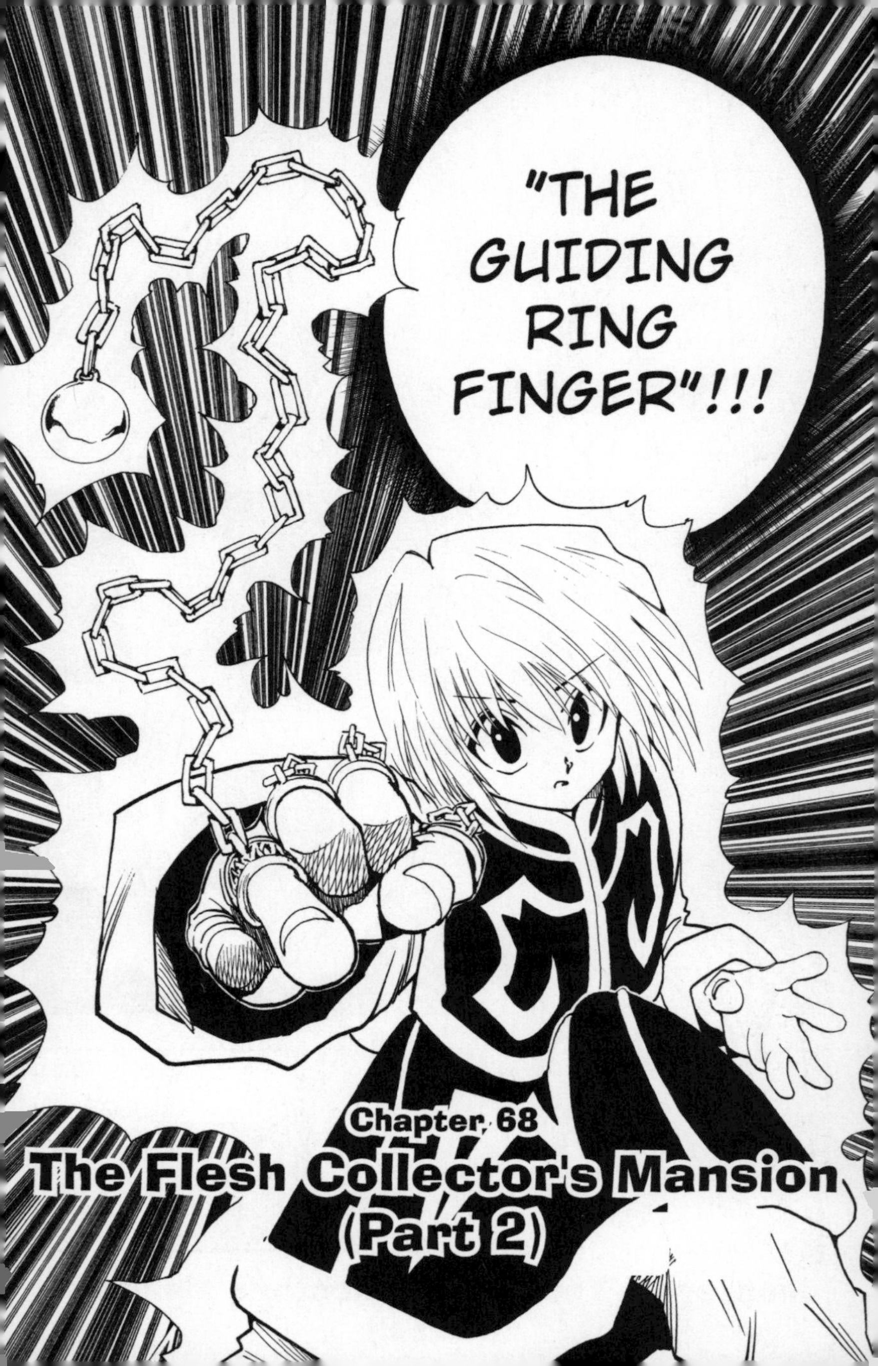
"THE GUIDING RING FINGER"!!!
Chapter 68
The Flesh Collector's Mansion (Part 2)

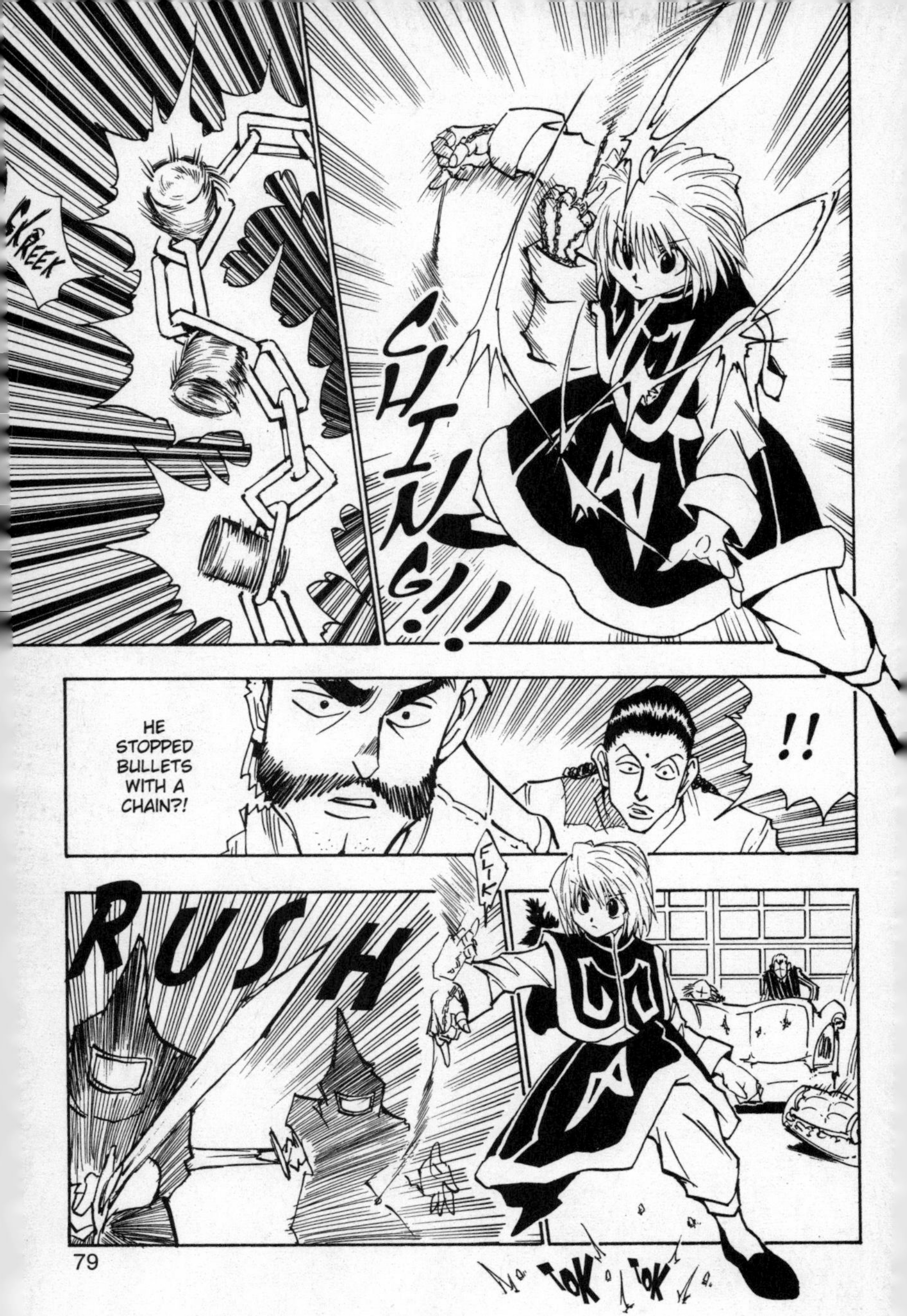
CHING!!
CKREEK
!!
HE STOPPED BULLETS WITH A CHAIN?!
FLIK
TOK TOK
RUSH

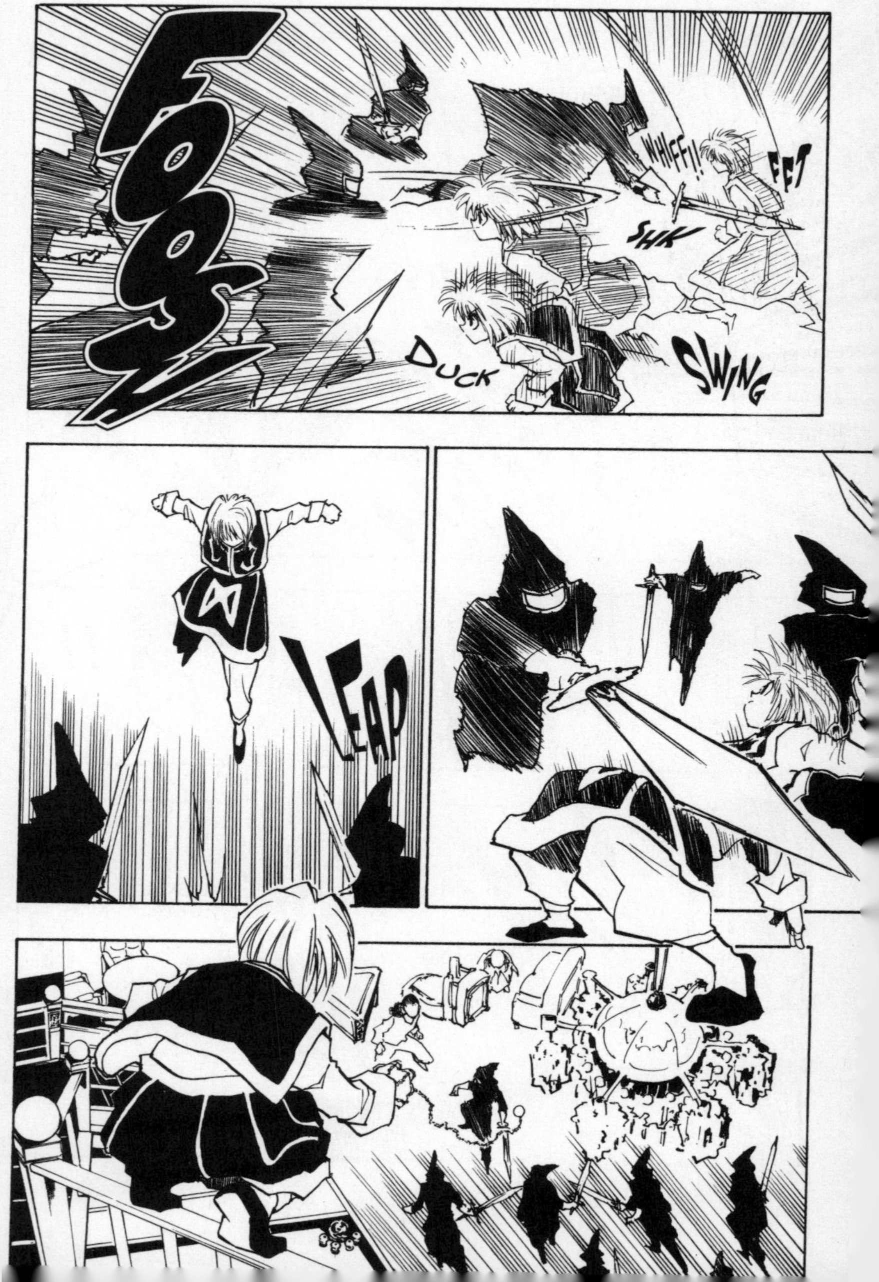
WHIFF!!
FFT
SHK
SWING
DUCK
FOOSH
LEAP

READ THIS WAY

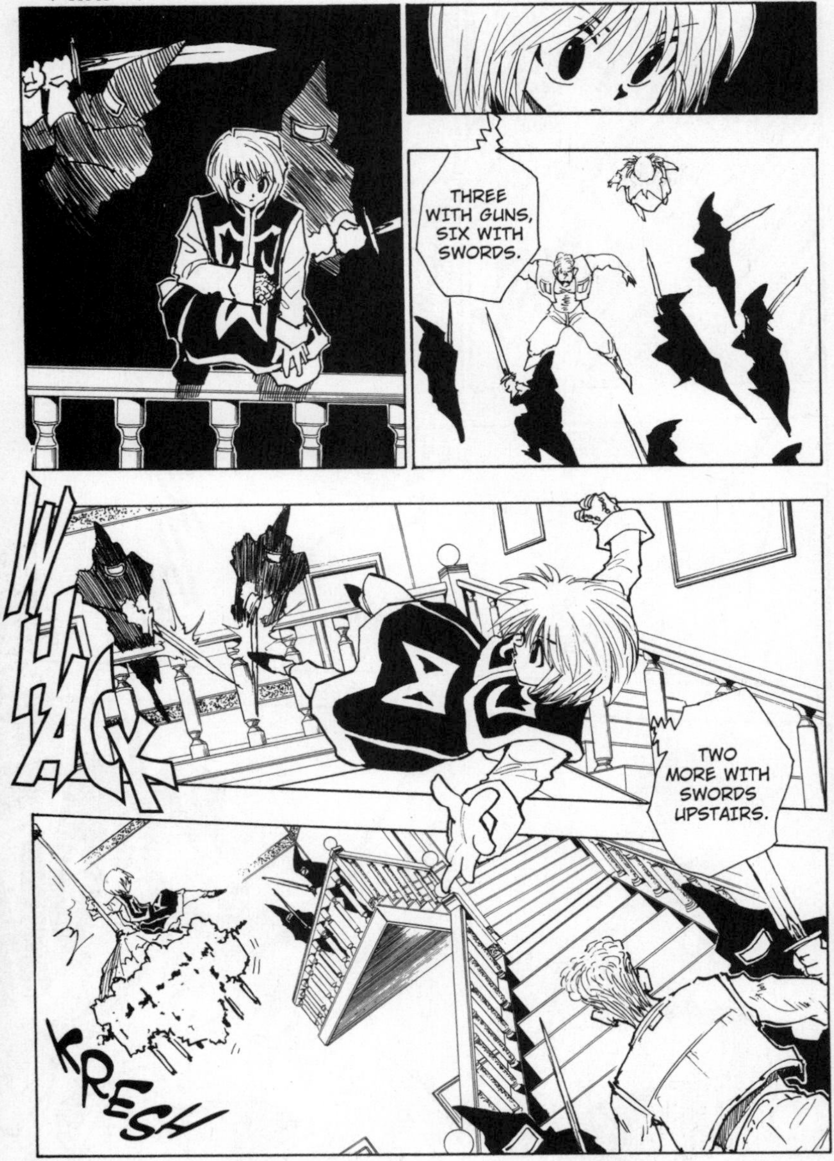

THREE WITH GUNS, SIX WITH SWORDS.
TWO MORE WITH SWORDS UPSTAIRS.
WHACK
KRESH

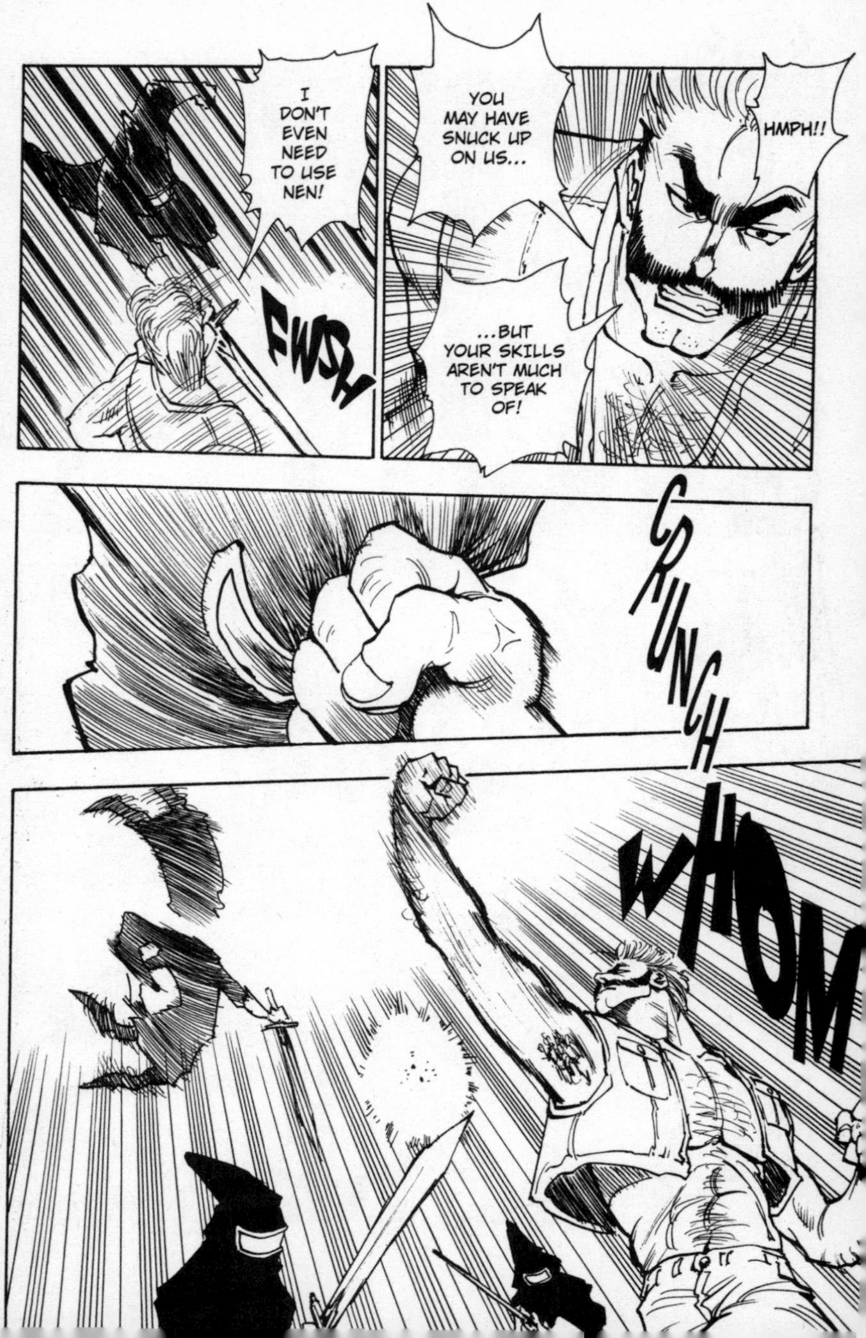
HMPH!!
YOU MAY HAVE SNUCK UP ON US...
...BUT YOUR SKILLS AREN'T MUCH TO SPEAK OF!
I DON'T EVEN NEED TO USE NEN!
FWSH
CRUNCH
WHOM

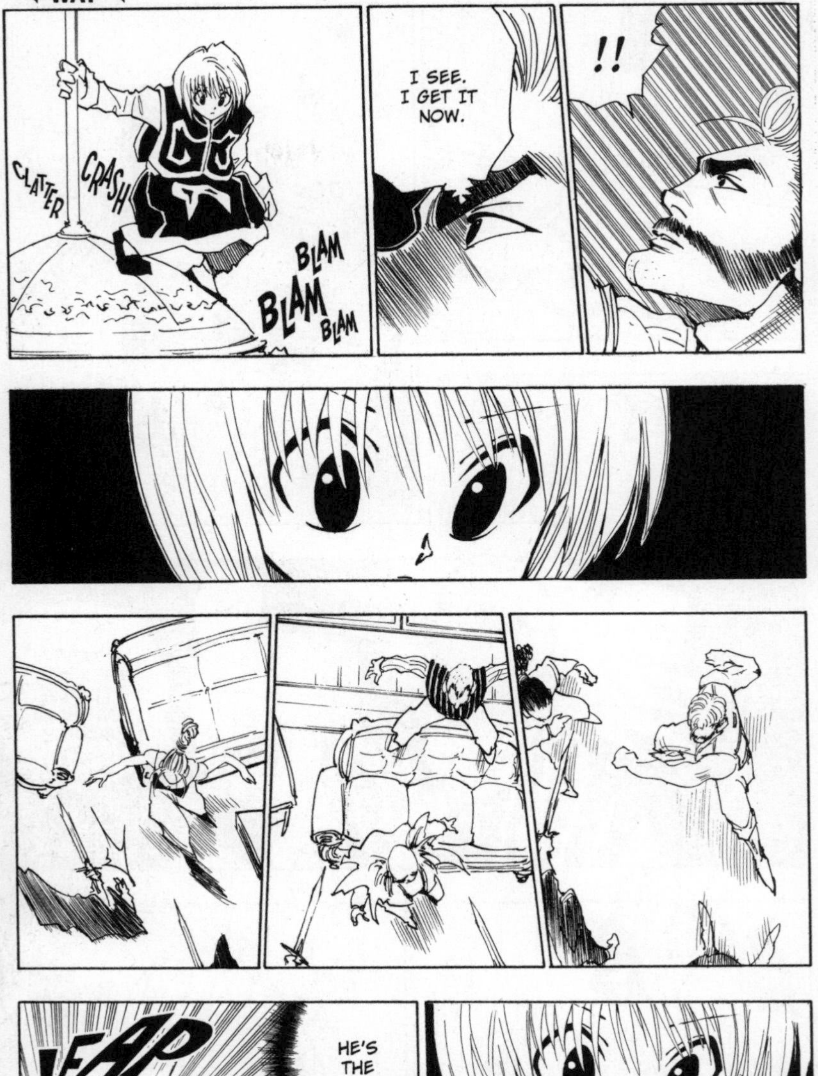
!!
I SEE. I GET IT NOW.
CRASH
CLATTER
BLAM
BLAM
BLAM
HE'S THE ONE!
LEAP

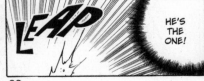

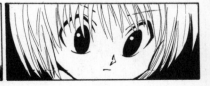

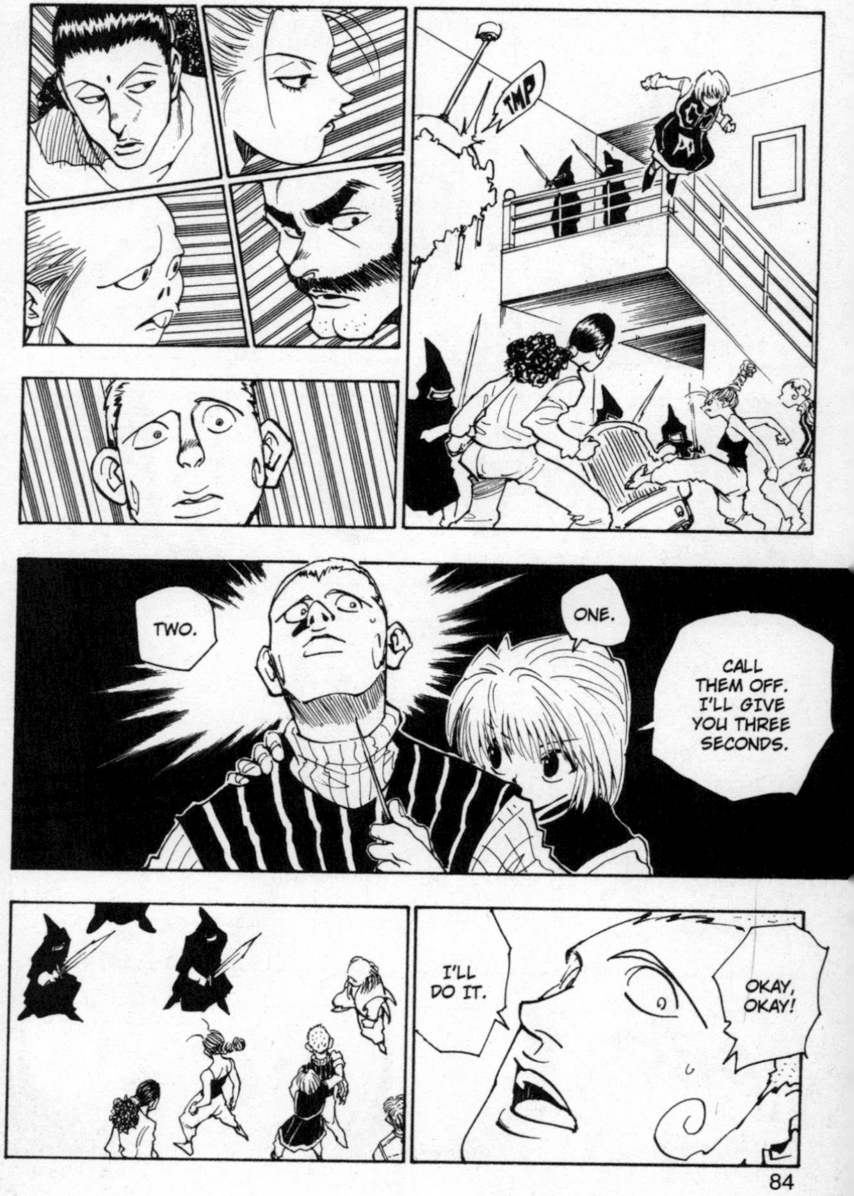
TMP
CALL THEM OFF. I'LL GIVE YOU THREE SECONDS.
ONE.
TWO.
OKAY, OKAY!
I'LL DO IT.

READ THIS WAY

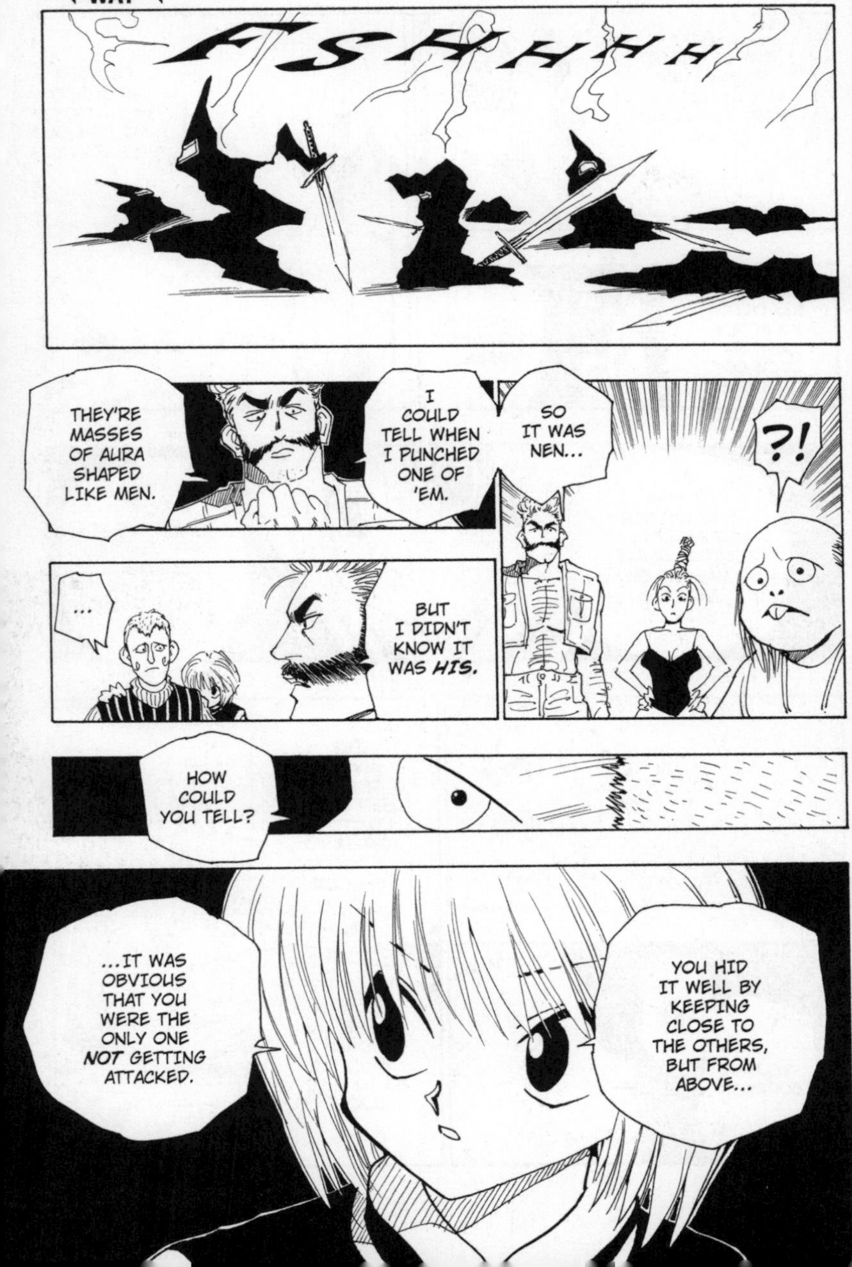
FSHHHH
SO IT WAS NEN...
?!
I COULD TELL WHEN I PUNCHED ONE OF 'EM.
THEY'RE MASSES OF AURA SHAPED LIKE MEN.
BUT I DIDN'T KNOW IT WAS *HIS.*
...
HOW COULD YOU TELL?
YOU HID IT WELL BY KEEPING CLOSE TO THE OTHERS, BUT FROM ABOVE...
...IT WAS OBVIOUS THAT YOU WERE THE ONLY ONE *NOT* GETTING ATTACKED.

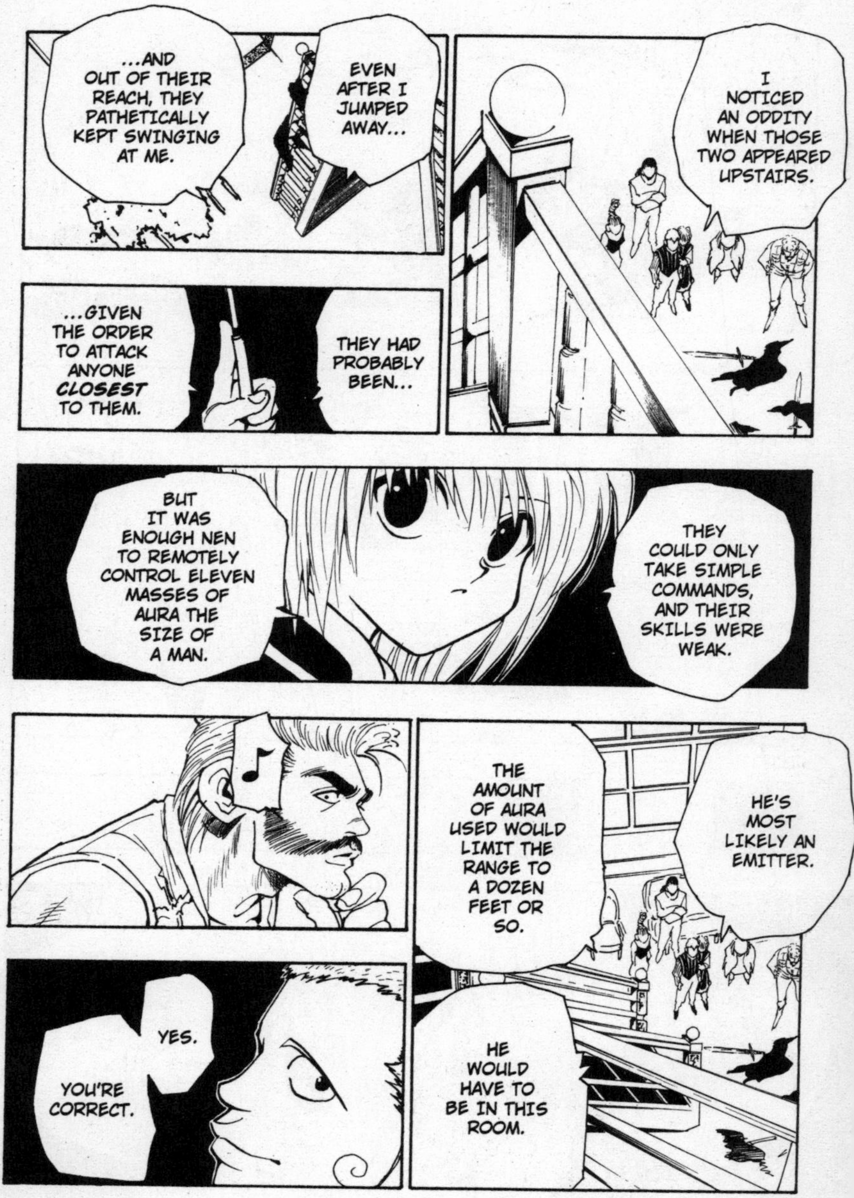
I NOTICED AN ODDITY WHEN THOSE TWO APPEARED UPSTAIRS.
EVEN AFTER I JUMPED AWAY...
...AND OUT OF THEIR REACH, THEY PATHETICALLY KEPT SWINGING AT ME.
THEY HAD PROBABLY BEEN...
...GIVEN THE ORDER TO ATTACK ANYONE *CLOSEST* TO THEM.
THEY COULD ONLY TAKE SIMPLE COMMANDS, AND THEIR SKILLS WERE WEAK.
BUT IT WAS ENOUGH NEN TO REMOTELY CONTROL ELEVEN MASSES OF AURA THE SIZE OF A MAN.
HE'S MOST LIKELY AN EMITTER.
THE AMOUNT OF AURA USED WOULD LIMIT THE RANGE TO A DOZEN FEET OR SO.
HE WOULD HAVE TO BE IN THIS ROOM.
♪
YES.
YOU'RE CORRECT.

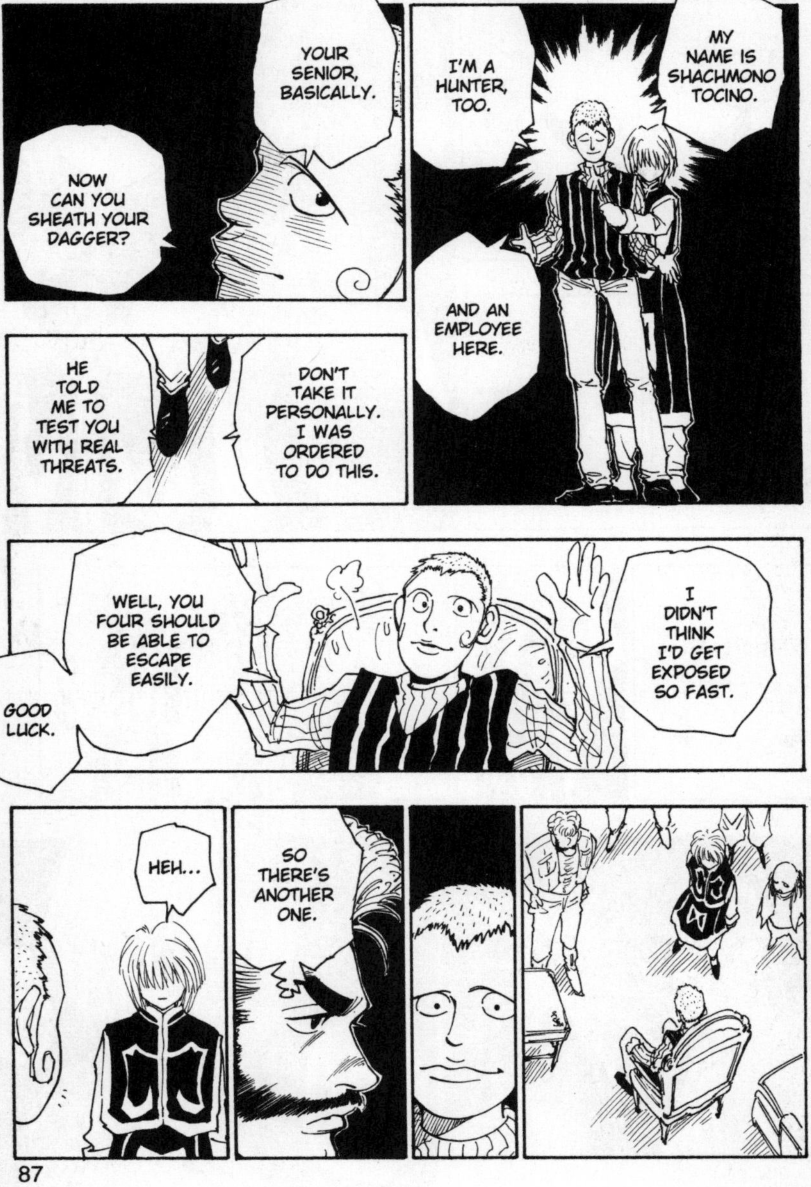
MY NAME IS SHACHMONO TOCINO.
I'M A HUNTER, TOO.
AND AN EMPLOYEE HERE.
YOUR SENIOR, BASICALLY.
NOW CAN YOU SHEATH YOUR DAGGER?
DON'T TAKE IT PERSONALLY. I WAS ORDERED TO DO THIS.
HE TOLD ME TO TEST YOU WITH REAL THREATS.
I DIDN'T THINK I'D GET EXPOSED SO FAST.
WELL, YOU FOUR SHOULD BE ABLE TO ESCAPE EASILY.
GOOD LUCK.
SO THERE'S ANOTHER ONE.
HEH...

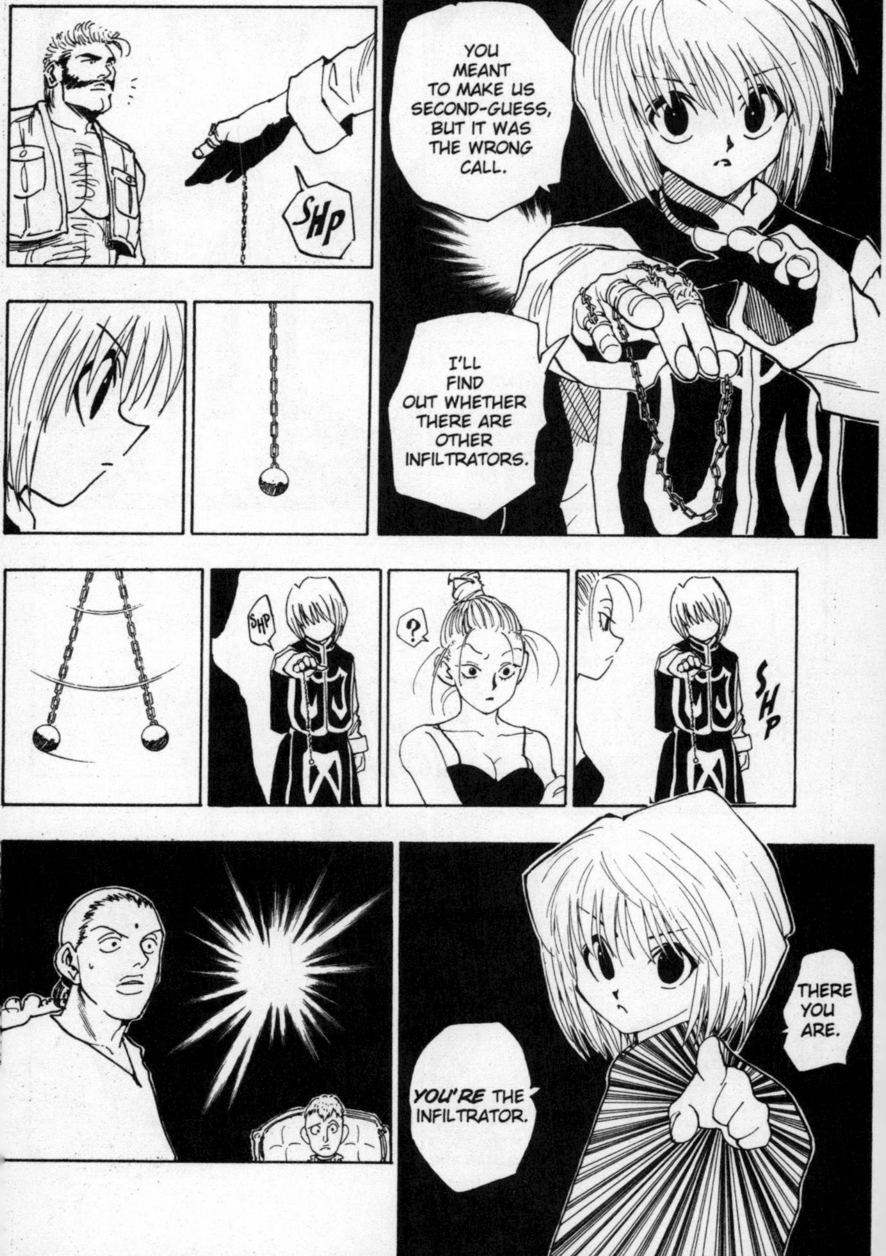
YOU MEANT TO MAKE US SECOND-GUESS, BUT IT WAS THE WRONG CALL.
I'LL FIND OUT WHETHER THERE ARE OTHER INFILTRATORS.
SHP
SHP
?
SHP
THERE YOU ARE.
YOU'RE THE INFILTRATOR.

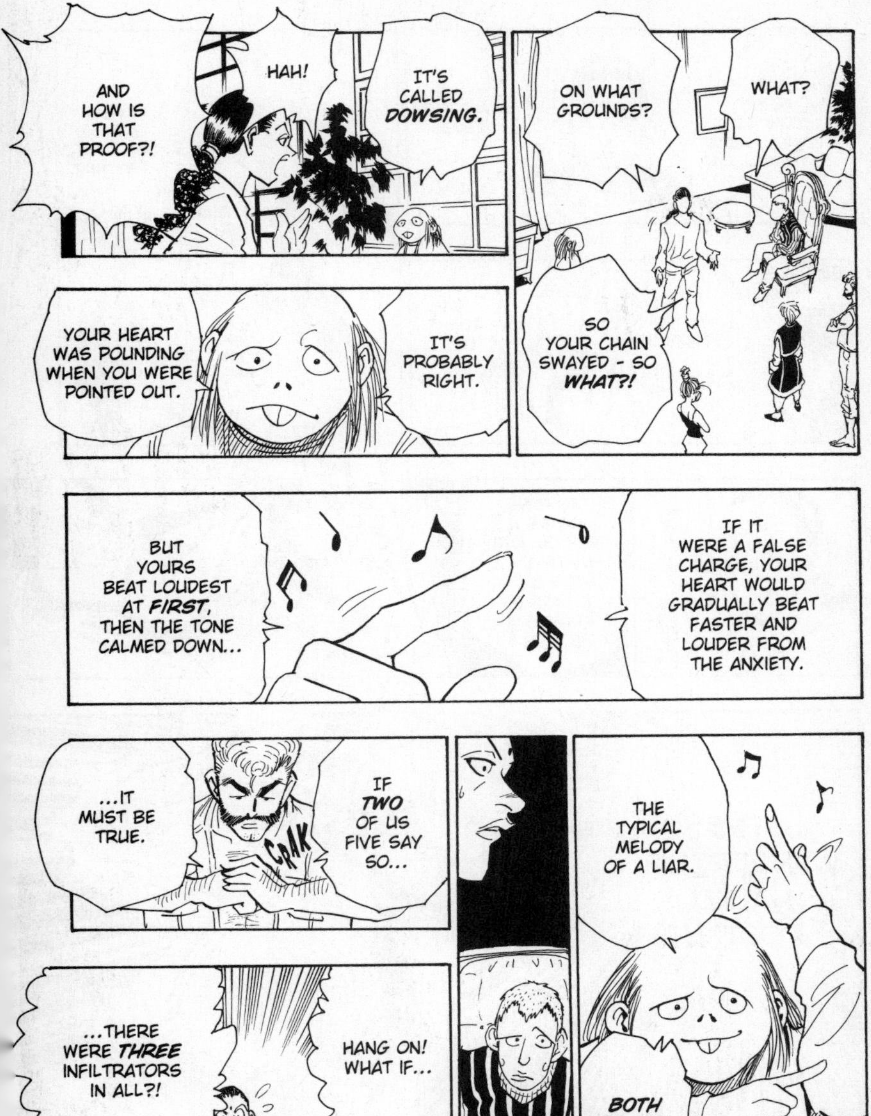
WHAT?
ON WHAT GROUNDS?
SO YOUR CHAIN SWAYED - SO WHAT?!
IT'S CALLED DOWSING.
HAH!
AND HOW IS THAT PROOF?!
IT'S PROBABLY RIGHT.
YOUR HEART WAS POUNDING WHEN YOU WERE POINTED OUT.
IF IT WERE A FALSE CHARGE, YOUR HEART WOULD GRADUALLY BEAT FASTER AND LOUDER FROM THE ANXIETY.
BUT YOURS BEAT LOUDEST AT FIRST, THEN THE TONE CALMED DOWN...
THE TYPICAL MELODY OF A LIAR.
BOTH OF YOU.
IF TWO OF US FIVE SAY SO...
CRAK
...IT MUST BE TRUE.
HANG ON! WHAT IF...
...THERE WERE THREE INFILTRATORS IN ALL?!

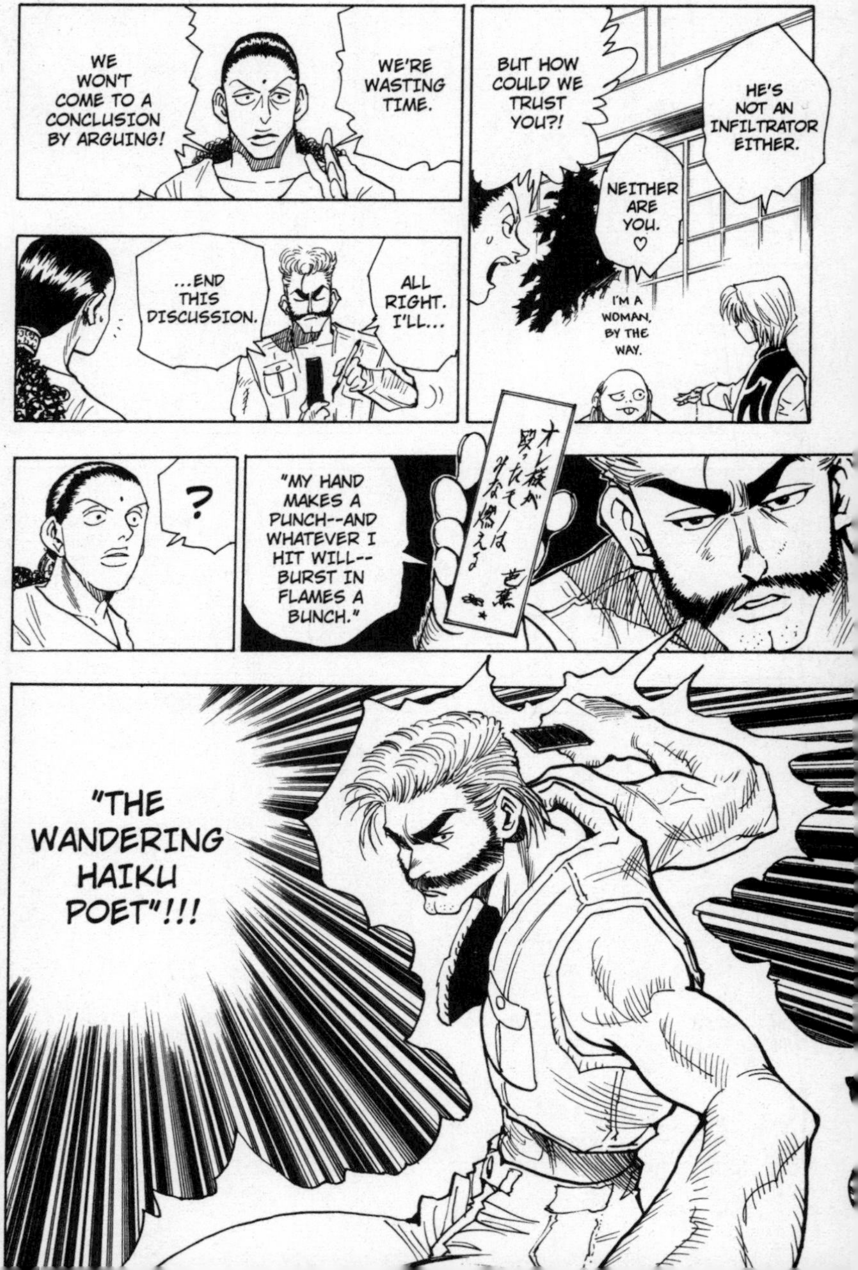
HE'S NOT AN INFILTRATOR EITHER.
BUT HOW COULD WE TRUST YOU?!
NEITHER ARE YOU. ♡
I'M A WOMAN, BY THE WAY.
WE'RE WASTING TIME.
WE WON'T COME TO A CONCLUSION BY ARGUING!
ALL RIGHT. I'LL...
...END THIS DISCUSSION.
オレ様が殴ったモノはみな燃える
芭蕉
"MY HAND MAKES A PUNCH--AND WHATEVER I HIT WILL--BURST IN FLAMES A BUNCH."
?
"THE WANDERING HAIKU POET"!!!

READ THIS WAY

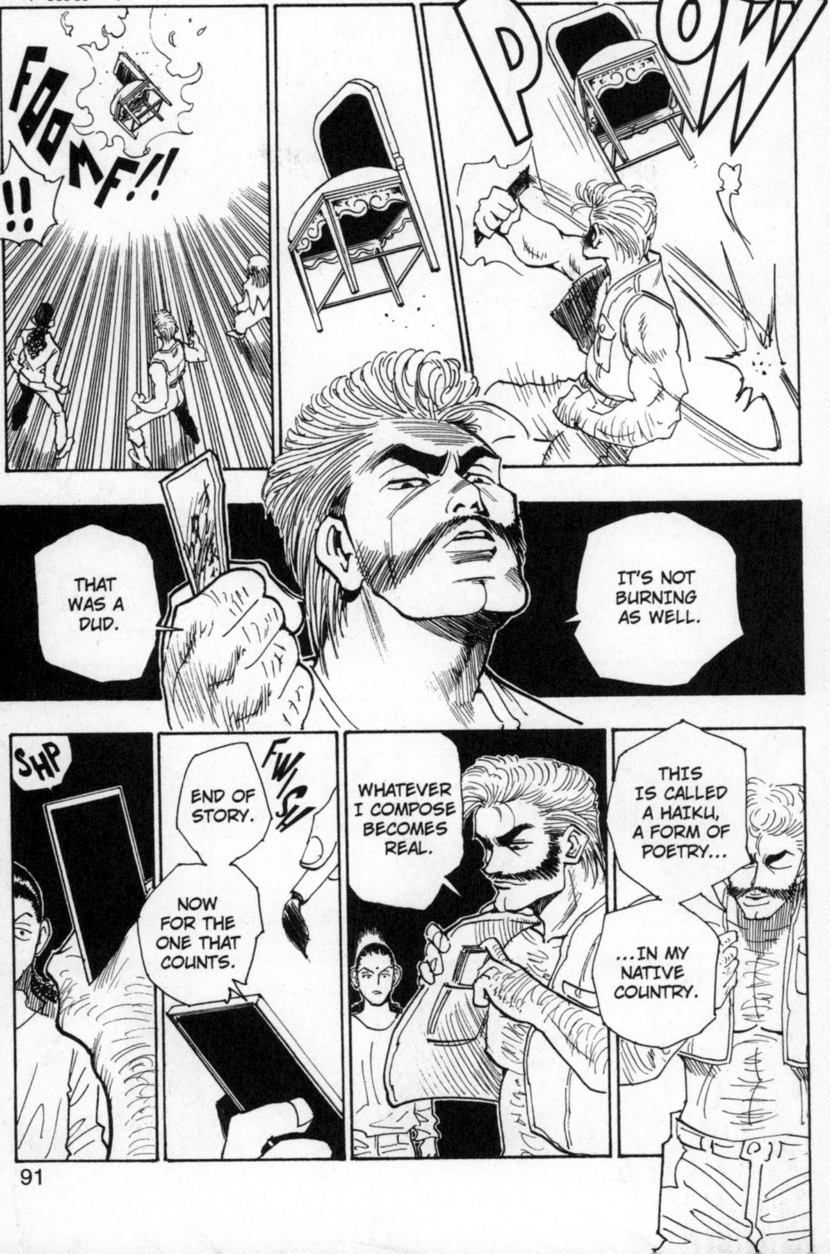

POW
FOOMF!!
!!
IT'S NOT BURNING AS WELL.
THAT WAS A DUD.
THIS IS CALLED A HAIKU, A FORM OF POETRY...
...IN MY NATIVE COUNTRY.
WHATEVER I COMPOSE BECOMES REAL.
END OF STORY.
FWISH
NOW FOR THE ONE THAT COUNTS.
SHP

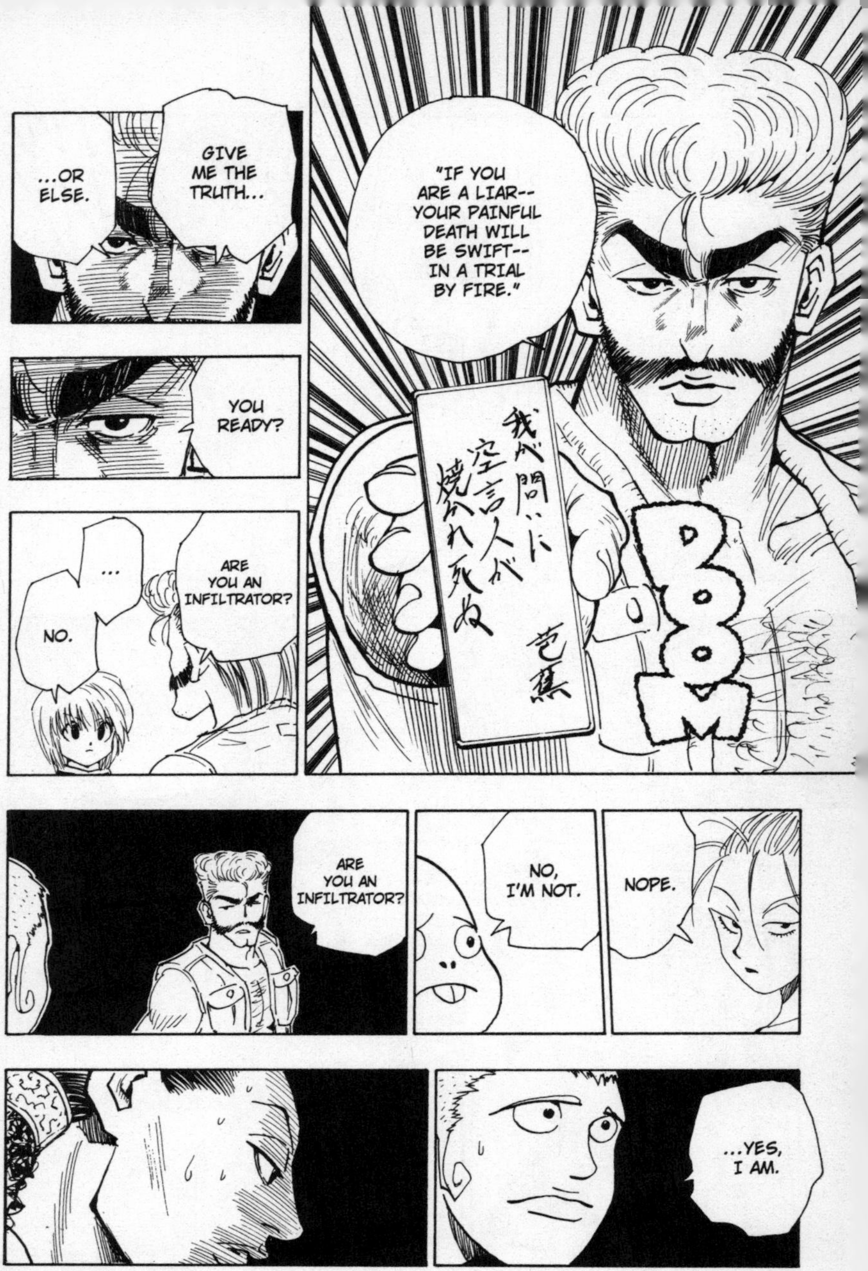
"IF YOU ARE A LIAR-- YOUR PAINFUL DEATH WILL BE SWIFT-- IN A TRIAL BY FIRE."
我が問いに
空言人が
焼かれ死ぬ
芭蕉
DOOM
GIVE ME THE TRUTH...
...OR ELSE.
YOU READY?
ARE YOU AN INFILTRATOR?
...
NO.
NOPE.
NO, I'M NOT.
ARE YOU AN INFILTRATOR?
...YES, I AM.

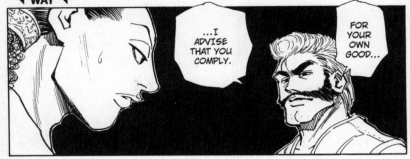

READ THIS WAY

FOR YOUR OWN GOOD...
...I ADVISE THAT YOU COMPLY.
ARE YOU AN INFILTRATOR?
LET'S HEAR YOUR ANSWER!!
我が問
FINE.
YES, I AM.
YOU GOT ME.

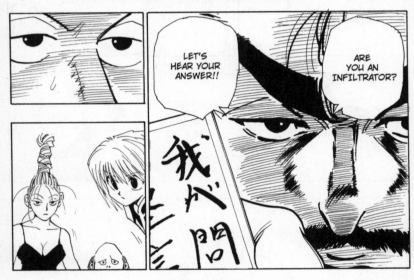

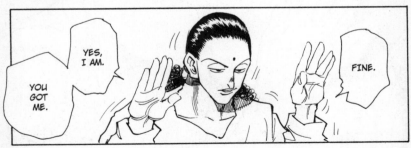

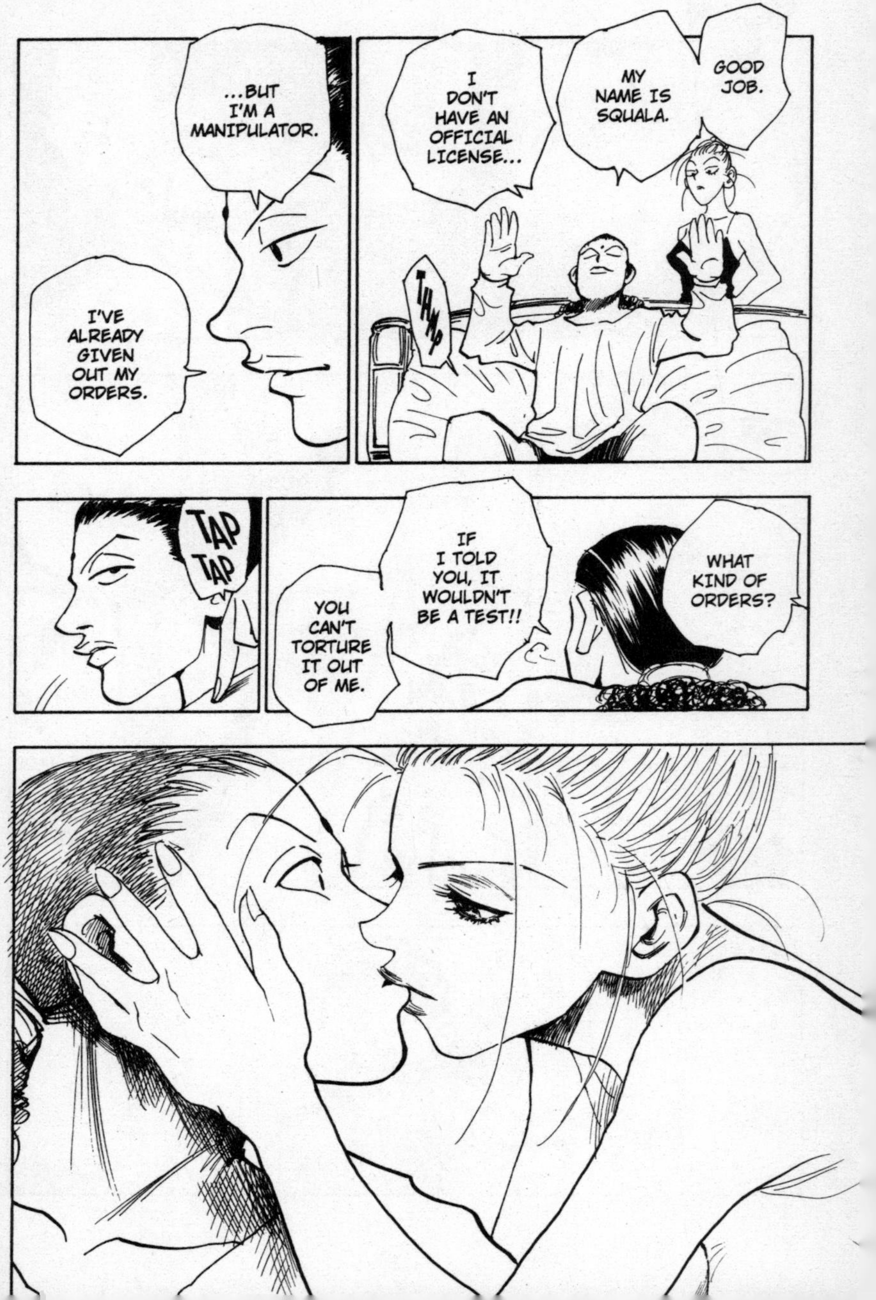
GOOD JOB.
MY NAME IS SQUALA.
I DON'T HAVE AN OFFICIAL LICENSE...
THMP
...BUT I'M A MANIPULATOR.
I'VE ALREADY GIVEN OUT MY ORDERS.
WHAT KIND OF ORDERS?
IF I TOLD YOU, IT WOULDN'T BE A TEST!!
YOU CAN'T TORTURE IT OUT OF ME.
TAP TAP

READ THIS WAY

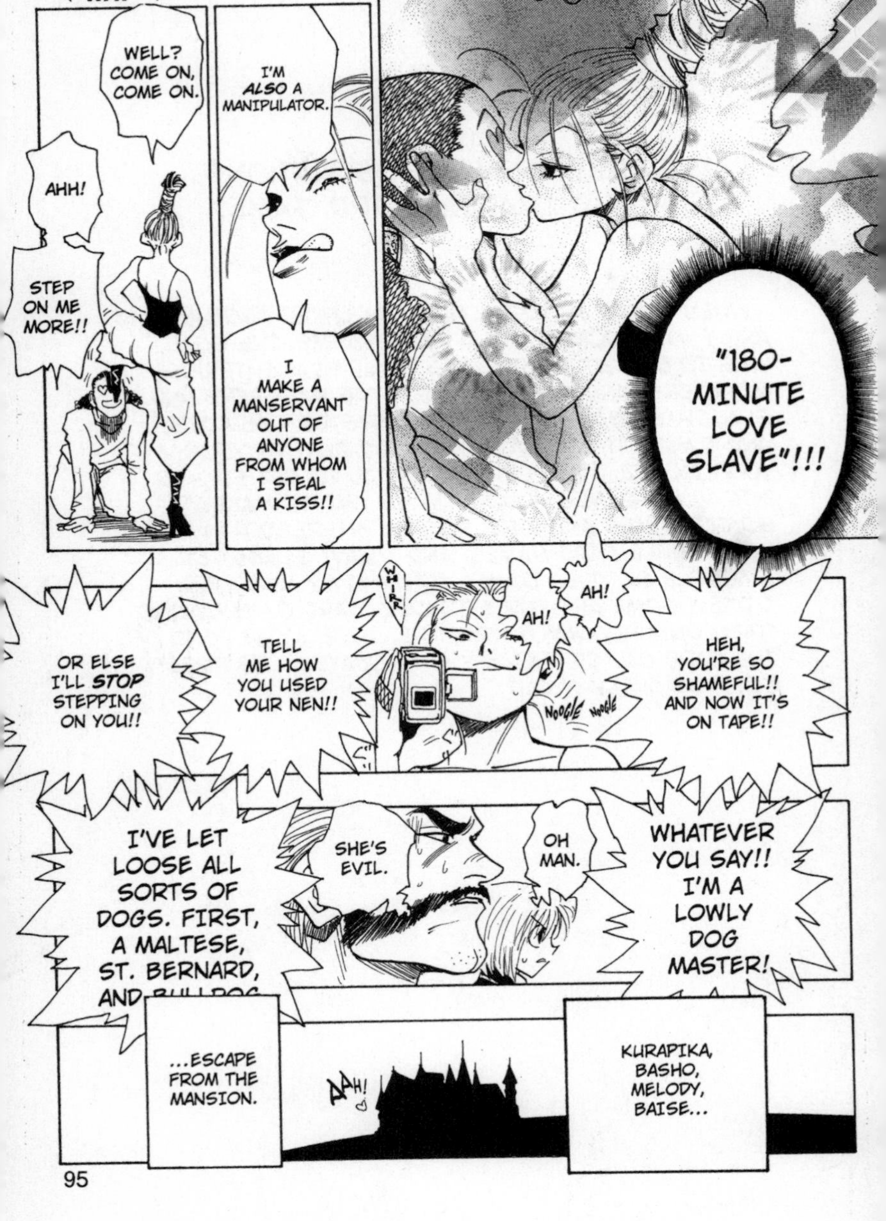

"180-MINUTE LOVE SLAVE"!!!
I'M ALSO A MANIPULATOR.
I MAKE A MANSERVANT OUT OF ANYONE FROM WHOM I STEAL A KISS!!
WELL? COME ON, COME ON.
AHH!
STEP ON ME MORE!!
HEH, YOU'RE SO SHAMEFUL!! AND NOW IT'S ON TAPE!!
AH!
AH!
WHIRR
NOOGIE NOOGIE
TELL ME HOW YOU USED YOUR NEN!!
OR ELSE I'LL STOP STEPPING ON YOU!!
WHATEVER YOU SAY!! I'M A LOWLY DOG MASTER!
OH MAN.
SHE'S EVIL.
I'VE LET LOOSE ALL SORTS OF DOGS. FIRST, A MALTESE, ST. BERNARD, AND
KURAPIKA, BASHO, MELODY, BAISE...
AAH!
...ESCAPE FROM THE MANSION.

I DREW SOME ILLUSTRATIONS FOR A TRADING CARD GAME.

WHEN I WAS IN JUNIOR HIGH, MY LITTLE BROTHER AND I MADE OURSELVES A BOARD GAME. THE GOAL WAS TO COLLECT TREASURES WHILE SLAUGHTERING MONSTERS, AND IT WAS CALLED "THE MASSACRE AND SLAUGHTER GAME." THE BATTLE SYSTEM USED DICE, AND I MADE IT SO THAT YOU COULD PLAY BY YOURSELF. YOU CAN SEE I HAD HIGH POTENTIAL TO GET SUCKED INTO VIDEO GAMES. I DON'T HAVE TIME TO MAKE BOARD GAMES ANYMORE, BUT I'M INTERESTED IN COLLECTIBLE CARD GAMES, AND I HAVE PLANS FOR A COUPLE OF VIDEO GAMES (ONLY IN MY MIND). SO, I DREW SOME ART FOR A TRADING CARD GAME CALLED "DRAGON KINGDOM"(© KRAFT.HEIL). I'M MOST FOND OF THE CARD CALLED "HERESY'S ADVOCATE." IT'S PRETTY CUTE, SO CHECK IT OUT.

Chapter 69 Greed Island

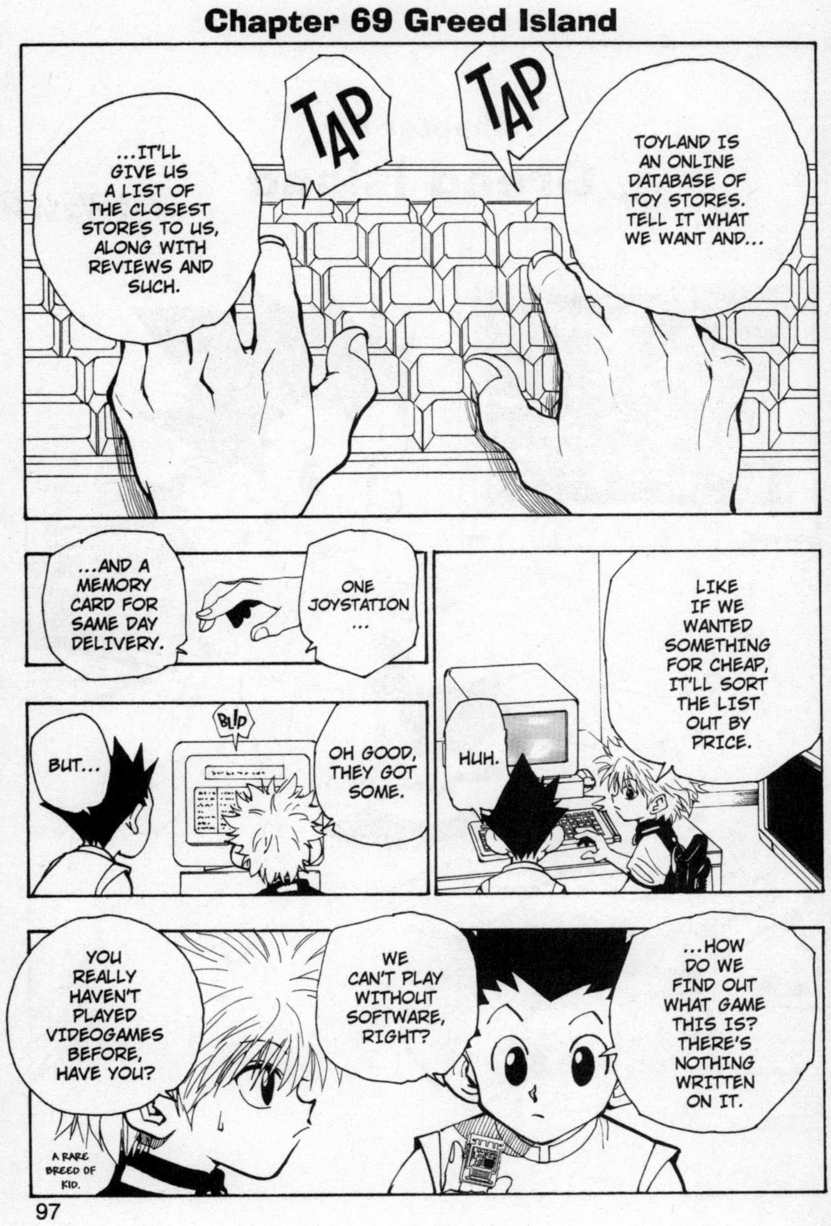

TOYLAND IS AN ONLINE DATABASE OF TOY STORES. TELL IT WHAT WE WANT AND...
TAP
TAP
...IT'LL GIVE US A LIST OF THE CLOSEST STORES TO US, ALONG WITH REVIEWS AND SUCH.
LIKE IF WE WANTED SOMETHING FOR CHEAP, IT'LL SORT THE LIST OUT BY PRICE.
HUH.
ONE JOYSTATION ...
...AND A MEMORY CARD FOR SAME DAY DELIVERY.
BLIP
OH GOOD, THEY GOT SOME.
BUT...
...HOW DO WE FIND OUT WHAT GAME THIS IS? THERE'S NOTHING WRITTEN ON IT.
WE CAN'T PLAY WITHOUT SOFTWARE, RIGHT?
YOU REALLY HAVEN'T PLAYED VIDEOGAMES BEFORE, HAVE YOU?
A RARE BREED OF KID.

Chapter 69
Greed Island

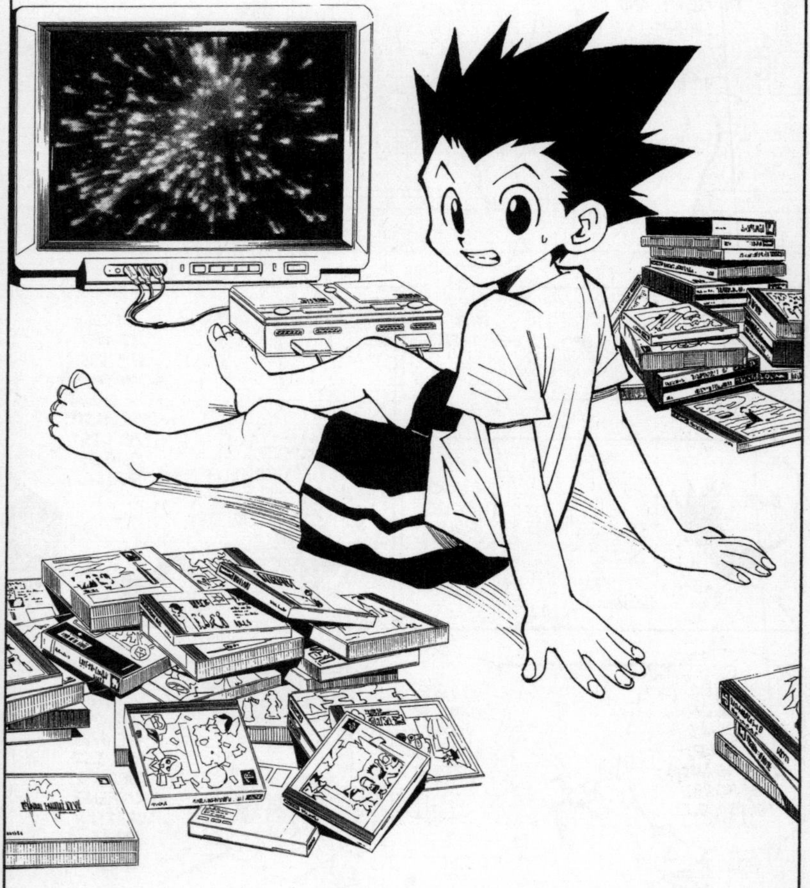

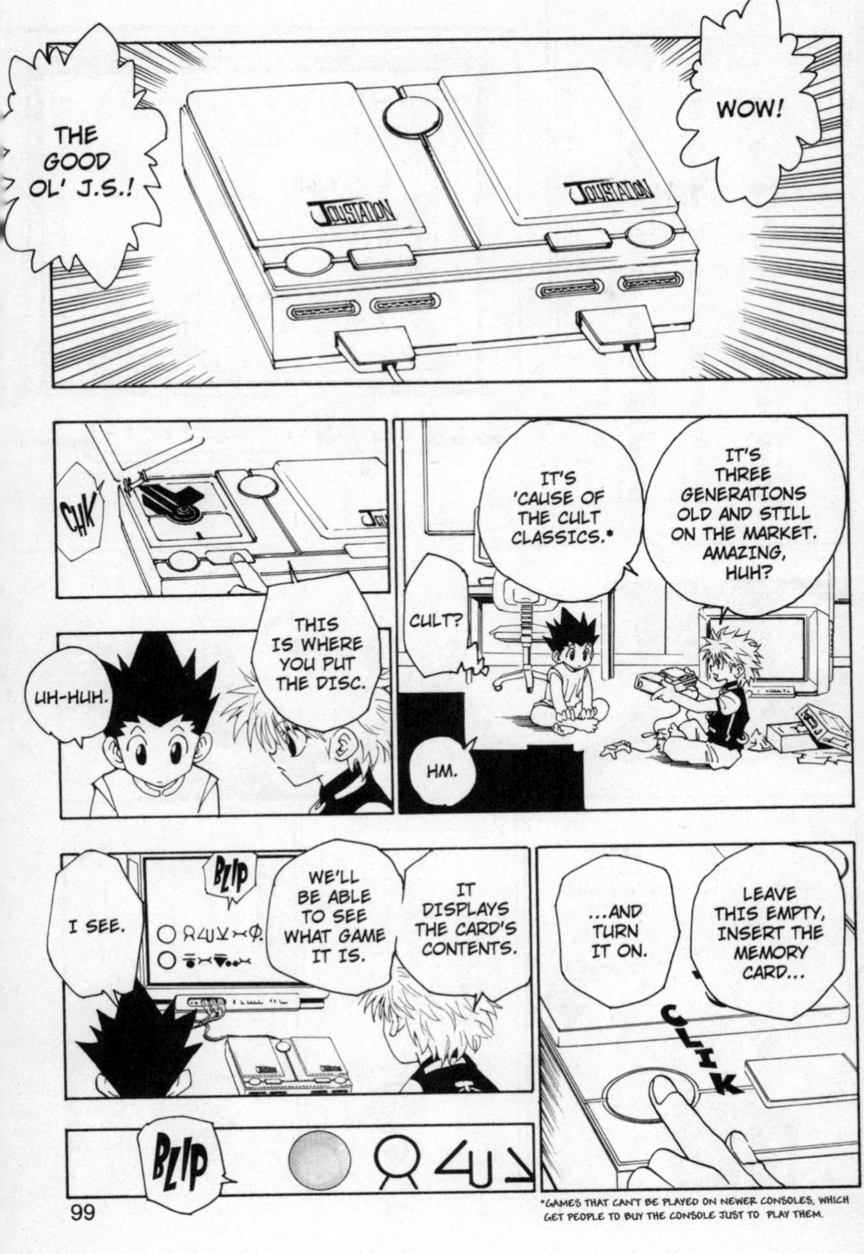
WOW!
THE GOOD OL' J.S.!
IT'S THREE GENERATIONS OLD AND STILL ON THE MARKET. AMAZING, HUH?
IT'S 'CAUSE OF THE CULT CLASSICS.*
CULT?
HM.
CHK
THIS IS WHERE YOU PUT THE DISC.
UH-HUH.
LEAVE THIS EMPTY, INSERT THE MEMORY CARD...
...AND TURN IT ON.
CLIK
IT DISPLAYS THE CARD'S CONTENTS.
WE'LL BE ABLE TO SEE WHAT GAME IT IS.
BLIP
I SEE.
BLIP

*GAMES THAT CAN'T BE PLAYED ON NEWER CONSOLES, WHICH GET PEOPLE TO BUY THE CONSOLE JUST TO PLAY THEM.

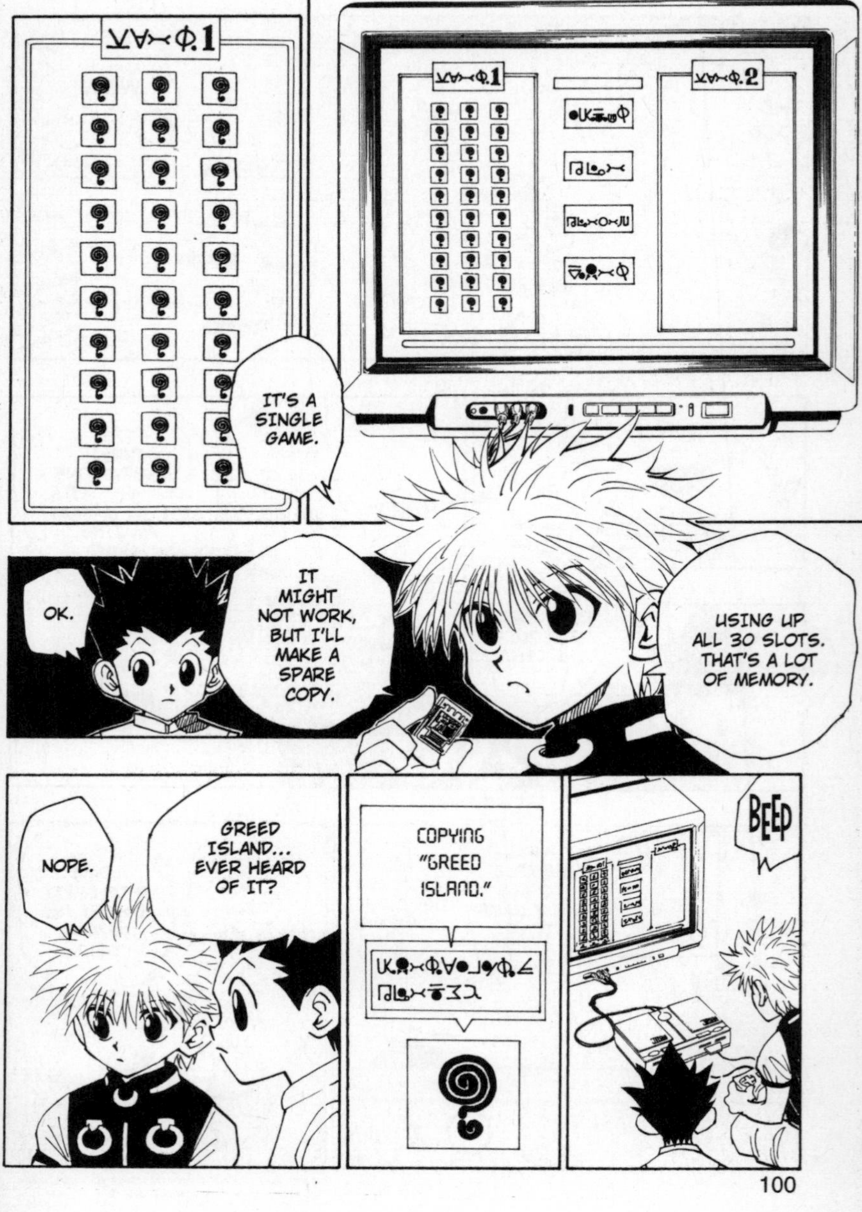
IT'S A SINGLE GAME.
USING UP ALL 30 SLOTS. THAT'S A LOT OF MEMORY.
IT MIGHT NOT WORK, BUT I'LL MAKE A SPARE COPY.
OK.
BEEP
COPYING "GREED ISLAND."
GREED ISLAND... EVER HEARD OF IT?
NOPE.

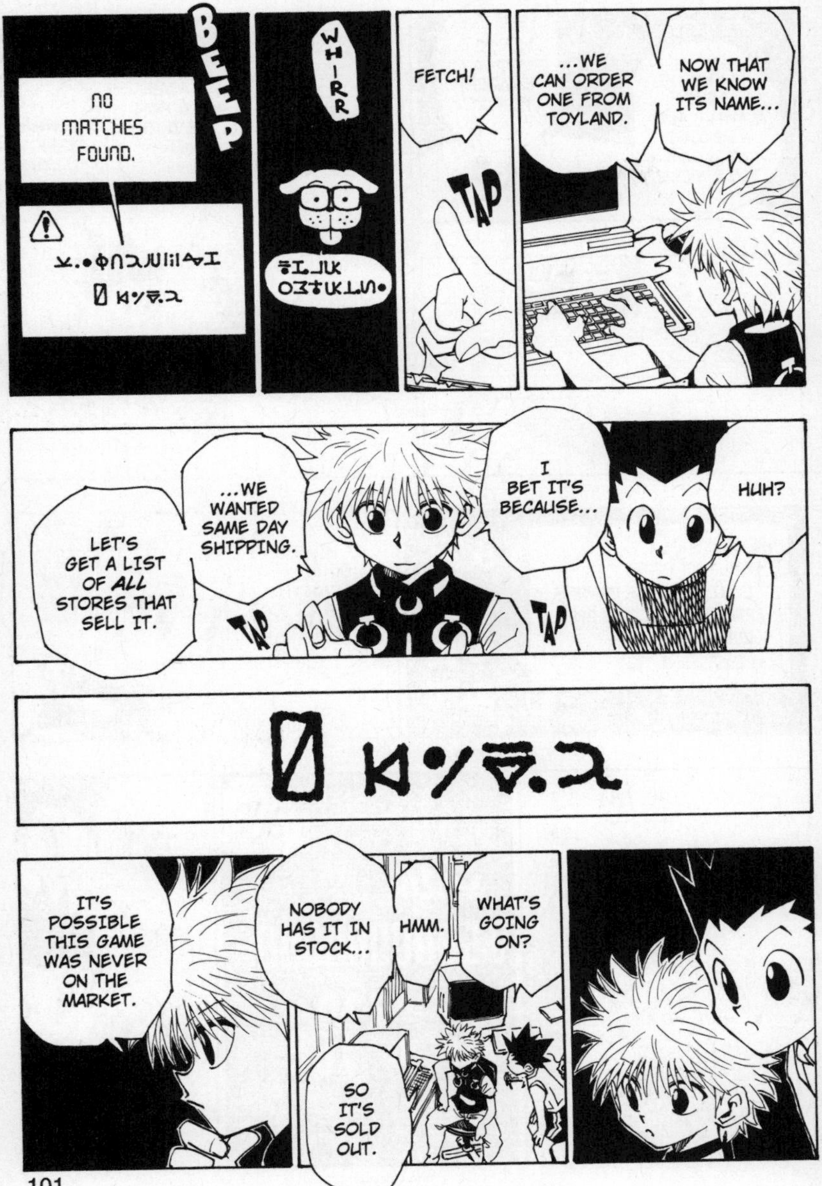
NOW THAT WE KNOW ITS NAME...
...WE CAN ORDER ONE FROM TOYLAND.
TAP
FETCH!
WHIRR
BEEP
NO MATCHES FOUND.
HUH?
I BET IT'S BECAUSE...
TAP
...WE WANTED SAME DAY SHIPPING.
LET'S GET A LIST OF ALL STORES THAT SELL IT.
TAP
WHAT'S GOING ON?
HMM.
NOBODY HAS IT IN STOCK...
SO IT'S SOLD OUT.
IT'S POSSIBLE THIS GAME WAS NEVER ON THE MARKET.

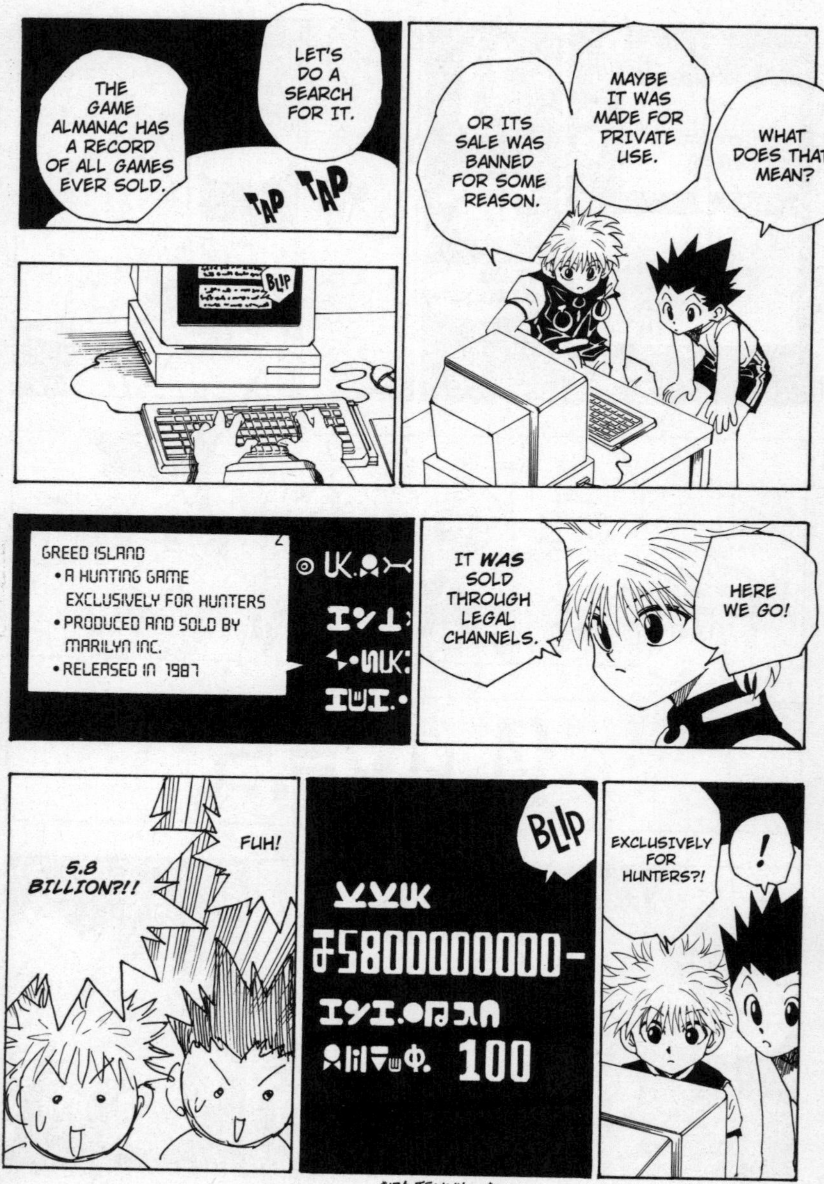
WHAT DOES THAT MEAN?
MAYBE IT WAS MADE FOR PRIVATE USE.
OR ITS SALE WAS BANNED FOR SOME REASON.
LET'S DO A SEARCH FOR IT.
THE GAME ALMANAC HAS A RECORD OF ALL GAMES EVER SOLD.
TAP TAP
BLIP
HERE WE GO!
IT *WAS* SOLD THROUGH LEGAL CHANNELS.
GREED ISLAND
• A HUNTING GAME EXCLUSIVELY FOR HUNTERS
• PRODUCED AND SOLD BY MARILYN INC.
• RELEASED IN 1987
!
EXCLUSIVELY FOR HUNTERS?!
BLIP
5800000000-
100
FUH!
5.8 BILLION?!!

*134 JENNY = $1

READ THIS WAY

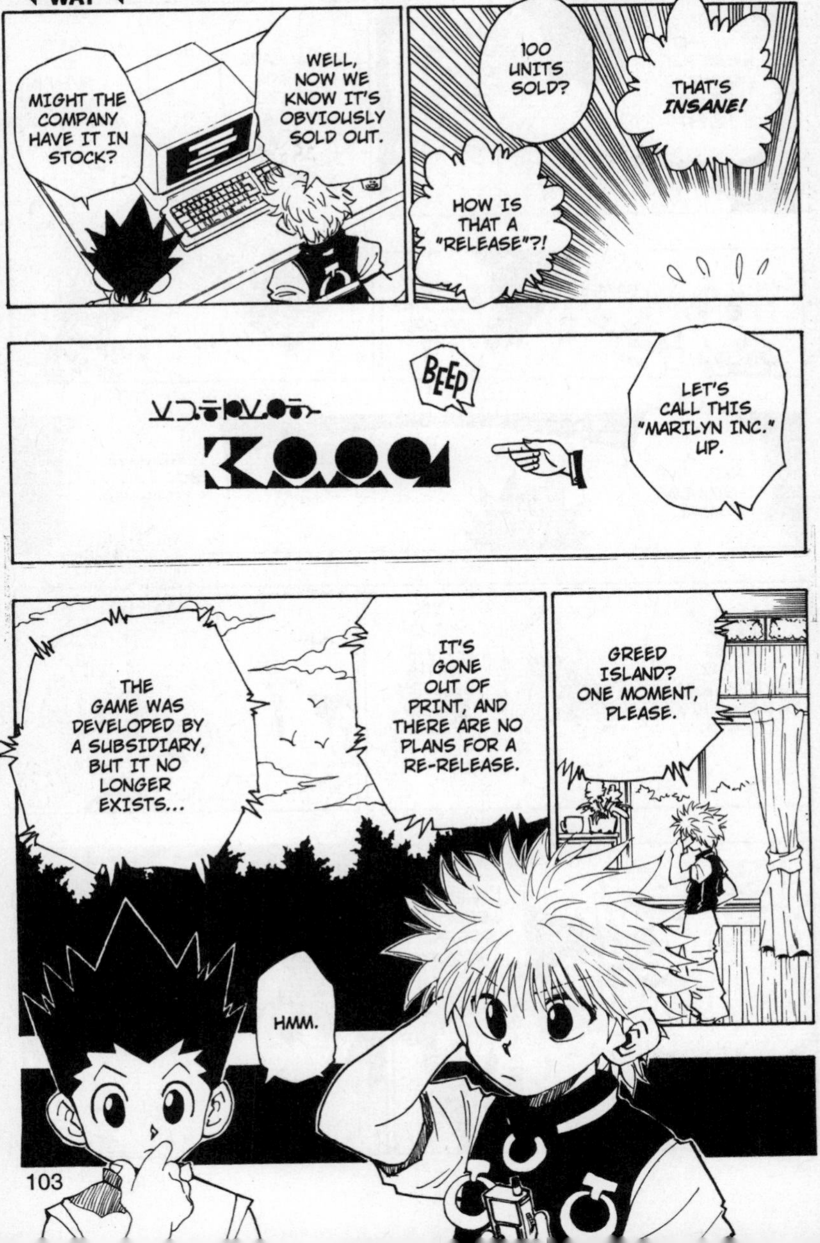

100 UNITS SOLD?
THAT'S *INSANE!*
HOW IS THAT A "RELEASE"?!
WELL, NOW WE KNOW IT'S OBVIOUSLY SOLD OUT.
MIGHT THE COMPANY HAVE IT IN STOCK?
LET'S CALL THIS "MARILYN INC." UP.
BEEP
GREED ISLAND? ONE MOMENT, PLEASE.
IT'S GONE OUT OF PRINT, AND THERE ARE NO PLANS FOR A RE-RELEASE.
THE GAME WAS DEVELOPED BY A SUBSIDIARY, BUT IT NO LONGER EXISTS...
HMM.

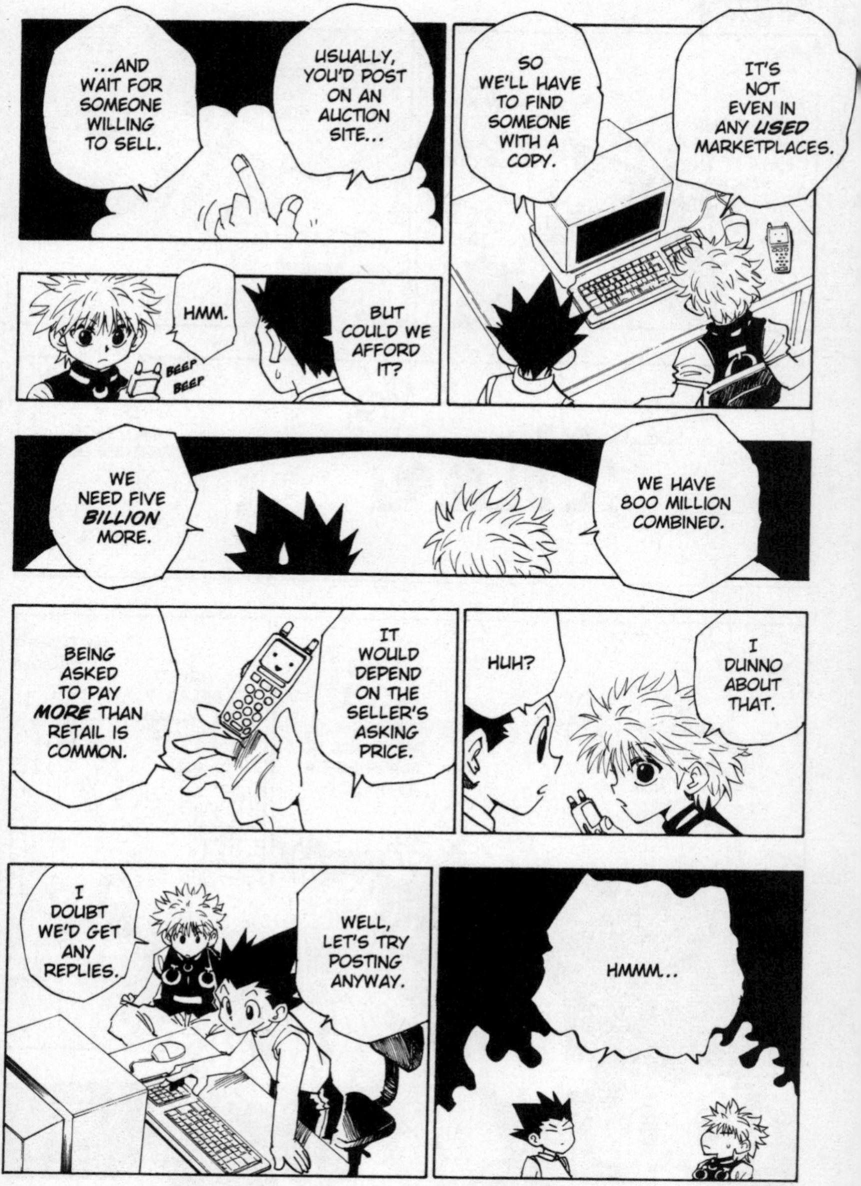
IT'S NOT EVEN IN ANY *USED* MARKETPLACES.
SO WE'LL HAVE TO FIND SOMEONE WITH A COPY.
USUALLY, YOU'D POST ON AN AUCTION SITE...
...AND WAIT FOR SOMEONE WILLING TO SELL.
BUT COULD WE AFFORD IT?
HMM.
BEEP BEEP
WE HAVE 800 MILLION COMBINED.
WE NEED FIVE *BILLION* MORE.
I DUNNO ABOUT THAT.
HUH?
IT WOULD DEPEND ON THE SELLER'S ASKING PRICE.
BEING ASKED TO PAY *MORE* THAN RETAIL IS COMMON.
HMMM...
WELL, LET'S TRY POSTING ANYWAY.
I DOUBT WE'D GET ANY REPLIES.

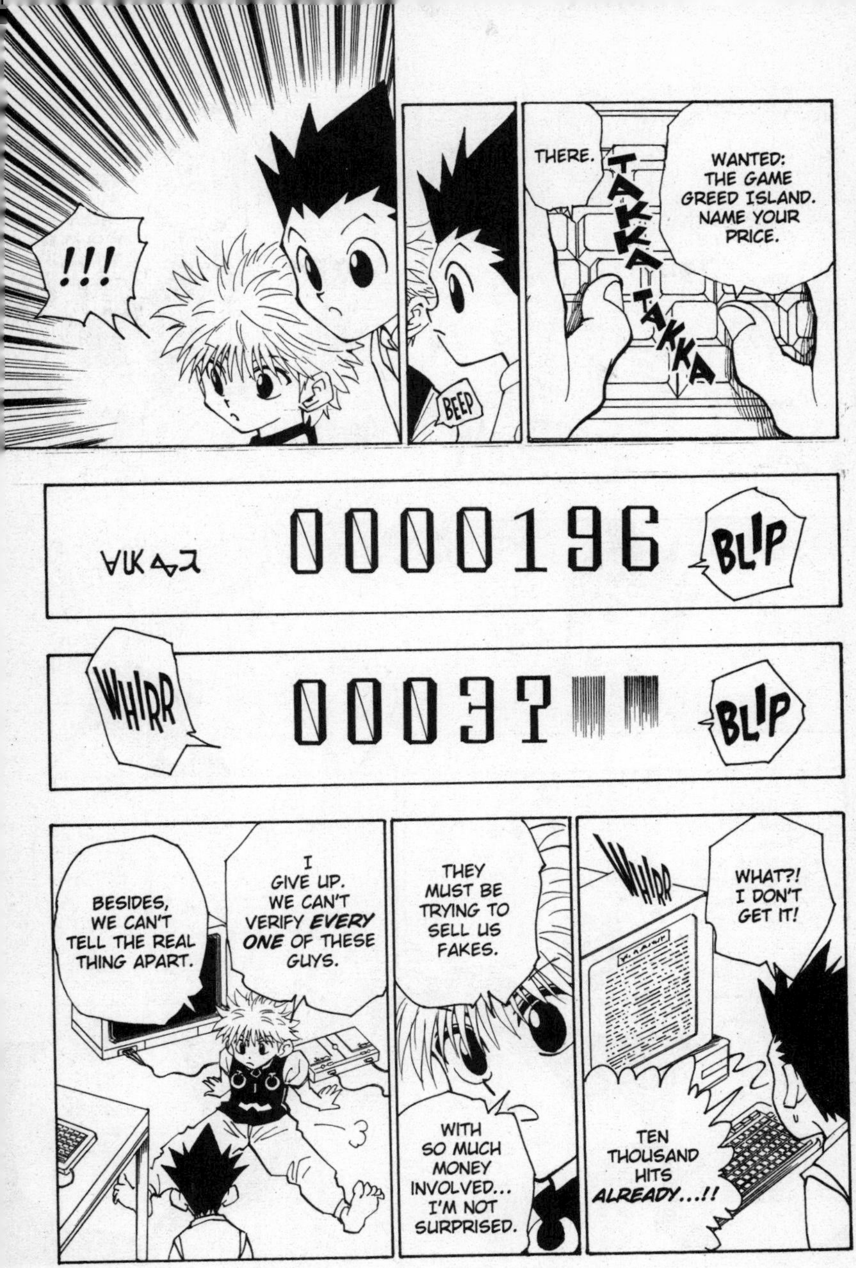
WANTED: THE GAME GREED ISLAND. NAME YOUR PRICE.
THERE.
TAKKA TAKKA
BEEP
!!!
BLIP
0000196
BLIP
00037
WHIRR
WHIRR
WHAT?! I DON'T GET IT!
TEN THOUSAND HITS *ALREADY*...!!
THEY MUST BE TRYING TO SELL US FAKES.
WITH SO MUCH MONEY INVOLVED... I'M NOT SURPRISED.
I GIVE UP. WE CAN'T VERIFY *EVERY ONE* OF THESE GUYS.
BESIDES, WE CAN'T TELL THE REAL THING APART.

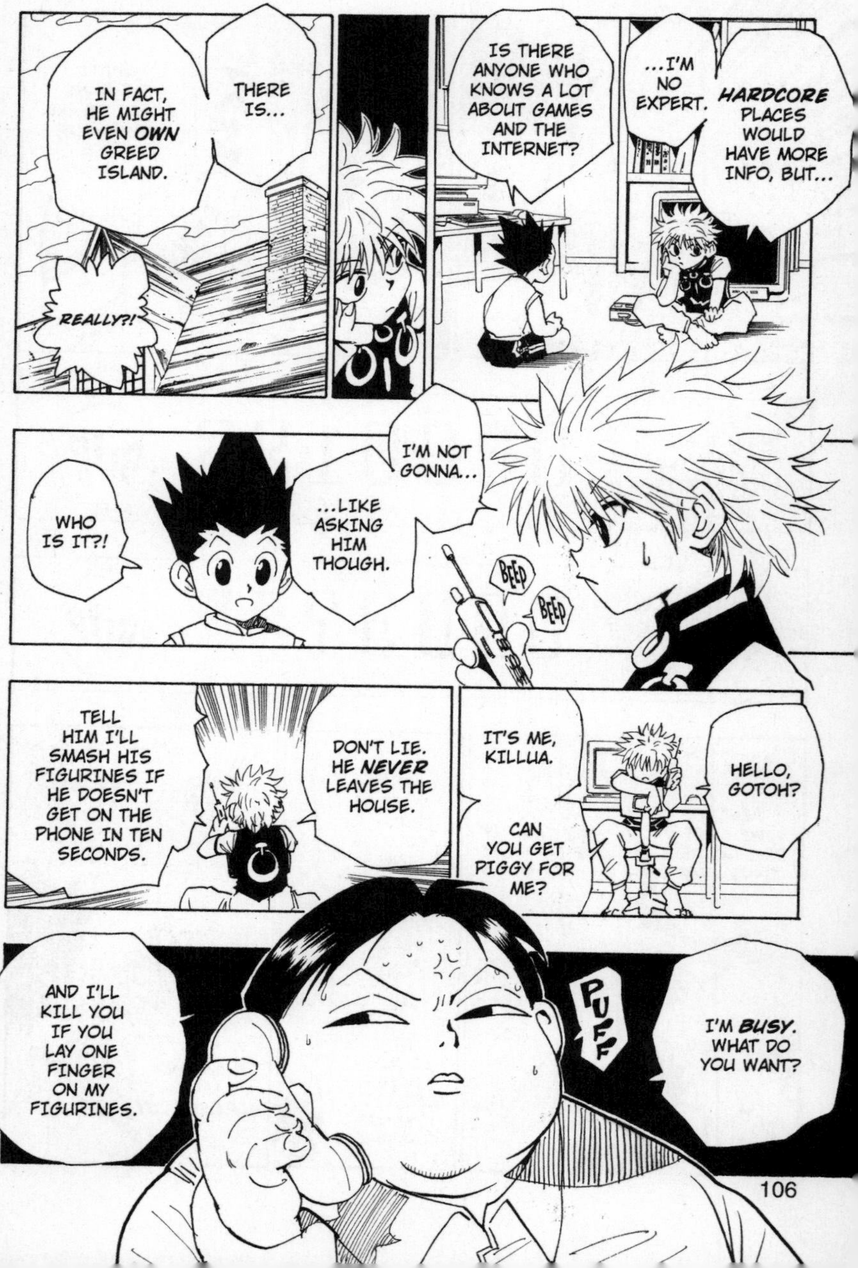

HARDCORE PLACES WOULD HAVE MORE INFO, BUT...
...I'M NO EXPERT.
IS THERE ANYONE WHO KNOWS A LOT ABOUT GAMES AND THE INTERNET?
THERE IS...
IN FACT, HE MIGHT EVEN OWN GREED ISLAND.
REALLY?!
I'M NOT GONNA...
...LIKE ASKING HIM THOUGH.
BEEP
BEEP
WHO IS IT?!
HELLO, GOTOH?
IT'S ME, KILLUA.
CAN YOU GET PIGGY FOR ME?
DON'T LIE. HE NEVER LEAVES THE HOUSE.
TELL HIM I'LL SMASH HIS FIGURINES IF HE DOESN'T GET ON THE PHONE IN TEN SECONDS.
I'M BUSY. WHAT DO YOU WANT?
PUFF
AND I'LL KILL YOU IF YOU LAY ONE FINGER ON MY FIGURINES.

READ THIS WAY

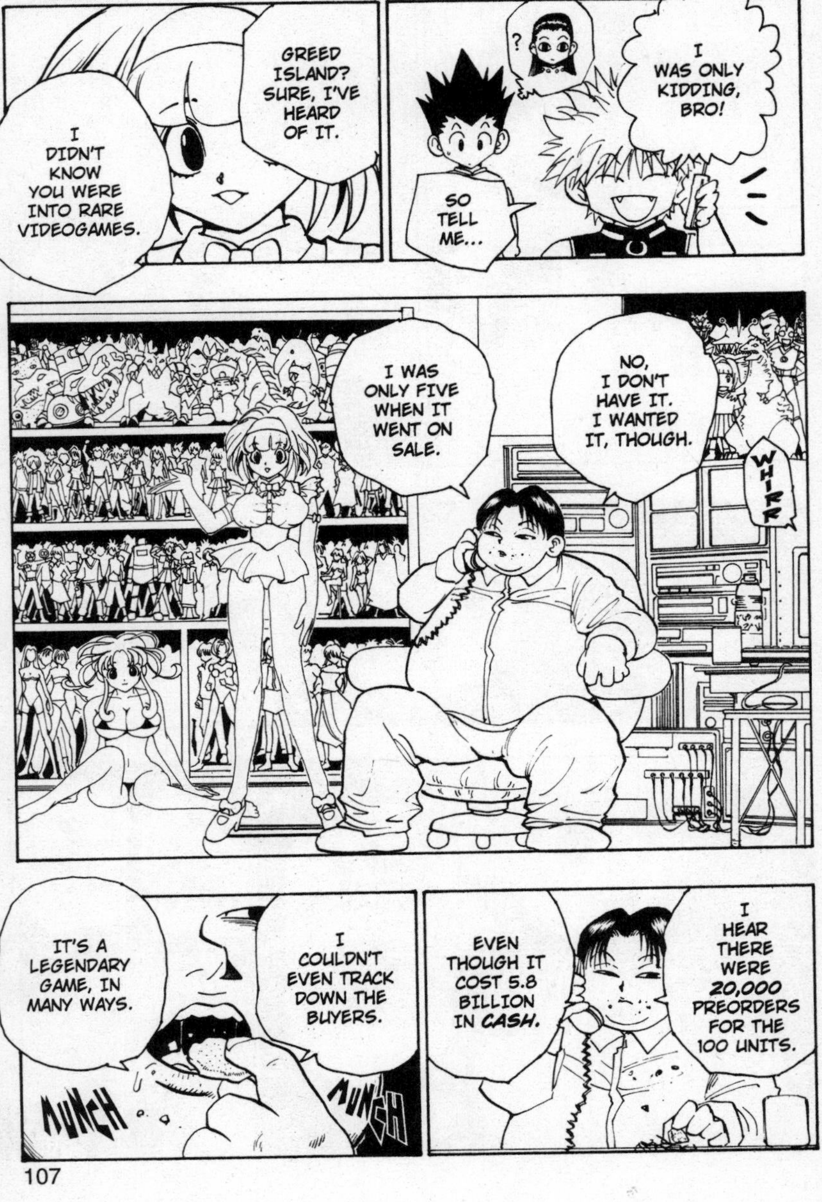
I WAS ONLY KIDDING, BRO!
?
SO TELL ME...
GREED ISLAND? SURE, I'VE HEARD OF IT.
I DIDN'T KNOW YOU WERE INTO RARE VIDEOGAMES.
NO, I DON'T HAVE IT. I WANTED IT, THOUGH.
WHIRR
I WAS ONLY FIVE WHEN IT WENT ON SALE.
I HEAR THERE WERE **20,000** PREORDERS FOR THE 100 UNITS.
EVEN THOUGH IT COST 5.8 BILLION IN ***CASH.***
I COULDN'T EVEN TRACK DOWN THE BUYERS.
MUNCH
IT'S A LEGENDARY GAME, IN MANY WAYS.
MUNCH

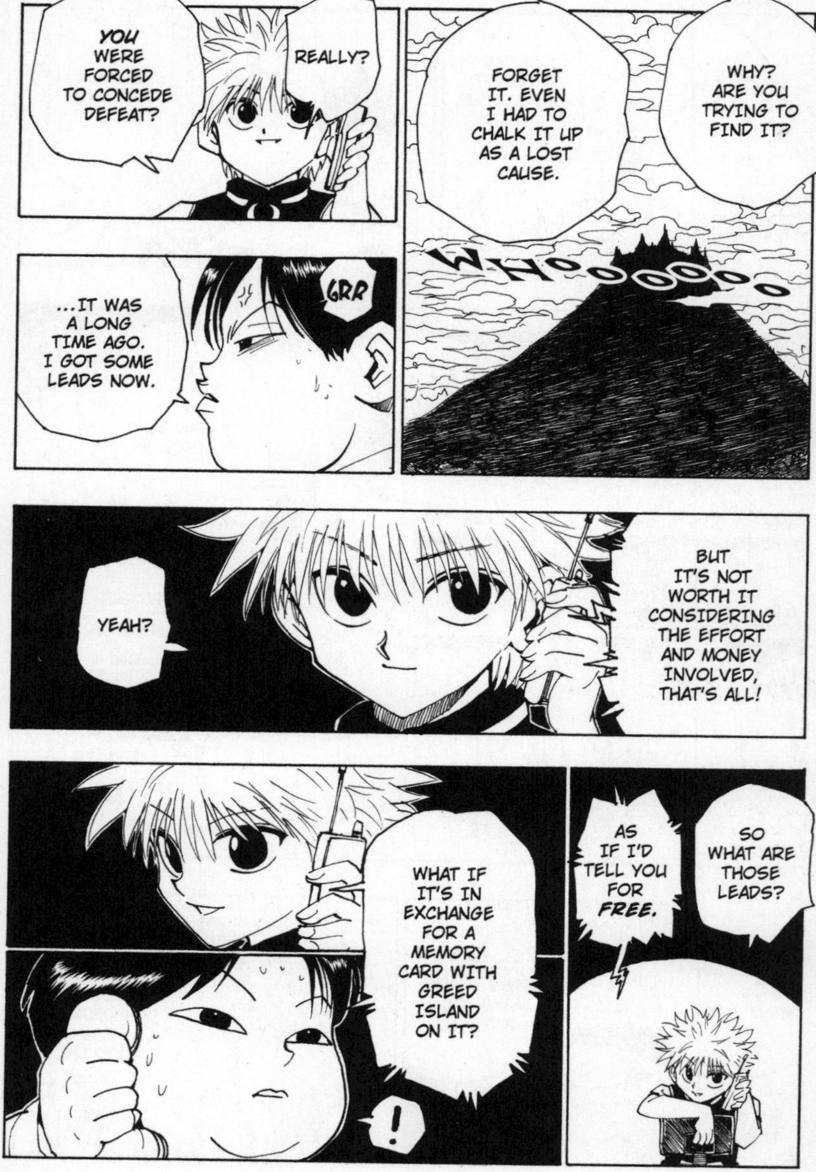

WHY? ARE YOU TRYING TO FIND IT?
FORGET IT. EVEN I HAD TO CHALK IT UP AS A LOST CAUSE.
WHOOOOOOOO
REALLY?
YOU WERE FORCED TO CONCEDE DEFEAT?
GRR
...IT WAS A LONG TIME AGO. I GOT SOME LEADS NOW.
BUT IT'S NOT WORTH IT CONSIDERING THE EFFORT AND MONEY INVOLVED, THAT'S ALL!
YEAH?
SO WHAT ARE THOSE LEADS?
AS IF I'D TELL YOU FOR *FREE.*
WHAT IF IT'S IN EXCHANGE FOR A MEMORY CARD WITH GREED ISLAND ON IT?
!

READ THIS WAY

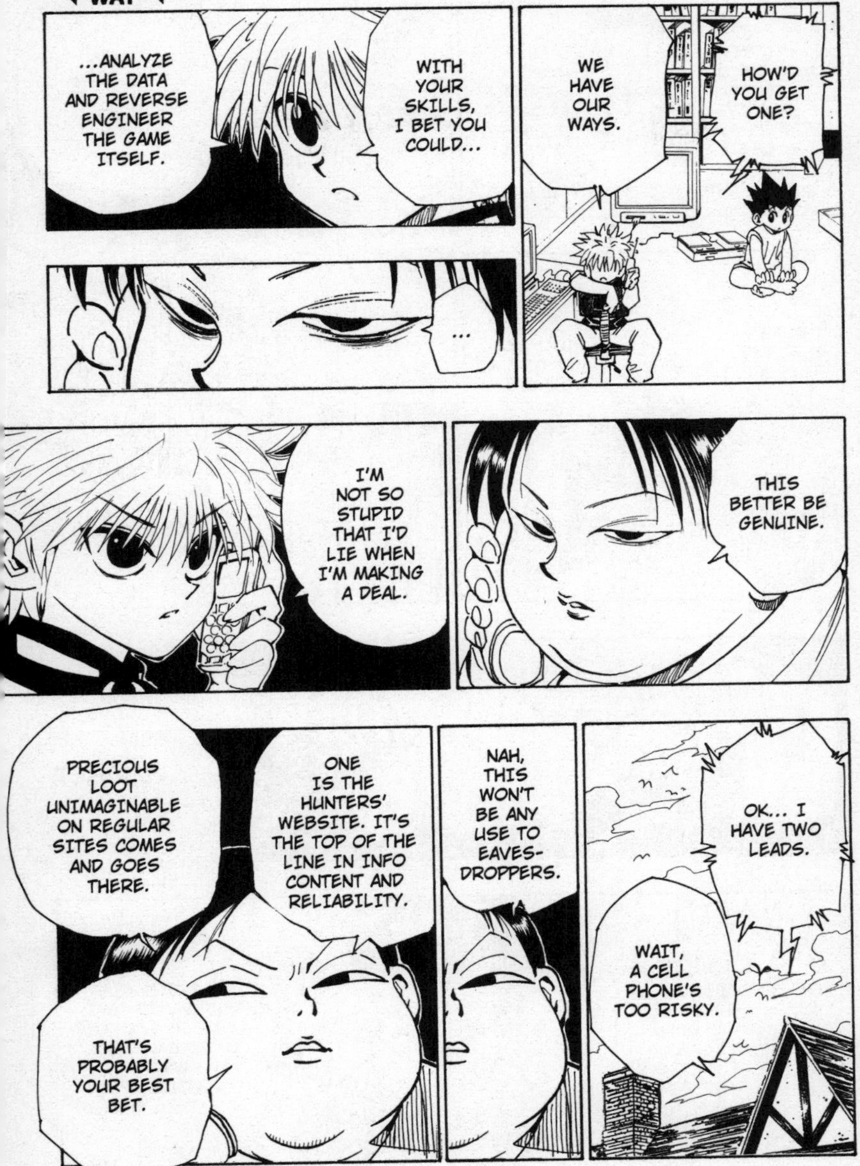
HOW'D YOU GET ONE?
WE HAVE OUR WAYS.
WITH YOUR SKILLS, I BET YOU COULD...
...ANALYZE THE DATA AND REVERSE ENGINEER THE GAME ITSELF.
...
THIS BETTER BE GENUINE.
I'M NOT SO STUPID THAT I'D LIE WHEN I'M MAKING A DEAL.
OK... I HAVE TWO LEADS.
WAIT, A CELL PHONE'S TOO RISKY.
NAH, THIS WON'T BE ANY USE TO EAVES-DROPPERS.
ONE IS THE HUNTERS' WEBSITE. IT'S THE TOP OF THE LINE IN INFO CONTENT AND RELIABILITY.
PRECIOUS LOOT UNIMAGINABLE ON REGULAR SITES COMES AND GOES THERE.
THAT'S PROBABLY YOUR BEST BET.

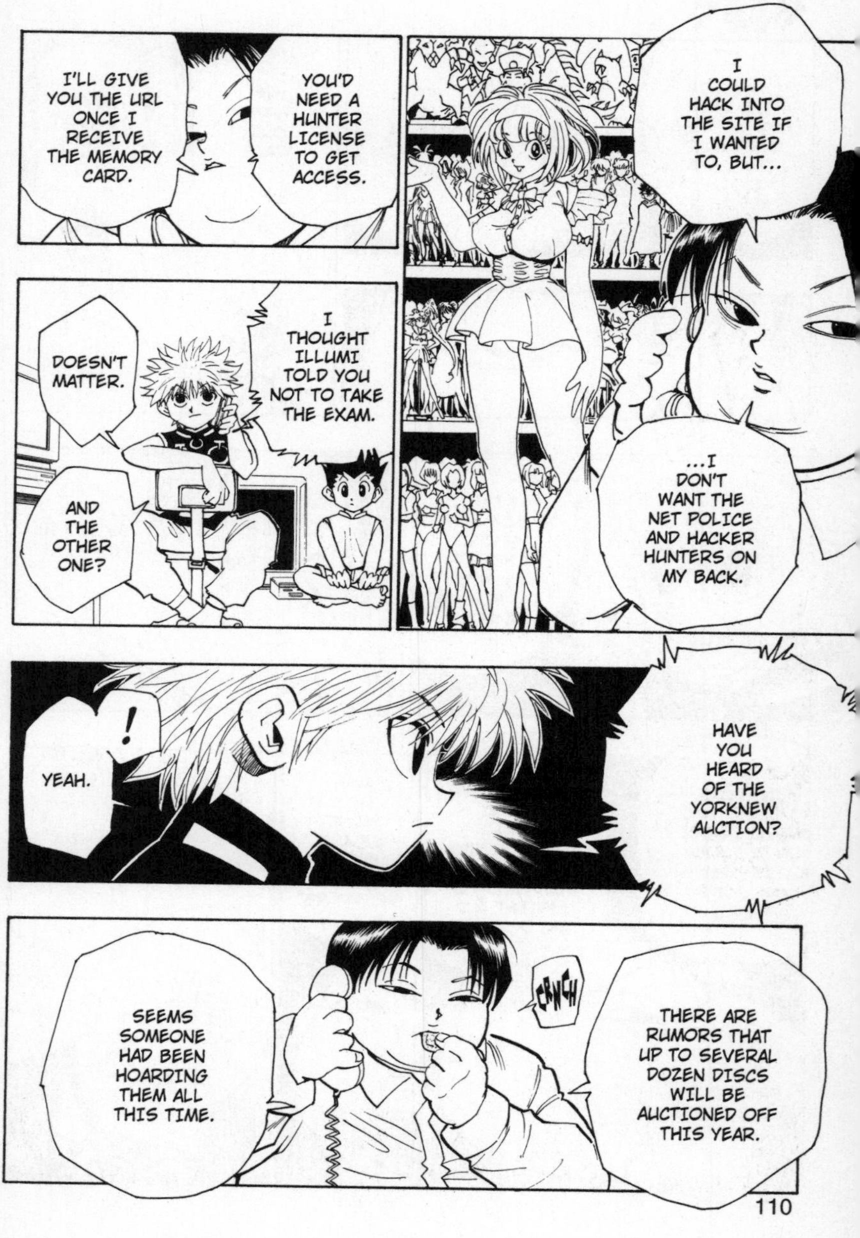
I COULD HACK INTO THE SITE IF I WANTED TO, BUT...
...I DON'T WANT THE NET POLICE AND HACKER HUNTERS ON MY BACK.
YOU'D NEED A HUNTER LICENSE TO GET ACCESS.
I'LL GIVE YOU THE URL ONCE I RECEIVE THE MEMORY CARD.
I THOUGHT ILLUMI TOLD YOU NOT TO TAKE THE EXAM.
DOESN'T MATTER.
AND THE OTHER ONE?
HAVE YOU HEARD OF THE YORKNEW AUCTION?
!
YEAH.
THERE ARE RUMORS THAT UP TO SEVERAL DOZEN DISCS WILL BE AUCTIONED OFF THIS YEAR.
CRNCH
SEEMS SOMEONE HAD BEEN HOARDING THEM ALL THIS TIME.

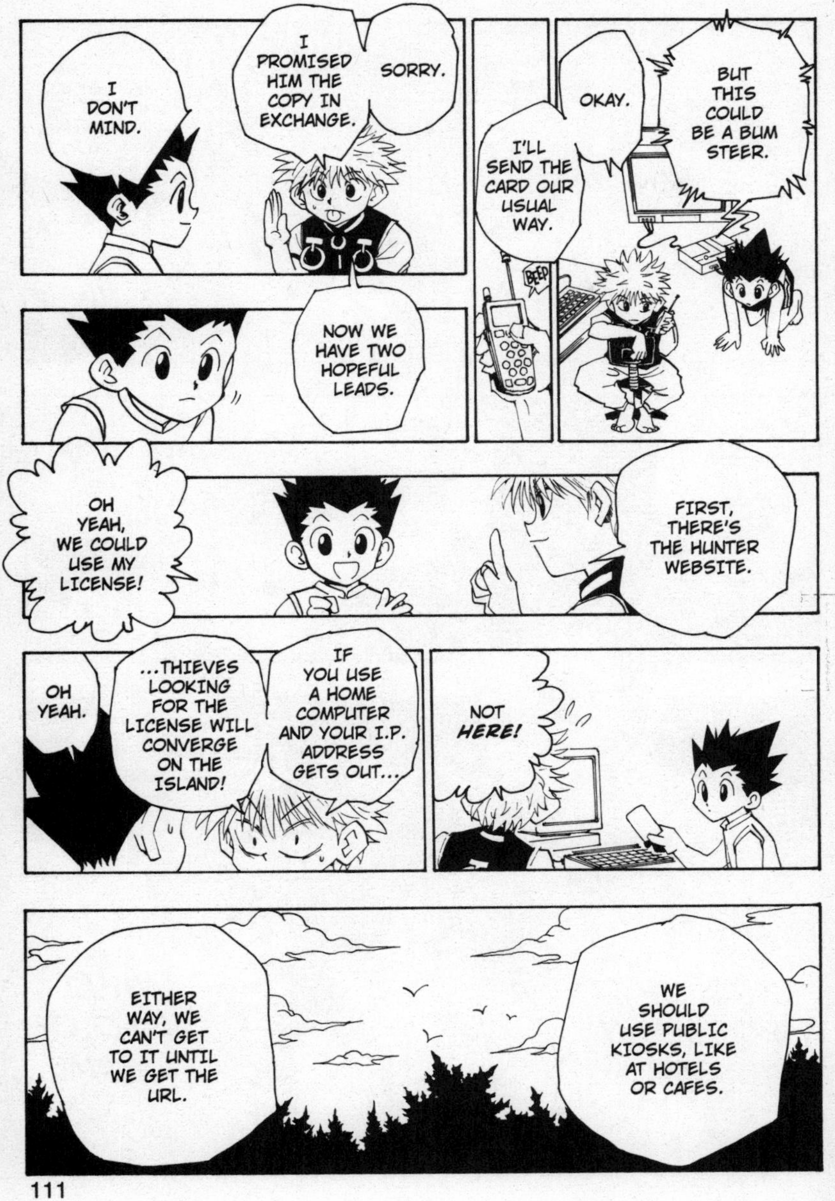
BUT THIS COULD BE A BUM STEER.
OKAY.
I'LL SEND THE CARD OUR USUAL WAY.
BEEP
SORRY.
I PROMISED HIM THE COPY IN EXCHANGE.
I DON'T MIND.
NOW WE HAVE TWO HOPEFUL LEADS.
FIRST, THERE'S THE HUNTER WEBSITE.
OH YEAH, WE COULD USE MY LICENSE!
NOT *HERE!*
IF YOU USE A HOME COMPUTER AND YOUR I.P. ADDRESS GETS OUT...
...THIEVES LOOKING FOR THE LICENSE WILL CONVERGE ON THE ISLAND!
OH YEAH.
WE SHOULD USE PUBLIC KIOSKS, LIKE AT HOTELS OR CAFES.
EITHER WAY, WE CAN'T GET TO IT UNTIL WE GET THE URL.

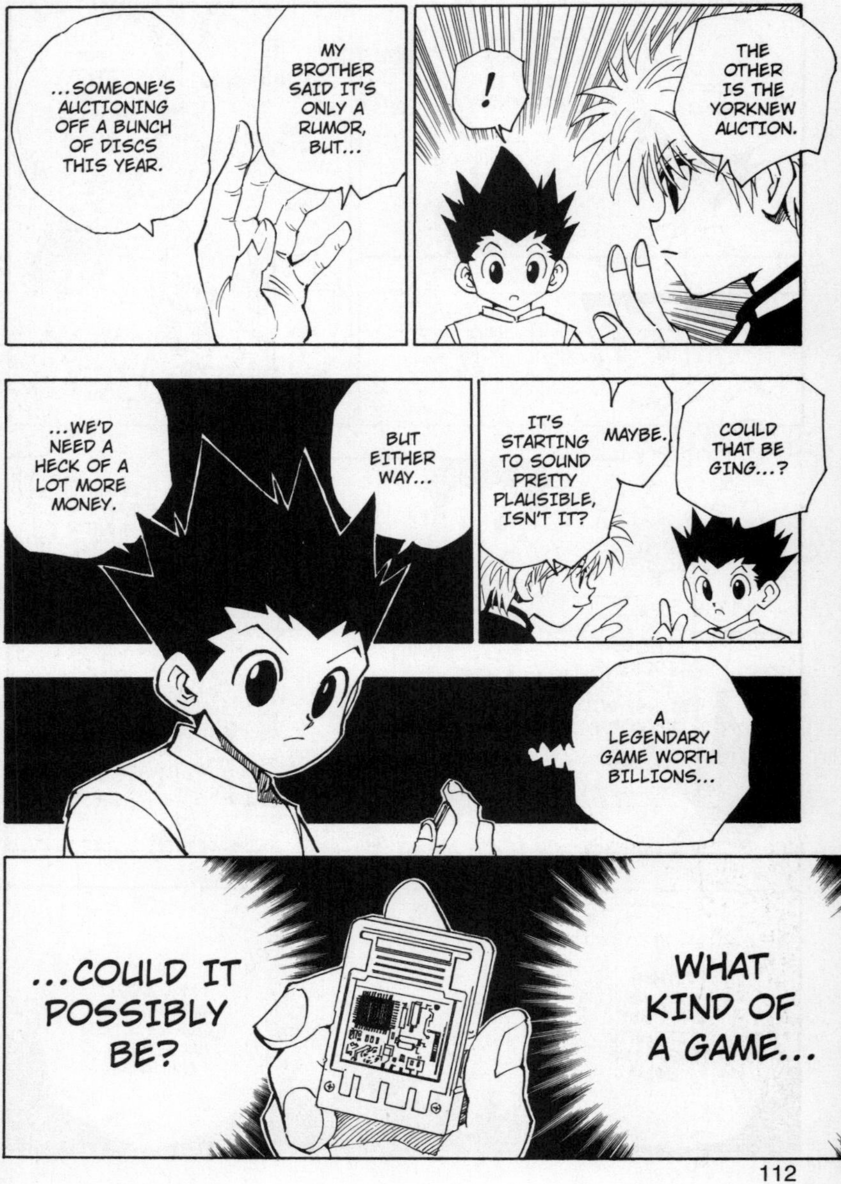
!
THE OTHER IS THE YORKNEW AUCTION.
MY BROTHER SAID IT'S ONLY A RUMOR, BUT...
...SOMEONE'S AUCTIONING OFF A BUNCH OF DISCS THIS YEAR.
COULD THAT BE GING...?
MAYBE.
IT'S STARTING TO SOUND PRETTY PLAUSIBLE, ISN'T IT?
BUT EITHER WAY...
...WE'D NEED A HECK OF A LOT MORE MONEY.
A LEGENDARY GAME WORTH BILLIONS...
WHAT KIND OF A GAME...
...COULD IT POSSIBLY BE?

…

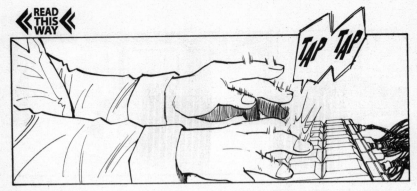

A HUNTING GAME EXCLUSIVELY FOR HUNTERS RELEASED IN 1987. ITS PRICE TAG AT 5.8 BILLION JENNY IS THE HIGHEST EVER FOR A VIDEOGAME, YET THERE WERE 20,000 PREORDERS FOR THE 100 UNITS PRODUCED. GREED ISLAND HAS DISAPPEARED FROM THE MARKET SINCE, AND IS NOW ONLY A TOPIC OF VARIOUS RUMORS FLYING ABOUT THE NET.

IN 1988, A REWARD WAS OFFERED BY A MR. BATTERA— 17 BILLION JENNY FOR THE GAME ITSELF, AND 50 BILLION FOR A MEMORY CARD WITH ENDGAME DATA. NOBODY HAS STEPPED FORWARD, A FACT THAT HAS SPAWNED FURTHER URBAN LEGENDS.

GREED ISLAND

BLIP

HEH.

THIS REWARD STILL REMAINS IN EFFECT...

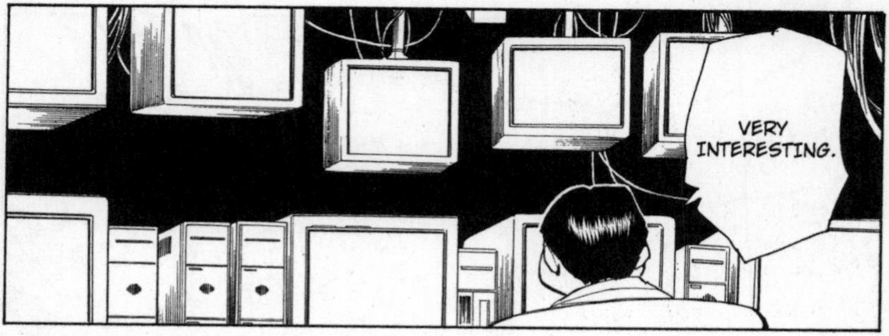
VERY INTERESTING.

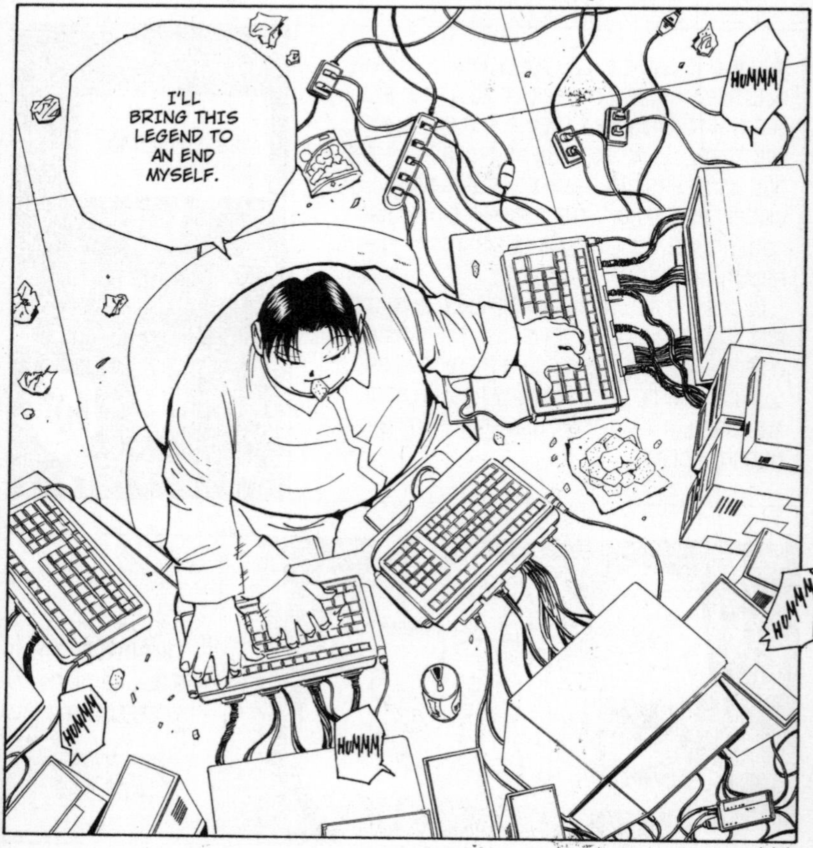
HUMMM
I'LL BRING THIS LEGEND TO AN END MYSELF.
HUMMM
HUMMM
HUMMM

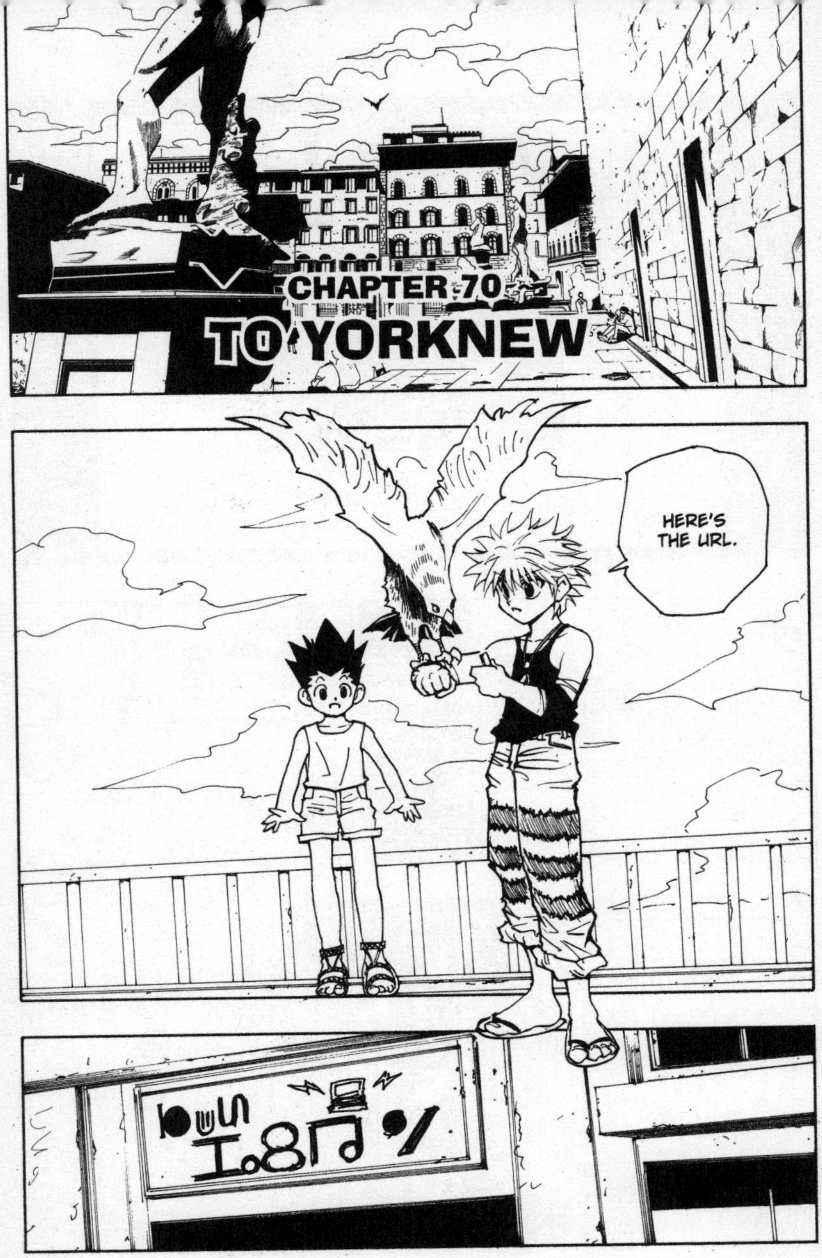
CHAPTER 70
TO YORKNEW
HERE'S THE URL.

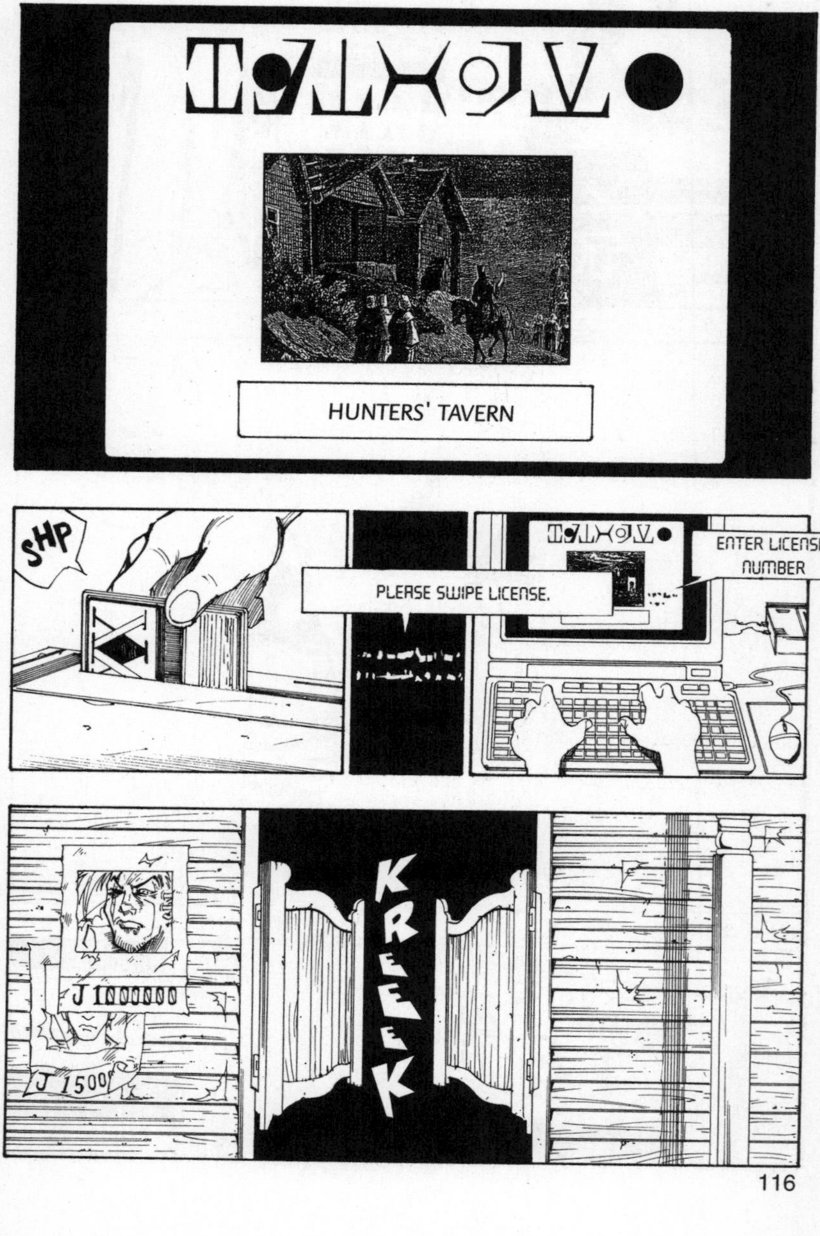
HUNTERS' TAVERN
ENTER LICENSE NUMBER
PLEASE SWIPE LICENSE.
SHP
KREEEK

READ THIS WAY

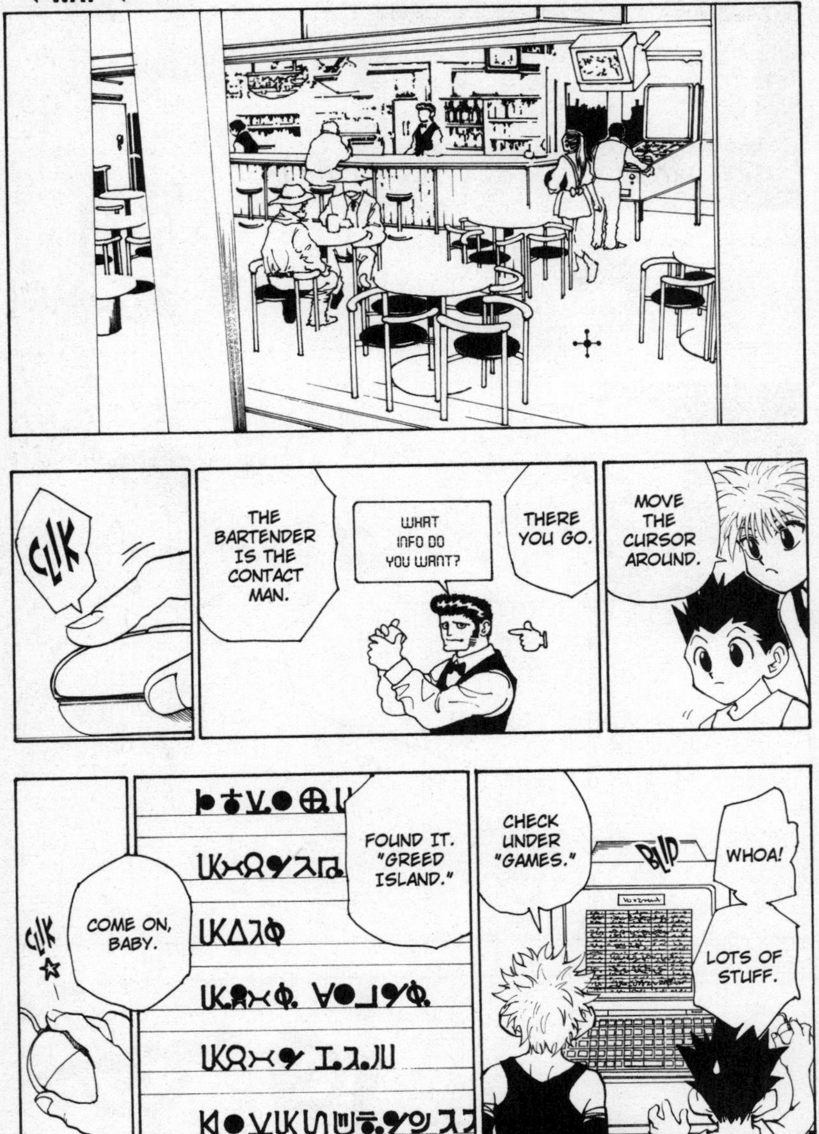
MOVE THE CURSOR AROUND.
THERE YOU GO.
WHAT INFO DO YOU WANT?
THE BARTENDER IS THE CONTACT MAN.
CLIK
WHOA!
LOTS OF STUFF.
BLIP
CHECK UNDER "GAMES."
FOUND IT. "GREED ISLAND."
COME ON, BABY.
CLIK☆

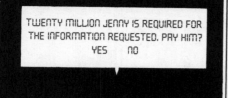

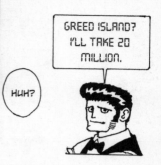

GREED ISLAND? I'LL TAKE 20 MILLION.
HUH?
TWENTY MILLION JENNY IS REQUIRED FOR THE INFORMATION REQUESTED. PAY HIM?
YES NO
GUESS NOTHING COMES FOR FREE.
NO SURPRISE.
I'M LOSING MY MONEY SENSE.
CHK
OK, LISTEN UP.
GREED ISLAND...

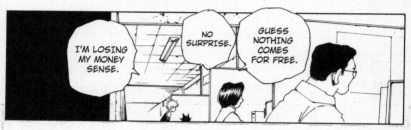

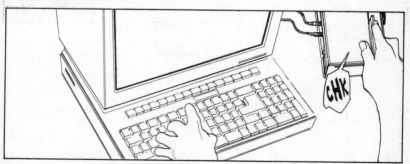

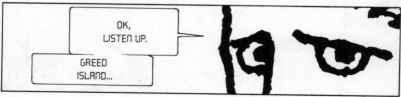

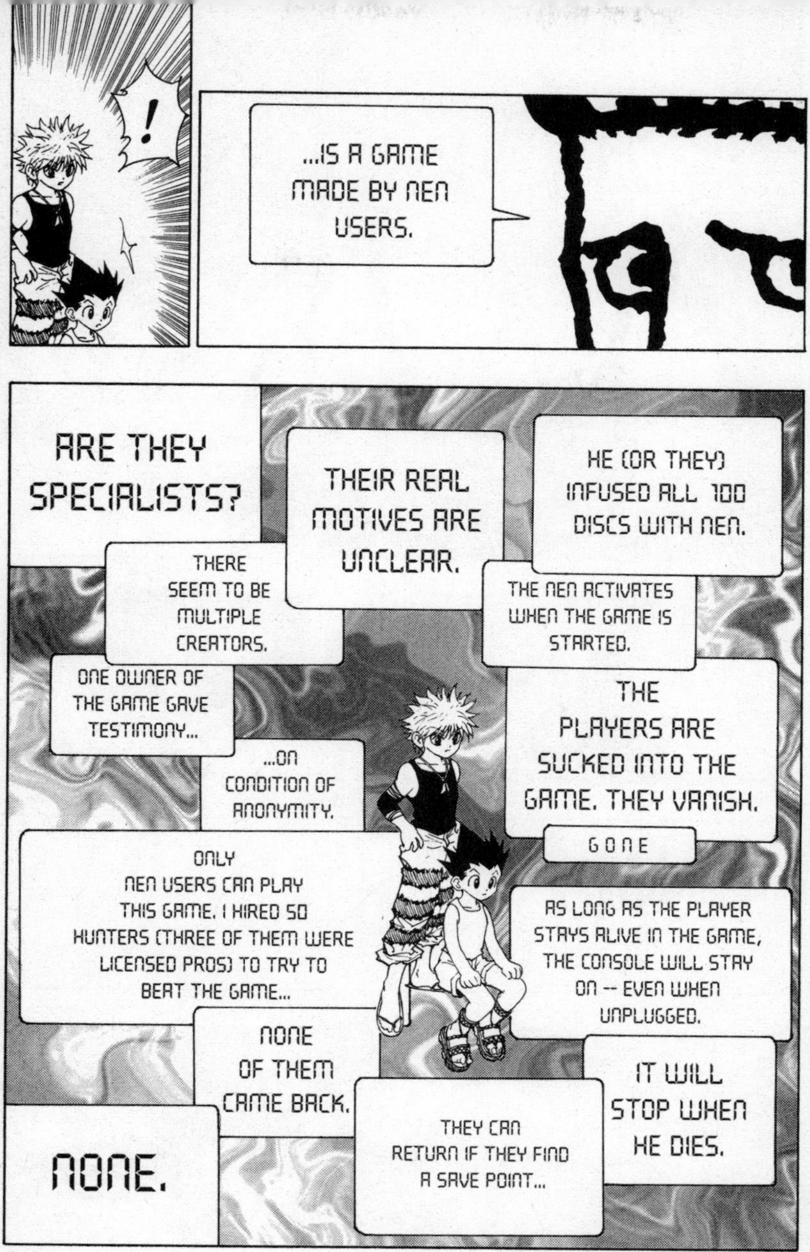
...IS A GAME MADE BY NEN USERS.
!
HE (OR THEY) INFUSED ALL 100 DISCS WITH NEN.
THEIR REAL MOTIVES ARE UNCLEAR.
ARE THEY SPECIALISTS?
THE NEN ACTIVATES WHEN THE GAME IS STARTED.
THERE SEEM TO BE MULTIPLE CREATORS.
THE PLAYERS ARE SUCKED INTO THE GAME. THEY VANISH.
GONE
ONE OWNER OF THE GAME GAVE TESTIMONY...
...ON CONDITION OF ANONYMITY.
AS LONG AS THE PLAYER STAYS ALIVE IN THE GAME, THE CONSOLE WILL STAY ON -- EVEN WHEN UNPLUGGED.
ONLY NEN USERS CAN PLAY THIS GAME. I HIRED 50 HUNTERS (THREE OF THEM WERE LICENSED PROS) TO TRY TO BEAT THE GAME...
IT WILL STOP WHEN HE DIES.
THEY CAN RETURN IF THEY FIND A SAVE POINT...
NONE OF THEM CAME BACK.
NONE.

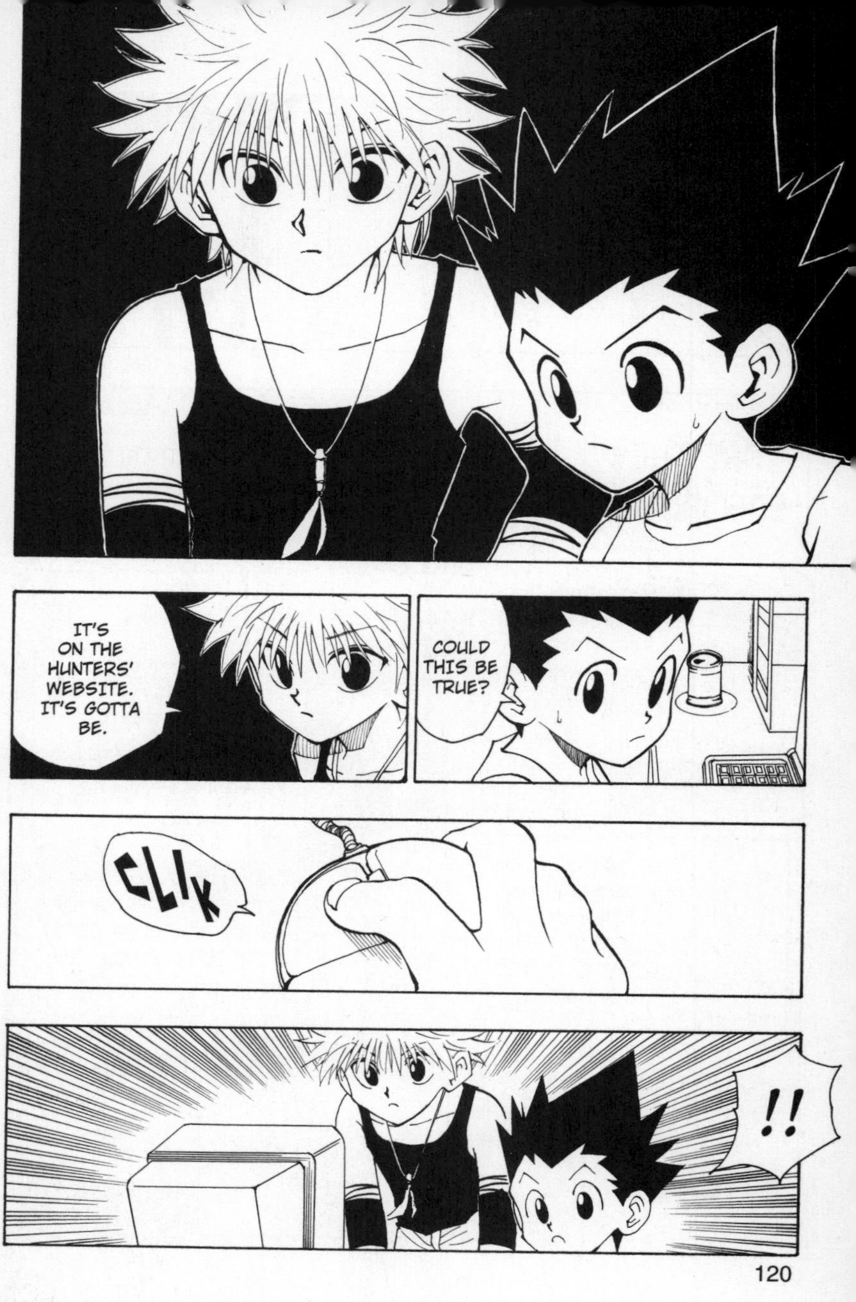
COULD THIS BE TRUE?
IT'S ON THE HUNTERS' WEBSITE. IT'S GOTTA BE.
CLIK
!!

READ THIS WAY

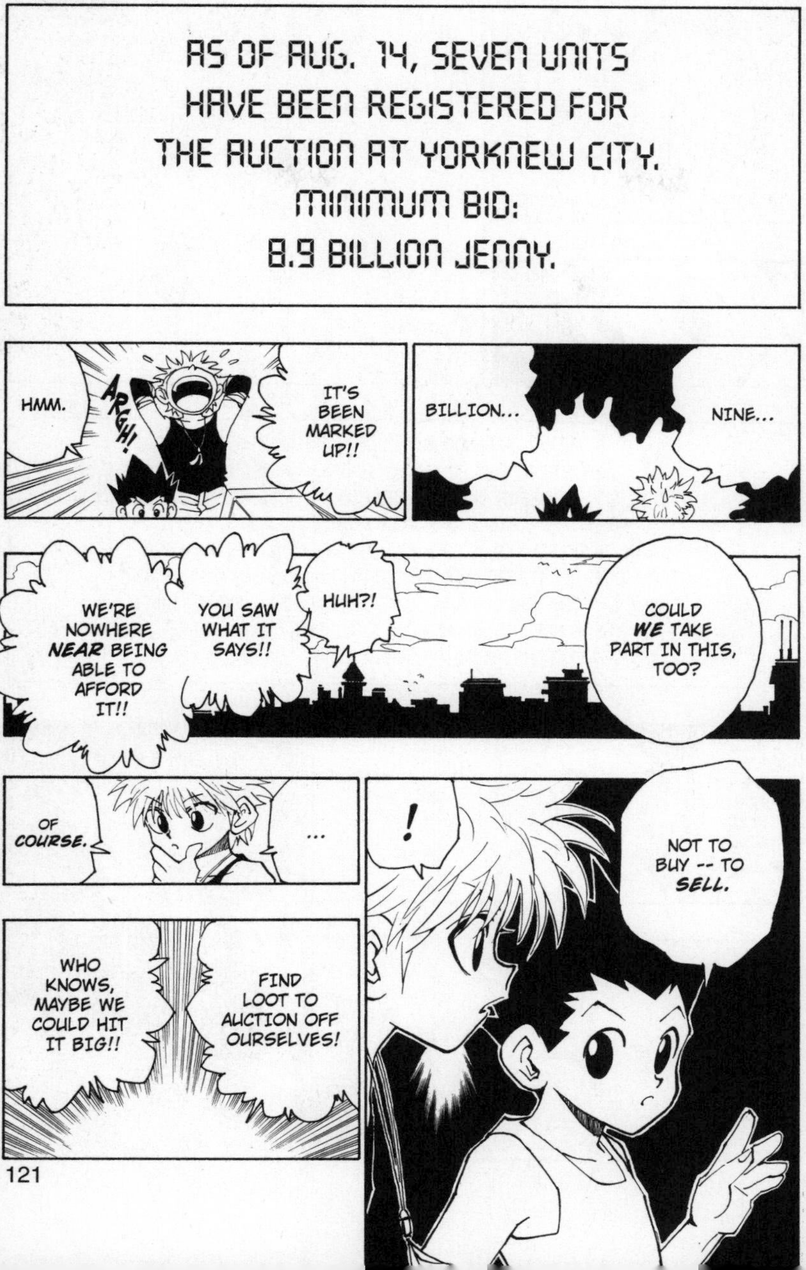

AS OF AUG. 14, SEVEN UNITS HAVE BEEN REGISTERED FOR THE AUCTION AT YORKNEW CITY. MINIMUM BID: 8.9 BILLION JENNY.
NINE...
BILLION...
IT'S BEEN MARKED UP!!
ARGH!!
HMM.
COULD WE TAKE PART IN THIS, TOO?
HUH?!
YOU SAW WHAT IT SAYS!!
WE'RE NOWHERE NEAR BEING ABLE TO AFFORD IT!!
NOT TO BUY -- TO SELL.
!
...
OF COURSE.
FIND LOOT TO AUCTION OFF OURSELVES!
WHO KNOWS, MAYBE WE COULD HIT IT BIG!!

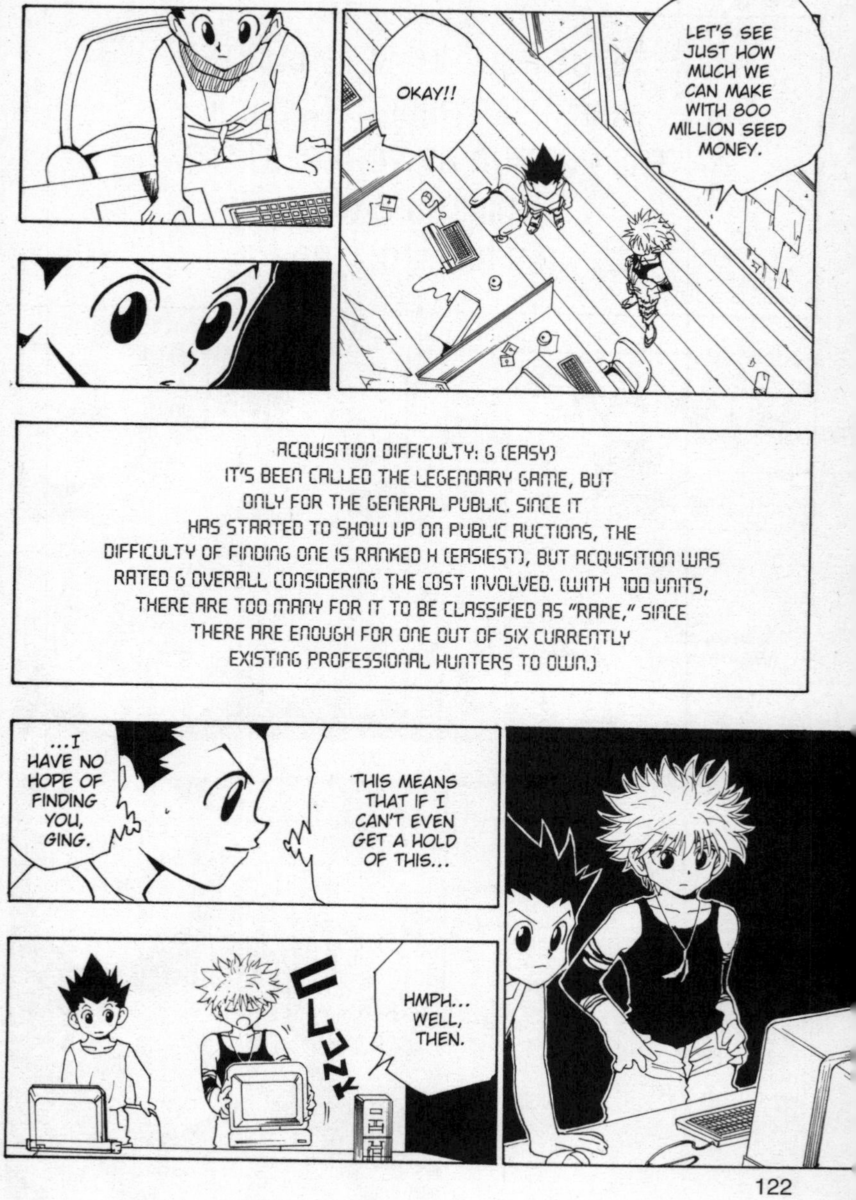
LET'S SEE JUST HOW MUCH WE CAN MAKE WITH 800 MILLION SEED MONEY.
OKAY!!
ACQUISITION DIFFICULTY: G (EASY)
IT'S BEEN CALLED THE LEGENDARY GAME, BUT ONLY FOR THE GENERAL PUBLIC. SINCE IT HAS STARTED TO SHOW UP ON PUBLIC AUCTIONS, THE DIFFICULTY OF FINDING ONE IS RANKED H (EASIEST), BUT ACQUISITION WAS RATED G OVERALL CONSIDERING THE COST INVOLVED. (WITH 100 UNITS, THERE ARE TOO MANY FOR IT TO BE CLASSIFIED AS "RARE," SINCE THERE ARE ENOUGH FOR ONE OUT OF SIX CURRENTLY EXISTING PROFESSIONAL HUNTERS TO OWN.)
THIS MEANS THAT IF I CAN'T EVEN GET A HOLD OF THIS...
...I HAVE NO HOPE OF FINDING YOU, GING.
HMPH... WELL, THEN.
CLUNK

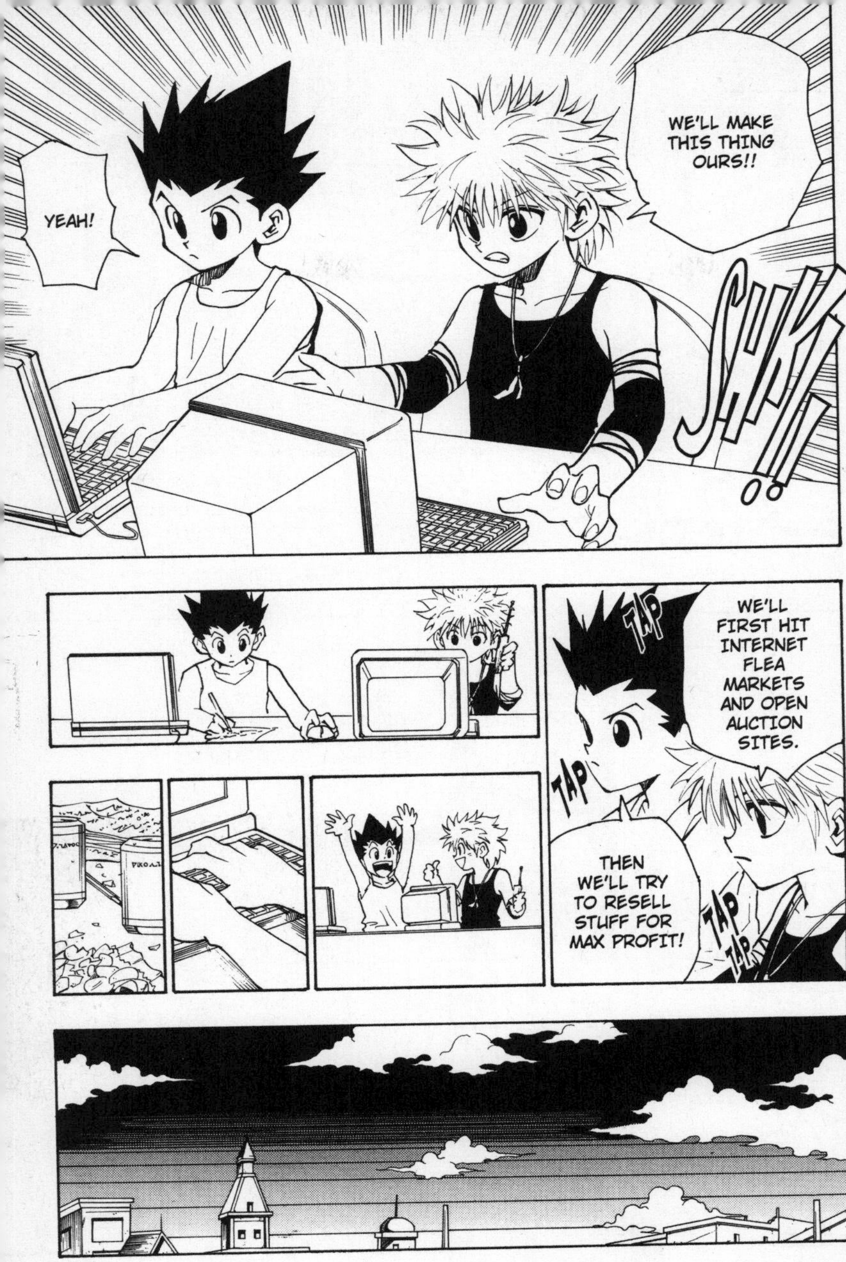
WE'LL MAKE THIS THING OURS!!
SHK!!
YEAH!
TAP
WE'LL FIRST HIT INTERNET FLEA MARKETS AND OPEN AUCTION SITES.
TAP
THEN WE'LL TRY TO RESELL STUFF FOR MAX PROFIT!
TAP TAP

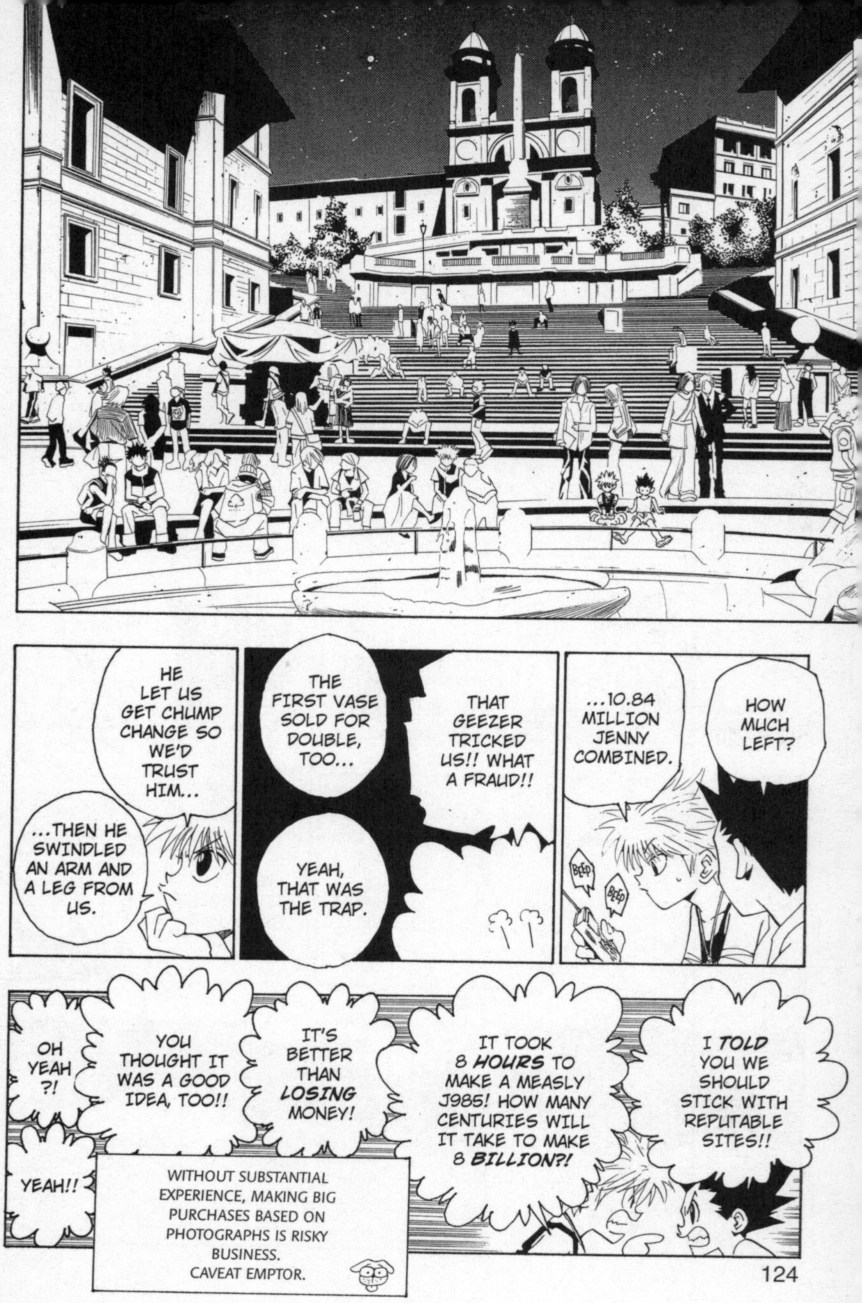
HOW MUCH LEFT?
...10.84 MILLION JENNY COMBINED.
BEEP
BEEP
THAT GEEZER TRICKED US!! WHAT A FRAUD!!
THE FIRST VASE SOLD FOR DOUBLE, TOO...
YEAH, THAT WAS THE TRAP.
HE LET US GET CHUMP CHANGE SO WE'D TRUST HIM...
...THEN HE SWINDLED AN ARM AND A LEG FROM US.
I *TOLD* YOU WE SHOULD STICK WITH REPUTABLE SITES!!
IT TOOK 8 ***HOURS*** TO MAKE A MEASLY J985! HOW MANY CENTURIES WILL IT TAKE TO MAKE 8 ***BILLION***?!
IT'S BETTER THAN ***LOSING*** MONEY!
YOU THOUGHT IT WAS A GOOD IDEA, TOO!!
OH YEAH ?!
YEAH!!

WITHOUT SUBSTANTIAL EXPERIENCE, MAKING BIG PURCHASES BASED ON PHOTOGRAPHS IS RISKY BUSINESS. CAVEAT EMPTOR.

READ THIS WAY

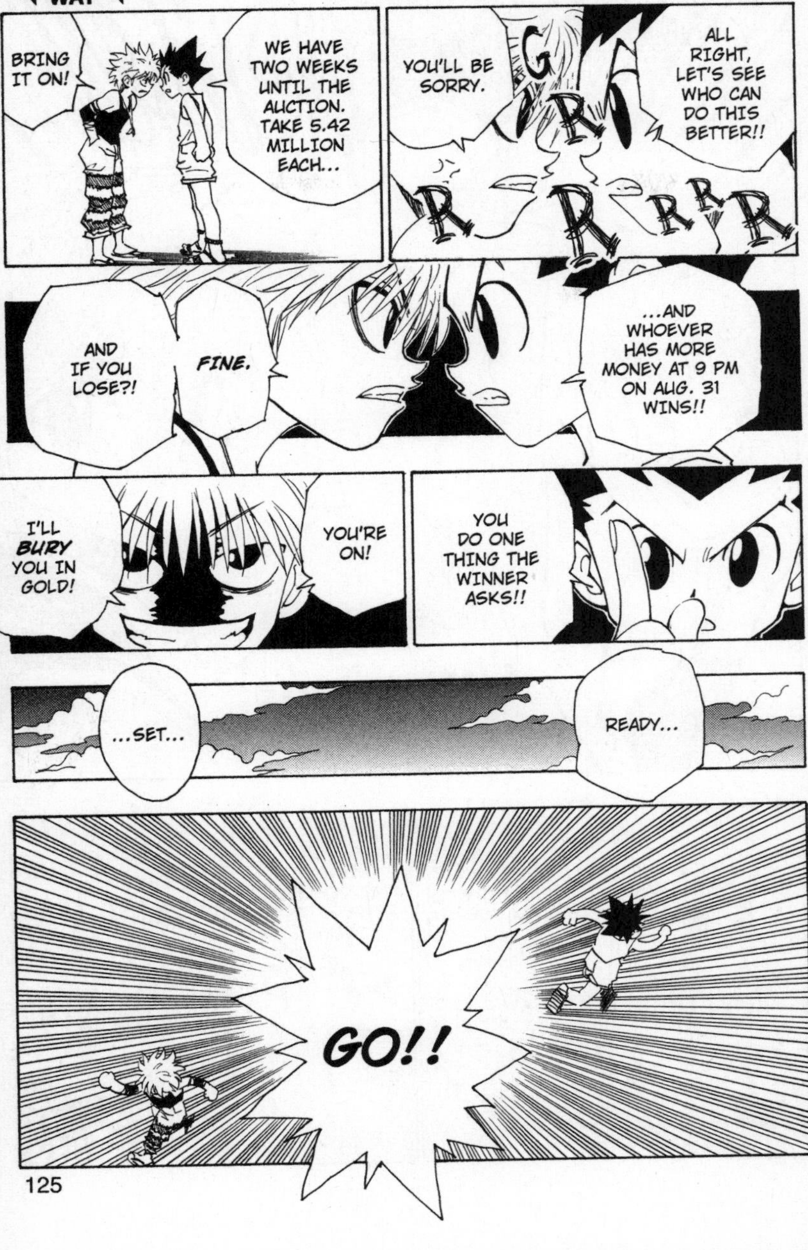
ALL RIGHT, LET'S SEE WHO CAN DO THIS BETTER!!
YOU'LL BE SORRY.
GRRRRRRR
WE HAVE TWO WEEKS UNTIL THE AUCTION. TAKE 5.42 MILLION EACH...
BRING IT ON!
...AND WHOEVER HAS MORE MONEY AT 9 PM ON AUG. 31 WINS!!
FINE.
AND IF YOU LOSE?!
YOU DO ONE THING THE WINNER ASKS!!
YOU'RE ON!
I'LL ***BURY*** YOU IN GOLD!
READY...
...SET...
GO!!

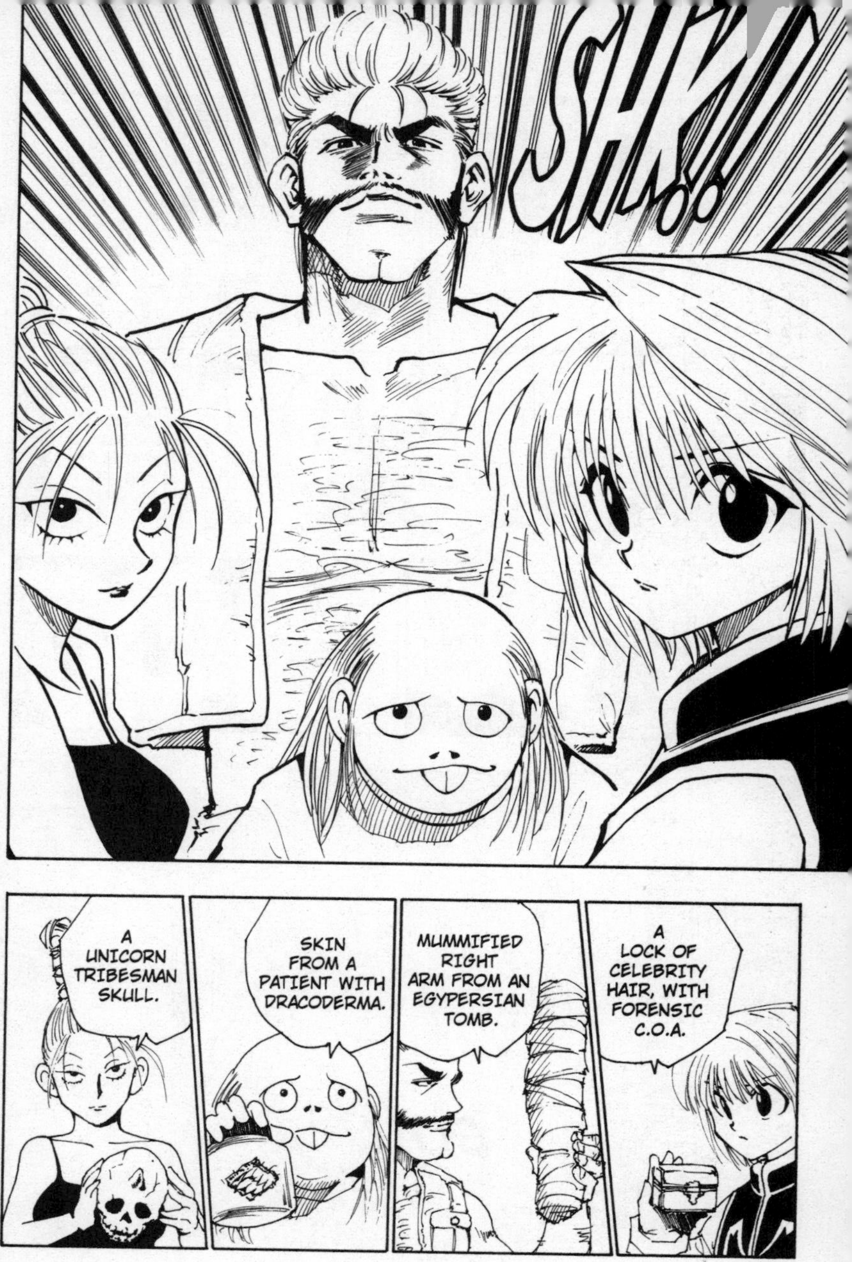
SHA..
A LOCK OF CELEBRITY HAIR, WITH FORENSIC C.O.A.
MUMMIFIED RIGHT ARM FROM AN EGYPERSIAN TOMB.
SKIN FROM A PATIENT WITH DRACODERMA.
A UNICORN TRIBESMAN SKULL.

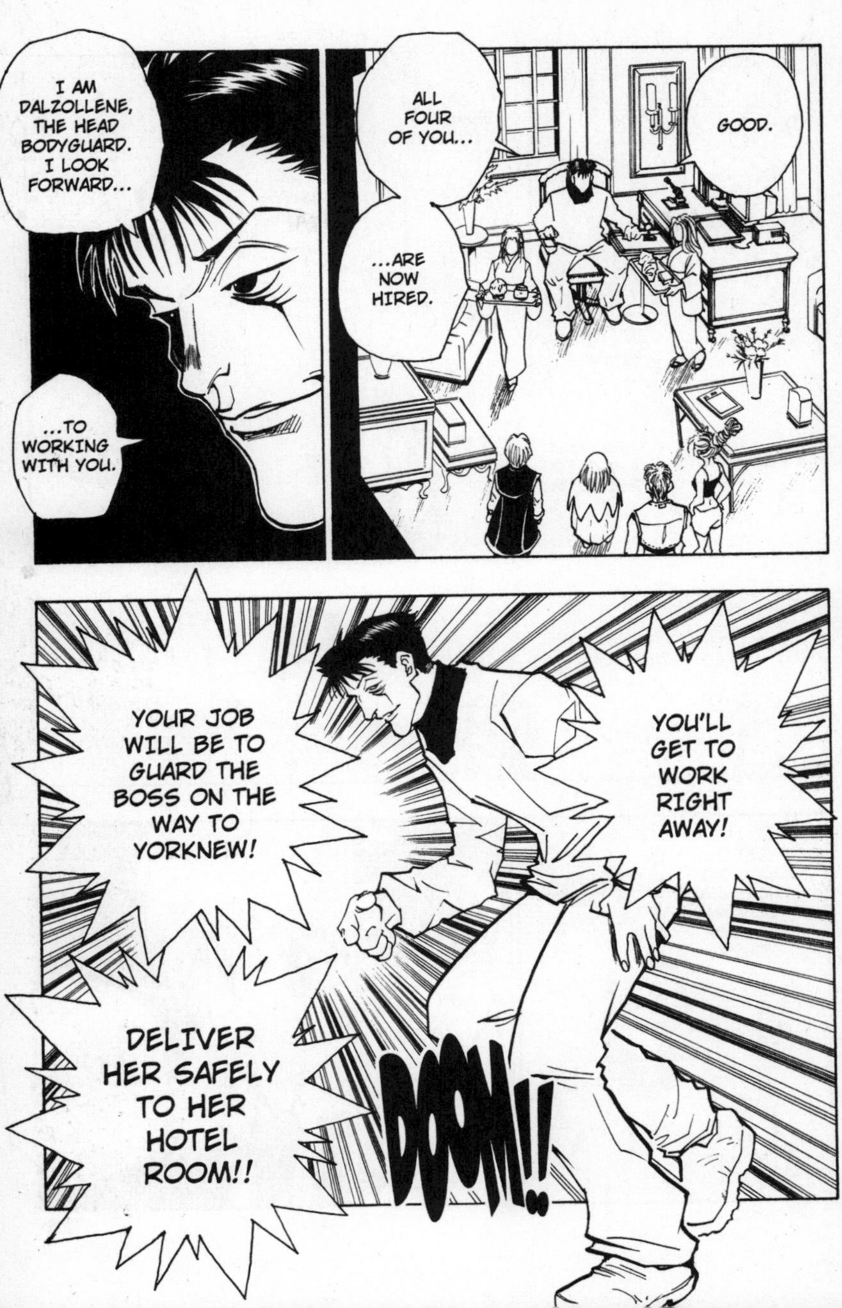
GOOD.
ALL FOUR OF YOU...
...ARE NOW HIRED.
I AM DALZOLLENE, THE HEAD BODYGUARD. I LOOK FORWARD...
...TO WORKING WITH YOU.
YOU'LL GET TO WORK RIGHT AWAY!
YOUR JOB WILL BE TO GUARD THE BOSS ON THE WAY TO YORKNEW!
DELIVER HER SAFELY TO HER HOTEL ROOM!!
DOOM!!

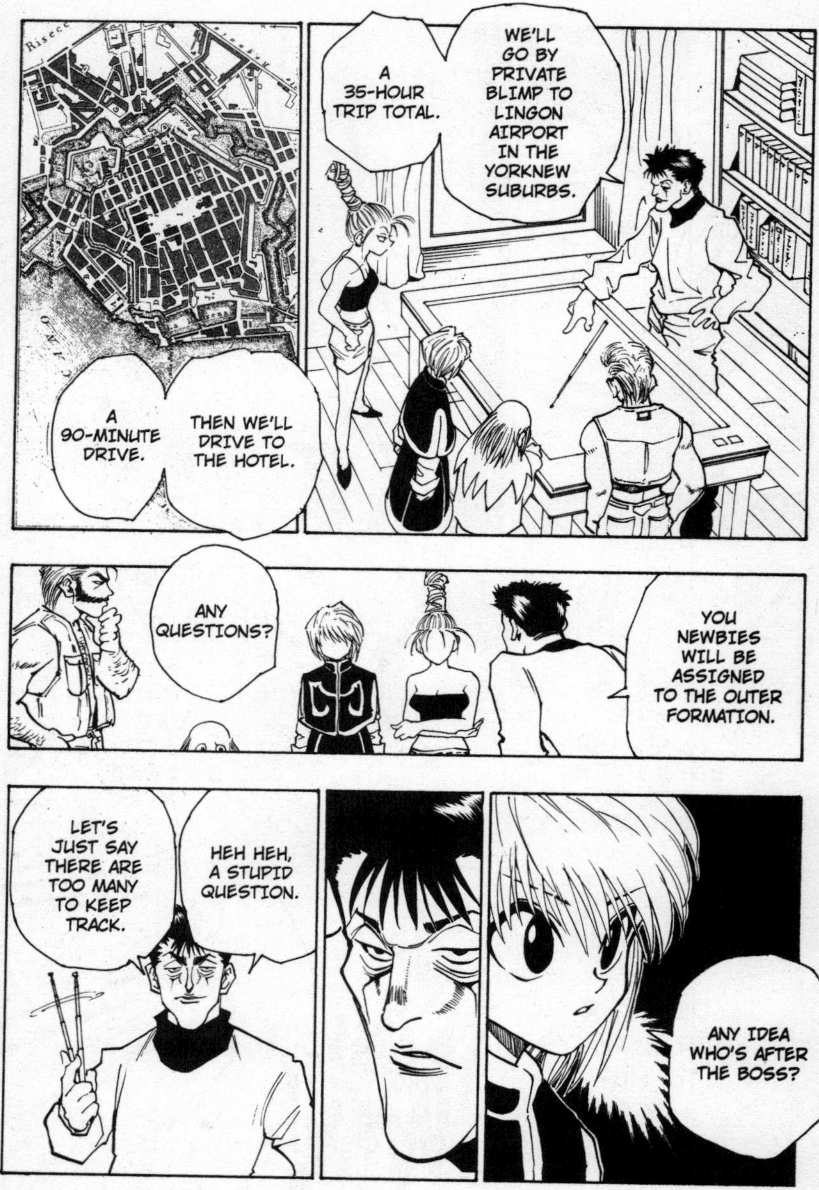
WE'LL GO BY PRIVATE BLIMP TO LINGON AIRPORT IN THE YORKNEW SUBURBS.
A 35-HOUR TRIP TOTAL.
THEN WE'LL DRIVE TO THE HOTEL.
A 90-MINUTE DRIVE.
YOU NEWBIES WILL BE ASSIGNED TO THE OUTER FORMATION.
ANY QUESTIONS?
ANY IDEA WHO'S AFTER THE BOSS?
HEH HEH, A STUPID QUESTION.
LET'S JUST SAY THERE ARE TOO MANY TO KEEP TRACK.

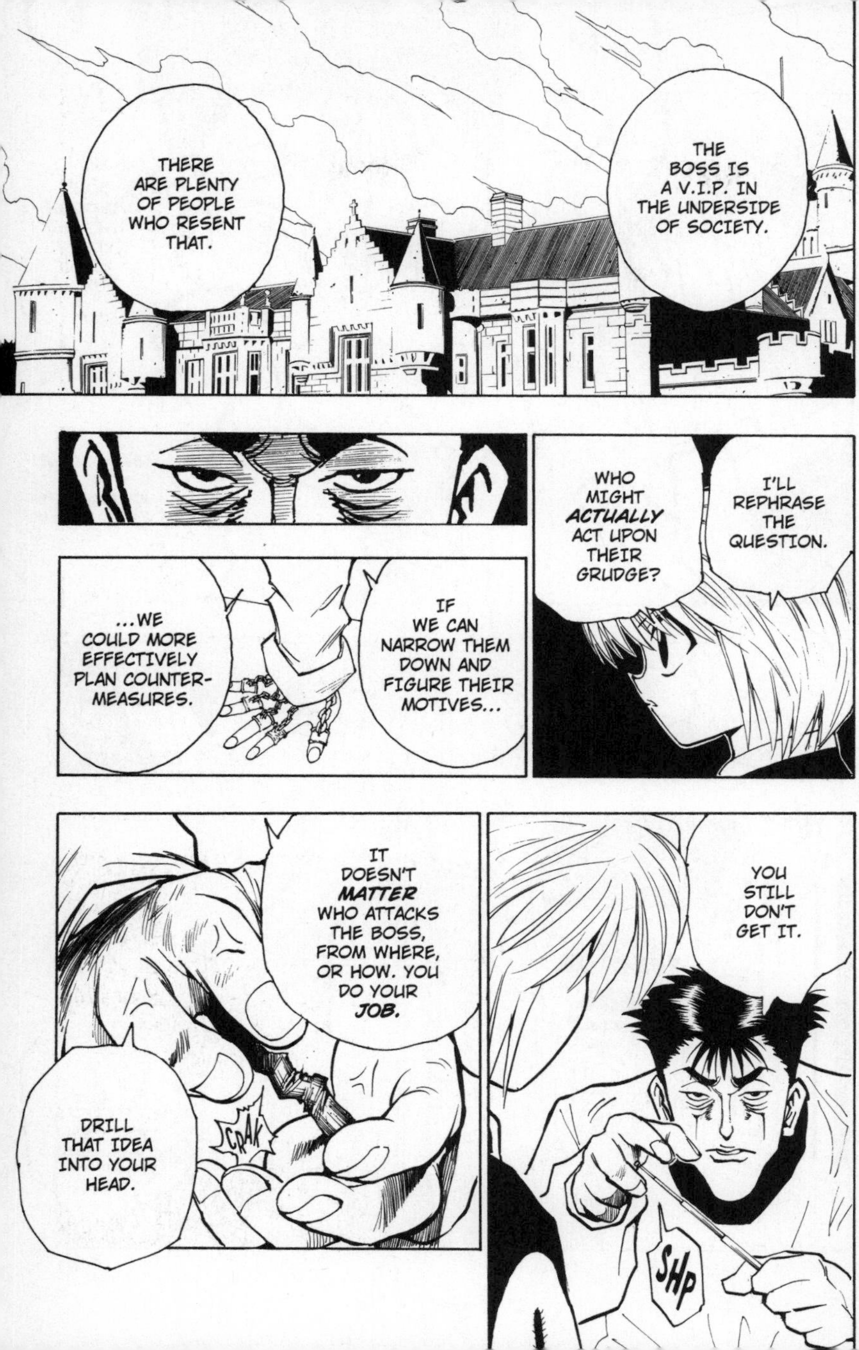
THE BOSS IS A V.I.P. IN THE UNDERSIDE OF SOCIETY.
THERE ARE PLENTY OF PEOPLE WHO RESENT THAT.
I'LL REPHRASE THE QUESTION.
WHO MIGHT *ACTUALLY* ACT UPON THEIR GRUDGE?
IF WE CAN NARROW THEM DOWN AND FIGURE THEIR MOTIVES...
...WE COULD MORE EFFECTIVELY PLAN COUNTER-MEASURES.
YOU STILL DON'T GET IT.
SHP
IT DOESN'T *MATTER* WHO ATTACKS THE BOSS, FROM WHERE, OR HOW. YOU DO YOUR *JOB.*
CRAK
DRILL THAT IDEA INTO YOUR HEAD.

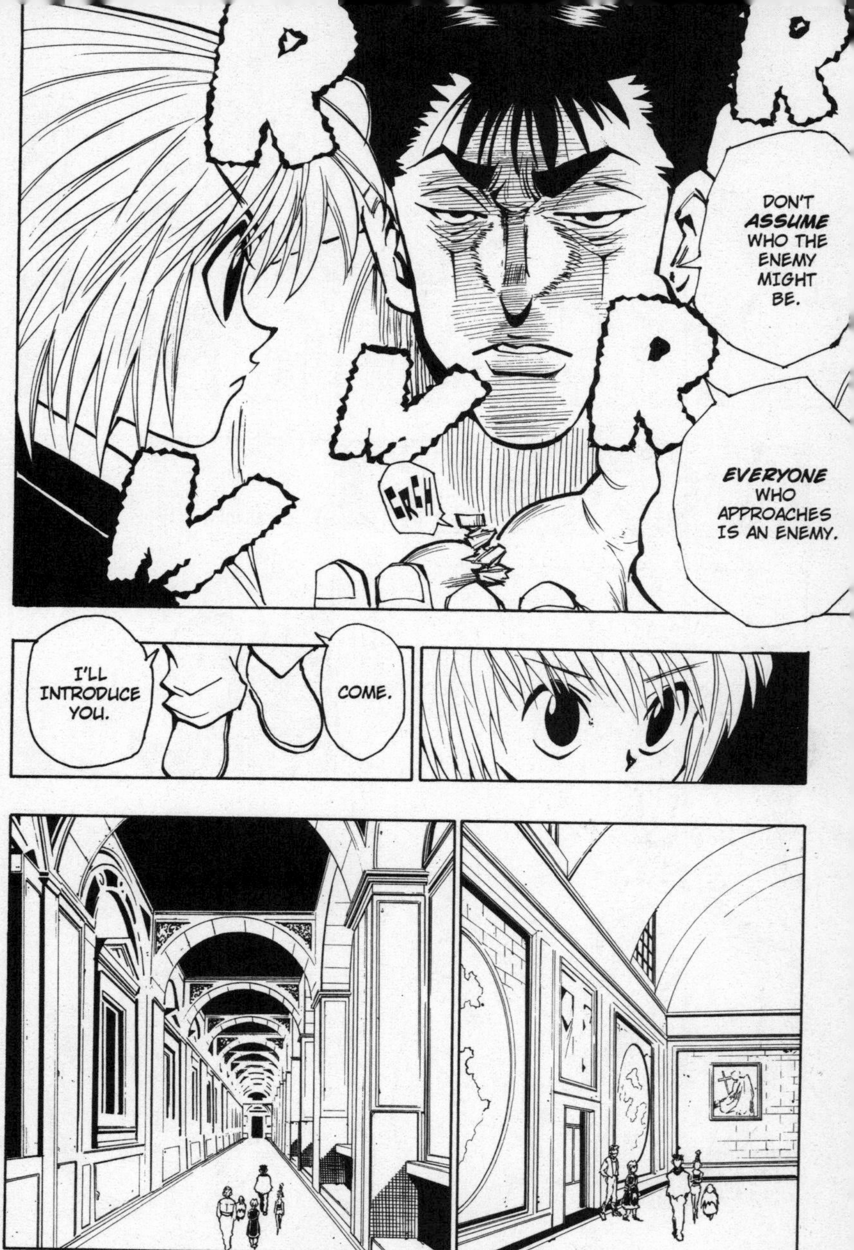
DON'T ASSUME WHO THE ENEMY MIGHT BE.
EVERYONE WHO APPROACHES IS AN ENEMY.
GRGH
COME.
I'LL INTRODUCE YOU.

READ THIS WAY

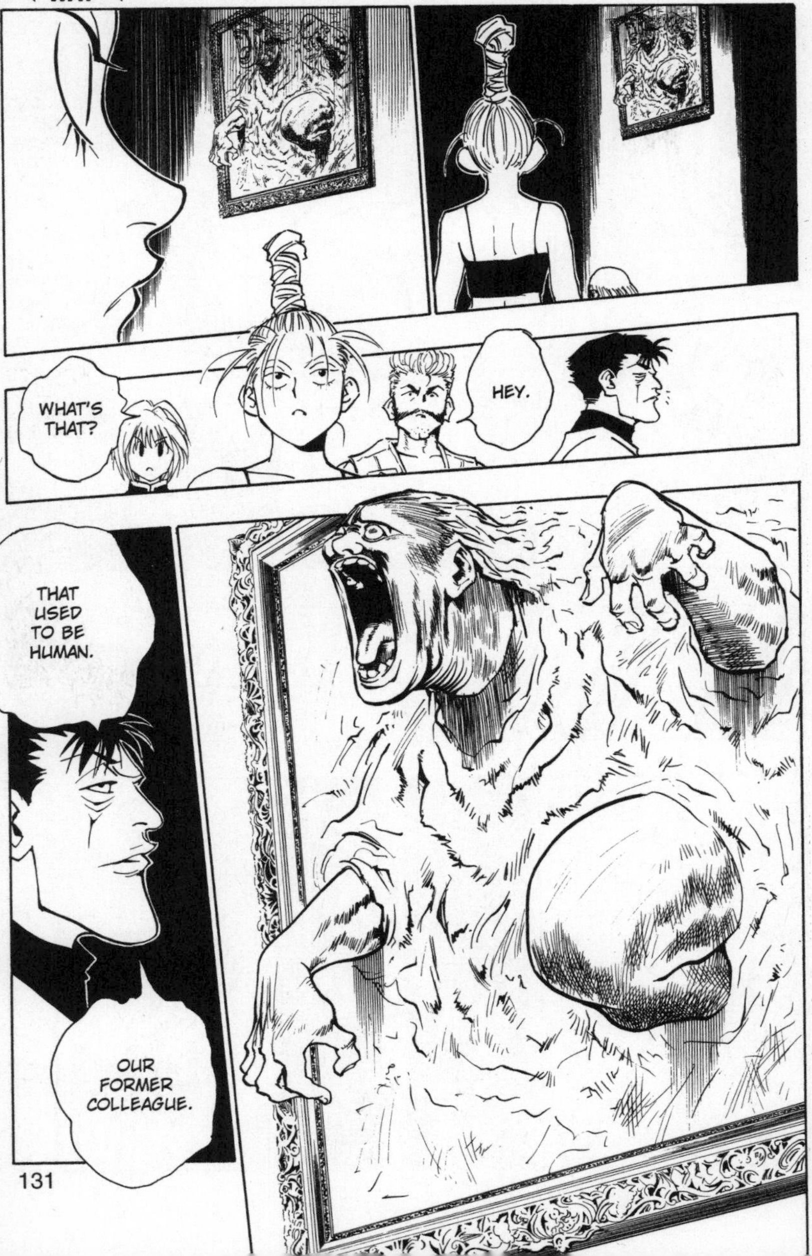

HEY.
WHAT'S THAT?
THAT USED TO BE HUMAN.
OUR FORMER COLLEAGUE.

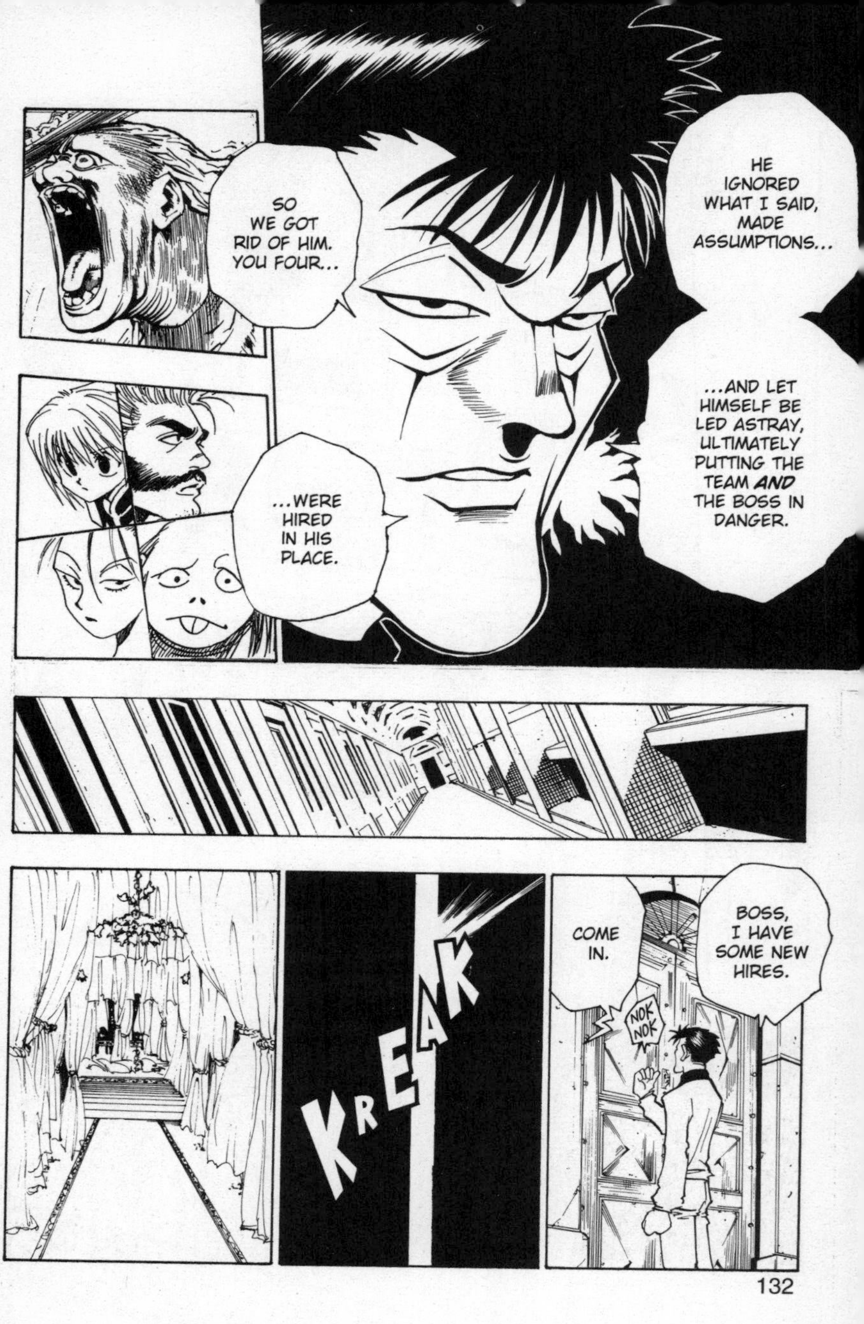
HE IGNORED WHAT I SAID, MADE ASSUMPTIONS...
...AND LET HIMSELF BE LED ASTRAY, ULTIMATELY PUTTING THE TEAM AND THE BOSS IN DANGER.
SO WE GOT RID OF HIM. YOU FOUR...
...WERE HIRED IN HIS PLACE.
BOSS, I HAVE SOME NEW HIRES.
NOK NOK
COME IN.
KREAK

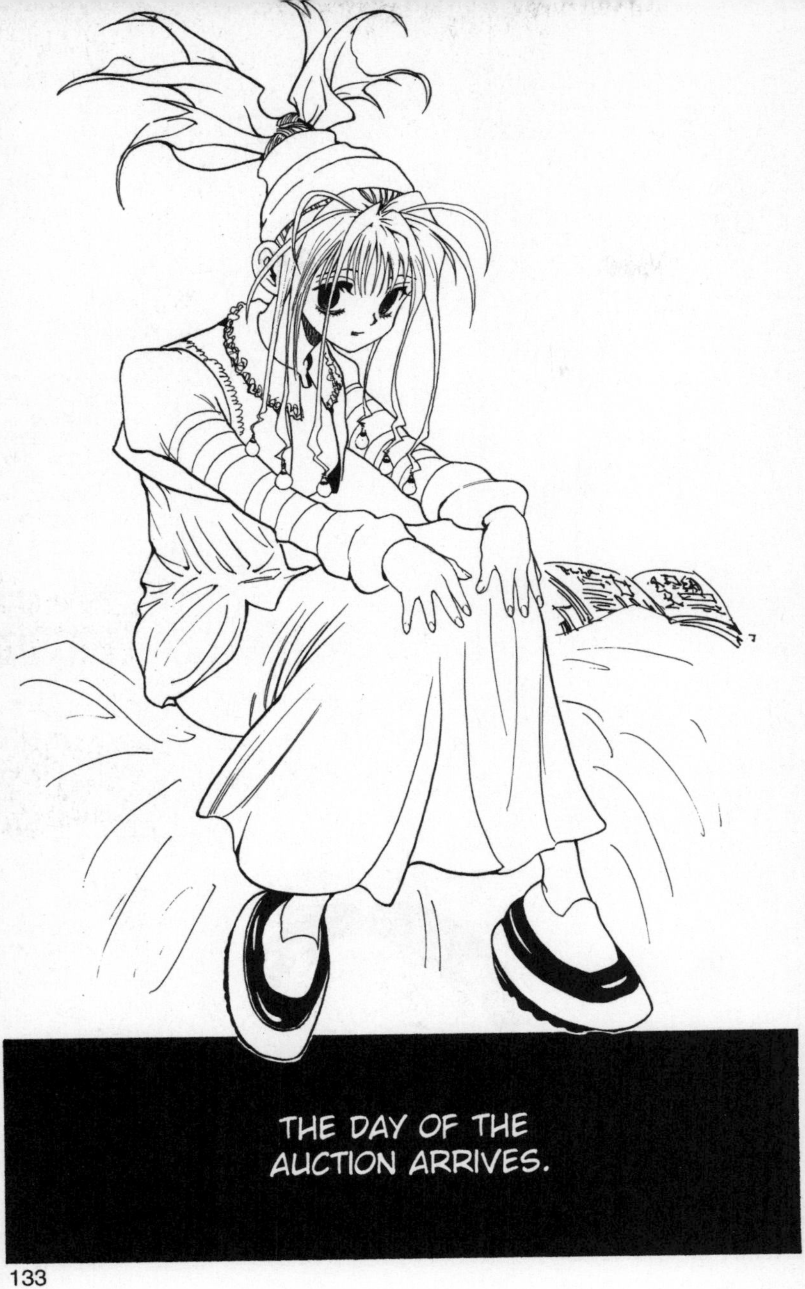
THE DAY OF THE
AUCTION ARRIVES.

CHAPTER 71 THE AUCTION BEGINS!!

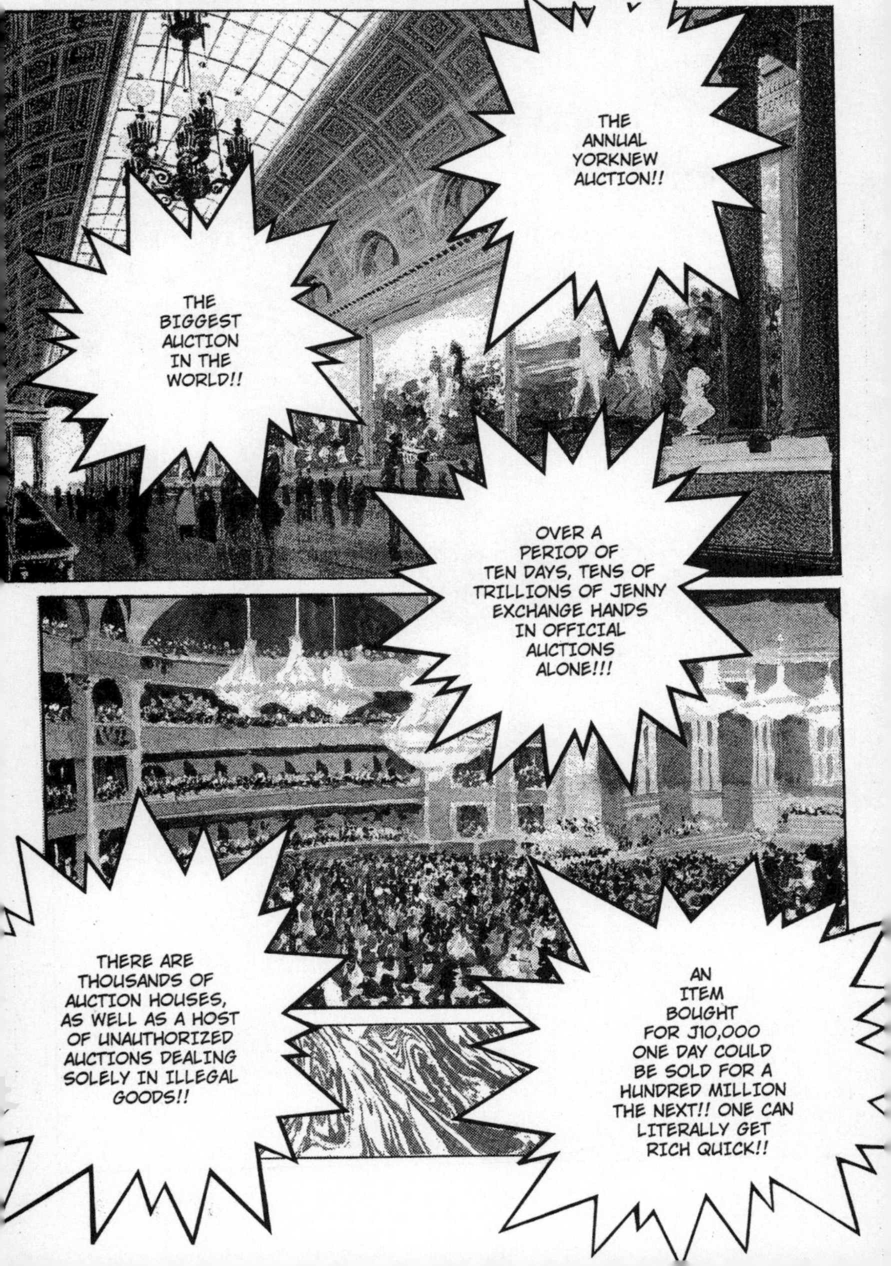
THE ANNUAL YORKNEW AUCTION!!
THE BIGGEST AUCTION IN THE WORLD!!
OVER A PERIOD OF TEN DAYS, TENS OF TRILLIONS OF JENNY EXCHANGE HANDS IN OFFICIAL AUCTIONS ALONE!!!
AN ITEM BOUGHT FOR J10,000 ONE DAY COULD BE SOLD FOR A HUNDRED MILLION THE NEXT!! ONE CAN LITERALLY GET RICH QUICK!!
THERE ARE THOUSANDS OF AUCTION HOUSES, AS WELL AS A HOST OF UNAUTHORIZED AUCTIONS DEALING SOLELY IN ILLEGAL GOODS!!

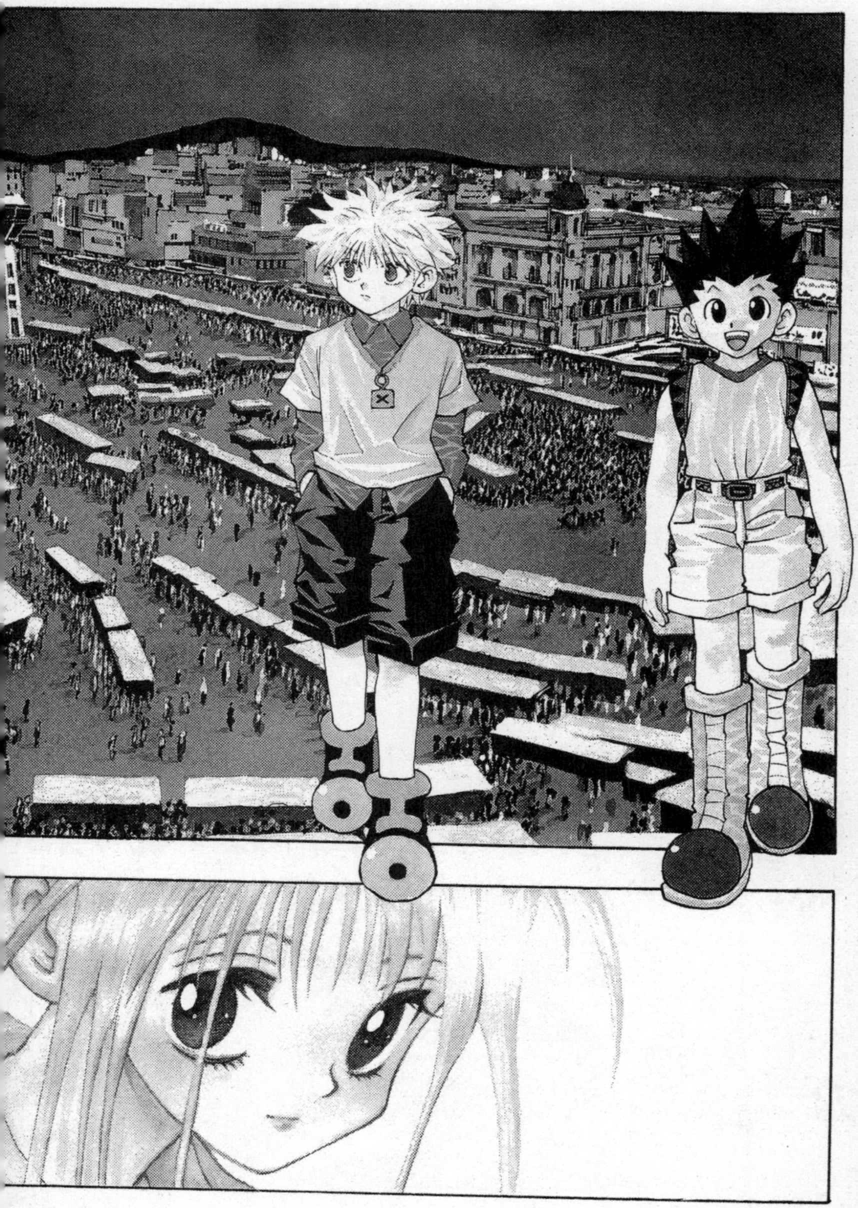

CHAPTER 71
THE AUCTION BEGINS!!

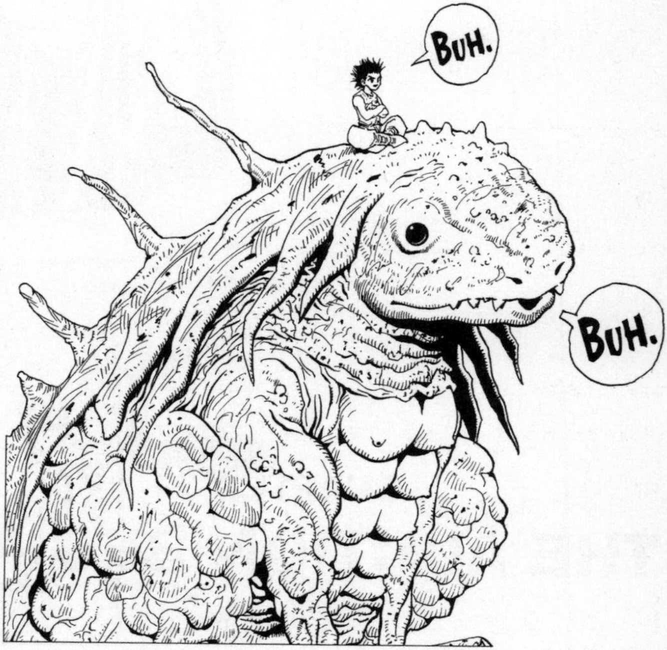
BUH.
BUH.

READ THIS WAY

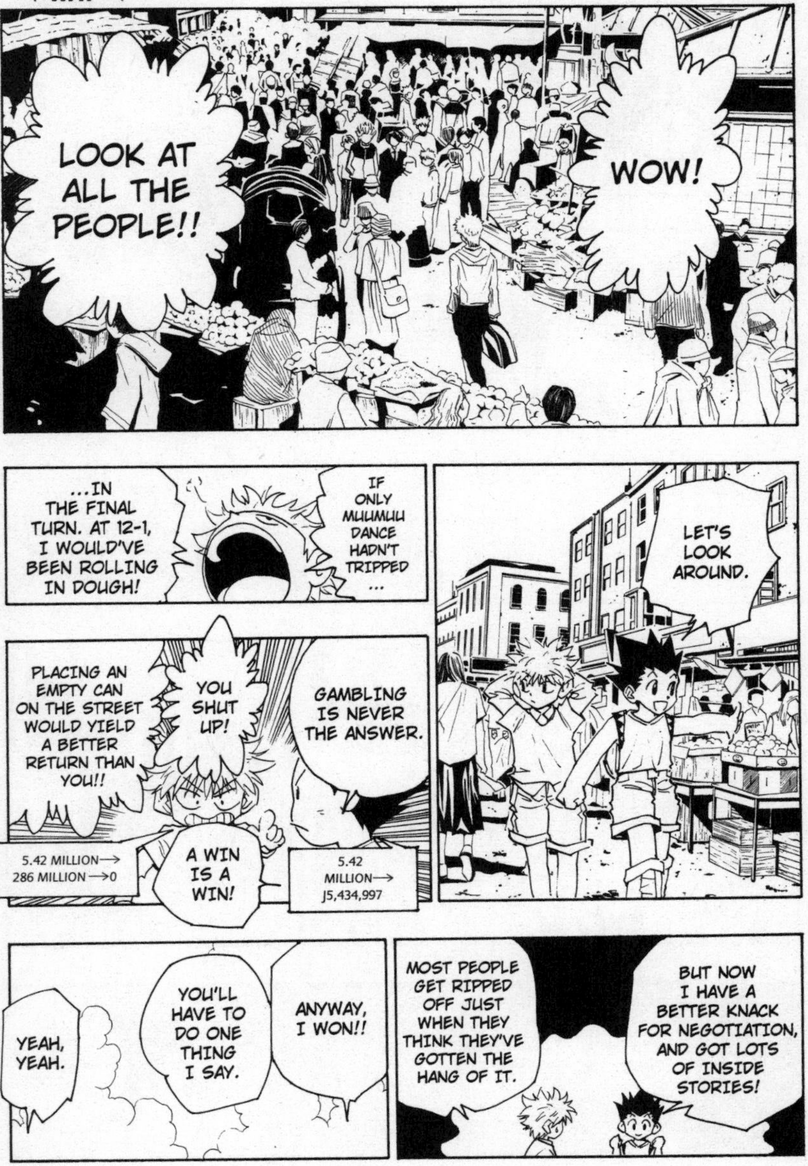
WOW!
LOOK AT ALL THE PEOPLE!!
LET'S LOOK AROUND.
IF ONLY MUUMUU DANCE HADN'T TRIPPED ...
...IN THE FINAL TURN. AT 12-1, I WOULD'VE BEEN ROLLING IN DOUGH!
GAMBLING IS NEVER THE ANSWER.
5.42 MILLION→ J5,434,997
YOU SHUT UP!
PLACING AN EMPTY CAN ON THE STREET WOULD YIELD A BETTER RETURN THAN YOU!!
A WIN IS A WIN!
5.42 MILLION→ 286 MILLION→0
BUT NOW I HAVE A BETTER KNACK FOR NEGOTIATION, AND GOT LOTS OF INSIDE STORIES!
MOST PEOPLE GET RIPPED OFF JUST WHEN THEY THINK THEY'VE GOTTEN THE HANG OF IT.
ANYWAY, I WON!!
YOU'LL HAVE TO DO ONE THING I SAY.
YEAH, YEAH.

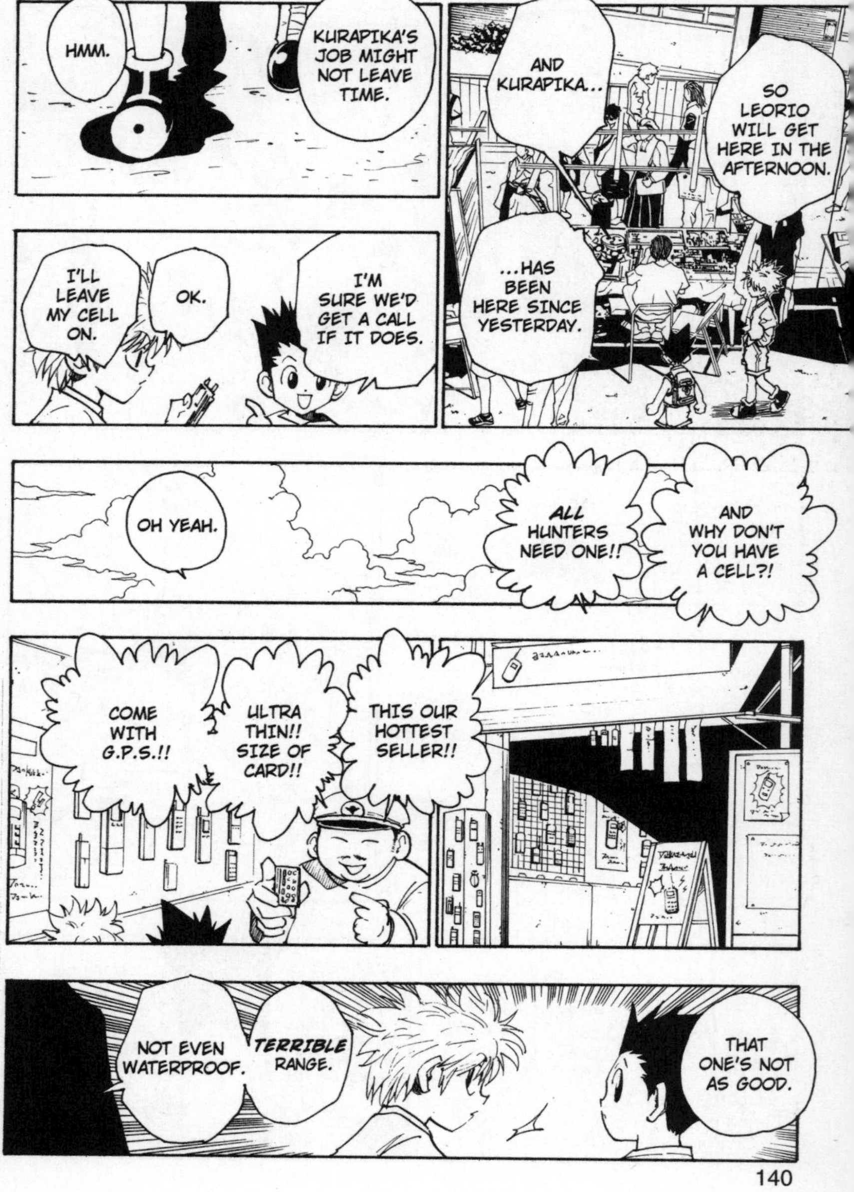
SO LEORIO WILL GET HERE IN THE AFTERNOON.
AND KURAPIKA...
...HAS BEEN HERE SINCE YESTERDAY.
KURAPIKA'S JOB MIGHT NOT LEAVE TIME.
HMM.
I'M SURE WE'D GET A CALL IF IT DOES.
OK.
I'LL LEAVE MY CELL ON.
AND WHY DON'T YOU HAVE A CELL?!
ALL HUNTERS NEED ONE!!
OH YEAH.
THIS OUR HOTTEST SELLER!!
ULTRA THIN!! SIZE OF CARD!!
COME WITH G.P.S.!!
THAT ONE'S NOT AS GOOD.
TERRIBLE RANGE.
NOT EVEN WATERPROOF.

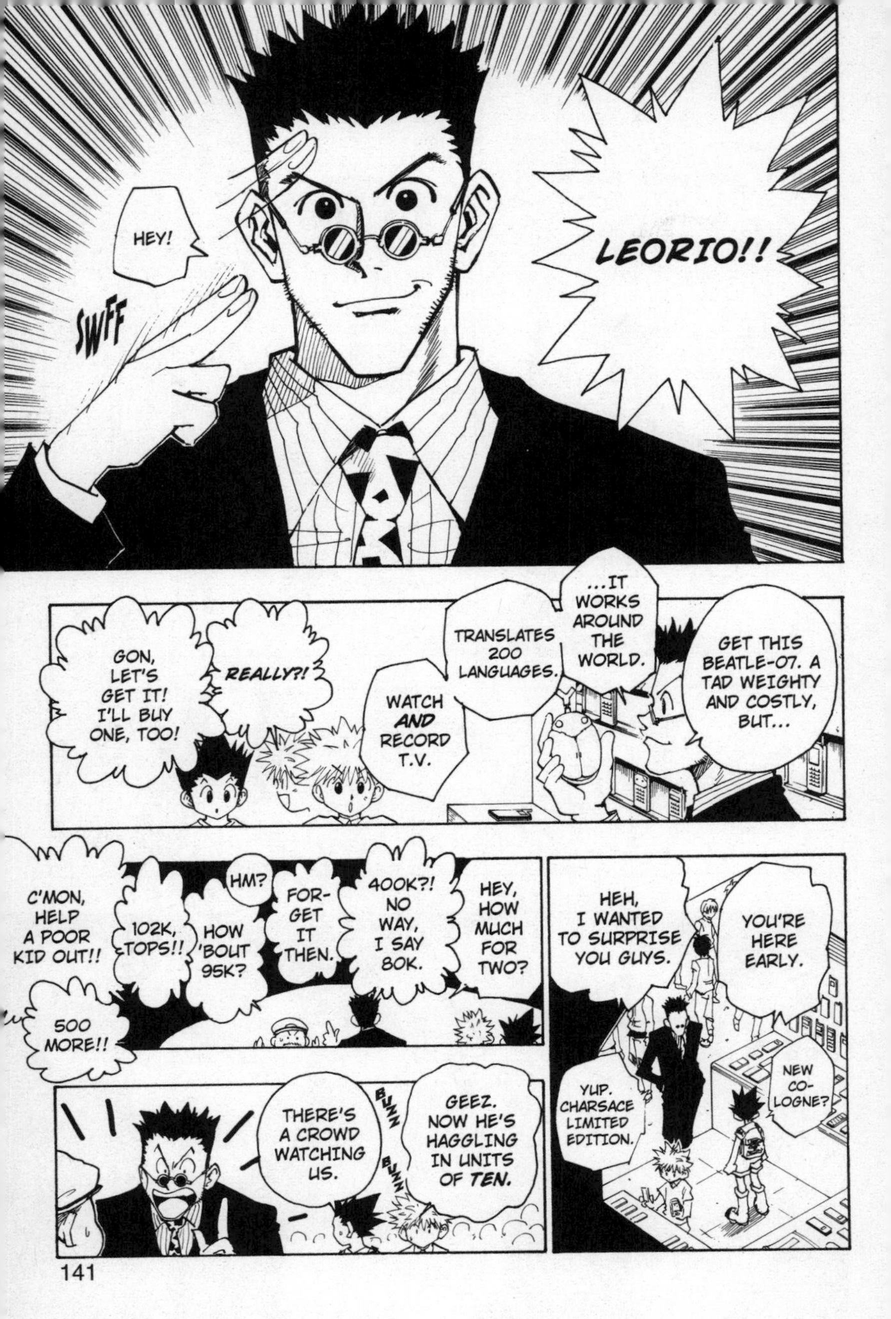
LEORIO!!
HEY!
SWFF
GET THIS BEATLE-07. A TAD WEIGHTY AND COSTLY, BUT...
...IT WORKS AROUND THE WORLD.
TRANSLATES 200 LANGUAGES.
WATCH AND RECORD T.V.
REALLY?!
GON, LET'S GET IT! I'LL BUY ONE, TOO!
YOU'RE HERE EARLY.
HEH, I WANTED TO SURPRISE YOU GUYS.
NEW CO-LOGNE?
YUP. CHARSACE LIMITED EDITION.
HEY, HOW MUCH FOR TWO?
400K?! NO WAY, I SAY 80K.
FOR-GET IT THEN.
HM?
HOW 'BOUT 95K?
102K, TOPS!!
C'MON, HELP A POOR KID OUT!!
500 MORE!!
GEEZ. NOW HE'S HAGGLING IN UNITS OF TEN.
BUZZ
BUZZ
THERE'S A CROWD WATCHING US.

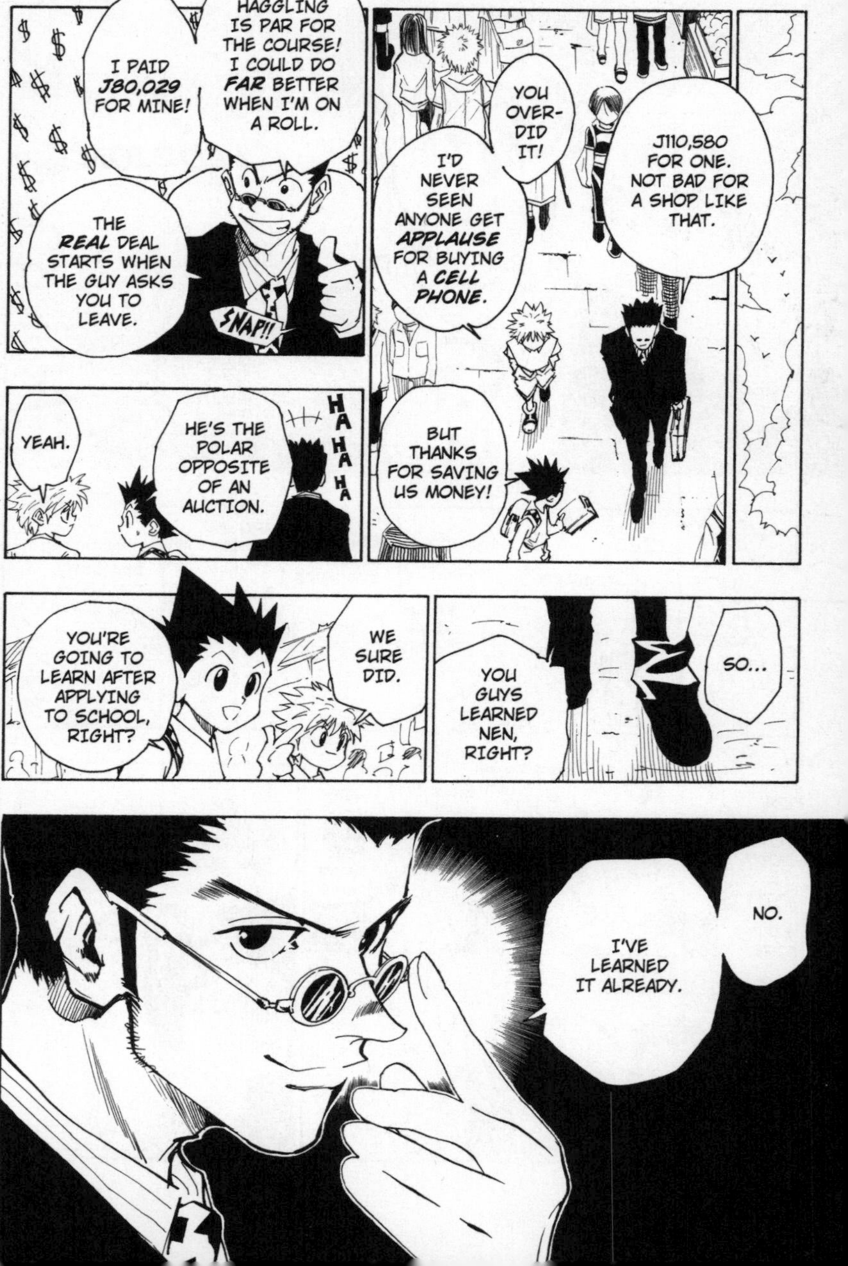
J110,580 FOR ONE. NOT BAD FOR A SHOP LIKE THAT.
YOU OVER-DID IT!
I'D NEVER SEEN ANYONE GET APPLAUSE FOR BUYING A CELL PHONE.
BUT THANKS FOR SAVING US MONEY!
HAGGLING IS PAR FOR THE COURSE! I COULD DO FAR BETTER WHEN I'M ON A ROLL.
I PAID J80,029 FOR MINE!
THE REAL DEAL STARTS WHEN THE GUY ASKS YOU TO LEAVE.
SNAP!!
HA HA HA HA
HE'S THE POLAR OPPOSITE OF AN AUCTION.
YEAH.
SO...
YOU GUYS LEARNED NEN, RIGHT?
WE SURE DID.
YOU'RE GOING TO LEARN AFTER APPLYING TO SCHOOL, RIGHT?
NO.
I'VE LEARNED IT ALREADY.

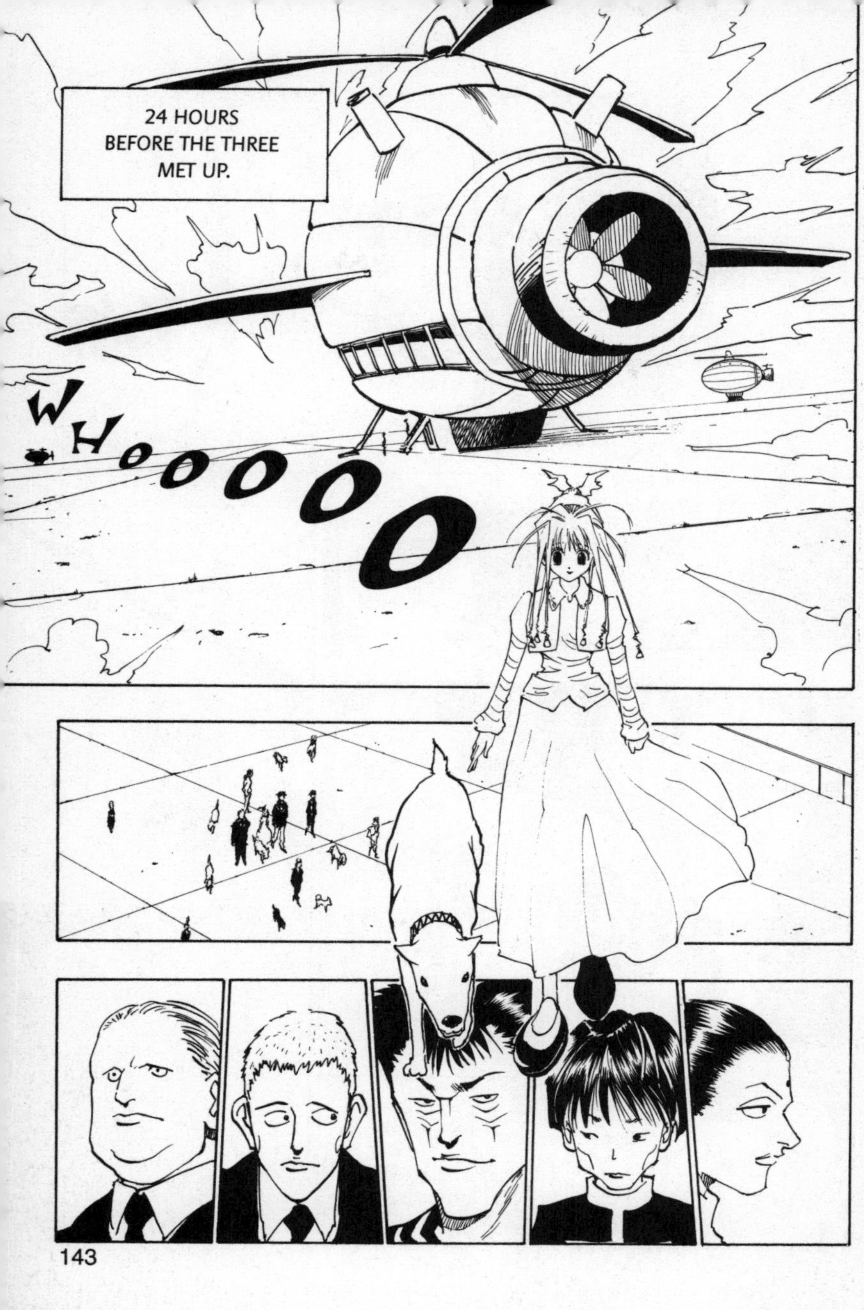
24 HOURS BEFORE THE THREE MET UP.
WHOOOOOO

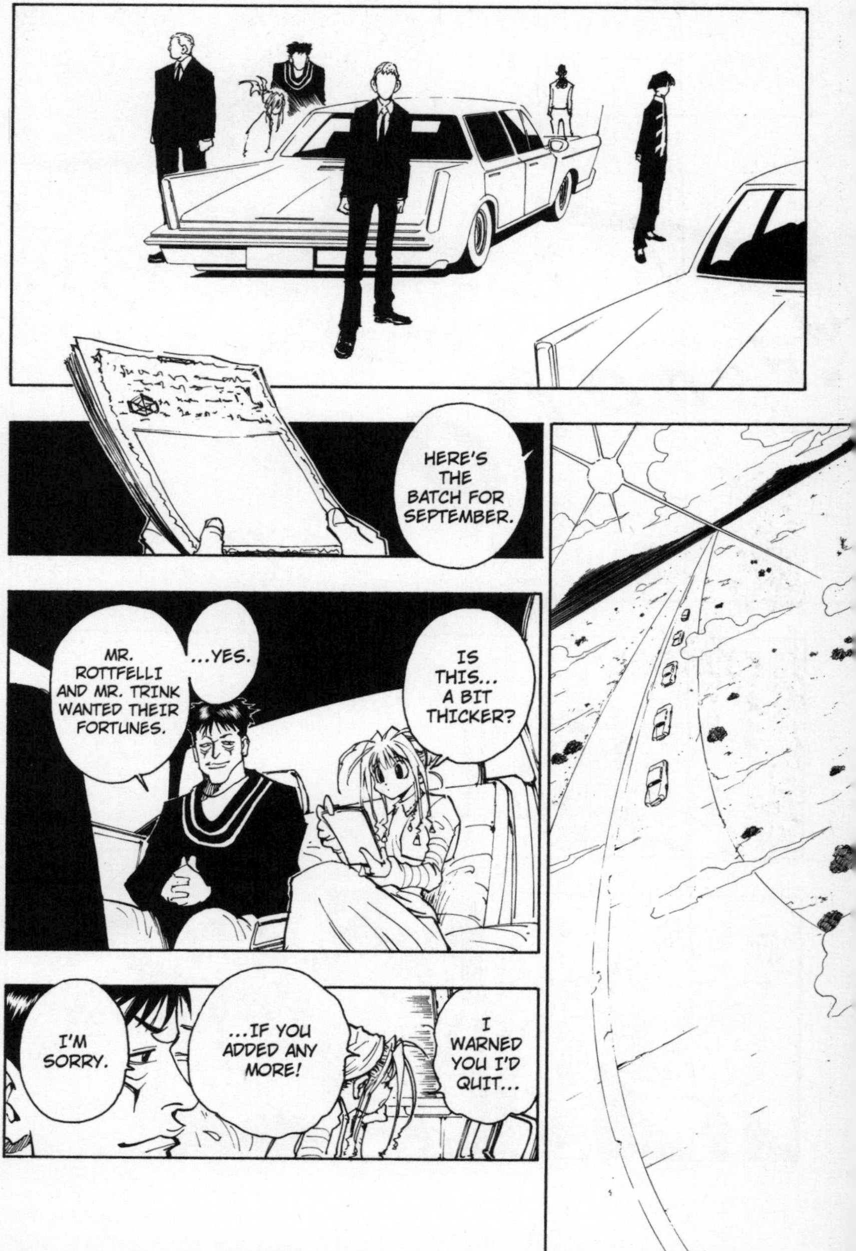
HERE'S THE BATCH FOR SEPTEMBER.
IS THIS... A BIT THICKER?
...YES.
MR. ROTTFELLI AND MR. TRINK WANTED THEIR FORTUNES.
I WARNED YOU I'D QUIT...
...IF YOU ADDED ANY MORE!
I'M SORRY.

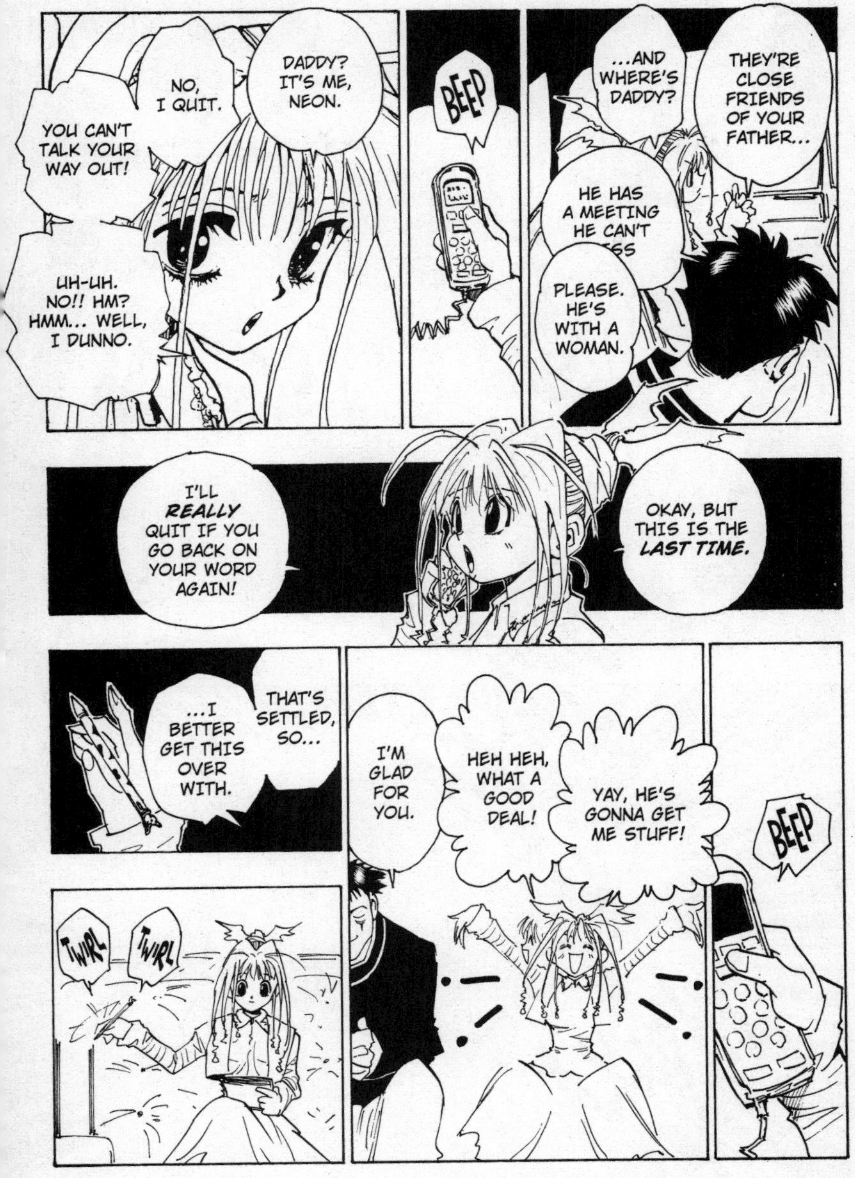
THEY'RE CLOSE FRIENDS OF YOUR FATHER...
...AND WHERE'S DADDY?
HE HAS A MEETING HE CAN'T
PLEASE. HE'S WITH A WOMAN.
BEEP
DADDY? IT'S ME, NEON.
NO, I QUIT.
YOU CAN'T TALK YOUR WAY OUT!
UH-UH. NO!! HM? HMM... WELL, I DUNNO.
OKAY, BUT THIS IS THE *LAST TIME.*
I'LL *REALLY* QUIT IF YOU GO BACK ON YOUR WORD AGAIN!
BEEP
YAY, HE'S GONNA GET ME STUFF!
HEH HEH, WHAT A GOOD DEAL!
I'M GLAD FOR YOU.
THAT'S SETTLED, SO...
...I BETTER GET THIS OVER WITH.
TWIRL
TWIRL

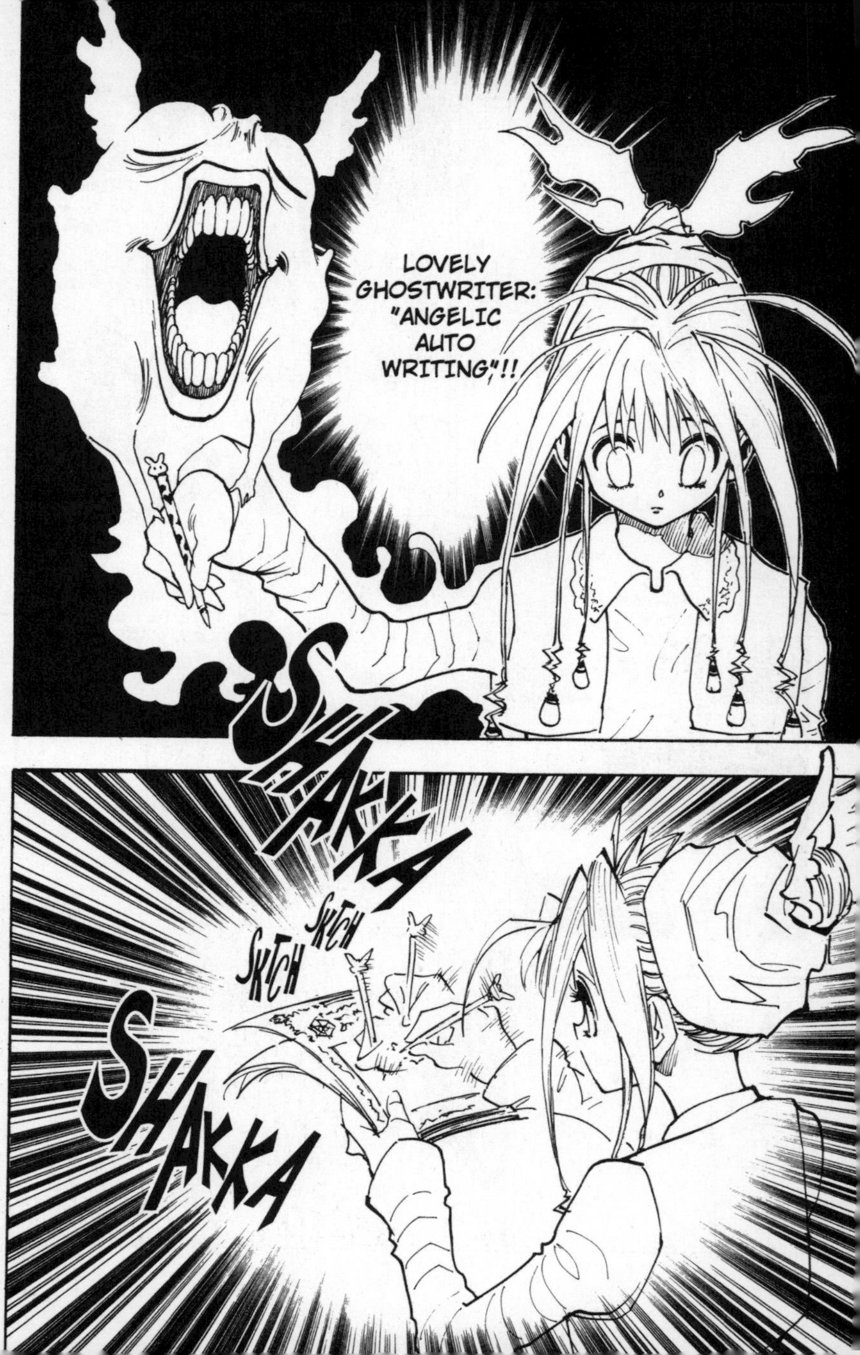
LOVELY GHOSTWRITER: "ANGELIC AUTO WRITING"!!
SHAKKA
SKTCH
SKTCH
SHAKKA

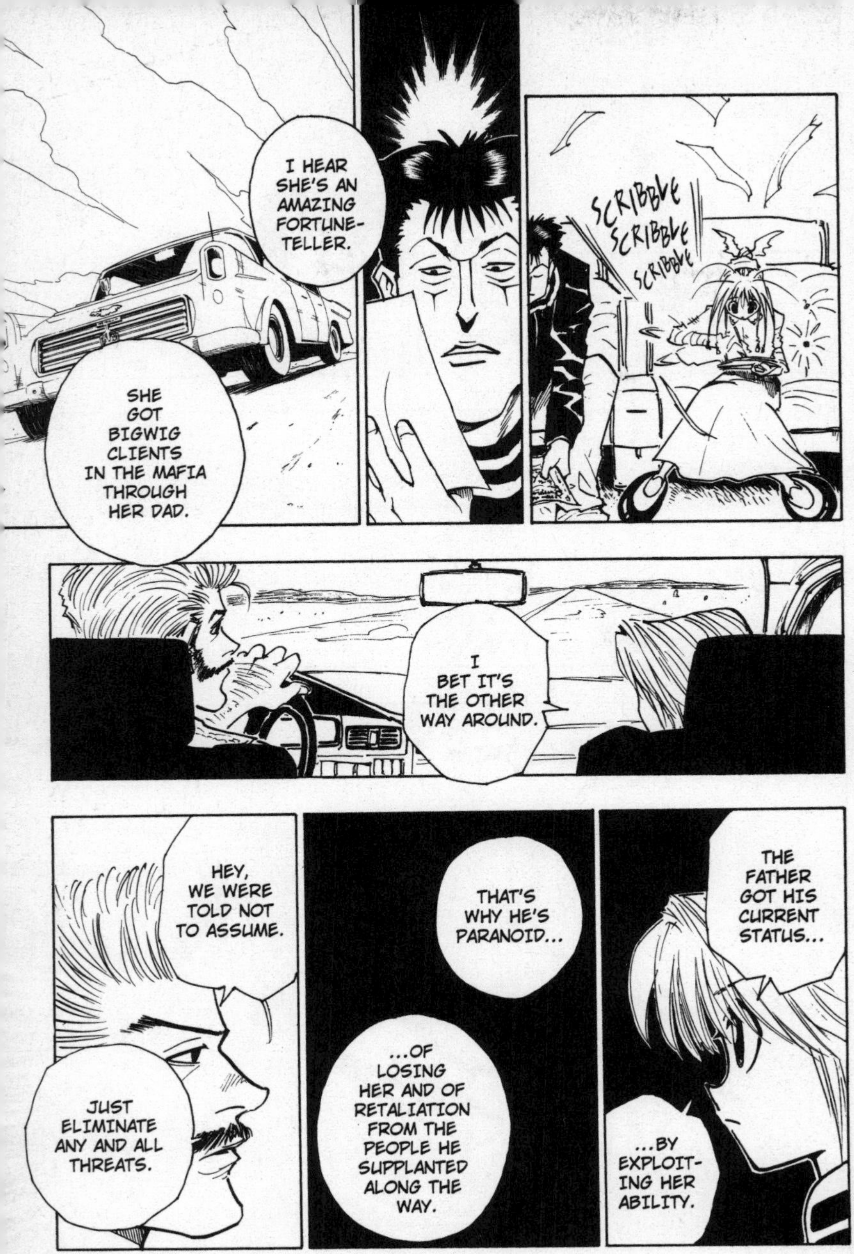
SCRIBBLE SCRIBBLE SCRIBBLE
I HEAR SHE'S AN AMAZING FORTUNE-TELLER.
SHE GOT BIGWIG CLIENTS IN THE MAFIA THROUGH HER DAD.
I BET IT'S THE OTHER WAY AROUND.
THE FATHER GOT HIS CURRENT STATUS...
...BY EXPLOITING HER ABILITY.
THAT'S WHY HE'S PARANOID...
...OF LOSING HER AND OF RETALIATION FROM THE PEOPLE HE SUPPLANTED ALONG THE WAY.
HEY, WE WERE TOLD NOT TO ASSUME.
JUST ELIMINATE ANY AND ALL THREATS.

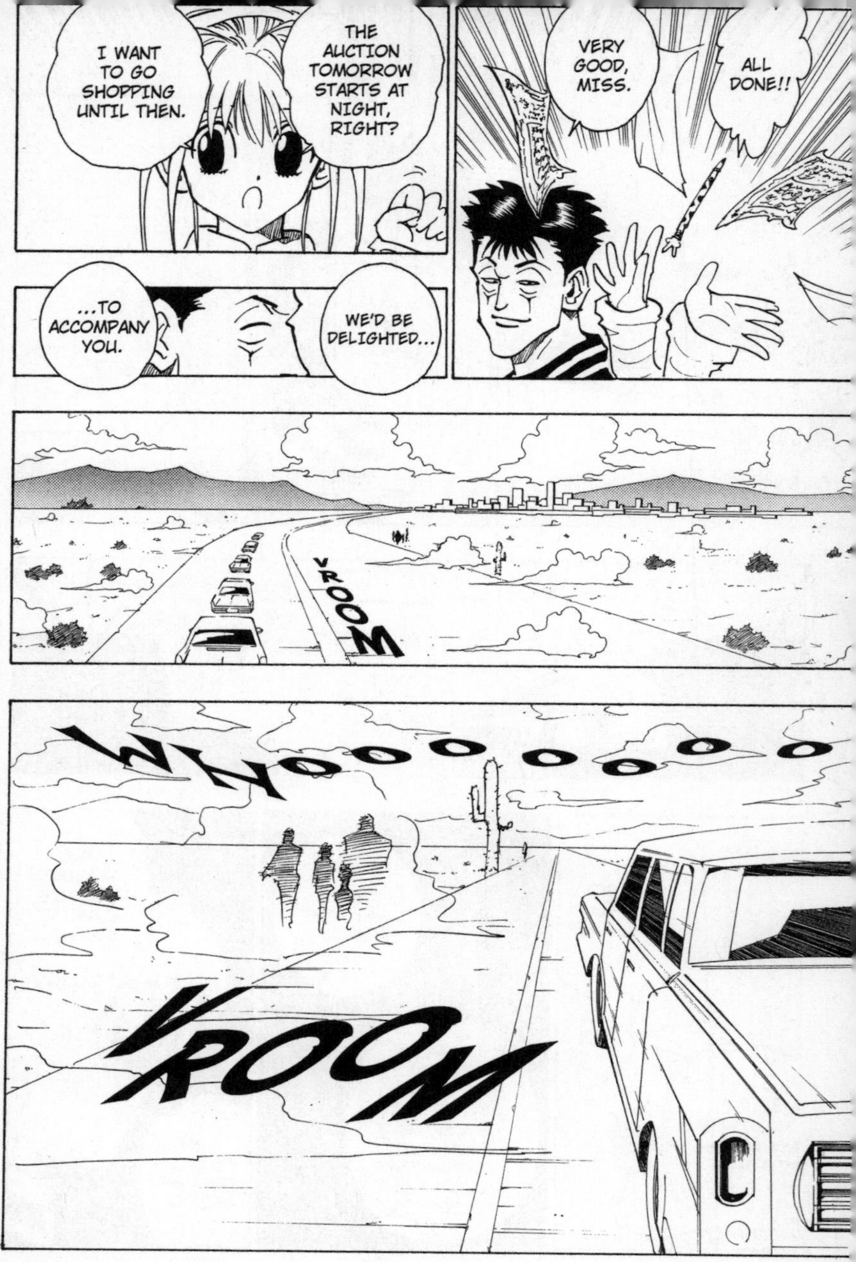
ALL DONE!!
VERY GOOD, MISS.
THE AUCTION TOMORROW STARTS AT NIGHT, RIGHT?
I WANT TO GO SHOPPING UNTIL THEN.
WE'D BE DELIGHTED...
...TO ACCOMPANY YOU.
VROOM
WHOOOOOOO
VROOM

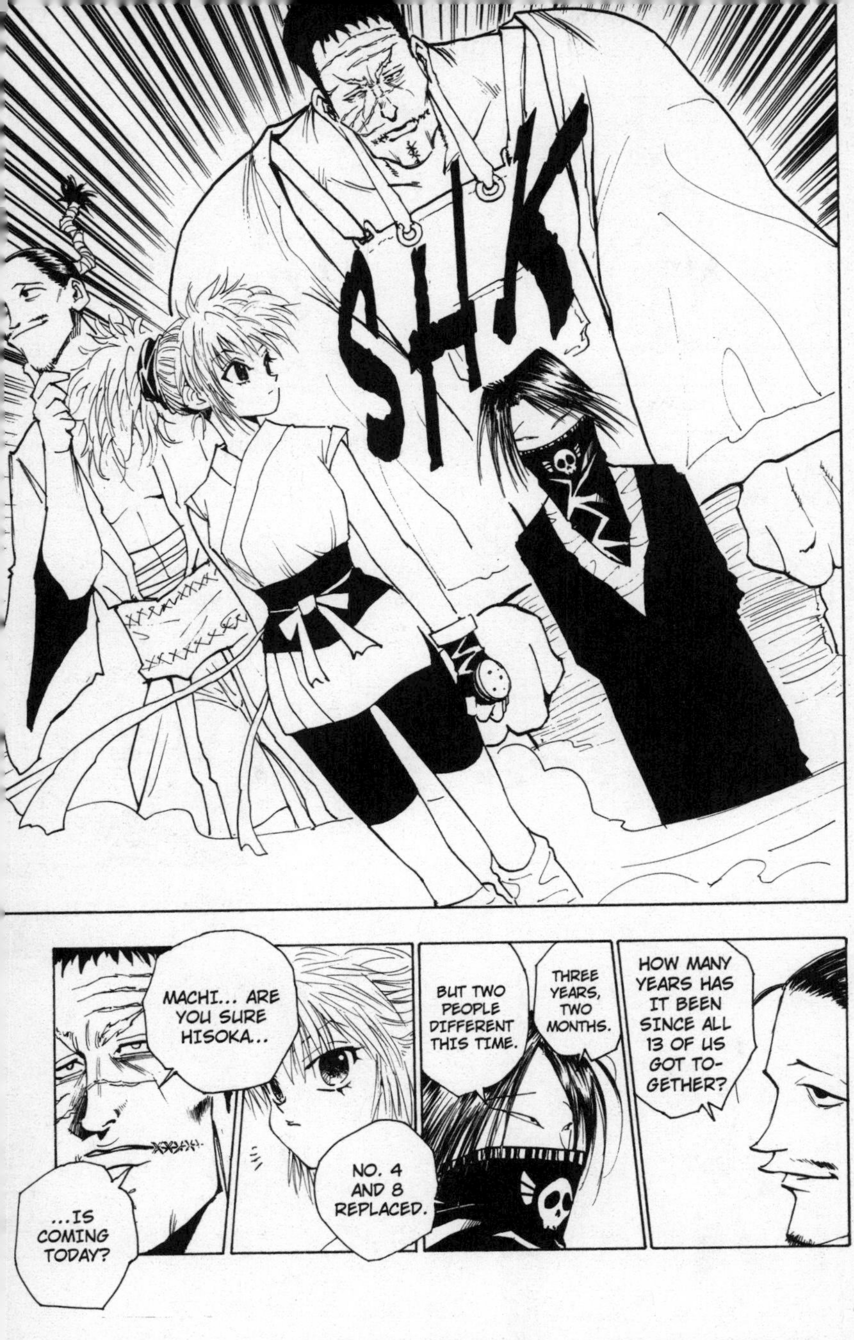
SHK
HOW MANY YEARS HAS IT BEEN SINCE ALL 13 OF US GOT TO-GETHER?
THREE YEARS, TWO MONTHS.
BUT TWO PEOPLE DIFFERENT THIS TIME.
NO. 4 AND 8 REPLACED.
MACHI... ARE YOU SURE HISOKA...
...IS COMING TODAY?

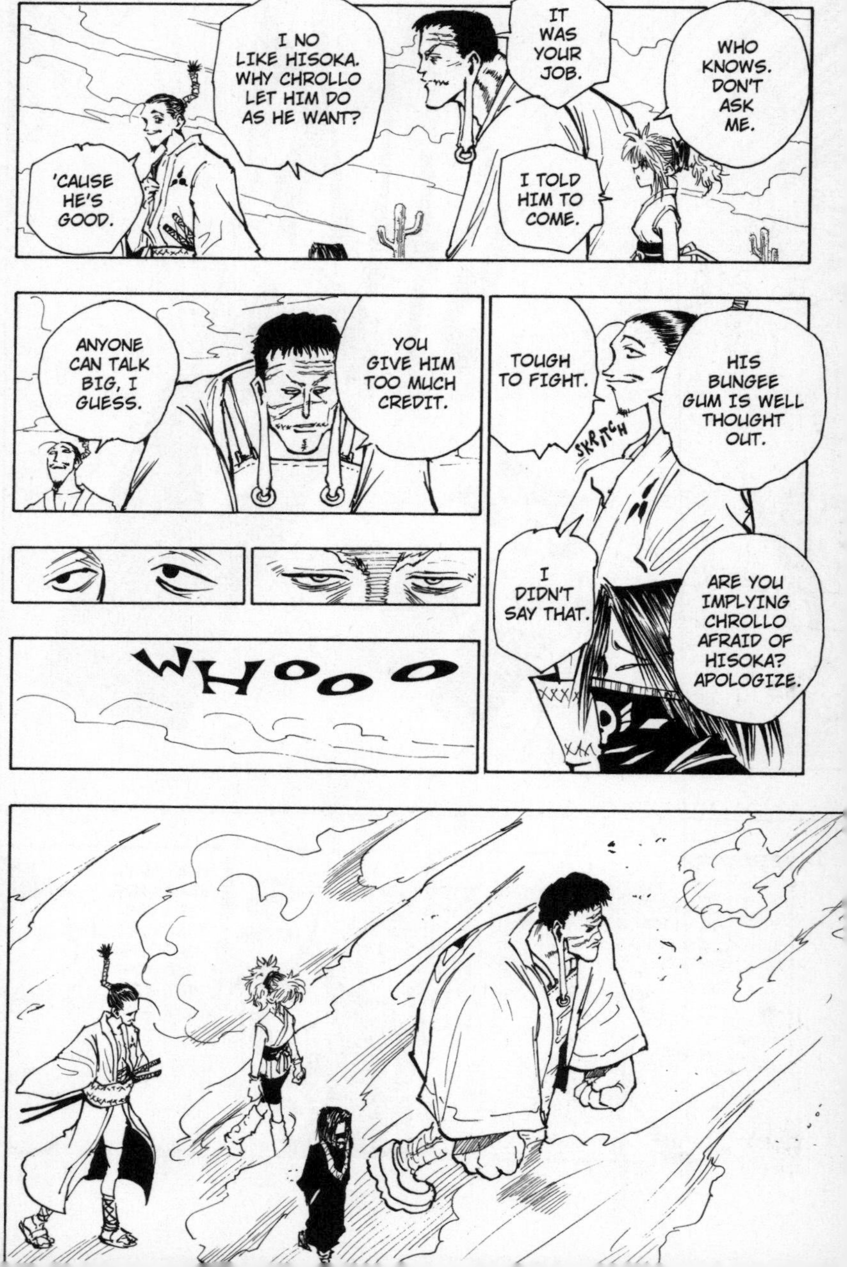
WHO KNOWS. DON'T ASK ME.
IT WAS YOUR JOB.
I NO LIKE HISOKA. WHY CHROLLO LET HIM DO AS HE WANT?
I TOLD HIM TO COME.
'CAUSE HE'S GOOD.
HIS BUNGEE GUM IS WELL THOUGHT OUT.
TOUGH TO FIGHT.
SKRITCH
ARE YOU IMPLYING CHROLLO AFRAID OF HISOKA? APOLOGIZE.
I DIDN'T SAY THAT.
YOU GIVE HIM TOO MUCH CREDIT.
ANYONE CAN TALK BIG, I GUESS.
WHOOO

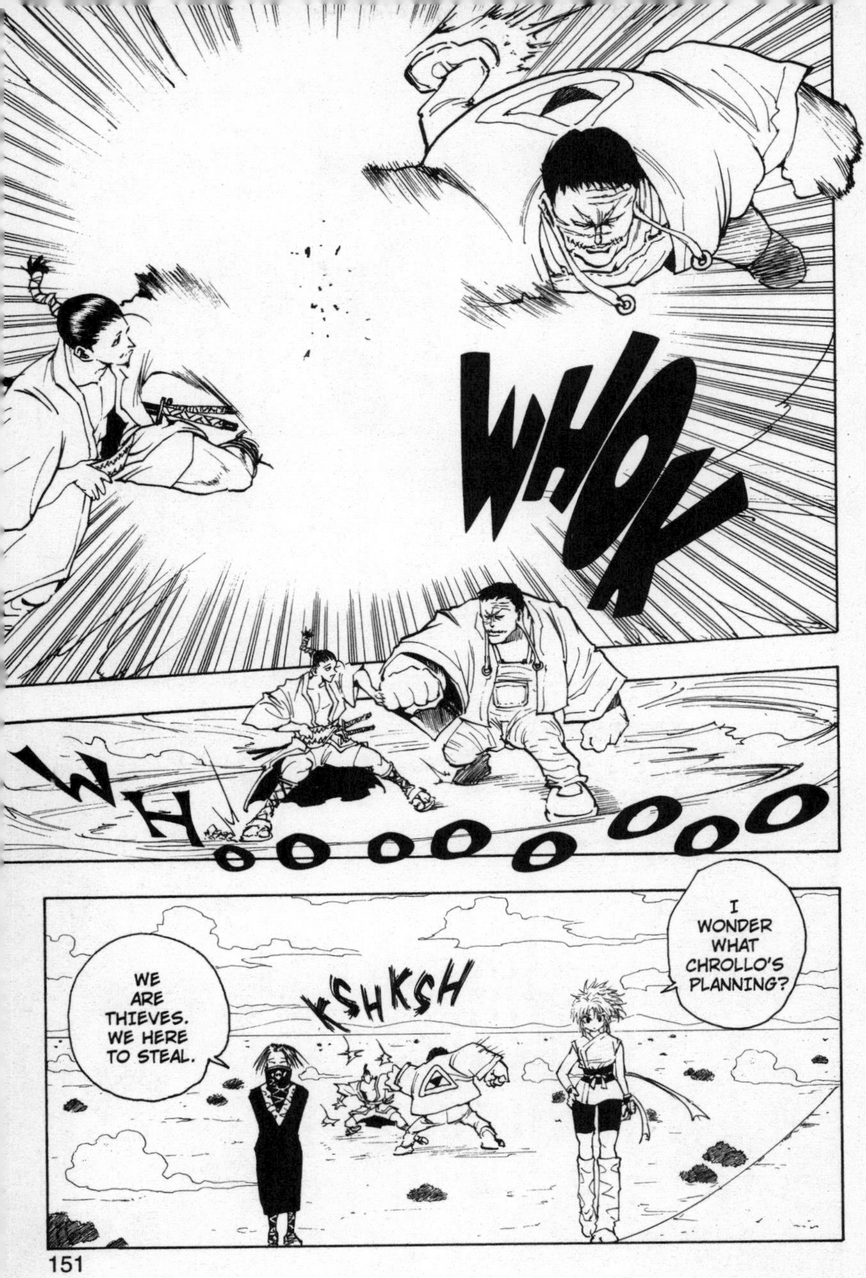
WHOA
WHOOOOOOOOO
I WONDER WHAT CHROLLO'S PLANNING?
KSHKSH
WE ARE THIEVES. WE HERE TO STEAL.

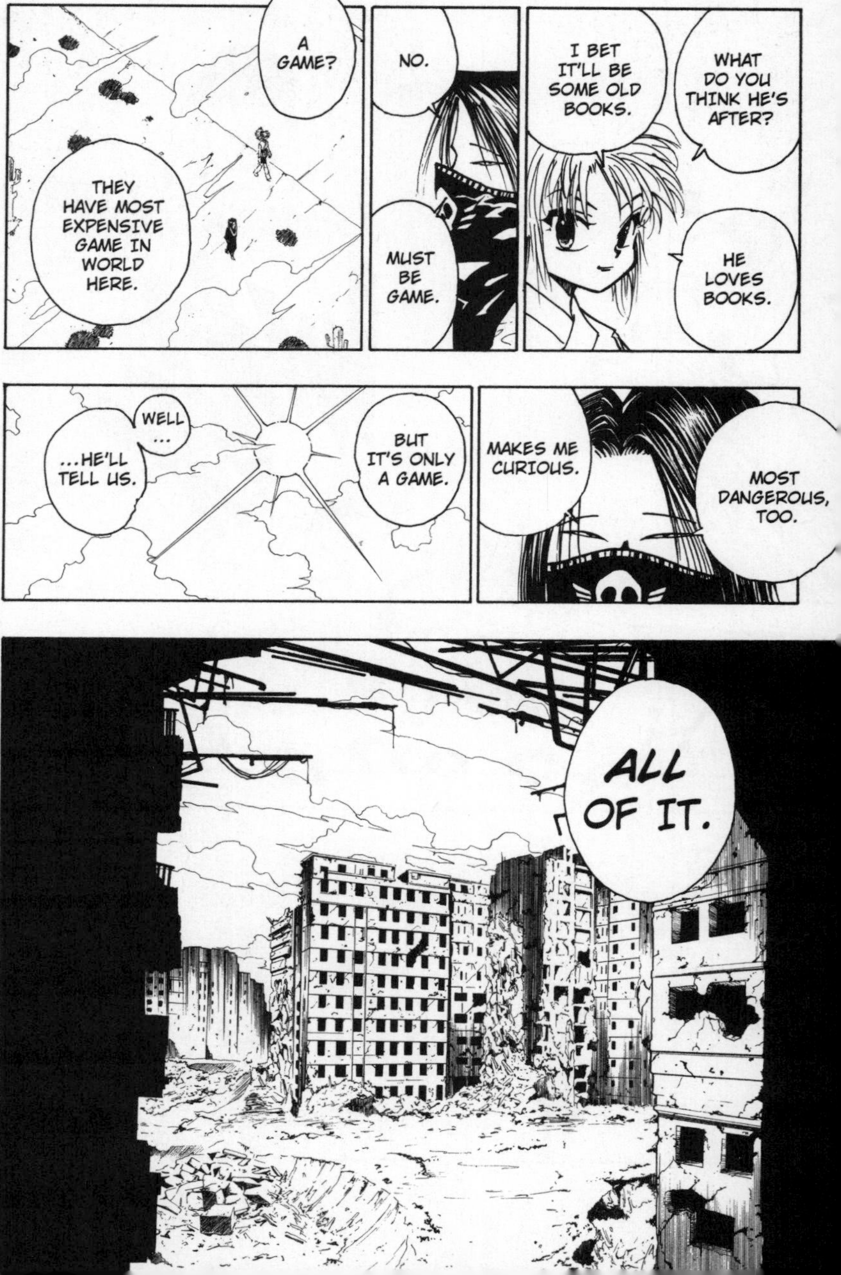
WHAT DO YOU THINK HE'S AFTER?
I BET IT'LL BE SOME OLD BOOKS.
HE LOVES BOOKS.
NO.
MUST BE GAME.
A GAME?
THEY HAVE MOST EXPENSIVE GAME IN WORLD HERE.
MOST DANGEROUS, TOO.
MAKES ME CURIOUS.
BUT IT'S ONLY A GAME.
WELL ...
...HE'LL TELL US.
ALL OF IT.

READ THIS WAY

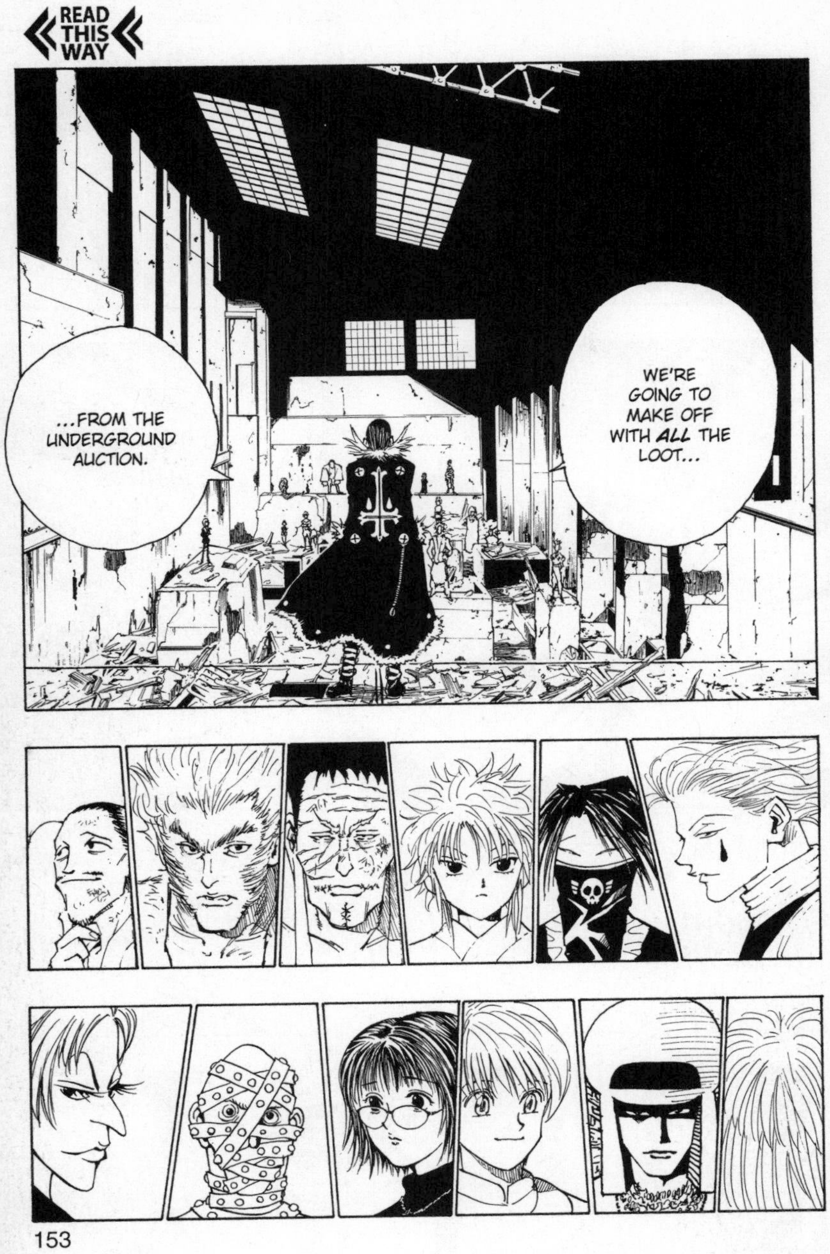
WE'RE GOING TO MAKE OFF WITH *ALL* THE LOOT...
...FROM THE UNDERGROUND AUCTION.

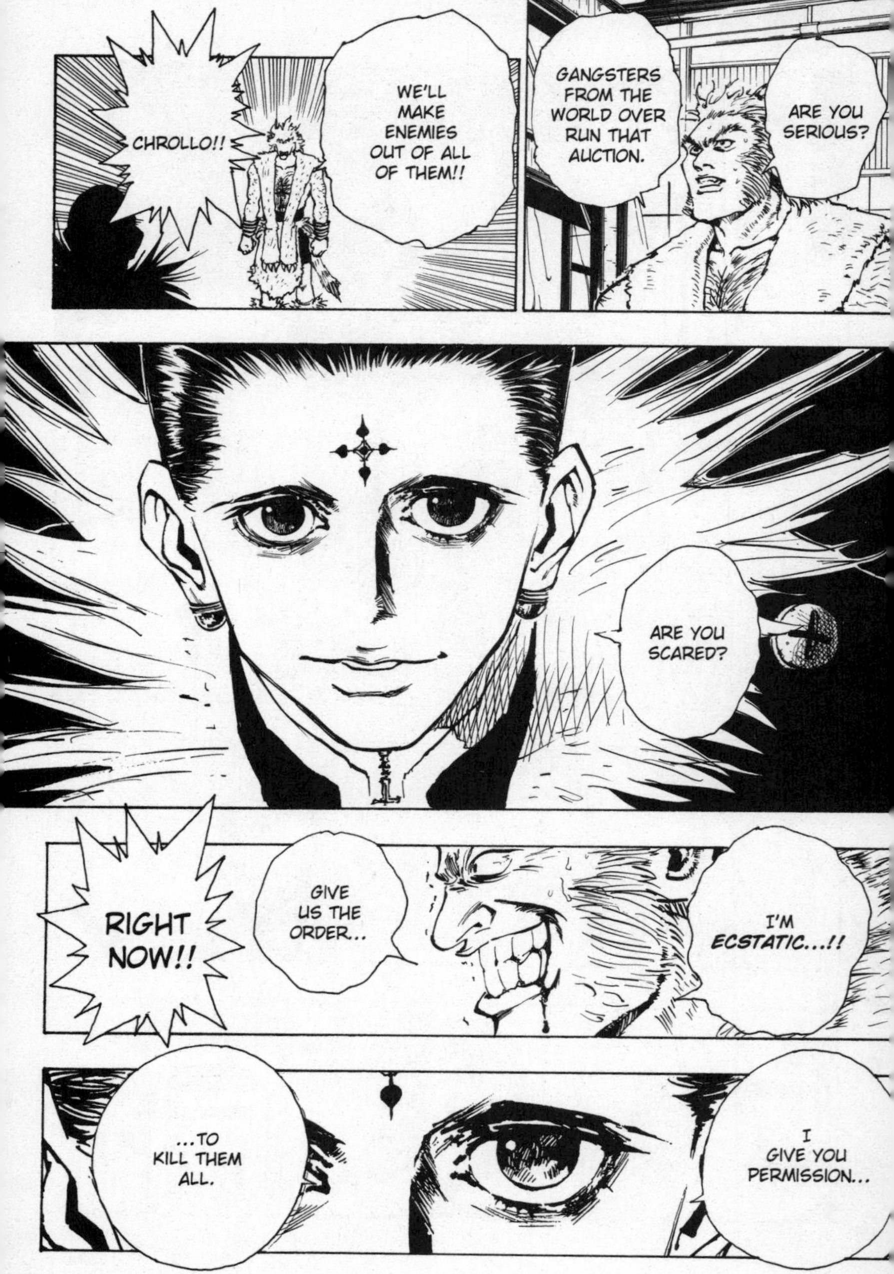
ARE YOU SERIOUS?
GANGSTERS FROM THE WORLD OVER RUN THAT AUCTION.
WE'LL MAKE ENEMIES OUT OF ALL OF THEM!!
CHROLLO!!
ARE YOU SCARED?
I'M *ECSTATIC*...!!
GIVE US THE ORDER...
RIGHT NOW!!
I GIVE YOU PERMISSION...
...TO KILL THEM ALL.

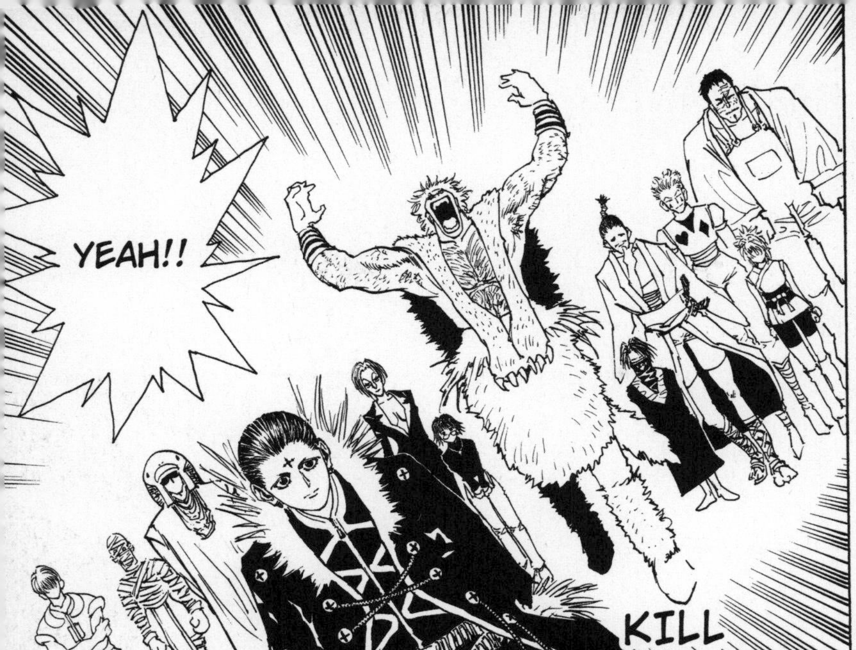
KILL ANYONE WHO GETS IN OUR WAY.
YEAH!!

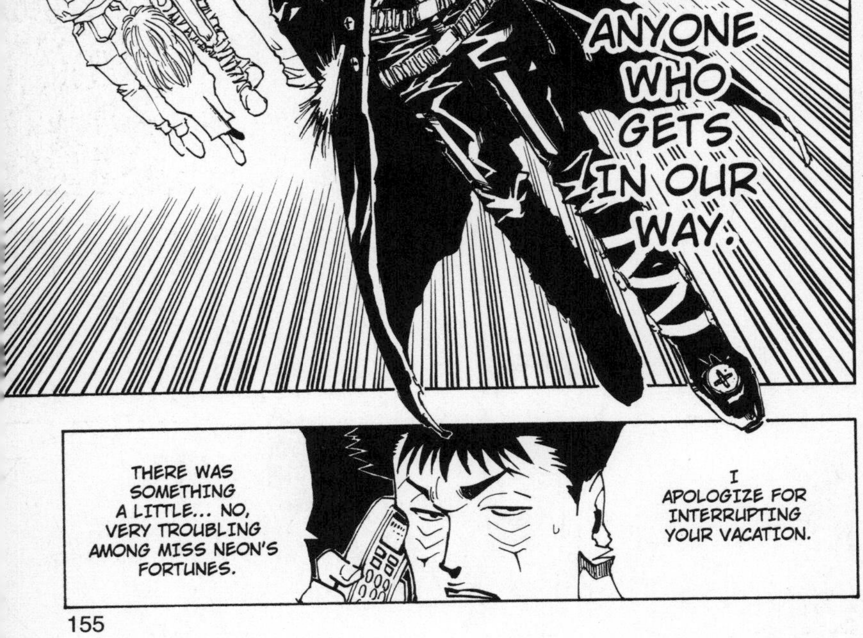
I APOLOGIZE FOR INTERRUPTING YOUR VACATION.
THERE WAS SOMETHING A LITTLE... NO, VERY TROUBLING AMONG MISS NEON'S FORTUNES.

Chapter 72 September 1st (Part 1)

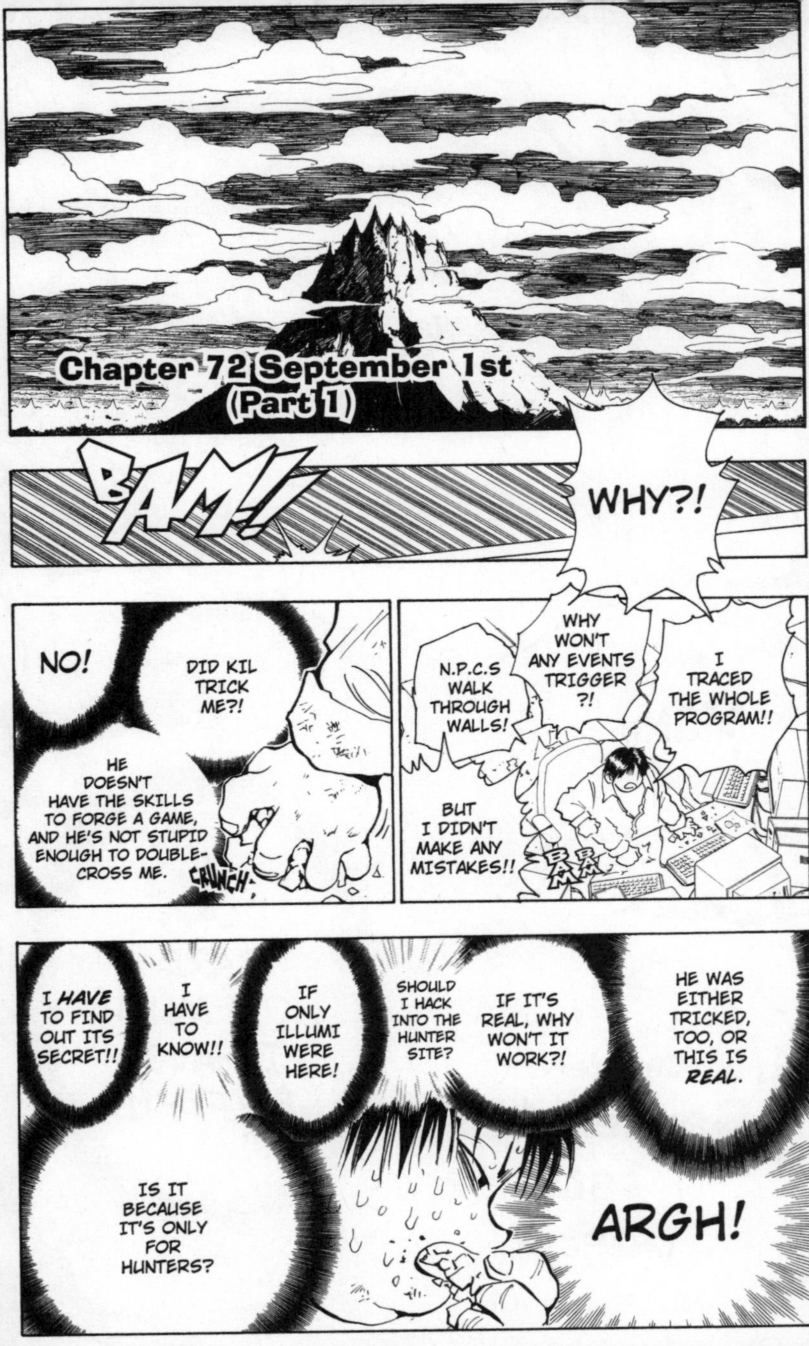

WHY?!
BAM!
I TRACED THE WHOLE PROGRAM!!
WHY WON'T ANY EVENTS TRIGGER ?!
N.P.C.S WALK THROUGH WALLS!
BUT I DIDN'T MAKE ANY MISTAKES!!
BAM BAM
DID KIL TRICK ME?!
NO!
HE DOESN'T HAVE THE SKILLS TO FORGE A GAME, AND HE'S NOT STUPID ENOUGH TO DOUBLE-CROSS ME.
CRUNCH
HE WAS EITHER TRICKED, TOO, OR THIS IS *REAL*.
IF IT'S REAL, WHY WON'T IT WORK?!
SHOULD I HACK INTO THE HUNTER SITE?
IF ONLY ILLUMI WERE HERE!
I HAVE TO KNOW!!
I *HAVE* TO FIND OUT ITS SECRET!!
ARGH!
IS IT BECAUSE IT'S ONLY FOR HUNTERS?

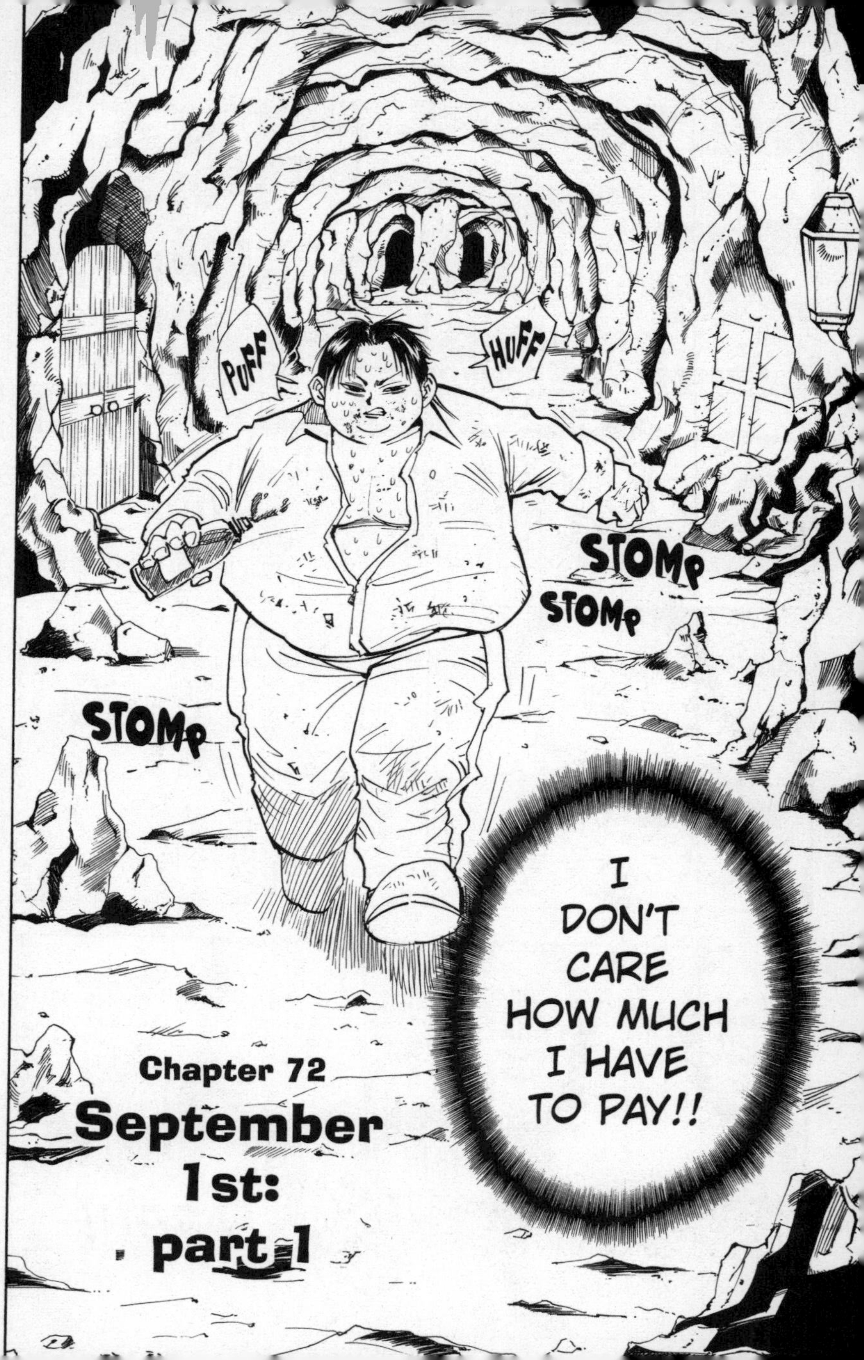
HUFF
PUFF
STOMP
STOMP
STOMP
I DON'T CARE HOW MUCH I HAVE TO PAY!!
Chapter 72
September 1st: part 1

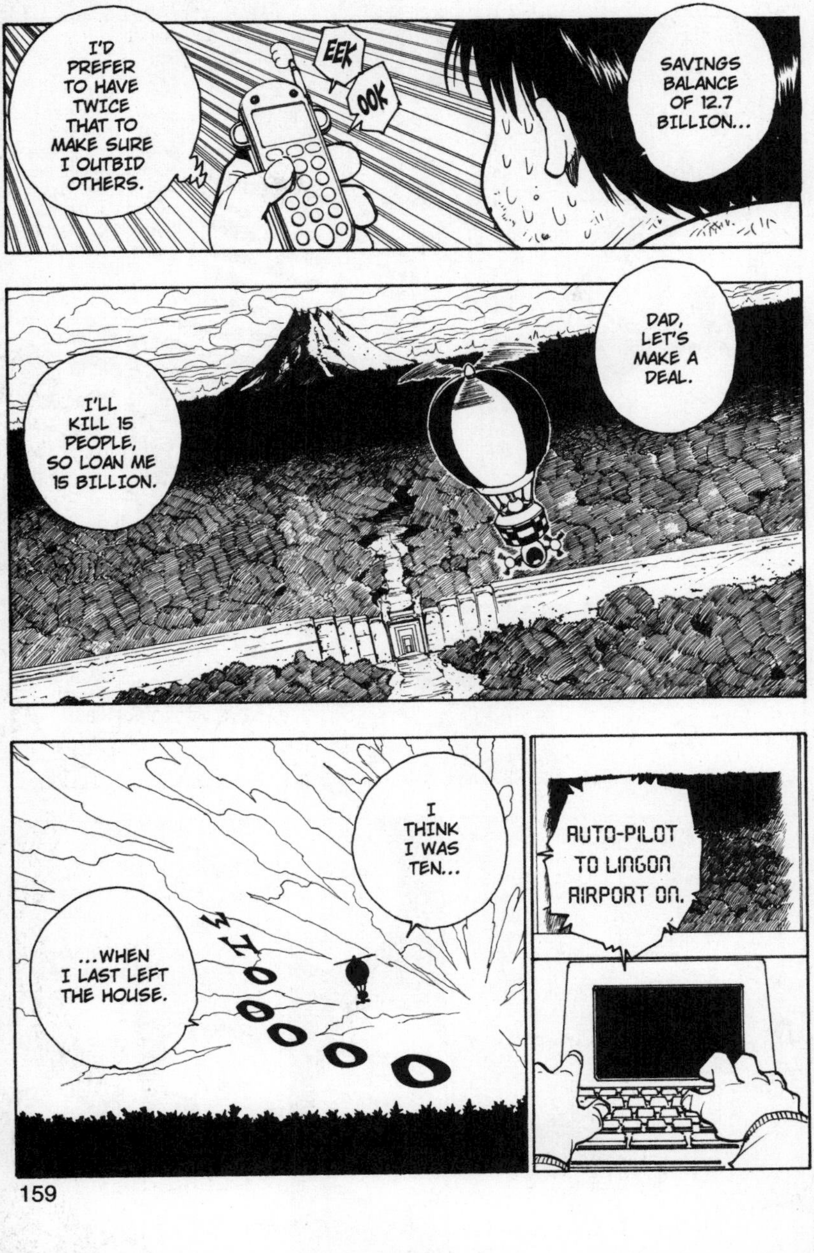
SAVINGS BALANCE OF 12.7 BILLION...
EEK
OOK
I'D PREFER TO HAVE TWICE THAT TO MAKE SURE I OUTBID OTHERS.
DAD, LET'S MAKE A DEAL.
I'LL KILL 15 PEOPLE, SO LOAN ME 15 BILLION.
AUTO-PILOT TO LINGON AIRPORT ON.
I THINK I WAS TEN...
...WHEN I LAST LEFT THE HOUSE.
ZHOOOOO

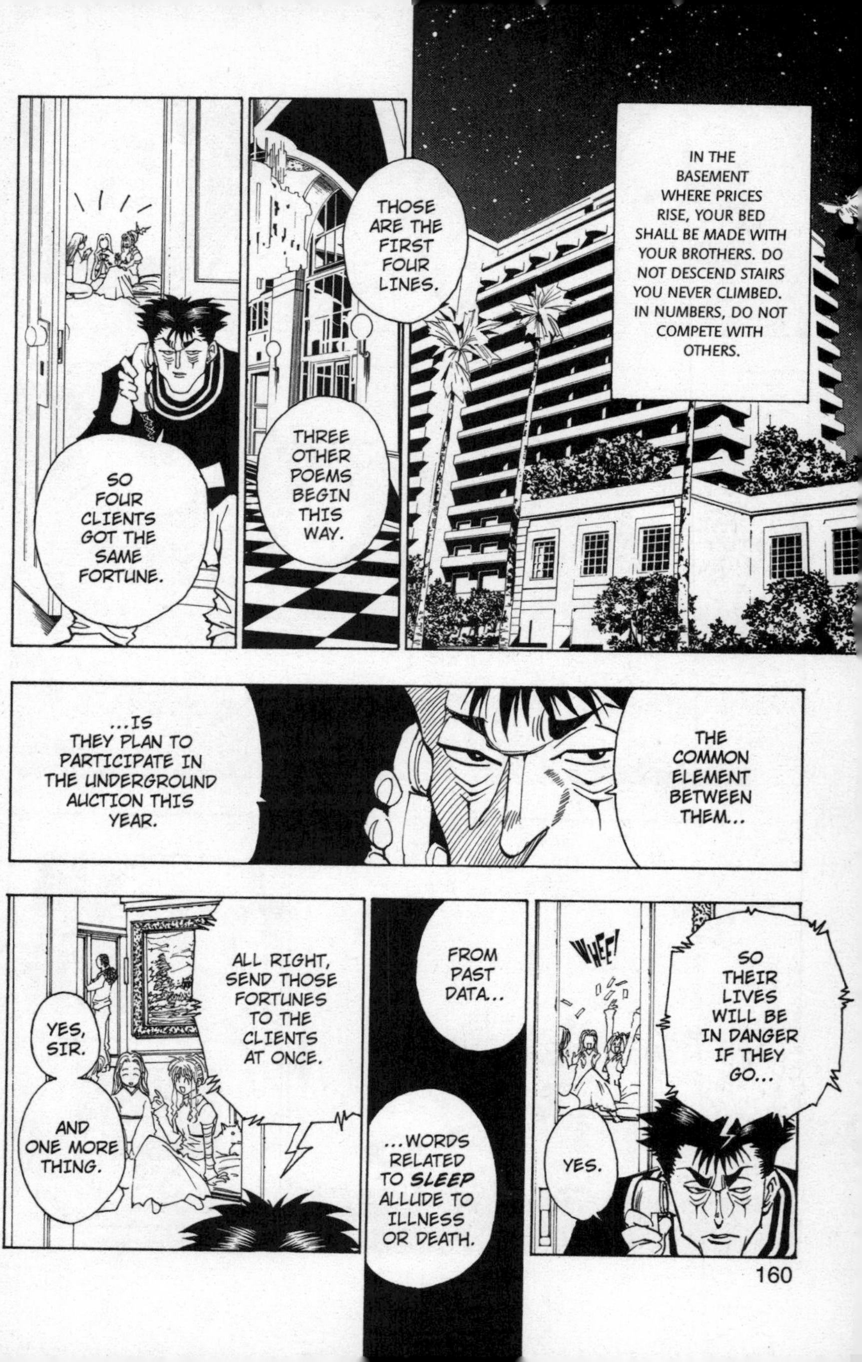
IN THE BASEMENT WHERE PRICES RISE, YOUR BED SHALL BE MADE WITH YOUR BROTHERS. DO NOT DESCEND STAIRS YOU NEVER CLIMBED. IN NUMBERS, DO NOT COMPETE WITH OTHERS.
THOSE ARE THE FIRST FOUR LINES.
THREE OTHER POEMS BEGIN THIS WAY.
SO FOUR CLIENTS GOT THE SAME FORTUNE.
THE COMMON ELEMENT BETWEEN THEM...
...IS THEY PLAN TO PARTICIPATE IN THE UNDERGROUND AUCTION THIS YEAR.
WHEE!
SO THEIR LIVES WILL BE IN DANGER IF THEY GO...
YES.
FROM PAST DATA...
...WORDS RELATED TO *SLEEP* ALLUDE TO ILLNESS OR DEATH.
ALL RIGHT, SEND THOSE FORTUNES TO THE CLIENTS AT ONCE.
YES, SIR.
AND ONE MORE THING.

READ THIS WAY

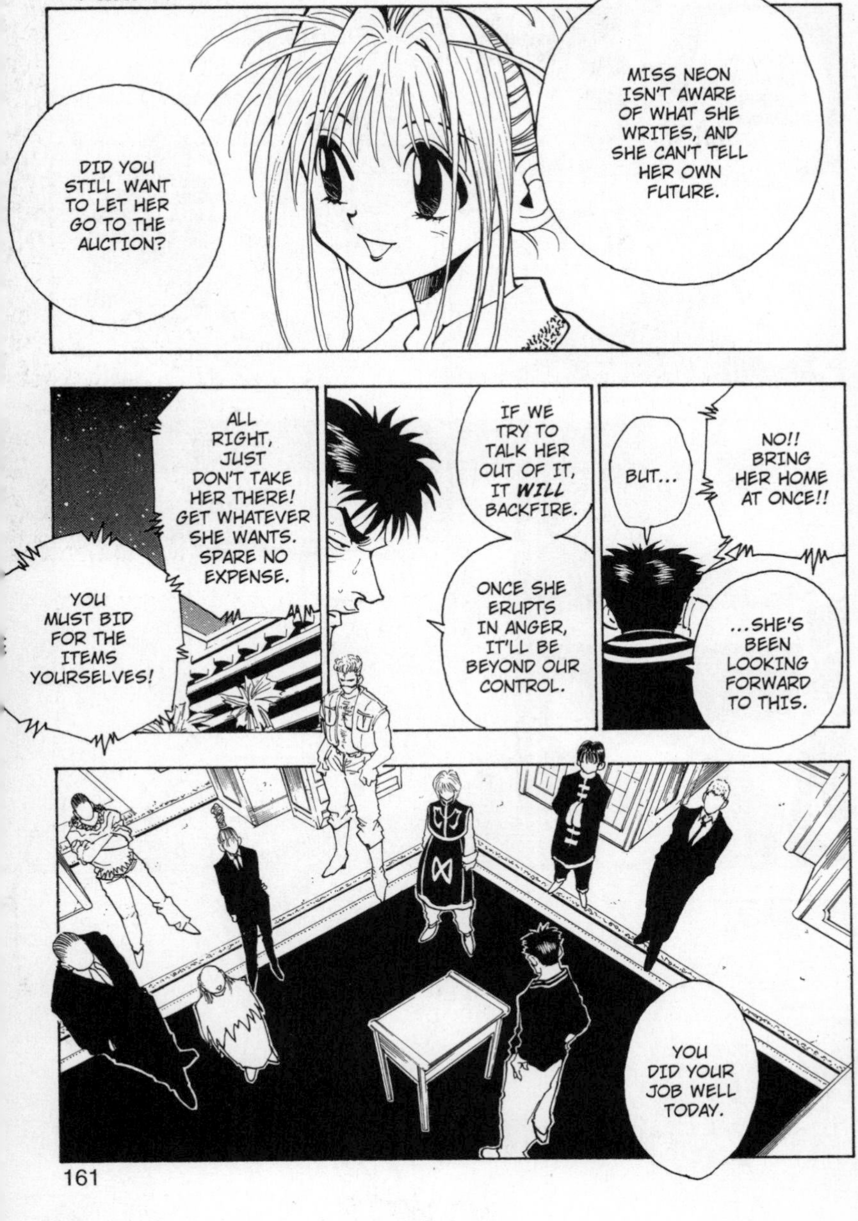

MISS NEON ISN'T AWARE OF WHAT SHE WRITES, AND SHE CAN'T TELL HER OWN FUTURE.
DID YOU STILL WANT TO LET HER GO TO THE AUCTION?
NO!! BRING HER HOME AT ONCE!!
BUT...
...SHE'S BEEN LOOKING FORWARD TO THIS.
IF WE TRY TO TALK HER OUT OF IT, IT *WILL* BACKFIRE.
ONCE SHE ERUPTS IN ANGER, IT'LL BE BEYOND OUR CONTROL.
ALL RIGHT, JUST DON'T TAKE HER THERE! GET WHATEVER SHE WANTS. SPARE NO EXPENSE.
YOU MUST BID FOR THE ITEMS YOURSELVES!
YOU DID YOUR JOB WELL TODAY.

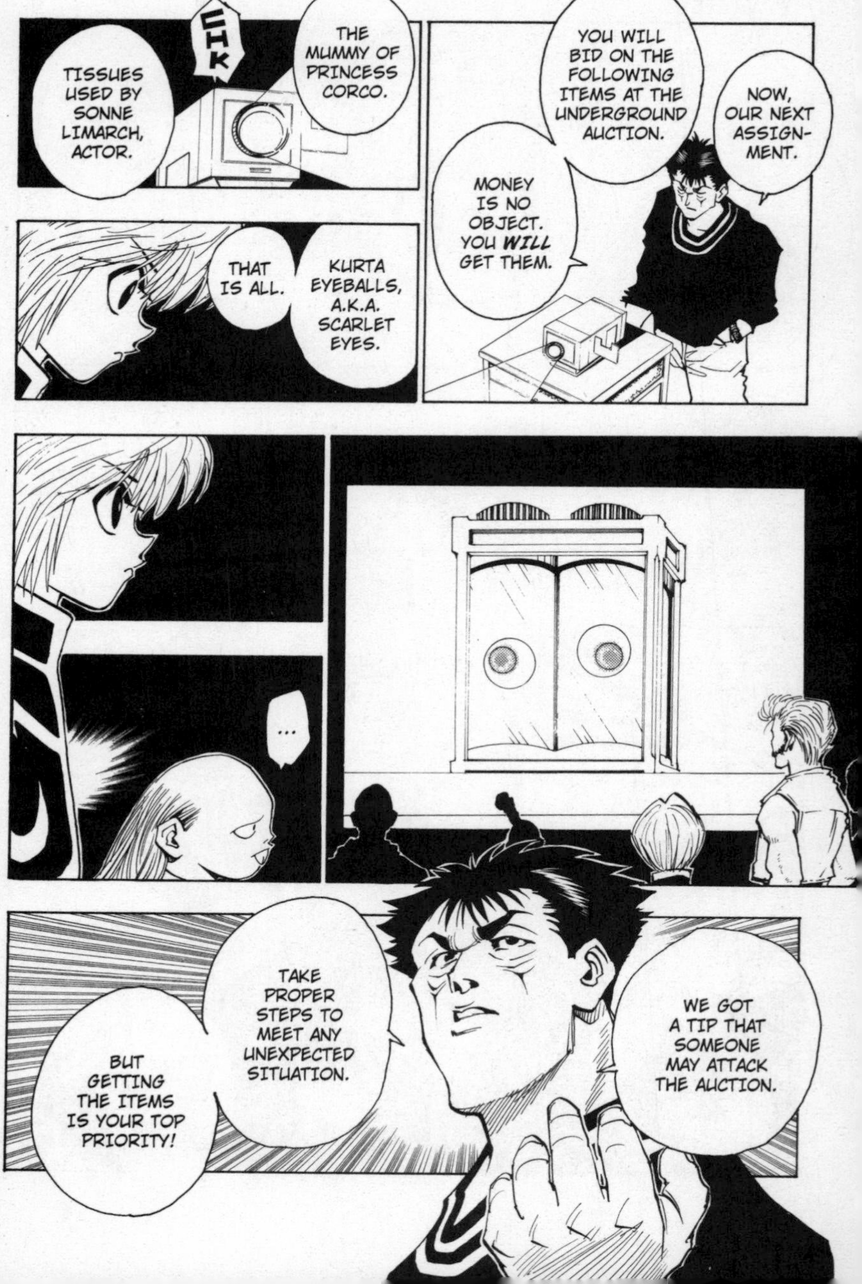
NOW, OUR NEXT ASSIGNMENT.
YOU WILL BID ON THE FOLLOWING ITEMS AT THE UNDERGROUND AUCTION.
MONEY IS NO OBJECT. YOU *WILL* GET THEM.
THE MUMMY OF PRINCESS CORCO.
CHK
TISSUES USED BY SONNE LIMARCH, ACTOR.
KURTA EYEBALLS, A.K.A. SCARLET EYES.
THAT IS ALL.
...
WE GOT A TIP THAT SOMEONE MAY ATTACK THE AUCTION.
TAKE PROPER STEPS TO MEET ANY UNEXPECTED SITUATION.
BUT GETTING THE ITEMS IS YOUR TOP PRIORITY!

READ THIS WAY

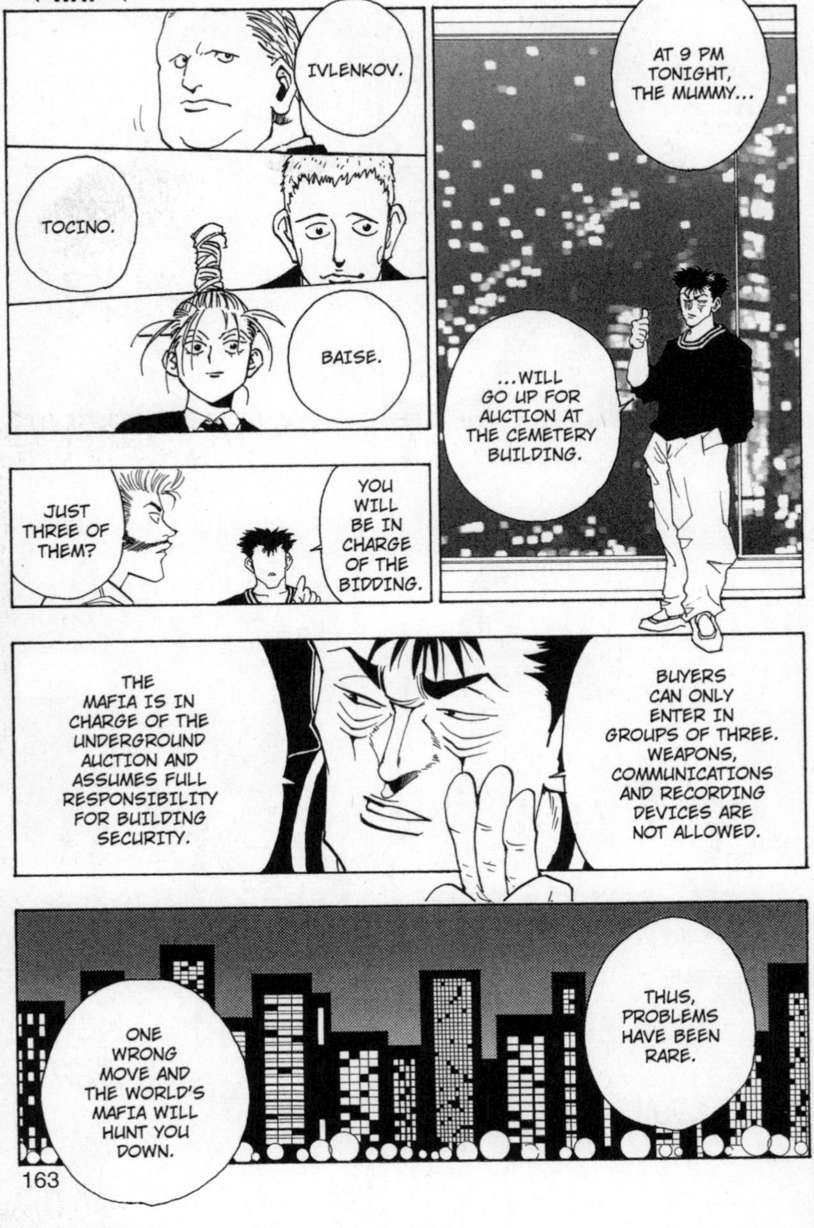

AT 9 PM TONIGHT, THE MUMMY...
...WILL GO UP FOR AUCTION AT THE CEMETERY BUILDING.
IVLENKOV.
TOCINO.
BAISE.
YOU WILL BE IN CHARGE OF THE BIDDING.
JUST THREE OF THEM?
BUYERS CAN ONLY ENTER IN GROUPS OF THREE. WEAPONS, COMMUNICATIONS AND RECORDING DEVICES ARE NOT ALLOWED.
THE MAFIA IS IN CHARGE OF THE UNDERGROUND AUCTION AND ASSUMES FULL RESPONSIBILITY FOR BUILDING SECURITY.
THUS, PROBLEMS HAVE BEEN RARE.
ONE WRONG MOVE AND THE WORLD'S MAFIA WILL HUNT YOU DOWN.

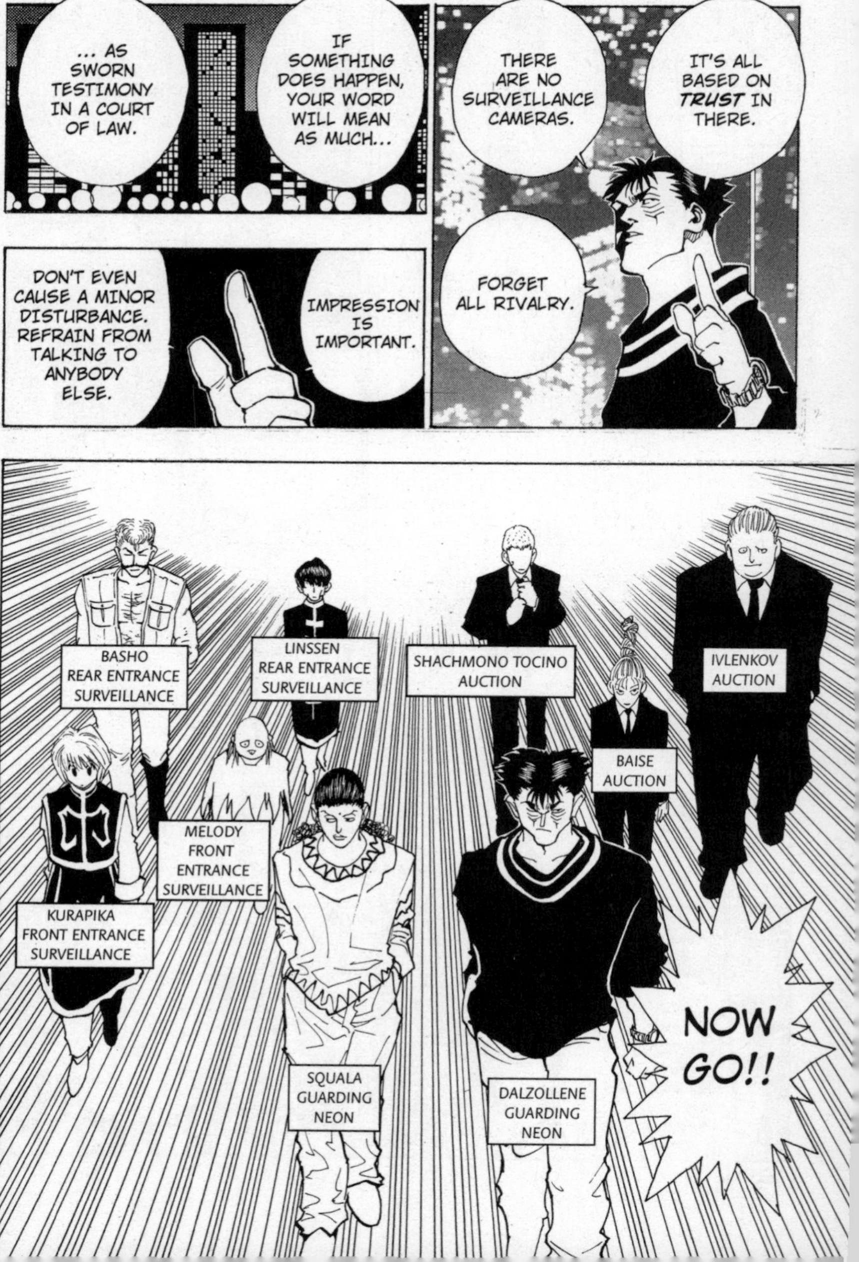
IT'S ALL BASED ON *TRUST* IN THERE.
THERE ARE NO SURVEILLANCE CAMERAS.
FORGET ALL RIVALRY.
IF SOMETHING DOES HAPPEN, YOUR WORD WILL MEAN AS MUCH...
... AS SWORN TESTIMONY IN A COURT OF LAW.
IMPRESSION IS IMPORTANT.
DON'T EVEN CAUSE A MINOR DISTURBANCE. REFRAIN FROM TALKING TO ANYBODY ELSE.
IVLENKOV AUCTION
SHACHMONO TOCINO AUCTION
LINSSEN REAR ENTRANCE SURVEILLANCE
BASHO REAR ENTRANCE SURVEILLANCE
BAISE AUCTION
MELODY FRONT ENTRANCE SURVEILLANCE
KURAPIKA FRONT ENTRANCE SURVEILLANCE
NOW GO!!
DALZOLLENE GUARDING NEON
SQUALA GUARDING NEON

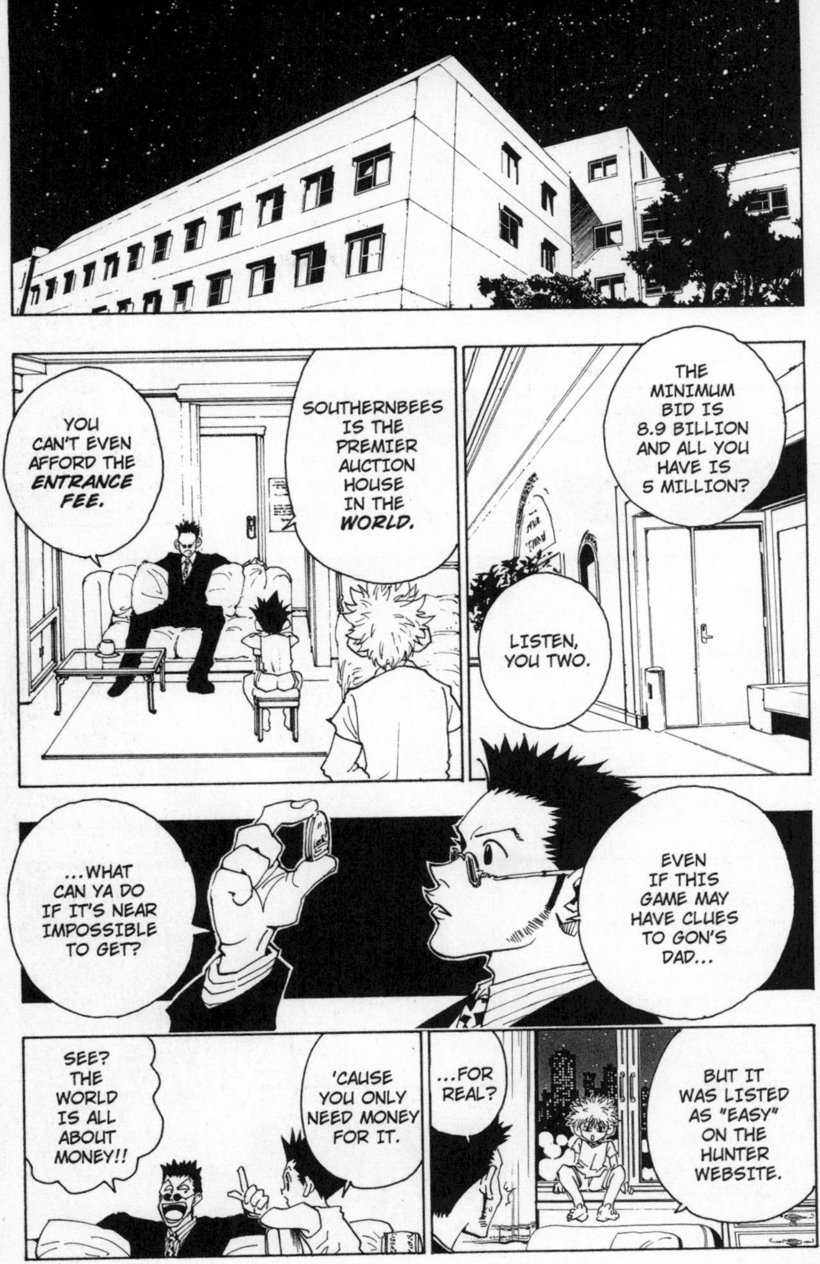
THE MINIMUM BID IS 8.9 BILLION AND ALL YOU HAVE IS 5 MILLION?
LISTEN, YOU TWO.
SOUTHERNBEES IS THE PREMIER AUCTION HOUSE IN THE *WORLD.*
YOU CAN'T EVEN AFFORD THE *ENTRANCE FEE.*
EVEN IF THIS GAME MAY HAVE CLUES TO GON'S DAD...
...WHAT CAN YA DO IF IT'S NEAR IMPOSSIBLE TO GET?
BUT IT WAS LISTED AS "EASY" ON THE HUNTER WEBSITE.
...FOR REAL?
'CAUSE YOU ONLY NEED MONEY FOR IT.
SEE? THE WORLD IS ALL ABOUT MONEY!!

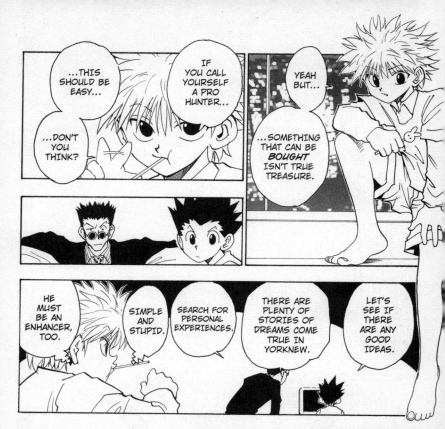

YEAH BUT...
...SOMETHING THAT CAN BE *BOUGHT* ISN'T TRUE TREASURE.
IF YOU CALL YOURSELF A PRO HUNTER...
...THIS SHOULD BE EASY...
...DON'T YOU THINK?
LET'S SEE IF THERE ARE ANY GOOD IDEAS.
THERE ARE PLENTY OF STORIES OF DREAMS COME TRUE IN YORKNEW.
SEARCH FOR PERSONAL EXPERIENCES.
SIMPLE AND STUPID.
HE MUST BE AN ENHANCER, TOO.
?
WHAT'S THIS?
BLIP
SWAP MEET: A GATHERING FOR THE AUCTION AND BARTER OF OBJECTS. THE BUYER EXHIBITS VARIOUS ITEMS, AND THE SELLER PICKS THE ONE HE LIKES AND OFFERS AN EXCHANGE WITH HIS OWN ITEM.
SEE ALSO: WINNER TAKE ALL, AND CONDITIONAL AUCTION

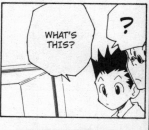

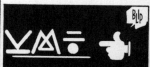

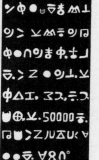

READ THIS WAY

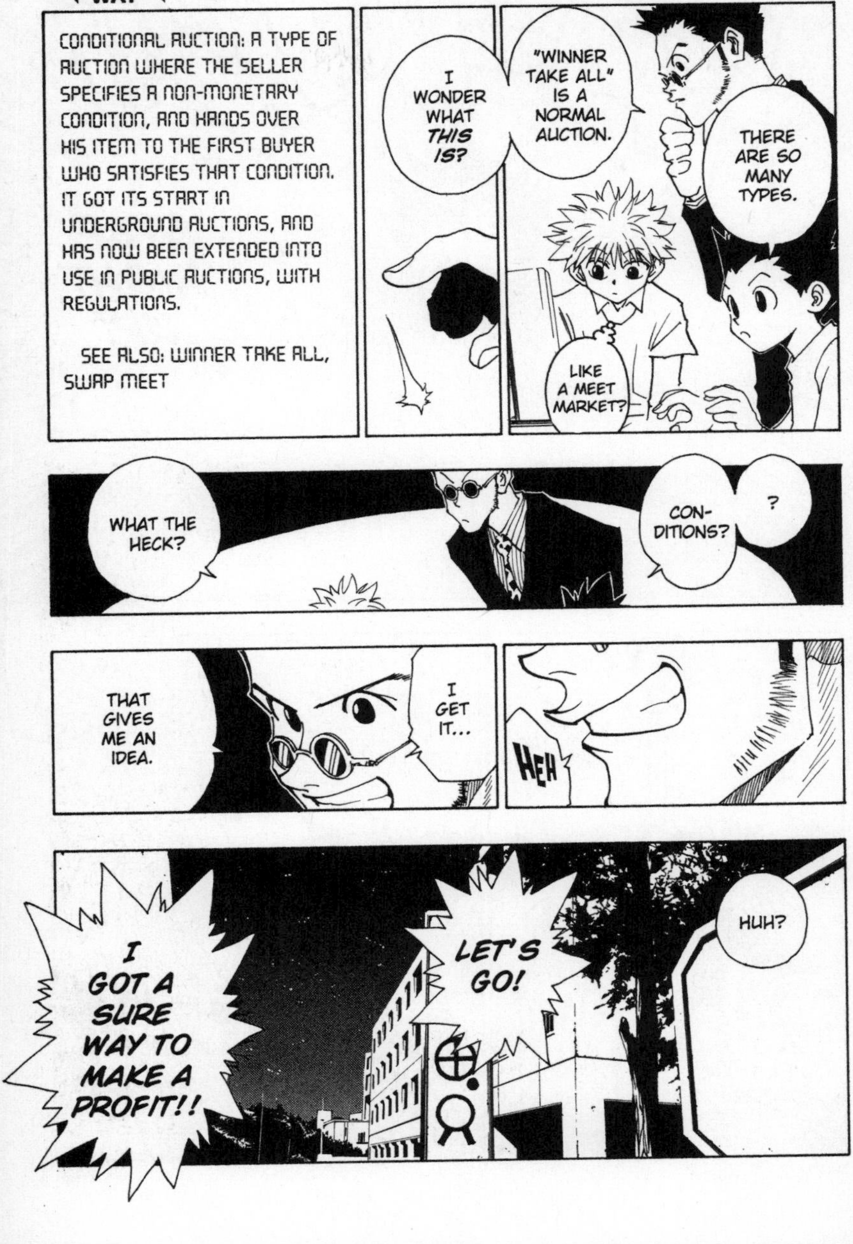
"WINNER TAKE ALL" IS A NORMAL AUCTION.
THERE ARE SO MANY TYPES.
LIKE A MEET MARKET?
I WONDER WHAT *THIS* IS?
CONDITIONAL AUCTION: A TYPE OF AUCTION WHERE THE SELLER SPECIFIES A NON-MONETARY CONDITION, AND HANDS OVER HIS ITEM TO THE FIRST BUYER WHO SATISFIES THAT CONDITION. IT GOT ITS START IN UNDERGROUND AUCTIONS, AND HAS NOW BEEN EXTENDED INTO USE IN PUBLIC AUCTIONS, WITH REGULATIONS.
SEE ALSO: WINNER TAKE ALL, SWAP MEET
?
CON-DITIONS?
WHAT THE HECK?
HEH
I GET IT...
THAT GIVES ME AN IDEA.
HUH?
LET'S GO!
I GOT A SURE WAY TO MAKE A PROFIT!!

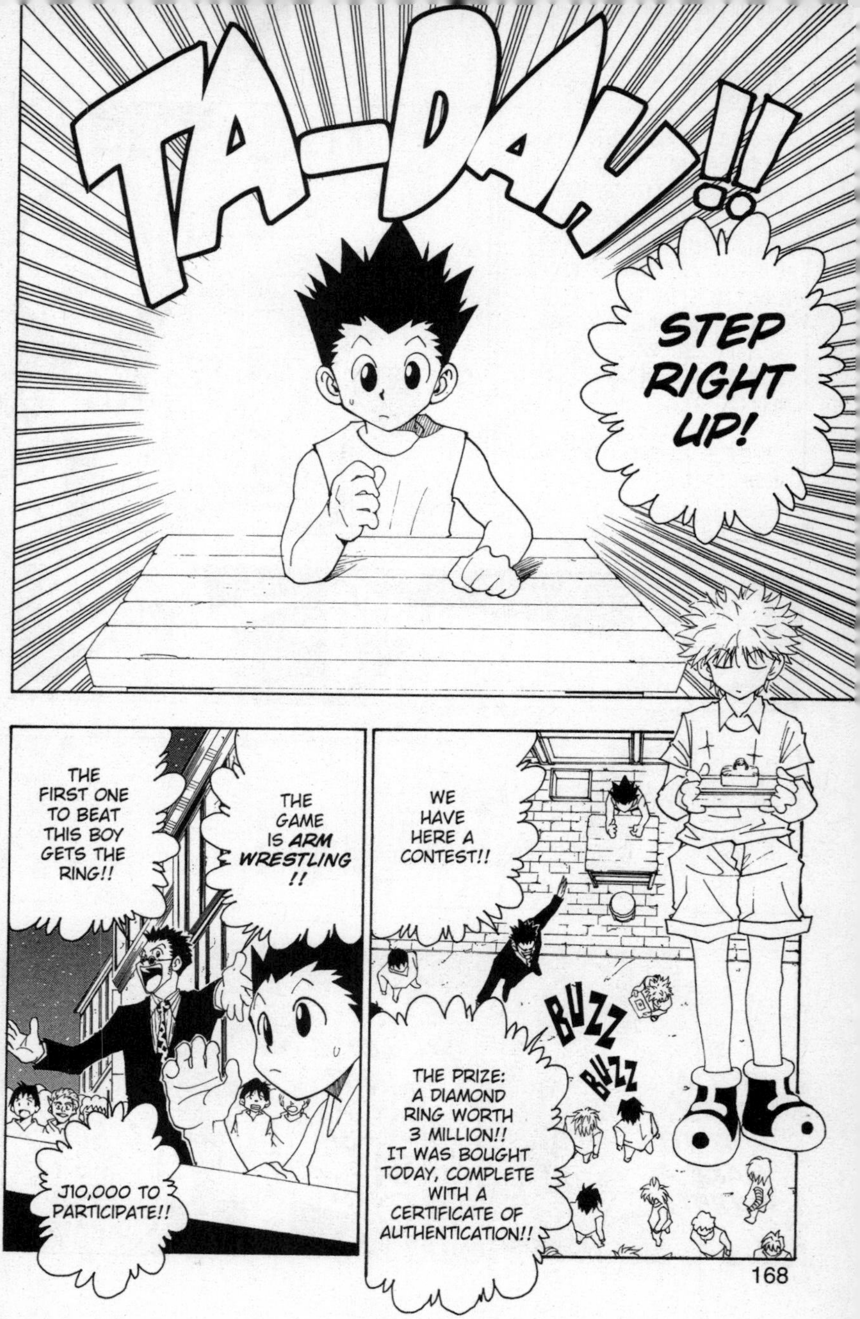
TA-DAH!!
STEP RIGHT UP!
WE HAVE HERE A CONTEST!!
BUZZ
BUZZ
THE PRIZE: A DIAMOND RING WORTH 3 MILLION!! IT WAS BOUGHT TODAY, COMPLETE WITH A CERTIFICATE OF AUTHENTICATION!!
THE GAME IS ARM WRESTLING!!
THE FIRST ONE TO BEAT THIS BOY GETS THE RING!!
J10,000 TO PARTICIPATE!!

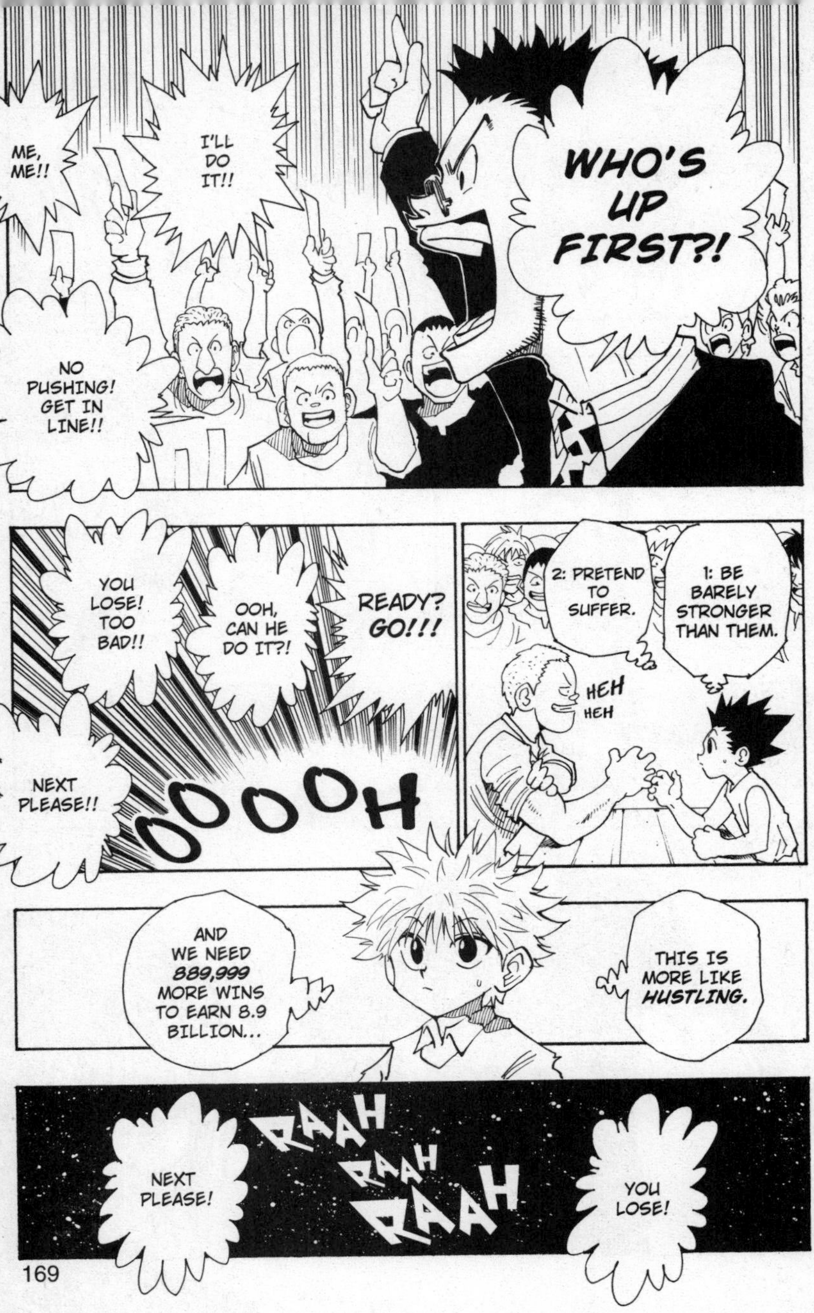
WHO'S UP FIRST?!
I'LL DO IT!!
ME, ME!!
NO PUSHING! GET IN LINE!!
1: BE BARELY STRONGER THAN THEM.
2: PRETEND TO SUFFER.
HEH HEH
READY? GO!!!
OOH, CAN HE DO IT?!
YOU LOSE! TOO BAD!!
OOOOH
NEXT PLEASE!!
THIS IS MORE LIKE HUSTLING.
AND WE NEED 889,999 MORE WINS TO EARN 8.9 BILLION...
YOU LOSE!
RAAH RAAH RAAH
NEXT PLEASE!

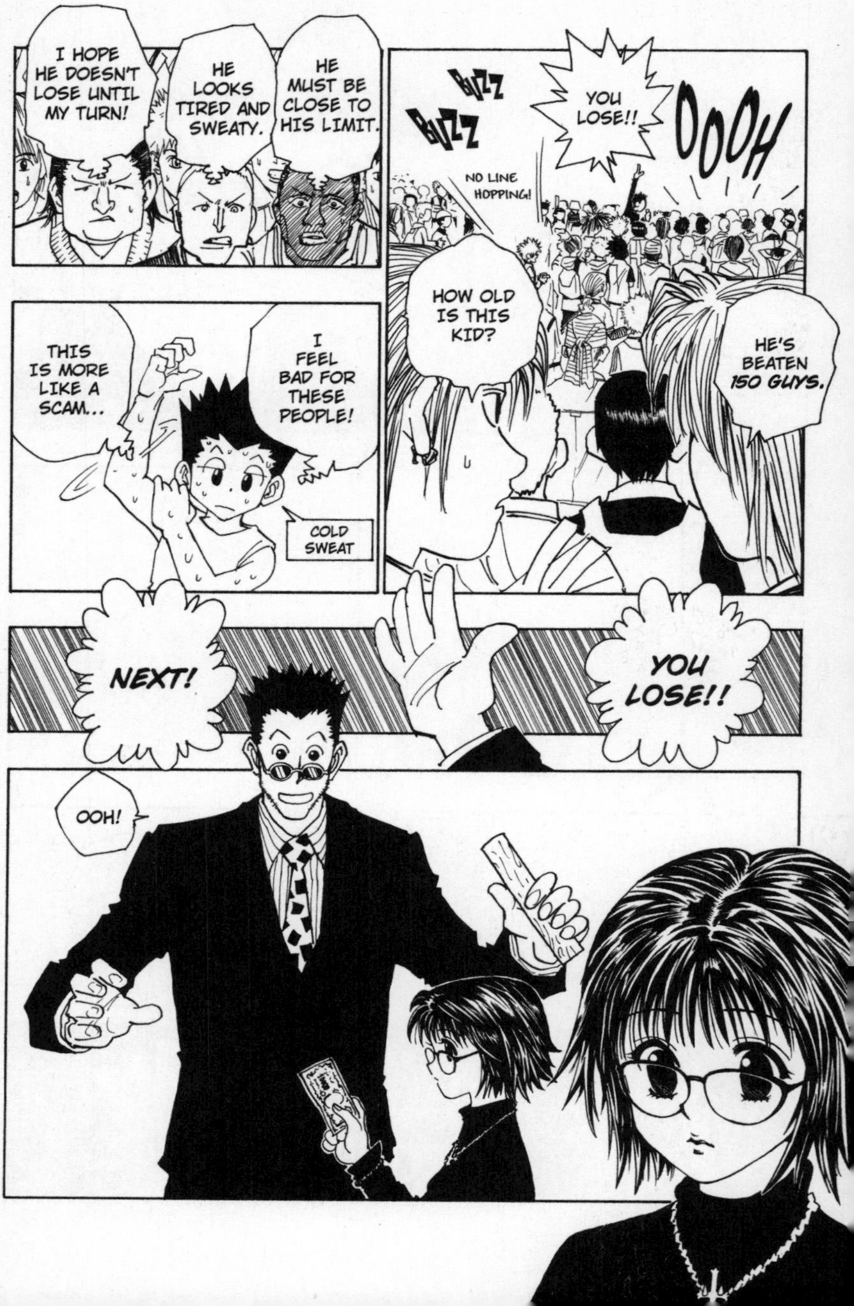
OOOH
YOU LOSE!!
BUZZ
BUZZ
NO LINE HOPPING!
HOW OLD IS THIS KID?
HE'S BEATEN 150 GUYS.
HE MUST BE CLOSE TO HIS LIMIT.
HE LOOKS TIRED AND SWEATY.
I HOPE HE DOESN'T LOSE UNTIL MY TURN!
I FEEL BAD FOR THESE PEOPLE!
COLD SWEAT
THIS IS MORE LIKE A SCAM...
YOU LOSE!!
NEXT!
OOH!

READ THIS WAY

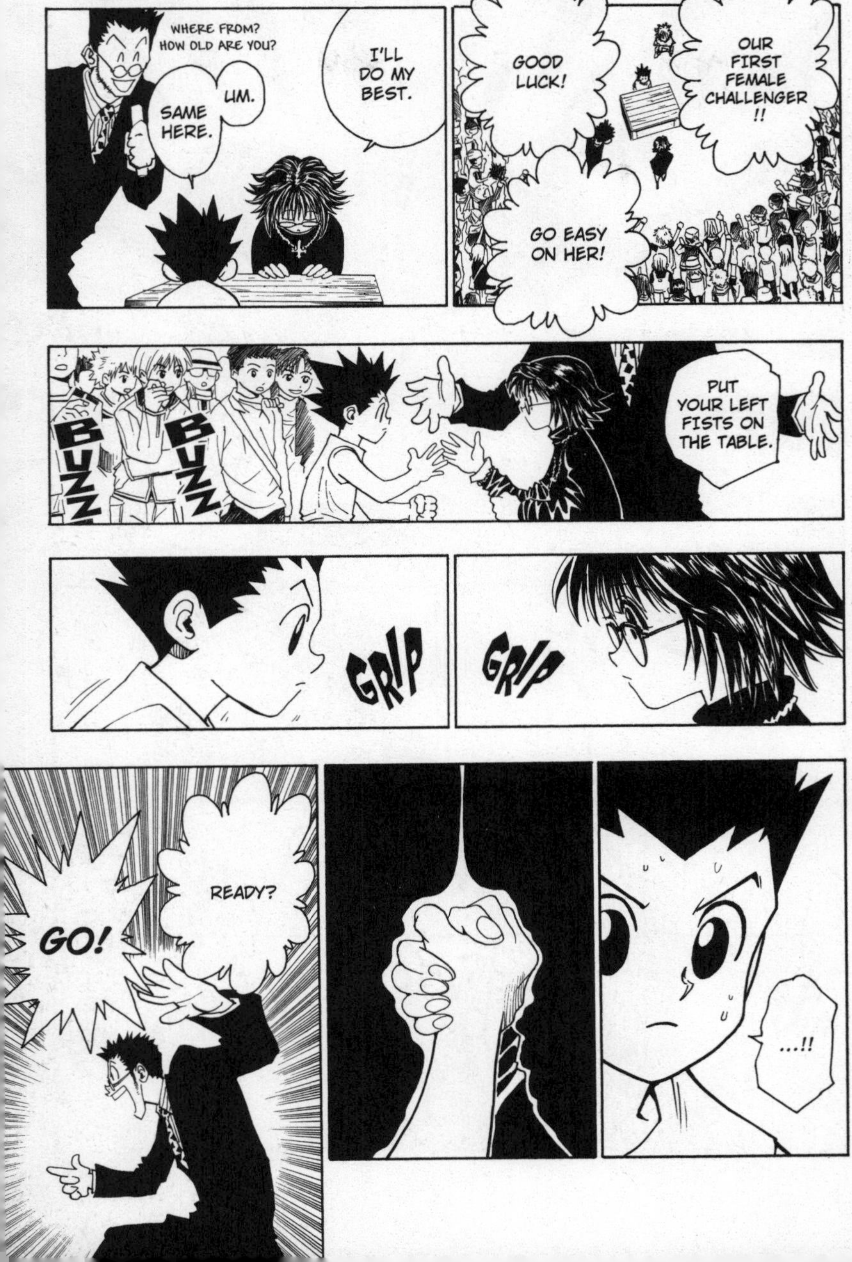
OUR FIRST FEMALE CHALLENGER !!
GOOD LUCK!
GO EASY ON HER!
WHERE FROM? HOW OLD ARE YOU?
UM.
I'LL DO MY BEST.
SAME HERE.
PUT YOUR LEFT FISTS ON THE TABLE.
BUZZ
BUZZ
GRIP
GRIP
...!!
READY?
GO!

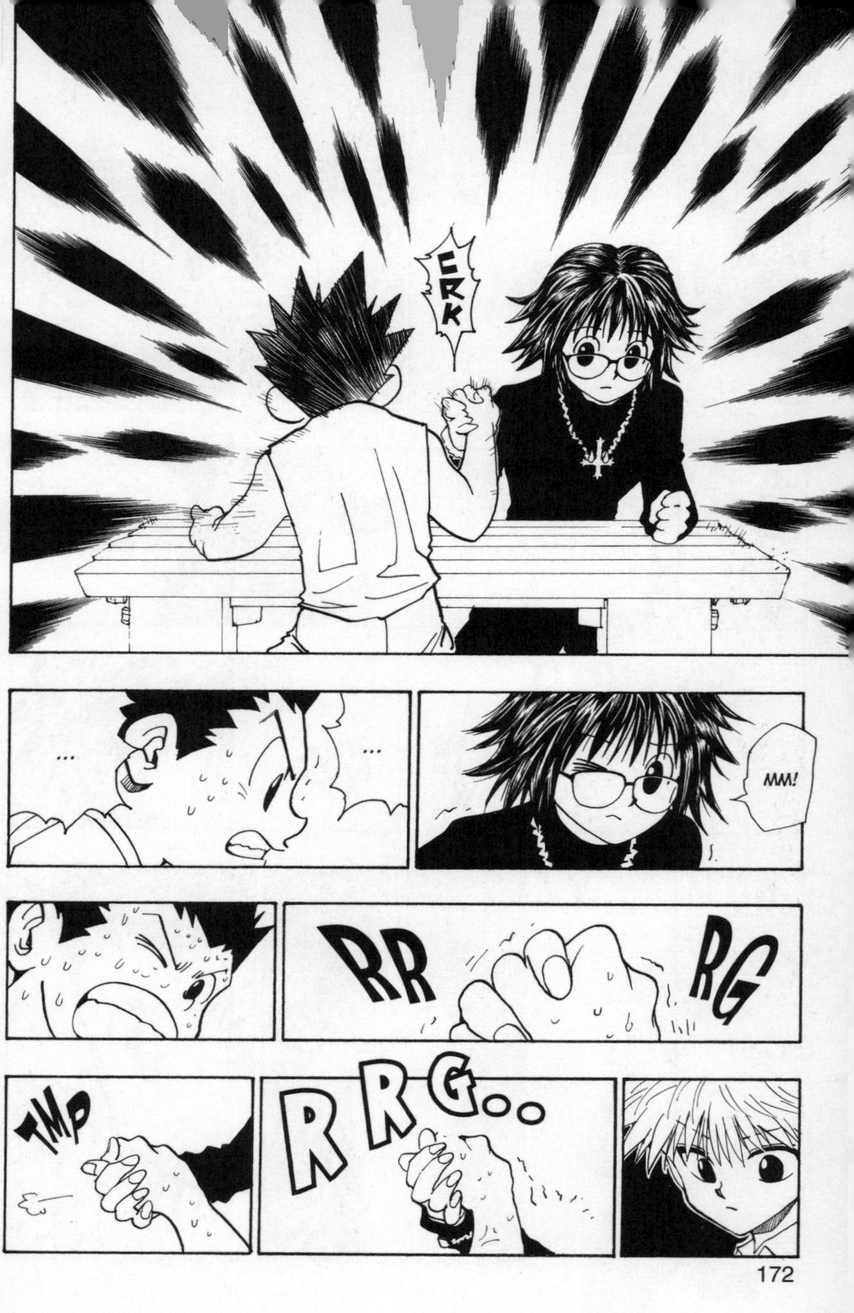
CRK
MM!
...
...
RR RG
RRG
TMP

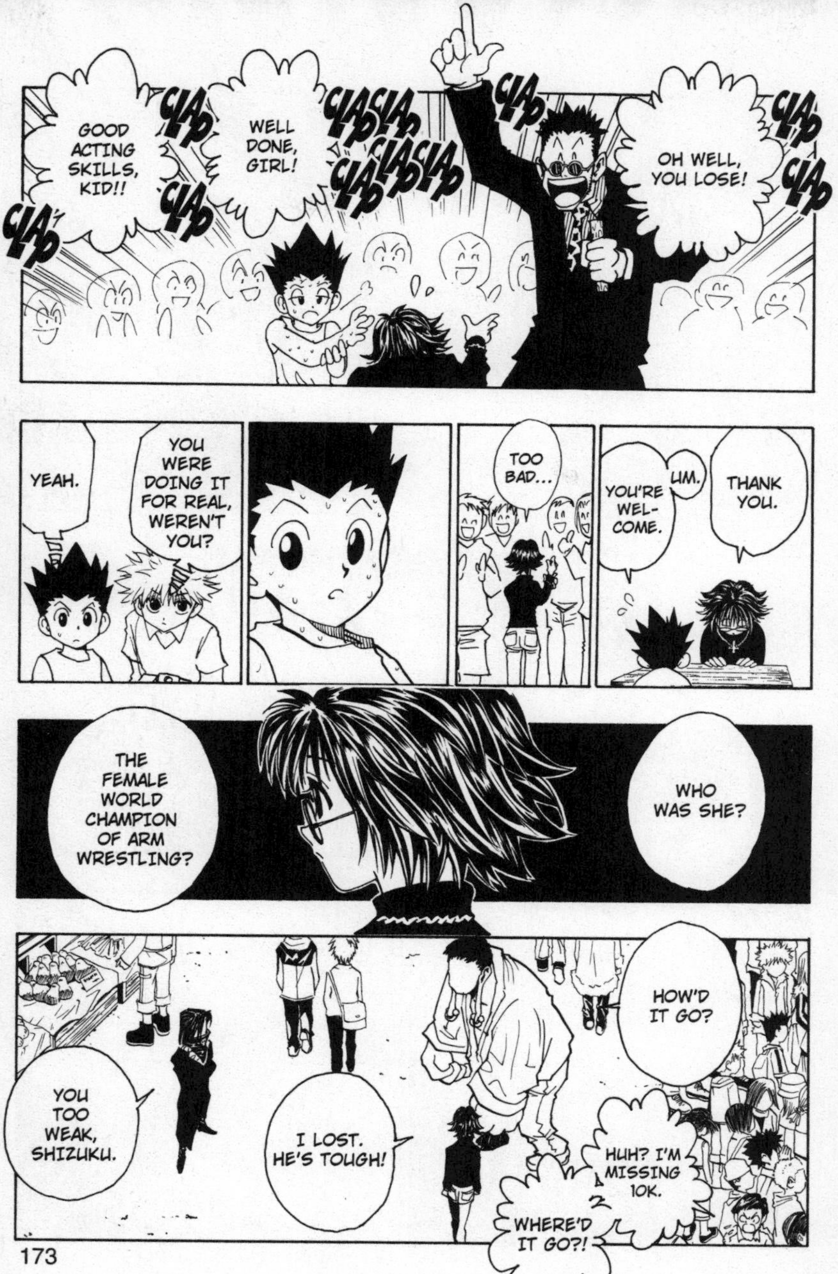
CLAP CLAP
OH WELL, YOU LOSE!
CLAP
CLAP CLAP CLAP CLAP
WELL DONE, GIRL!
CLAP CLAP
GOOD ACTING SKILLS, KID!!
CLAP
THANK YOU.
UM.
YOU'RE WEL-COME.
TOO BAD...
YOU WERE DOING IT FOR REAL, WEREN'T YOU?
YEAH.
WHO WAS SHE?
THE FEMALE WORLD CHAMPION OF ARM WRESTLING?
HOW'D IT GO?
HUH? I'M MISSING 10K.
WHERE'D IT GO?!
I LOST. HE'S TOUGH!
YOU TOO WEAK, SHIZUKU.

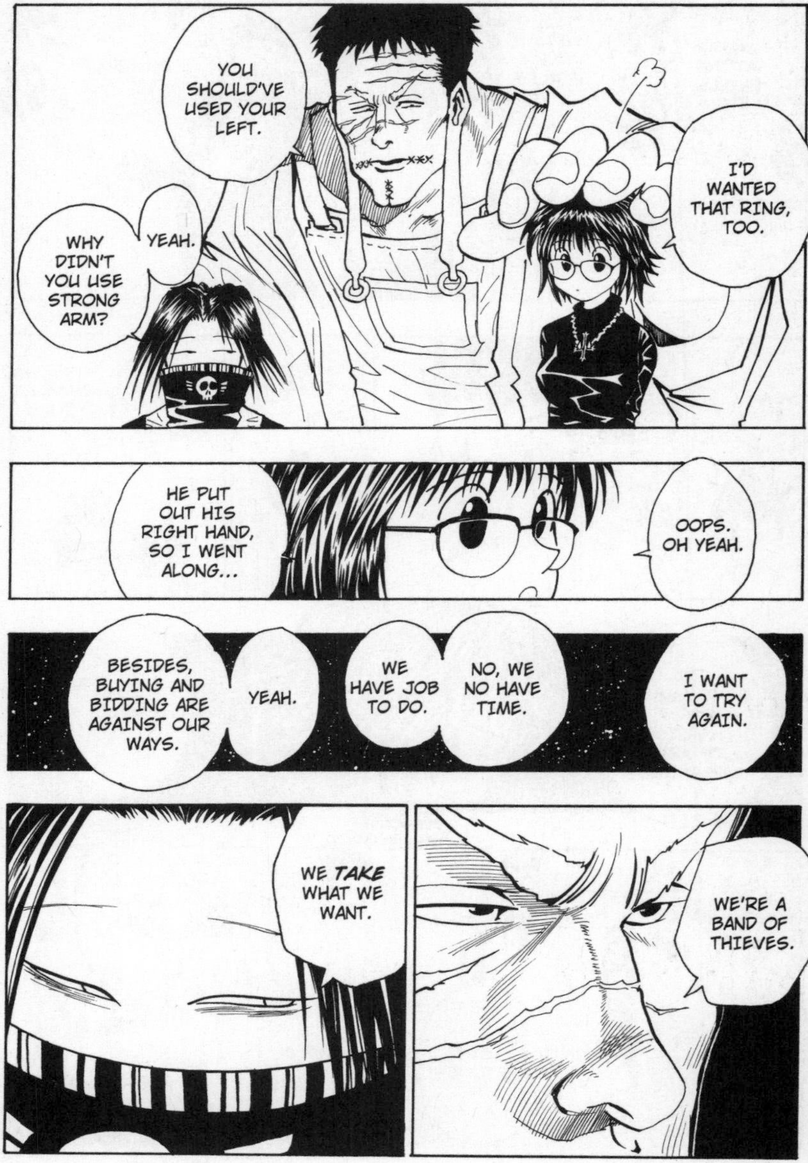
I'D WANTED THAT RING, TOO.
YOU SHOULD'VE USED YOUR LEFT.
YEAH.
WHY DIDN'T YOU USE STRONG ARM?
OOPS. OH YEAH.
HE PUT OUT HIS RIGHT HAND, SO I WENT ALONG...
I WANT TO TRY AGAIN.
NO, WE NO HAVE TIME.
WE HAVE JOB TO DO.
YEAH.
BESIDES, BUYING AND BIDDING ARE AGAINST OUR WAYS.
WE'RE A BAND OF THIEVES.
WE *TAKE* WHAT WE WANT.

READ THIS WAY

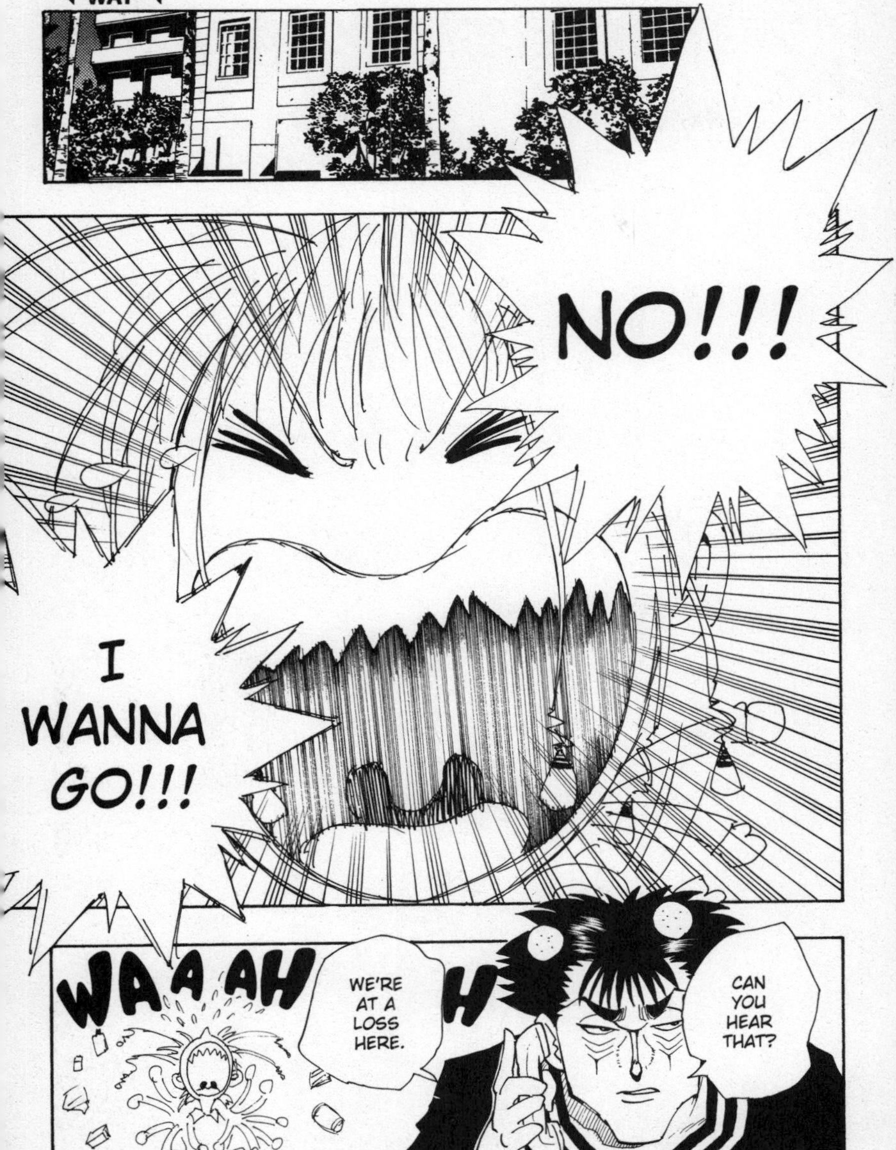
NO!!!
I WANNA GO!!!
CAN YOU HEAR THAT?
WE'RE AT A LOSS HERE.
WAAAHH

Chapter 73

September 1st (Part 2)

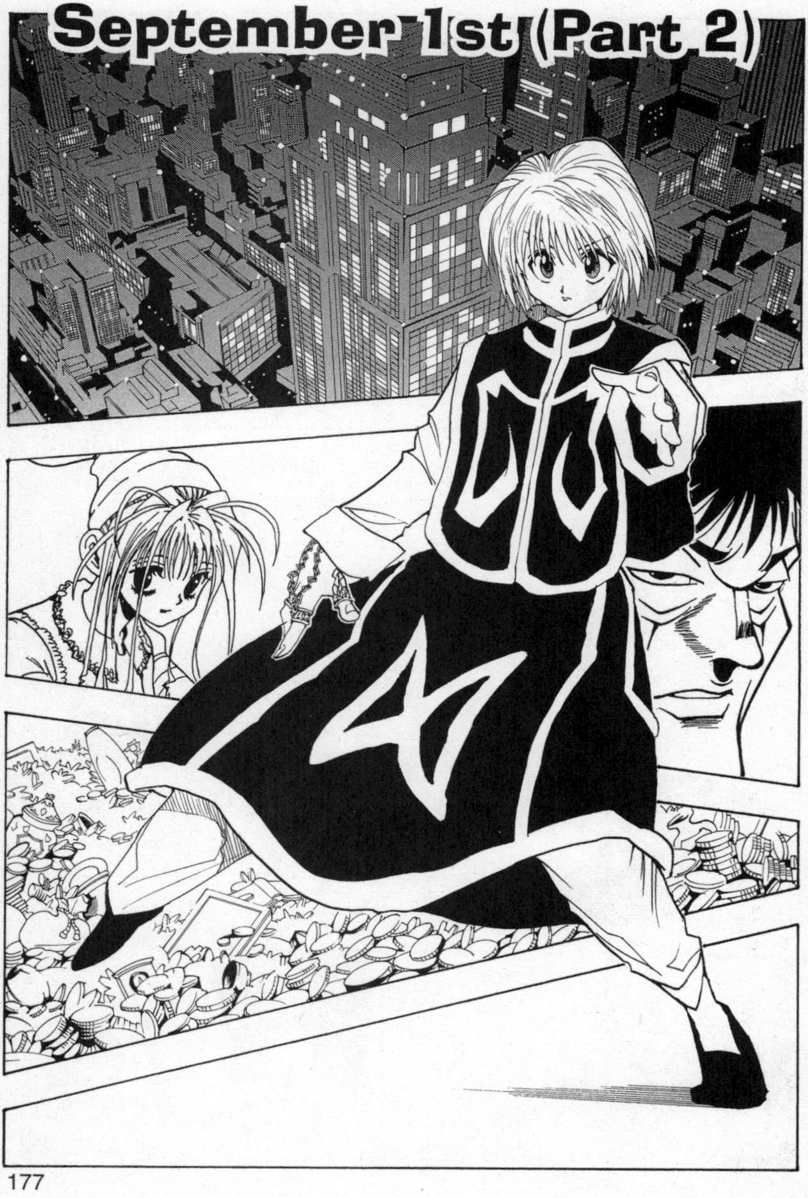

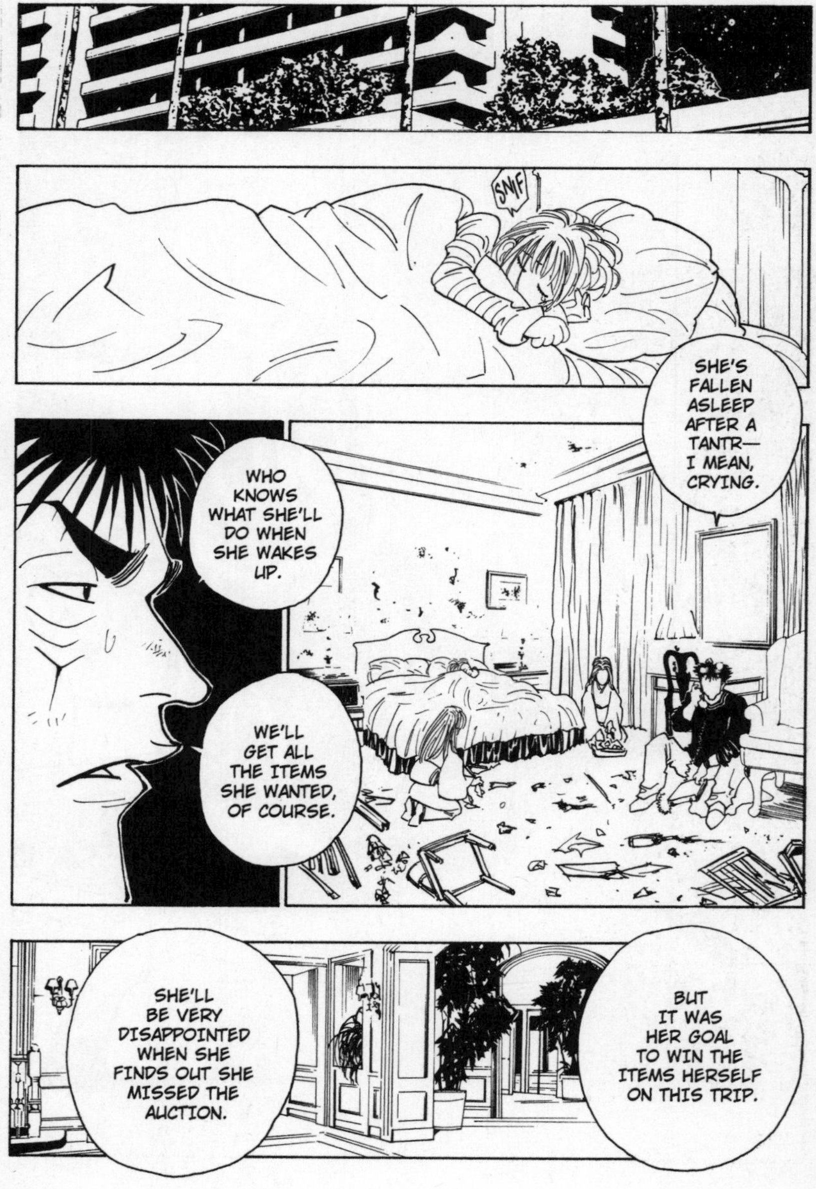
SNIF
SHE'S FALLEN ASLEEP AFTER A TANTR— I MEAN, CRYING.
WHO KNOWS WHAT SHE'LL DO WHEN SHE WAKES UP.
WE'LL GET ALL THE ITEMS SHE WANTED, OF COURSE.
BUT IT WAS HER GOAL TO WIN THE ITEMS HERSELF ON THIS TRIP.
SHE'LL BE VERY DISAPPOINTED WHEN SHE FINDS OUT SHE MISSED THE AUCTION.

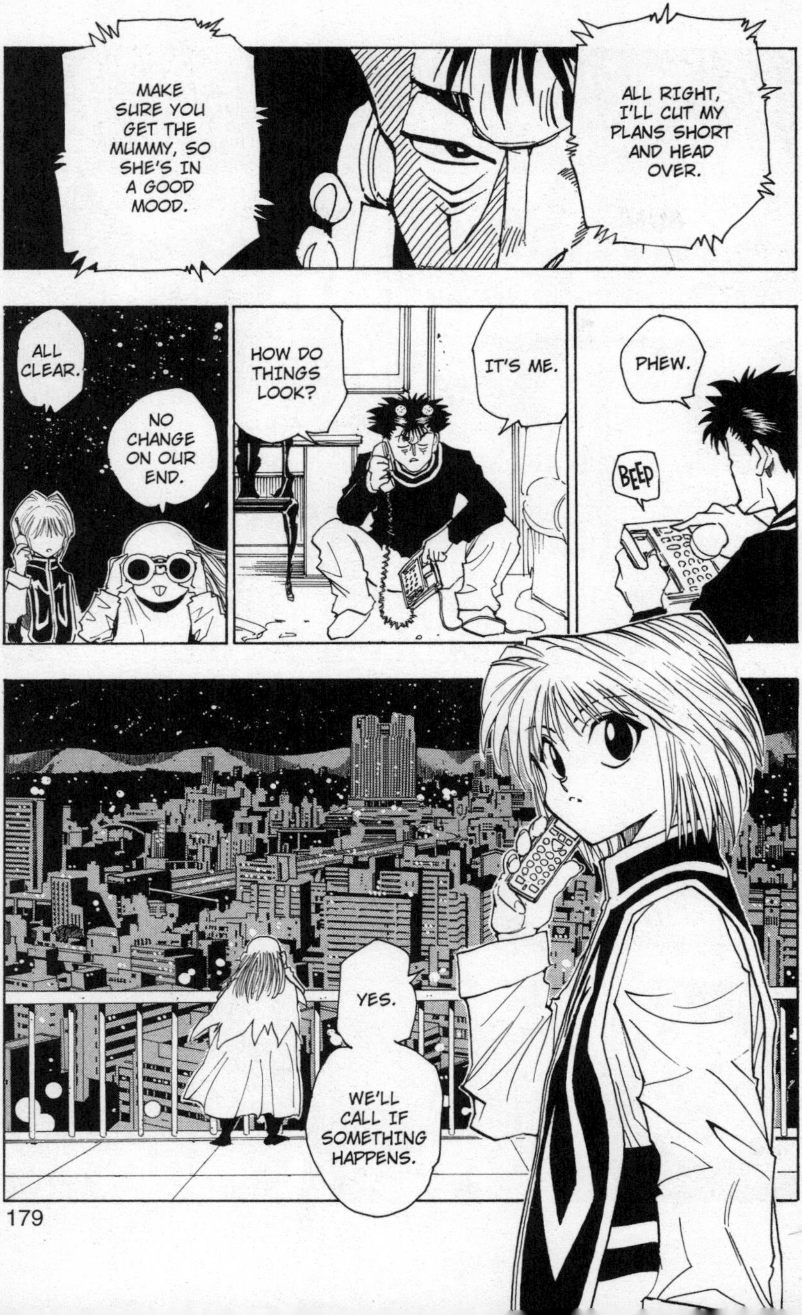
ALL RIGHT, I'LL CUT MY PLANS SHORT AND HEAD OVER.
MAKE SURE YOU GET THE MUMMY, SO SHE'S IN A GOOD MOOD.
PHEW.
BEEP
IT'S ME.
HOW DO THINGS LOOK?
ALL CLEAR.
NO CHANGE ON OUR END.
YES.
WE'LL CALL IF SOMETHING HAPPENS.

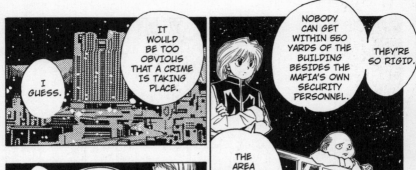

NOBODY CAN GET WITHIN 550 YARDS OF THE BUILDING BESIDES THE MAFIA'S OWN SECURITY PERSONNEL.
THEY'RE SO RIGID.
THE AREA WOULD BE OVERRUN BY THUGS OTHERWISE.
IT WOULD BE TOO OBVIOUS THAT A CRIME IS TAKING PLACE.
I GUESS.
...
MAY I ASK YOU A QUESTION?
SURE.
THE SCARLET EYES.
WHAT DO THEY MEAN TO YOU?
...
WHY DO YOU ASK?

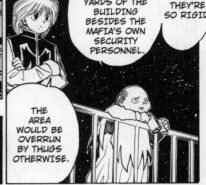

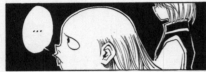

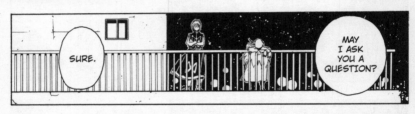

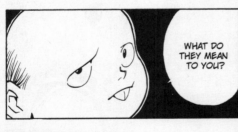

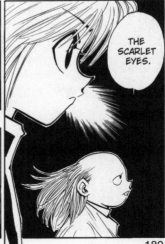

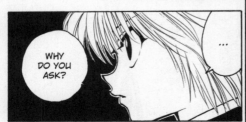

READ THIS WAY

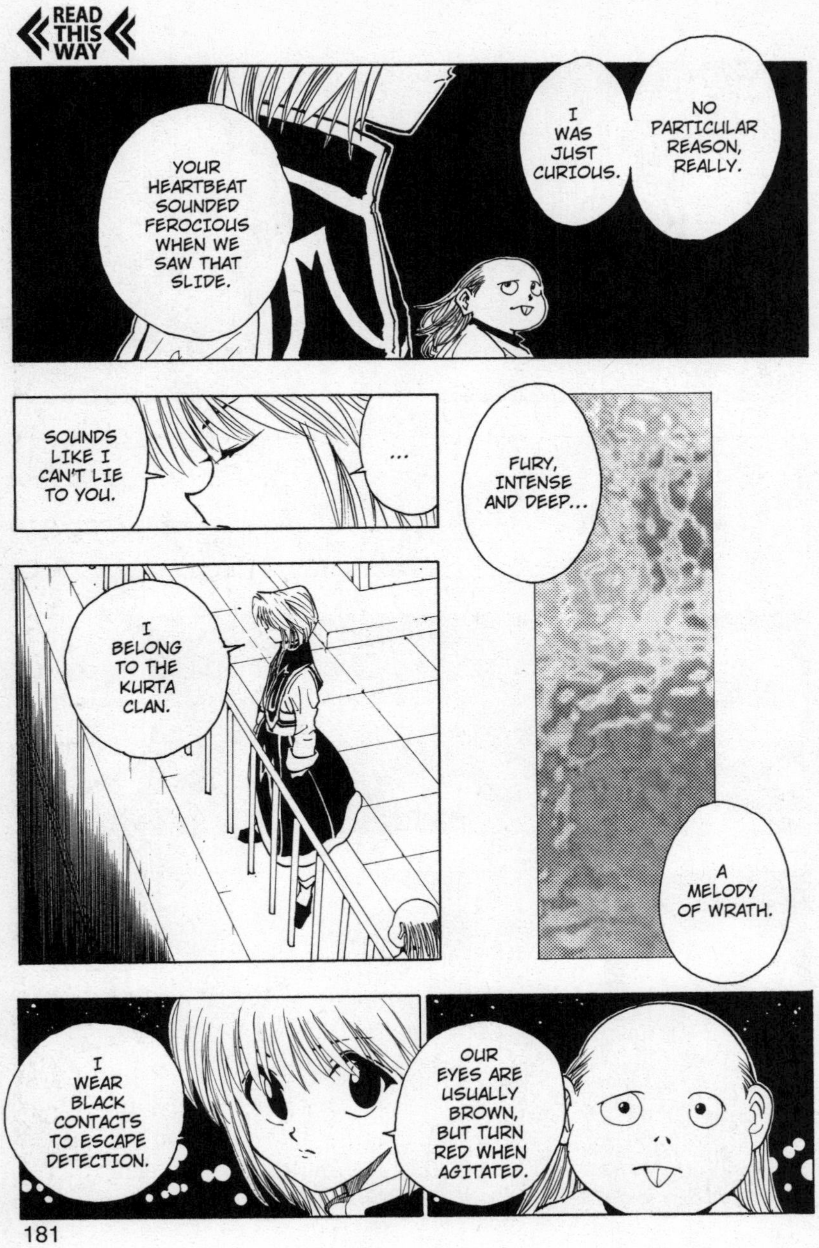
NO PARTICULAR REASON, REALLY.
I WAS JUST CURIOUS.
YOUR HEARTBEAT SOUNDED FEROCIOUS WHEN WE SAW THAT SLIDE.
FURY, INTENSE AND DEEP...
A MELODY OF WRATH.
...
SOUNDS LIKE I CAN'T LIE TO YOU.
I BELONG TO THE KURTA CLAN.
OUR EYES ARE USUALLY BROWN, BUT TURN RED WHEN AGITATED.
I WEAR BLACK CONTACTS TO ESCAPE DETECTION.

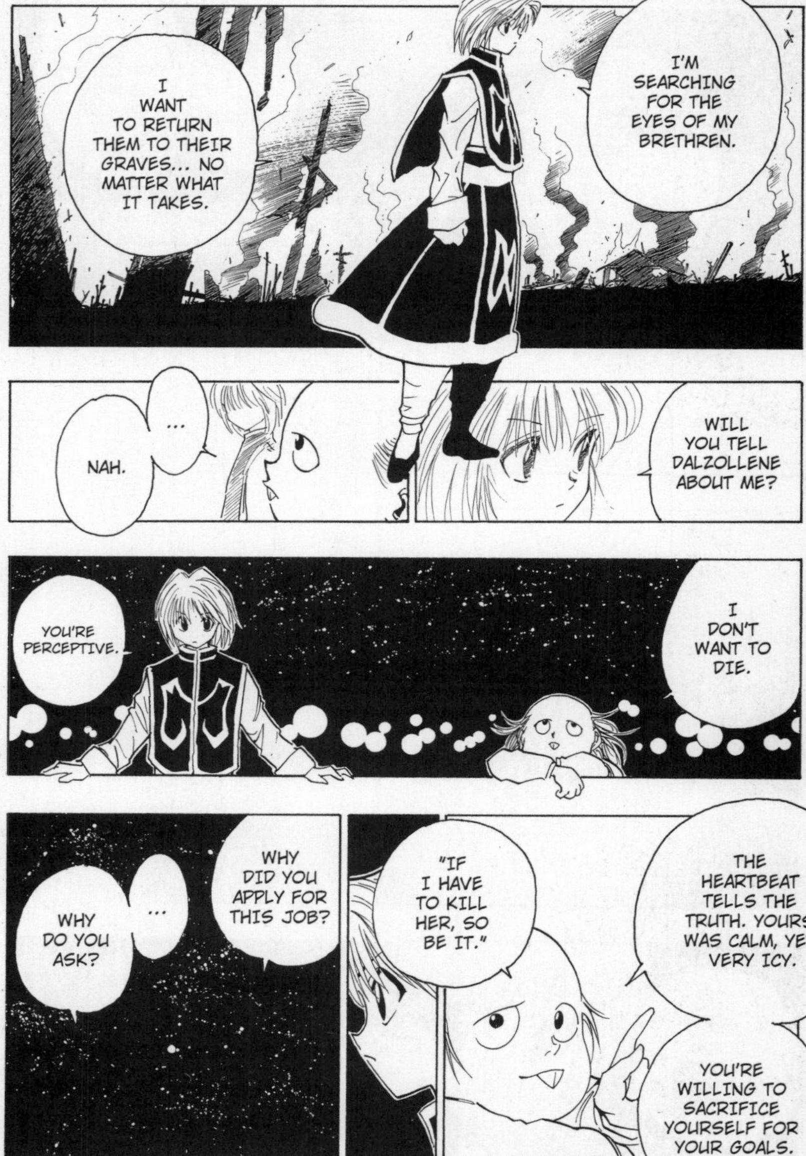
I'M SEARCHING FOR THE EYES OF MY BRETHREN.
I WANT TO RETURN THEM TO THEIR GRAVES... NO MATTER WHAT IT TAKES.
WILL YOU TELL DALZOLLENE ABOUT ME?
...
NAH.
I DON'T WANT TO DIE.
YOU'RE PERCEPTIVE.
THE HEARTBEAT TELLS THE TRUTH. YOURS WAS CALM, YET VERY ICY.
YOU'RE WILLING TO SACRIFICE YOURSELF FOR YOUR GOALS.
"IF I HAVE TO KILL HER, SO BE IT."
WHY DID YOU APPLY FOR THIS JOB?
...
WHY DO YOU ASK?

READ THIS WAY

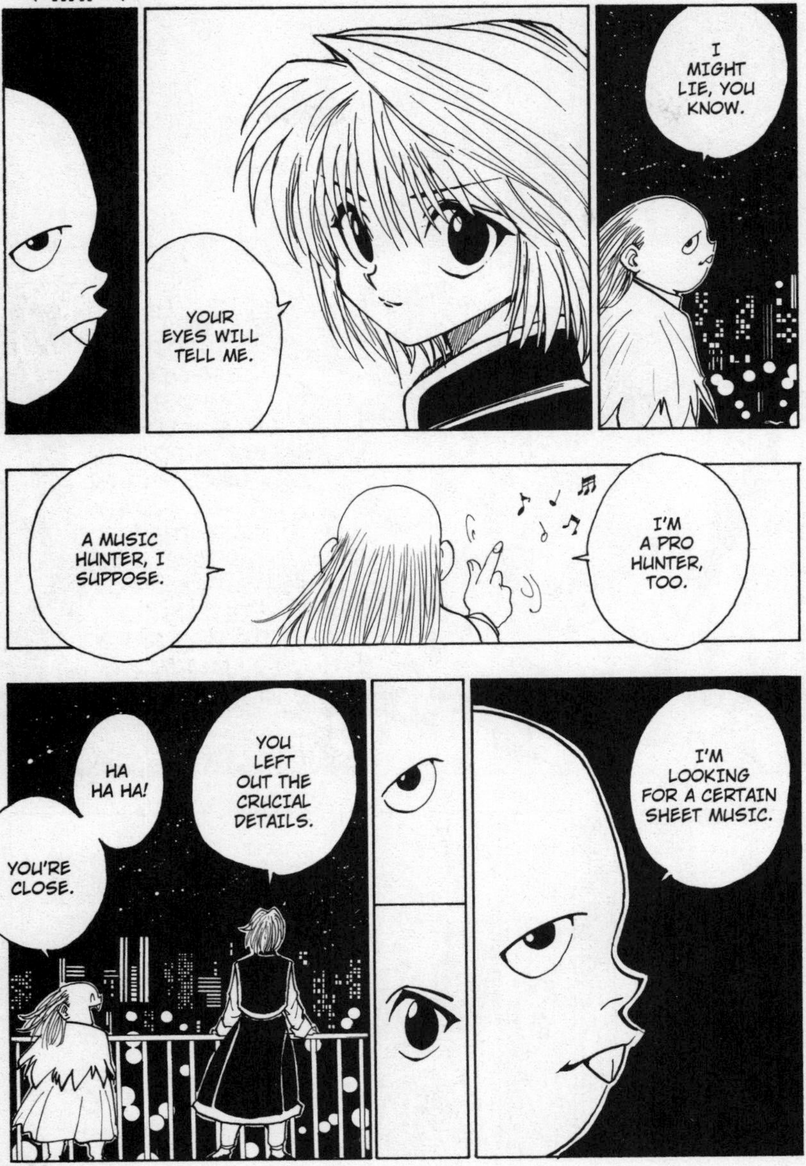
I MIGHT LIE, YOU KNOW.
YOUR EYES WILL TELL ME.
I'M A PRO HUNTER, TOO.
A MUSIC HUNTER, I SUPPOSE.
I'M LOOKING FOR A CERTAIN SHEET MUSIC.
YOU LEFT OUT THE CRUCIAL DETAILS.
HA HA HA!
YOU'RE CLOSE.

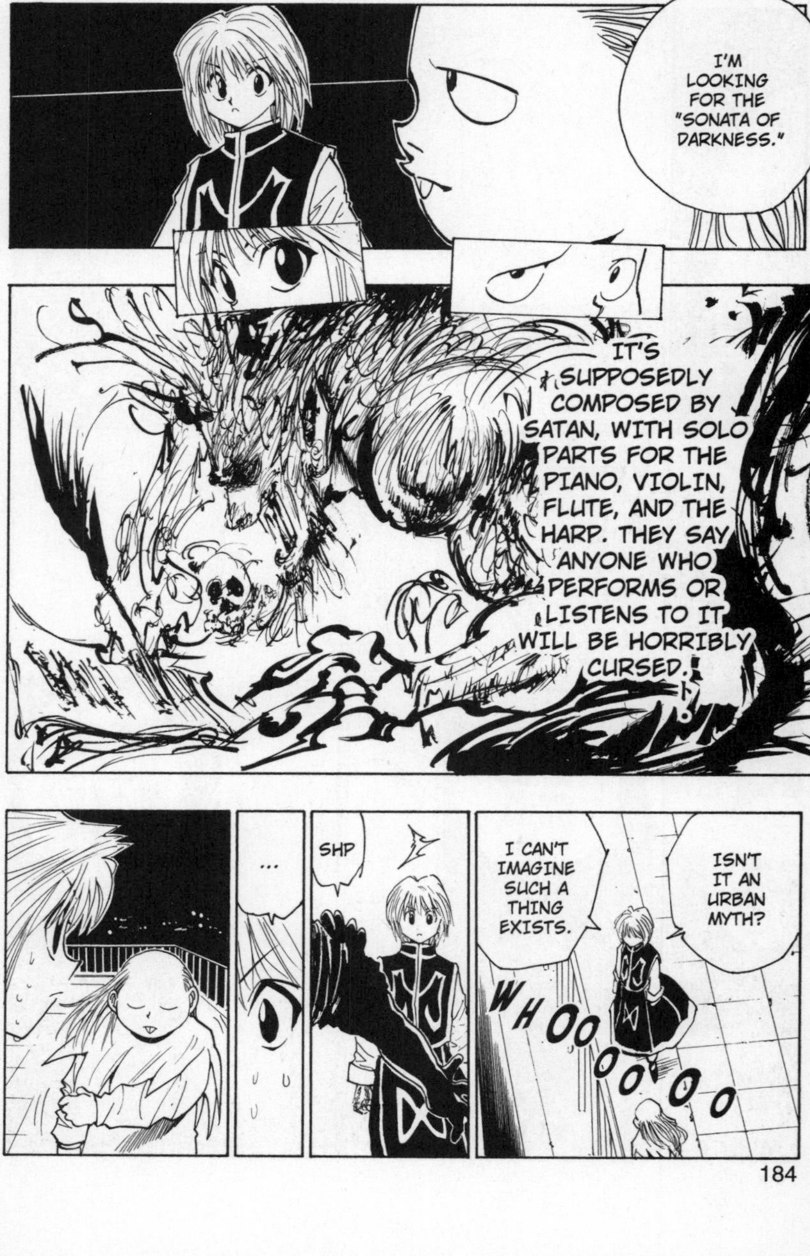
I'M LOOKING FOR THE "SONATA OF DARKNESS."
IT'S SUPPOSEDLY COMPOSED BY SATAN, WITH SOLO PARTS FOR THE PIANO, VIOLIN, FLUTE, AND THE HARP. THEY SAY ANYONE WHO PERFORMS OR LISTENS TO IT WILL BE HORRIBLY CURSED.
ISN'T IT AN URBAN MYTH?
I CAN'T IMAGINE SUCH A THING EXISTS.
WHOOOOOOOOO
SHP
...

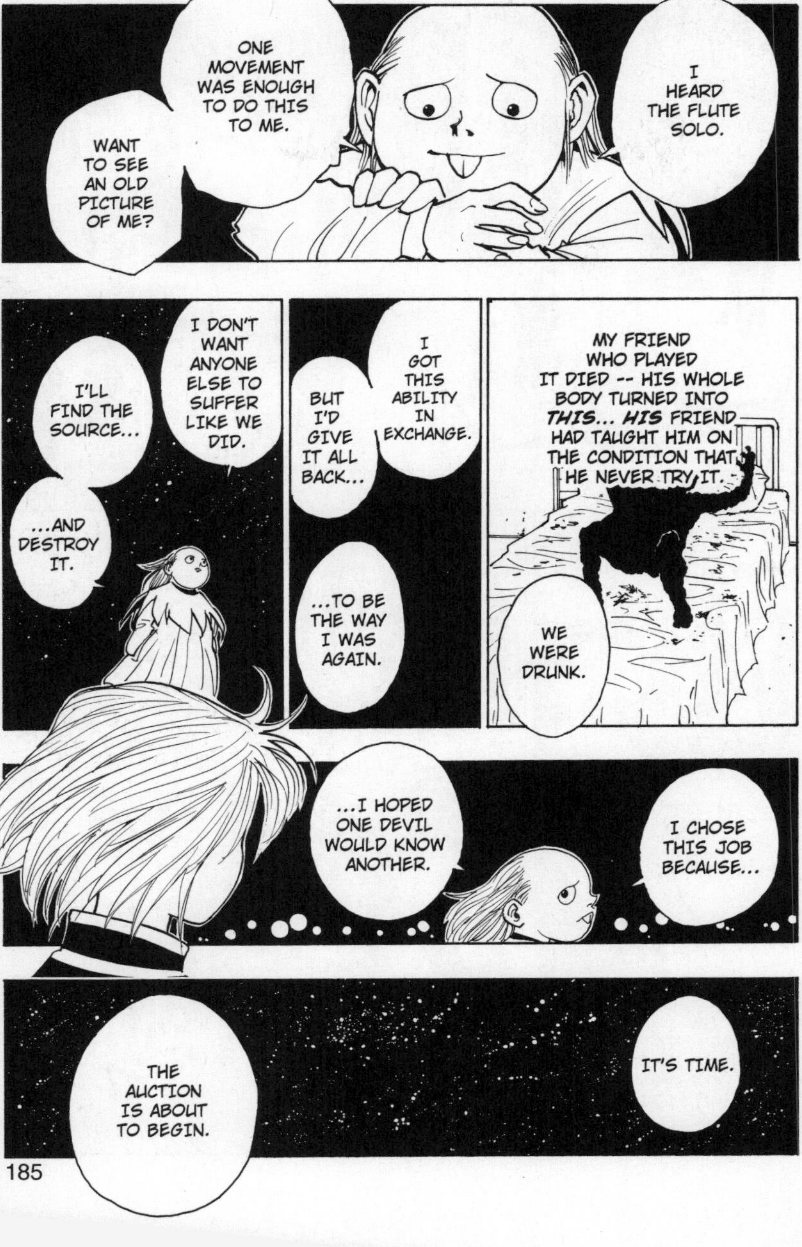
I HEARD THE FLUTE SOLO.
ONE MOVEMENT WAS ENOUGH TO DO THIS TO ME.
WANT TO SEE AN OLD PICTURE OF ME?
MY FRIEND WHO PLAYED IT DIED -- HIS WHOLE BODY TURNED INTO *THIS*... *HIS* FRIEND HAD TAUGHT HIM ON THE CONDITION THAT HE NEVER TRY IT.
WE WERE DRUNK.
I GOT THIS ABILITY IN EXCHANGE.
BUT I'D GIVE IT ALL BACK...
...TO BE THE WAY I WAS AGAIN.
I DON'T WANT ANYONE ELSE TO SUFFER LIKE WE DID.
I'LL FIND THE SOURCE...
...AND DESTROY IT.
I CHOSE THIS JOB BECAUSE...
...I HOPED ONE DEVIL WOULD KNOW ANOTHER.
IT'S TIME.
THE AUCTION IS ABOUT TO BEGIN.

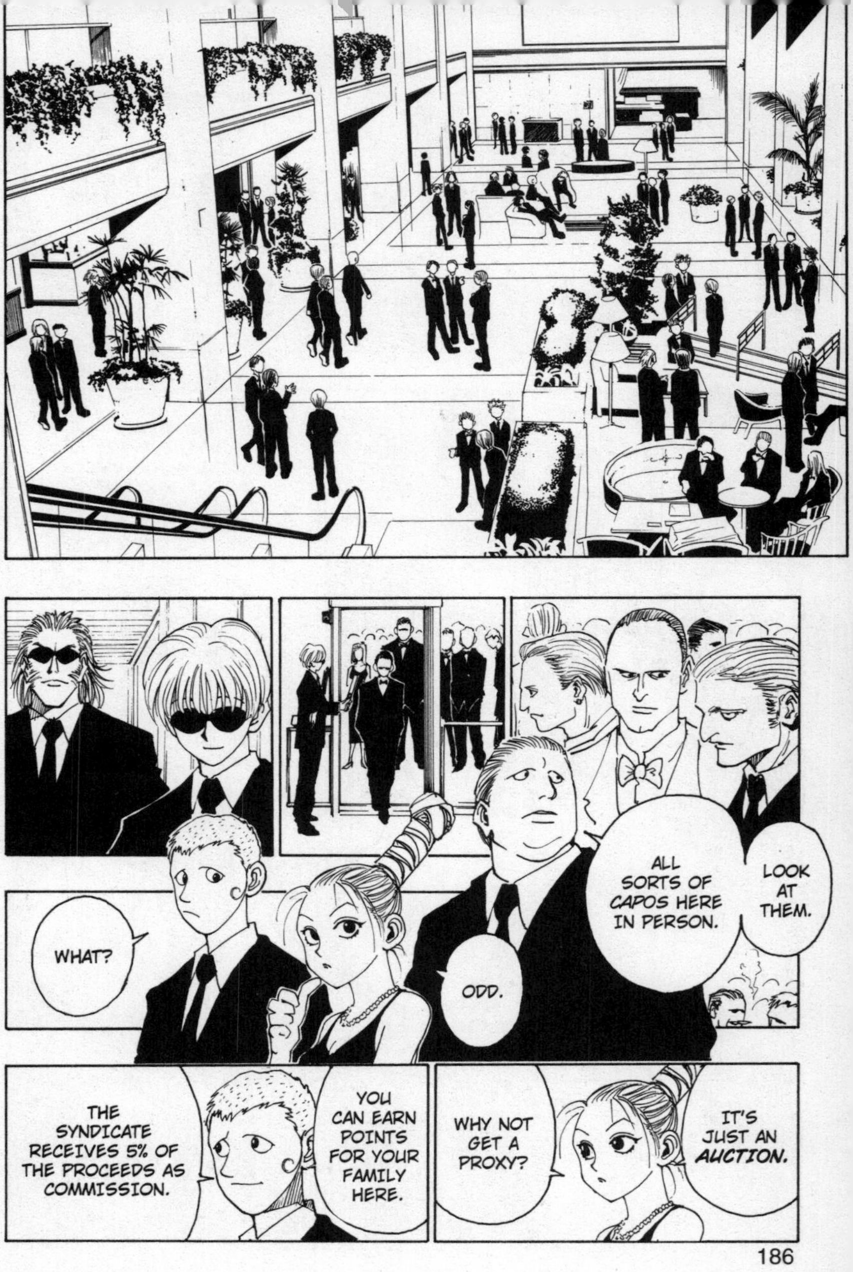
LOOK AT THEM.
ALL SORTS OF CAPOS HERE IN PERSON.
ODD.
WHAT?
IT'S JUST AN AUCTION.
WHY NOT GET A PROXY?
YOU CAN EARN POINTS FOR YOUR FAMILY HERE.
THE SYNDICATE RECEIVES 5% OF THE PROCEEDS AS COMMISSION.

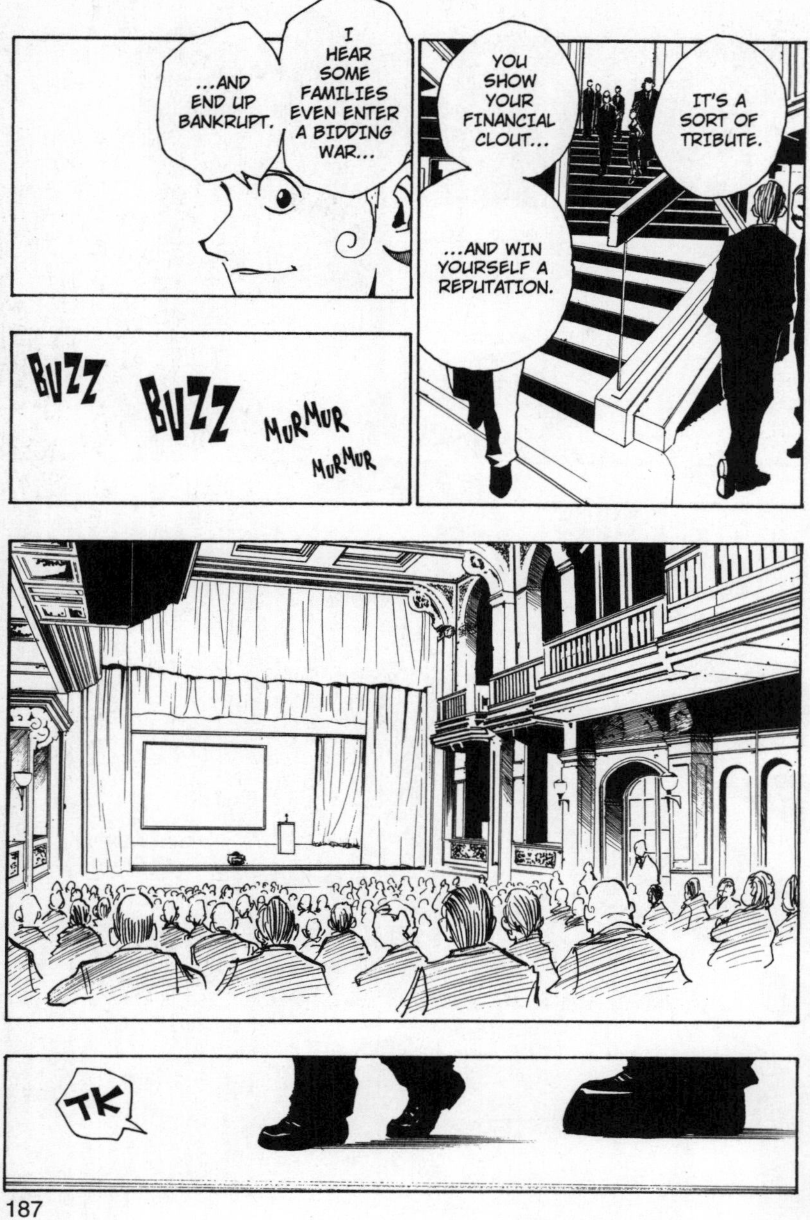
IT'S A SORT OF TRIBUTE.
YOU SHOW YOUR FINANCIAL CLOUT...
...AND WIN YOURSELF A REPUTATION.
I HEAR SOME FAMILIES EVEN ENTER A BIDDING WAR...
...AND END UP BANKRUPT.
BUZZ
BUZZ
MURMUR
MURMUR
TK

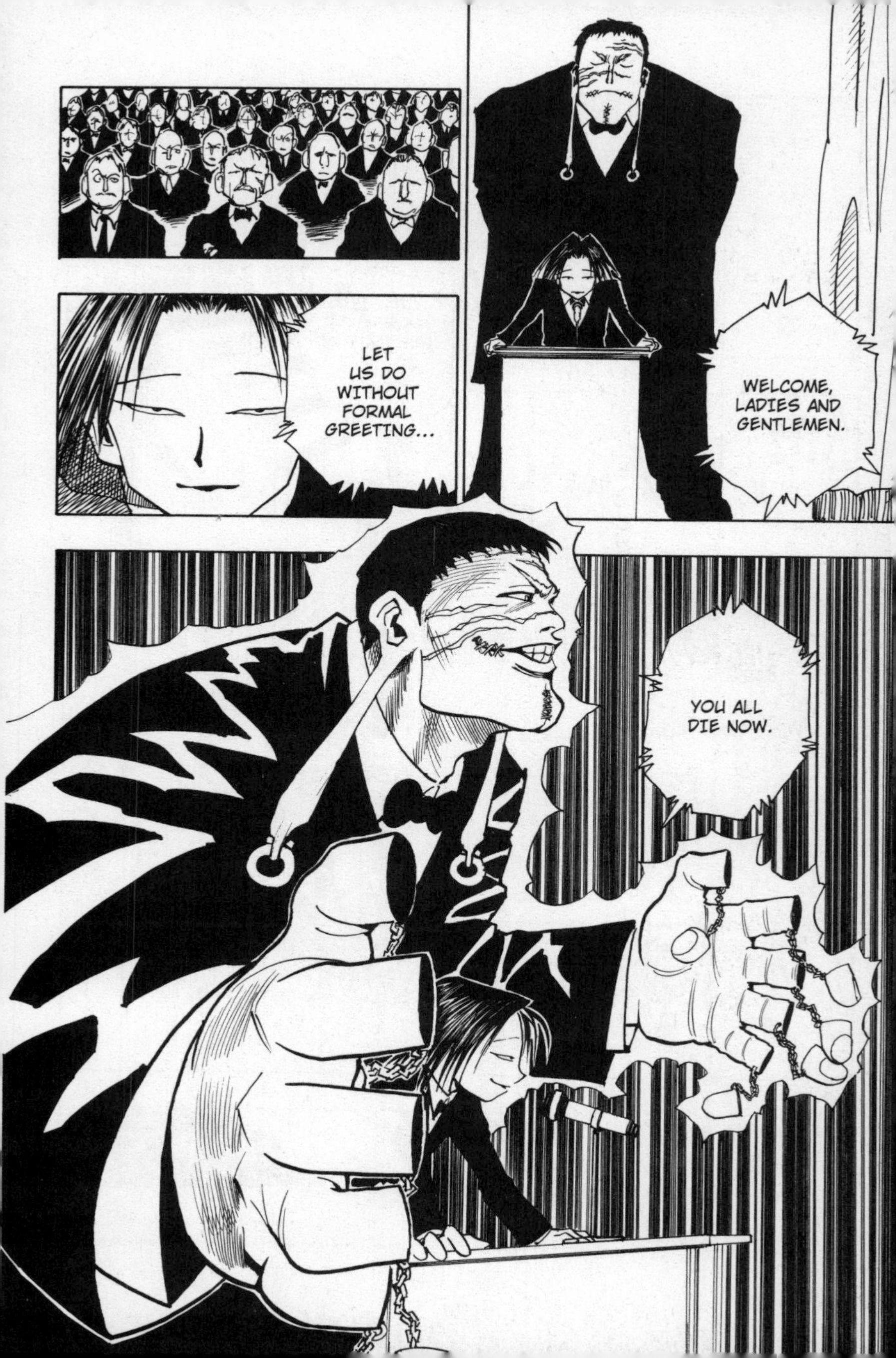
WELCOME, LADIES AND GENTLEMEN.
LET US DO WITHOUT FORMAL GREETING...
YOU ALL DIE NOW.

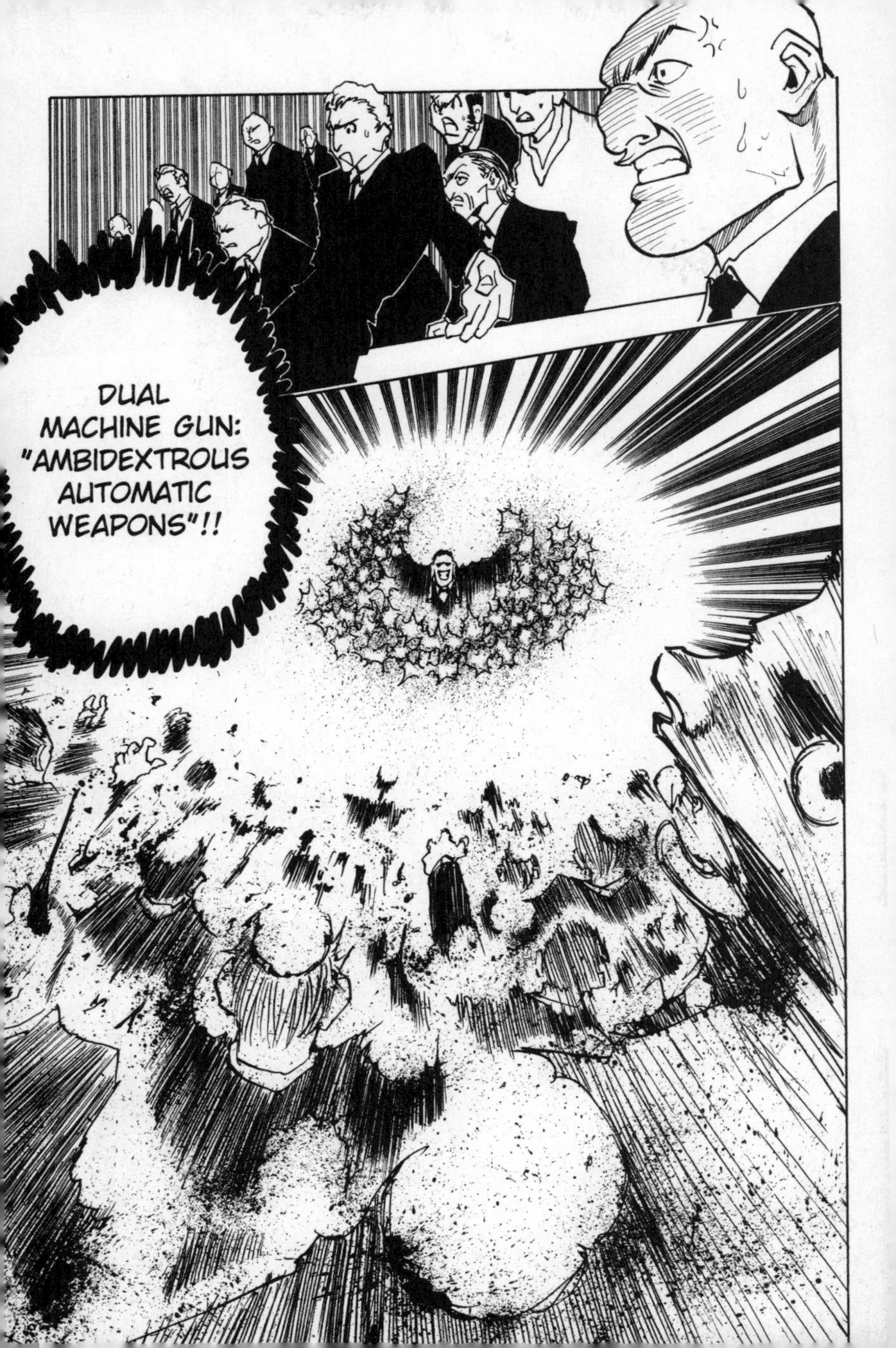
DUAL MACHINE GUN: "AMBIDEXTROUS AUTOMATIC WEAPONS"!!

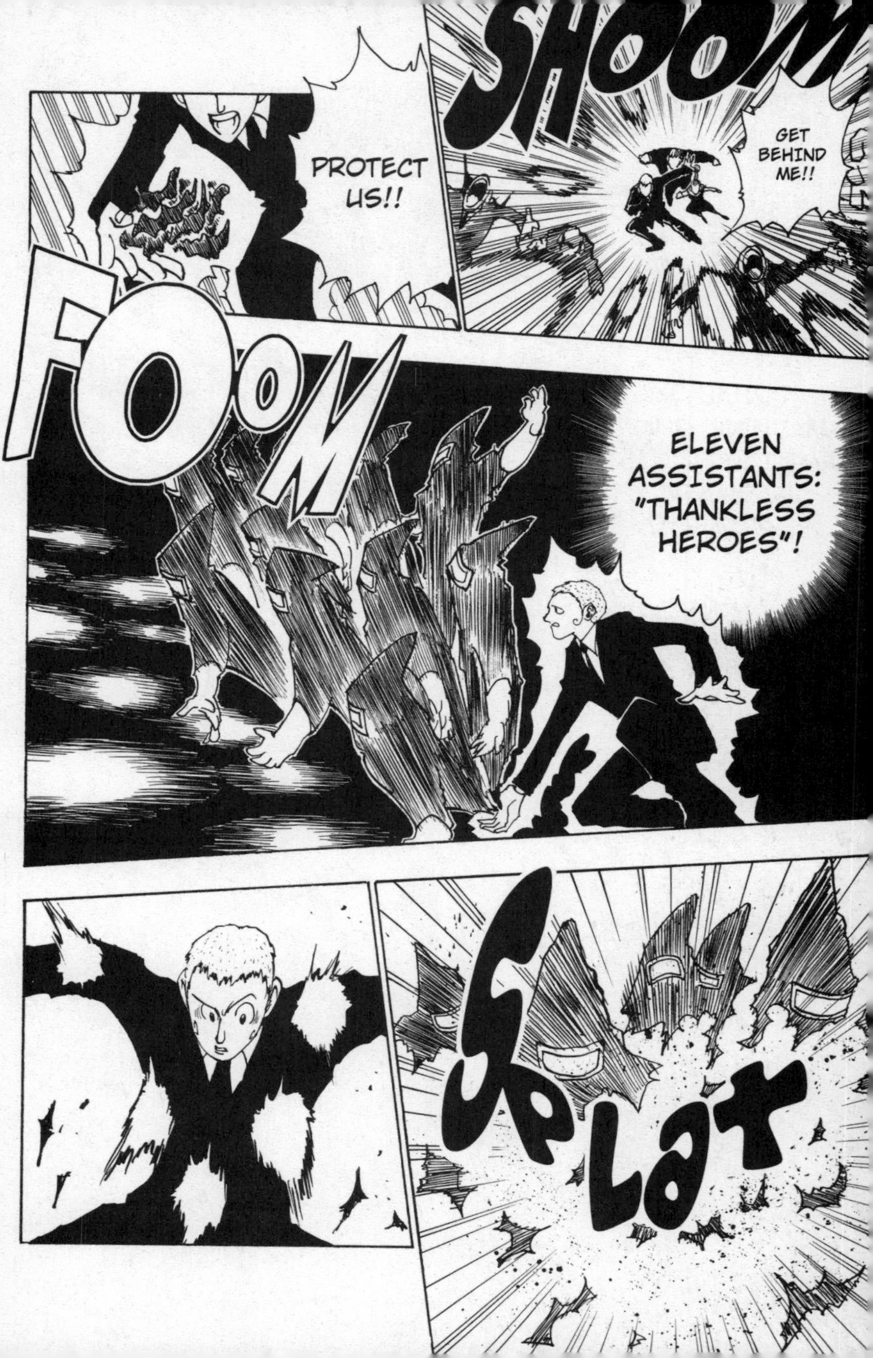
SHOOM
GET BEHIND ME!!
PROTECT US!!
FOOM
ELEVEN ASSISTANTS: "THANKLESS HEROES"!
SPLAT

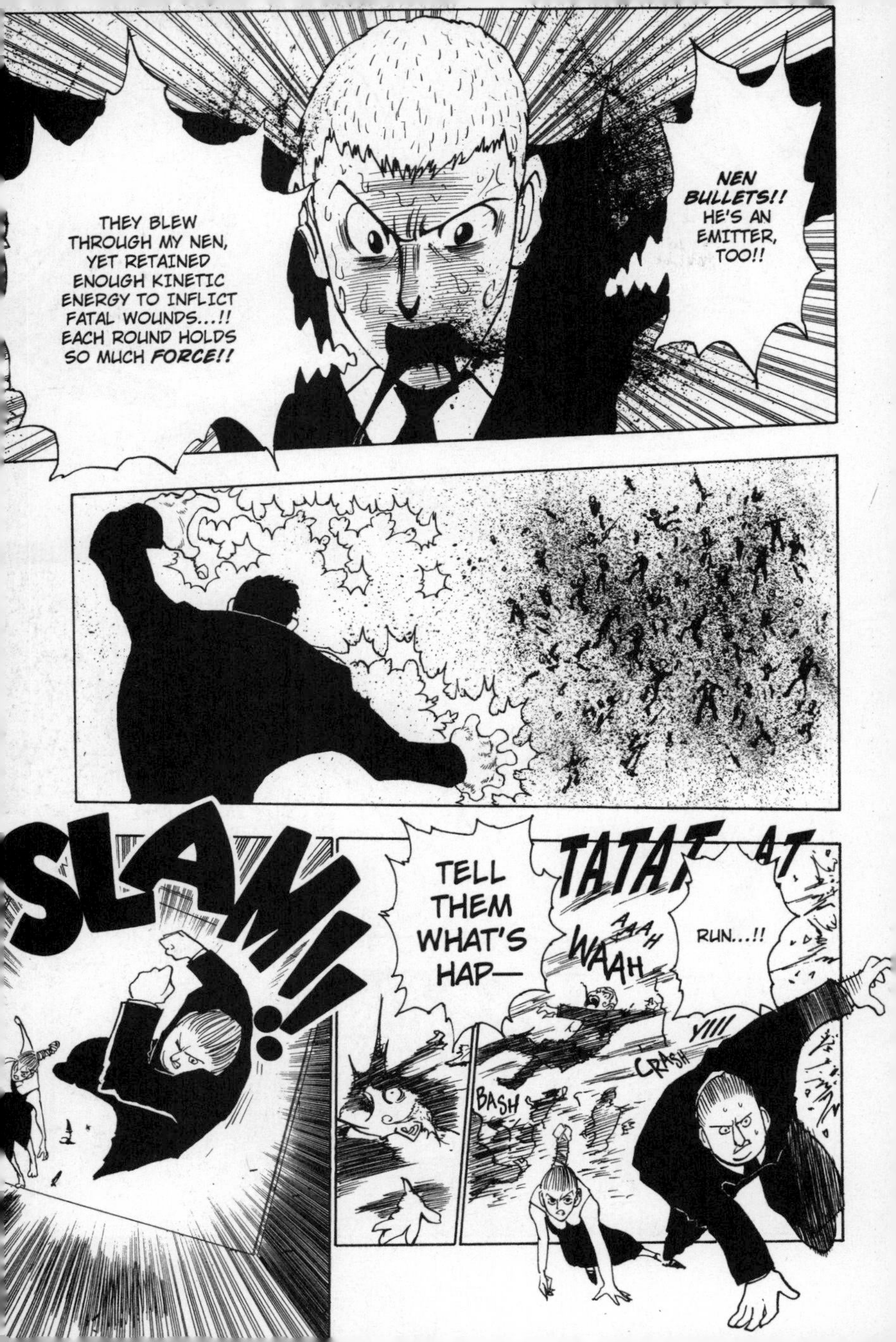
NEN BULLETS!! HE'S AN EMITTER, TOO!!
THEY BLEW THROUGH MY NEN, YET RETAINED ENOUGH KINETIC ENERGY TO INFLICT FATAL WOUNDS...!! EACH ROUND HOLDS SO MUCH FORCE!!
TATATAT
RUN...!!
TELL THEM WHAT'S HAP—
AAAH
WAAAH
YIII
CRASH
BASH
SLAM!!

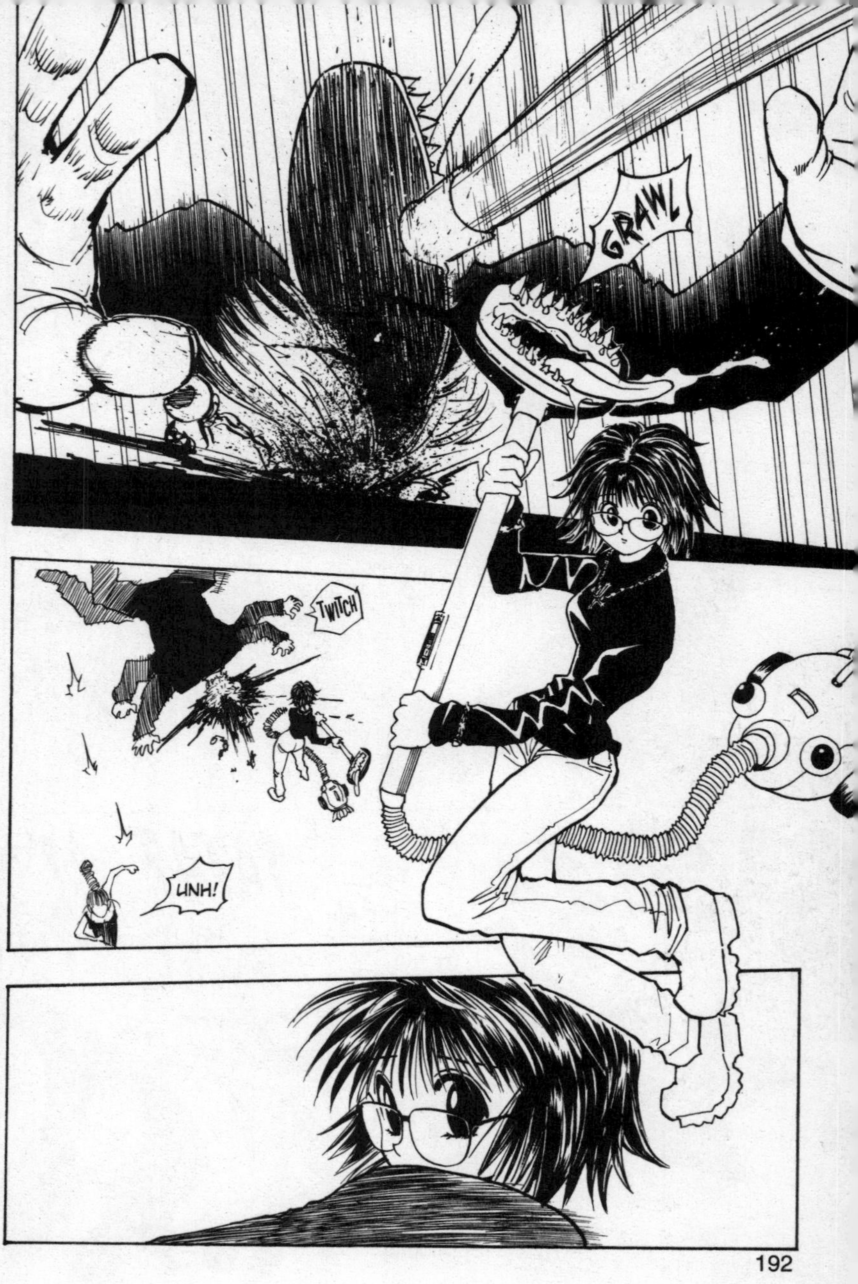
GRAWL
TWITCH
UNH!

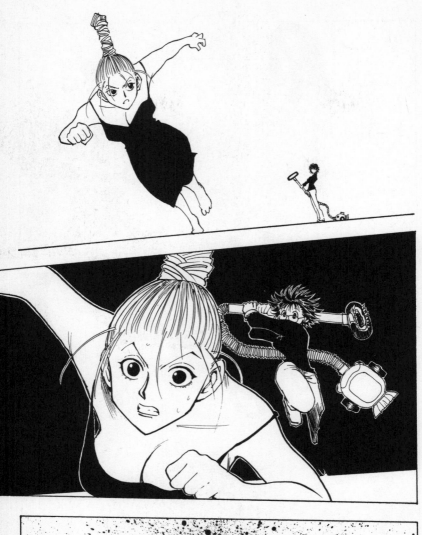

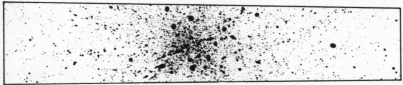

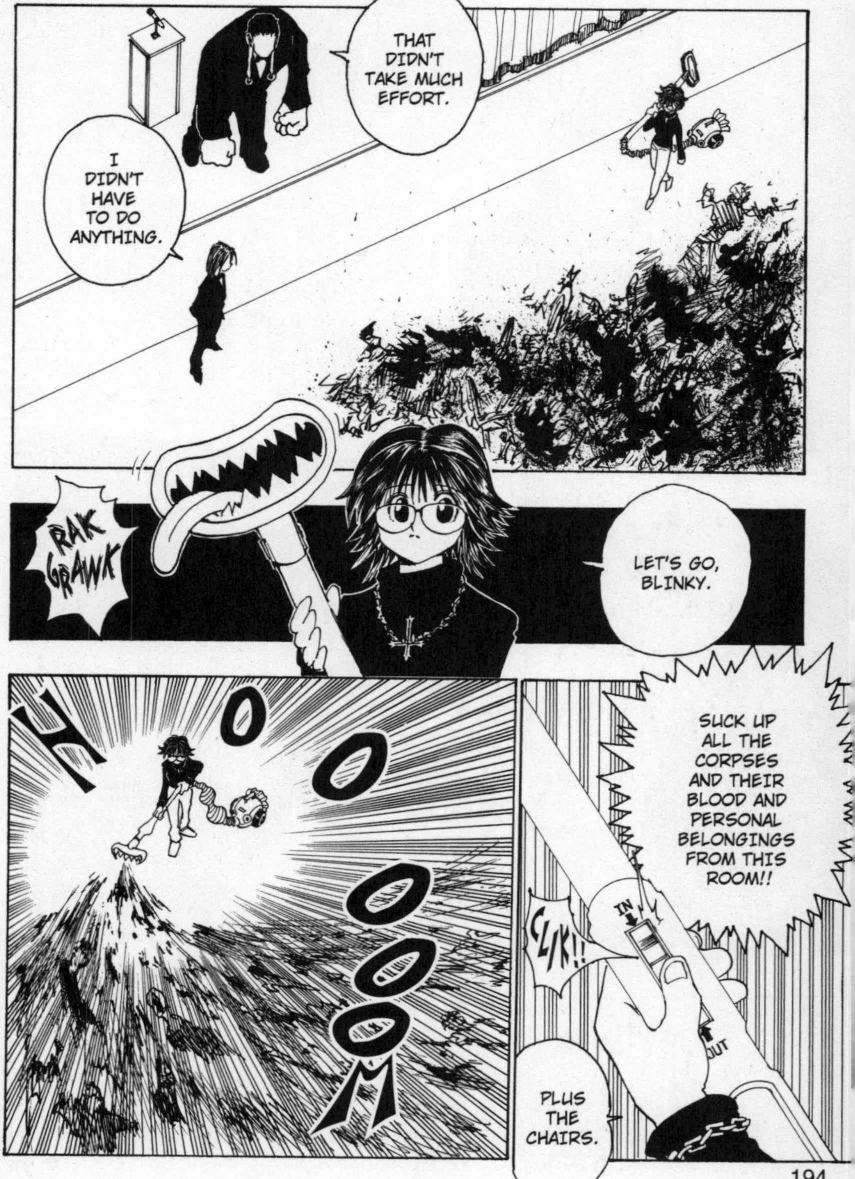
THAT DIDN'T TAKE MUCH EFFORT.
I DIDN'T HAVE TO DO ANYTHING.
LET'S GO, BLINKY.
RAK GRAWK
SUCK UP ALL THE CORPSES AND THEIR BLOOD AND PERSONAL BELONGINGS FROM THIS ROOM!!
IN
CLIK!!
OUT
PLUS THE CHAIRS.
HOOOOOOOM

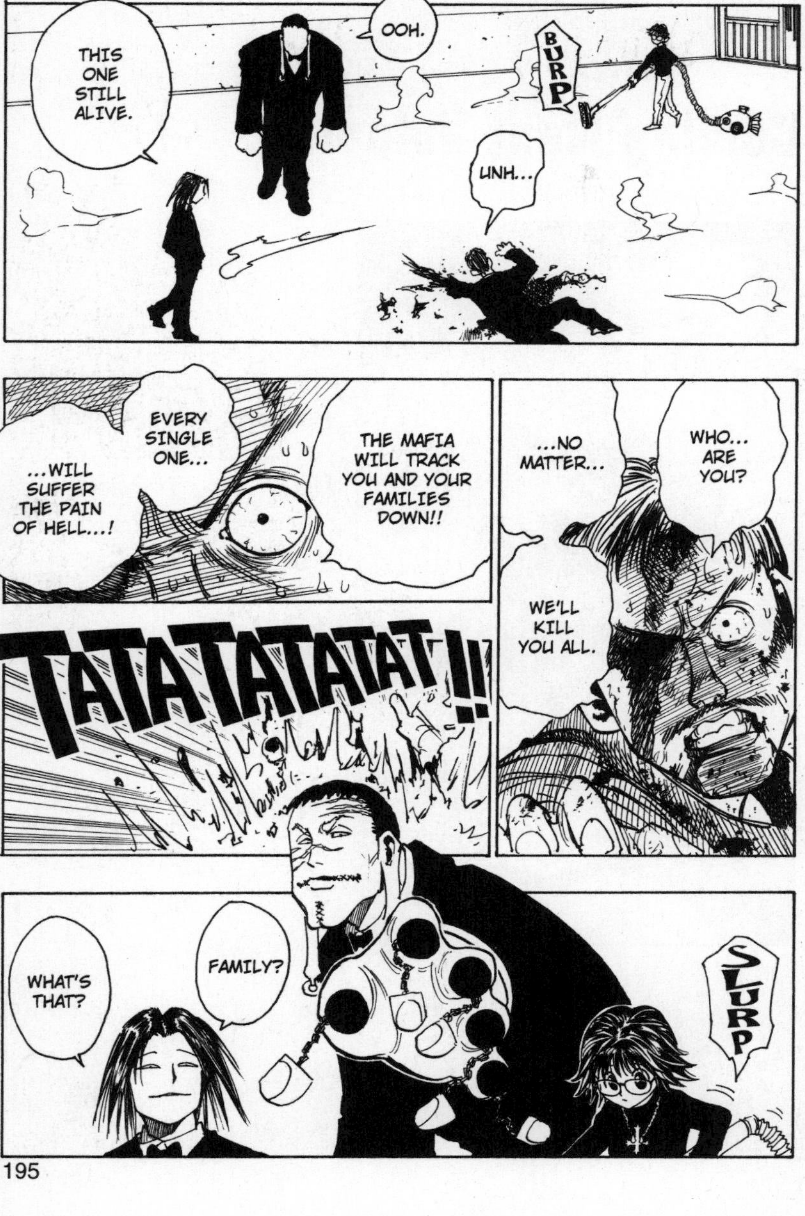
BURP
OOH.
THIS ONE STILL ALIVE.
UNH...
WHO... ARE YOU?
...NO MATTER...
WE'LL KILL YOU ALL.
THE MAFIA WILL TRACK YOU AND YOUR FAMILIES DOWN!!
EVERY SINGLE ONE...
...WILL SUFFER THE PAIN OF HELL...!
TATATATATAT!!
SLURP
FAMILY?
WHAT'S THAT?

Coming Next Volume...

When items that were supposed to be auctioned off appear to have disappeared, everyone wonders who pulled off the heist. Will Gon get one step closer to finding the mysterious video game?

Available now!

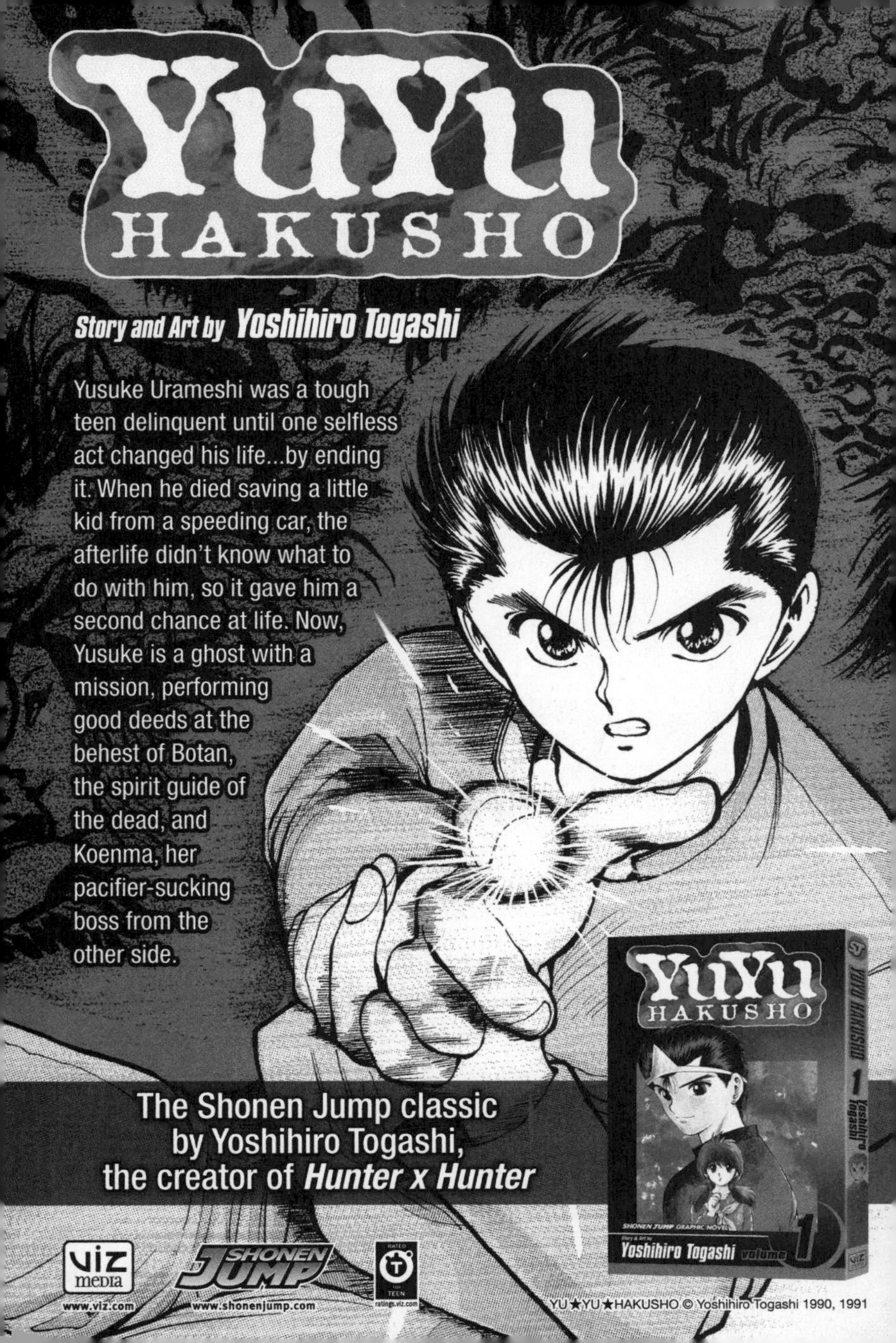
YuYu HAKUSHO
Story and Art by Yoshihiro Togashi
Yusuke Urameshi was a tough teen delinquent until one selfless act changed his life...by ending it. When he died saving a little kid from a speeding car, the afterlife didn't know what to do with him, so it gave him a second chance at life. Now, Yusuke is a ghost with a mission, performing good deeds at the behest of Botan, the spirit guide of the dead, and Koenma, her pacifier-sucking boss from the other side.
YuYu HAKUSHO
SHONEN JUMP GRAPHIC NOVEL
Yoshihiro Togashi volume 1
The Shonen Jump classic by Yoshihiro Togashi, the creator of Hunter x Hunter
viz media
www.viz.com
SHONEN JUMP
www.shonenjump.com
RATED T TEEN
ratings.viz.com
YU★YU★HAKUSHO © Yoshihiro Togashi 1990, 1991

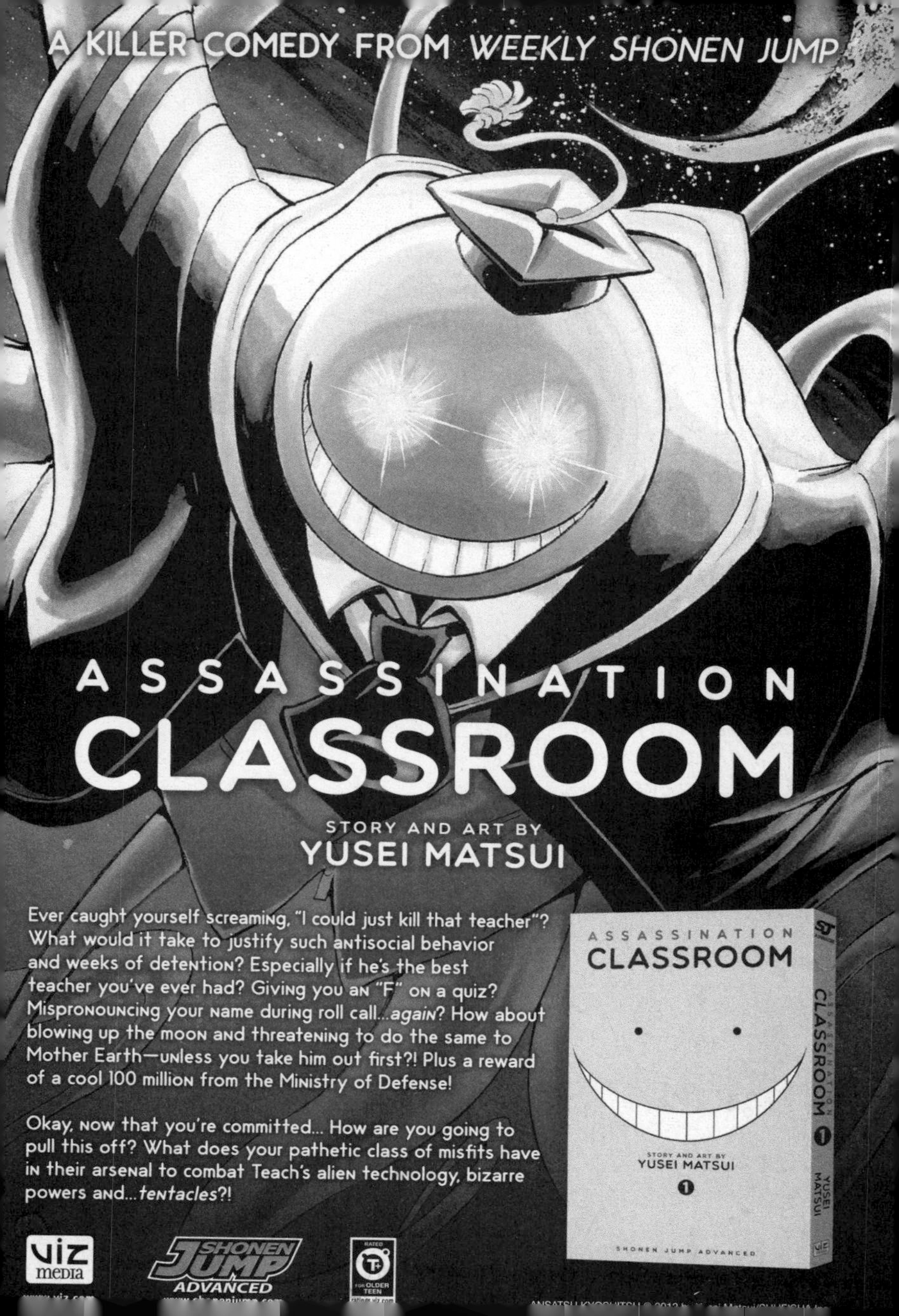
A KILLER COMEDY FROM WEEKLY SHONEN JUMP
ASSASSINATION CLASSROOM
STORY AND ART BY
YUSEI MATSUI
Ever caught yourself screaming, "I could just kill that teacher"? What would it take to justify such antisocial behavior and weeks of detention? Especially if he's the best teacher you've ever had? Giving you an "F" on a quiz? Mispronouncing your name during roll call...*again*? How about blowing up the moon and threatening to do the same to Mother Earth—unless you take him out first?! Plus a reward of a cool 100 million from the Ministry of Defense!
Okay, now that you're committed... How are you going to pull this off? What does your pathetic class of misfits have in their arsenal to combat Teach's alien technology, bizarre powers and...*tentacles*?!
ASSASSINATION CLASSROOM
STORY AND ART BY
YUSEI MATSUI
1
SHONEN JUMP ADVANCED
viz media
SHONEN JUMP ADVANCED
RATED T+ FOR OLDER TEEN
ratings.viz.com

EYESHIELD 21

STORY BY RIICHIRO INAGAKI
ART BY YUSUKE MURATA

From the artist of *One-Punch Man!*

Wimpy Sena Kobayakawa has been running away from bullies all his life. But when the football gear comes on, things change—Sena's speed and uncanny ability to elude big bullies just might give him what it takes to become a great high school football hero! Catch all the bone-crushing action and slapstick comedy of Japan's hottest football manga!

VIZ MEDIA

SHONEN JUMP ADVANCED

RATED T FOR OLDER TEEN
ratings.viz.com

www.viz.com   www.shonenjump.com

You're Reading in the Wrong Direction!!

Whoops! Guess what? You're starting at the wrong end of the comic!

...It's true! In keeping with the original Japanese format, **Hunter x Hunter** is meant to be read from right to left, starting in the upper-right corner.

Unlike English, which is read from left to right, Japanese is read from right to left, meaning that action, sound effects and word-balloon order are completely reversed... something which can make readers unfamiliar with Japanese feel pretty backwards themselves. For this reason, manga or Japanese comics published in the U.S. in English have sometimes been published "flopped"—that is, printed in exact reverse order, as though seen from the other side of a mirror.

By flopping pages, U.S. publishers can avoid confusing readers, but the compromise is not without its downside. For one thing, a character in a flopped manga series who once wore in the original Japanese version a T-shirt emblazoned with "M A Y" (as in "the merry month of") now wears one which reads "Y A M"! Additionally, many manga creators in Japan are themselves unhappy with the process, as some feel the mirror-imaging of their art skews their original intentions.

We are proud to bring you Yoshihiro Togashi's **Hunter x Hunter** in the original unflopped format. For now, though, turn to the other side of the book and let the adventure begin...!

—Editor